Praise for Eric Alterman's
SOUND & FURY

"Savagely witty and incisive. Alterman does a remarkable job of deflating the aura of omniscience many pundits project."
—Neil A Grauer, *Baltimore Sun*

"Alterman attempts to give the invisible influence [of the punditocracy] a face, and succeeds surprisingly well, given the difficulty of proof. Candid, biting, disarming…[*Sound & Fury*] is great entertainment."
—Steve Weinberg, *St. Louis Post-Dispatch*

"Eric Alterman takes [political pundits] on in this informative, entertaining, sometimes hilarious, always well-written book. [*Sound & Fury*] should be required reading for every politician and every voter."
—Leo McConnell, *Hudson Daily Sun*

"Anyone who cares about the media will be troubled by Alterman's conclusions of what he calls the Punditocracy."
—O. Casey Corr, *Seattle Times*

"Alterman puts punditry in perspective, giving a history of its development and analyzing its current effect on politics….An engaging and knowledgeable analysis."
—*Kirkus Reviews*

"[*Sound & Fury*] is a scathing, humor-filled exposé. Successful both as a political history and media criticism, this work deserves a wide audience."
—*Publishers Weekly*

"Alterman writes with verve and humor."—Don Kazak, *Palo Alto Weekly*

"A witty examination of the punditocracy….Devastating."
—Mel Small, *Detroit News*

"Alterman's willingness to offer unambiguous political criticism is his book's greatest strength." —Geoffrey Stokes, *Boston Sunday Globe*

SOUND AND FURY

THE WASHINGTON PUNDITOCRACY AND THE COLLAPSE OF AMERICAN POLITICS

ERIC ALTERMAN

HarperPerennial

A Division of HarperCollinsPublishers

A hardcover edition of this book was published in 1992 by HarperCollins Publishers.

HarperCollins books may be purchased for educational, business, or sales promotional use. For information please write: Special Markets Department, HarperCollins Publishers, Inc., 10 East 53rd Street, New York, NY 10022.

First HarperPerennial edition published 1993.

Designed by Alma Hochhauser Orenstein

LIBRARY OF CONGRESS CATALOG CARD NUMBER 91-59934

ISBN 0-06-092427-6

93 94 95 96 97 AC/RRD 10 9 8 7 6 5 4 3 2 1

To my parents and to the memory of their parents.

לְדֹר וָדֹר

CONTENTS

SECTION III
Consequences: The Bush Years

ACKNOWLEDGMENTS

Ever since *Harper's* published the acknowledgment pages from Michael Ledeen's *Grave New World* under the title "The Courtier's Art," authors have been forewarned that there is a downside to thanking too profusely in too many high places. This is not a bad thing and I have tried to keep it in mind. While I am on the defensive here, I should like to add that to any wits or lazy headline writers who had been planning to call this book "a tale told by an idiot . . . signifying nothing," it's been done.

That out of the way, I have a great many people to thank, most of them far more illustrious than myself. First among these is the late I. F. Stone. Through his example, his friendship and his encouragement of my work, Izzy, together with Esther Stone, helped give me the confidence to sustain this project. It is my most profound regret upon finishing that Izzy is no longer around to see the work he helped inspire.

If this book accomplishes nothing else, I should like to blow the whistle on my friend and colleague at the World Policy Institute, Sherle R. Schwenninger, who for my money is the most thoughtful, knowledgeable, and original unsung strategic genius in American political and intellectual life today. I am not wholly certain where my ideas begin and Sherle's leave off in these pages, and I am only grateful to whatever providential powers placed him on my side. Arch Gillies, the Institute's president during most of this period, was also a source of limitless inspiration, education, and good humor. I will always be in his debt. Thanks also go to Erika Burk, Shareen Hertel, Vivienne Bariffe, and Carol Greenberg of the Institute's staff.

I am also unspeakably indebted to those friends and colleagues who braved through an entire draft of the book, and thereby helped me discover what I had intended to say in the first place. This was not always as much fun as it sounds like, particularly since I am not always as grateful as I ought to be for constructive criticism. Into this category falls first and foremost my saintly wife, Patricia Caplan, followed by my friends: Kai Bird, Michael Kazin, Michael Waldman, Patti Cohen, and Richard Barnet; my editor, Rick Kot, and my agent, Kathy Robbins. Thanks also to Kathy's terrific staff, most notably the indefatigable Elizabeth Mackey, Lauren Marino, Julia Null, and Steve Bromage. My appreciation as well to Michael Carlisle.

David Rieff helped get me off the ground, weighing in at crucial moments with important editorial suggestions and intellectual challenges. The book might never have happened had it not been for his help. I am triply grateful to Ronald Steel: first, for writing his magnificent Lippmann biography, which saved me a great deal of work; second for taking the time on a frigid Christmas Eve a few years back to come to my apartment and disabuse me of many of my misperceptions about the man; and third, for giving me one hell of a tough time on the Lippmann-related aspects of the manuscript. No doubt the book does not reflect Ron's criticism nearly as well as it should. Paul Kennedy also deserves special gratitude for his role in helping me to decide to convert a 1988 article-length treatment of this subject in *World Policy Journal* into *Sound and Fury*.

Other friends who read sections of the book and contributed helpful comments include Isaac Shapiro, Tina Rosenberg, and David Handelman. Friends who are waiting for the hardcover but who probably ought to be thanked anyway include Joel Friedman, Lisa Murray McGovern, David Rudd, Ricki Seidman, Melissa Block, Beryl Bucher, Mike Mosettig, Monique Currie, Sarah Sewall, Jeff Porro, Myra Pilson, Elise O'Shaughnessy, Don Guttenplan, Marcus Raskin, Nel van Beusekom, Evy Rosen, my hero—Loring Henderson—and as they say at the Oscars, too many people to mention here.

I'd like to say thanks also to those editors whose assignments helped shape the work or finance parts of my research. Among these are, of course, the amazing Mr. Kot, the already noted Sherle Schwenninger, Amanda Spake and Bob Thompson of *The Washington Post Magazine*, Kathleen Quinn, formerly of *The New York Times* Op-Ed page, Jack Limpert of *The Washingtonian*, and Victor Navasky of *The Nation*. (The financing part obviously does not apply to the Wily and Parsimonious One.) For additional financial and logistical support, I heartily thank the World Policy Institute at the New School for Social Research, the W. H. Ferry Foundation, and the Fund for Constitutional Journalism.

I am obviously grateful to the many people who took the time to be interviewed by me for this book, particularly those who were well aware that I was unlikely to be sympathetic to their politics but were sufficiently generous—or confident—to give me a clear line of fire nevertheless. A special thanks in this department goes to Charles Krauthammer, who helped me quite early in the process to understand the moral and intellectual complications of the task I had undertaken and who deserves an apology for a callous imputation I once made on a Washington, D.C., radio program regarding his friendship with a dishonest U.S. government official. As for those who believe themselves to have been misquoted or otherwise abused, please feel free to challenge whatever I've written, but keep in mind, I probably have it on tape.

Though it's almost unbelievably hokey, I would like also to offer my appreciation to some of the teachers I've had over the years for what must have seemed a painfully thankless task at the time. In rough chronological order they are: Ed Grossman, Neil Maloney, Werner Feig, Richard Liebowitz, Richard Polenberg, Isaac Kramnick, John Najemy, Benedict Anderson, Richard and Barbara Rosecrance, Paul Kennedy, Robert Dahl, Mac Destler, Edward Said, Donald Kagan, Miles Kahler, Bart Bernstein, Steve Zipperstein, and Max Tiktin. Thanks too to the reference staffs at the Library of Congress, George Washington University Library, Georgetown University Library, *The Washington Post* Library, and particularly, Bob Garber, Barbara Vandegrift, and Barbara Van Woerkom at the National Press Club Library. More thanks to Sheila Gillooly, Rick Kot's charming and able assistant. Thanks, too, to my copy editor, Ann Adelman.

Boy-wonder George Stephanopoulos, the best man at my wedding, read some of the book between campaigns and insists on being mentioned here. Fine. George contributed absolutely nothing of value to this work and probably held it up with his idiosyncratic questions and baseless complaints. Whatever mistakes remain in the final version are his responsibility.

Finally, I should like to thank my parents, Carl and Ruth Alterman. They paid for this book many times over, and they deserved better.

ERA
Stanford, California
April 1992

PREFACE

A preface," Joseph Alsop and Turner Catledge explained in 1938, "is a form of self-indulgence which can only be excused when there is a need to explain a book's limitations." Since all books, like all authors, have limitations, this does not seem to me to be too onerous a standard to uphold. Here are a few of mine:

Sound and Fury is organized into three distinct sections. In Section I, I offer an abridged critical history of the pundit profession, beginning in prerevolutionary times and closing with the birth of what I call the Reagan punditocracy. Section II is a combination *tour d'horizon* of the central pundit personalities and institutions of the Reagan years as well as an examination of their respective roles in the shaping of the politics of the era. Section III resumes the historical narrative and carries us through the first three years of the Bush presidency. It focuses on the long-term political, economic, social, and environmental consequences of the punditocracy's stranglehold upon our national political dialogue as viewed through the prisms of the rise of Mikhail Gorbachev, the end of the Cold War, and the Persian Gulf War. The conclusion picks up with a brief discussion of the primary campaign of 1992.

For Section I, I relied primarily on original columns, memoirs, interviews, secondary historical sources, and a limited number of private papers available in library collections. Section II relies heavily on interviews with the principals involved, as well as their published writings and television performances. Section III is based primarily on a combination of published pundit writings and television appearances discussed in the context of what I consider to be reliable news reports regarding the issues in question. In this section, I made every effort to employ widely available mainstream journalistic sources, i.e., *The New York Times, The Washington Post, The Wall Street Journal, The Economist, Foreign Policy,* and so forth, on the theory that if the facts discussed in these publications were so easily available to me, they were just as easily available to the people whose work I was critiquing.

A final word regarding personal disclosure: It is all but impossible to live and work in the world of Washington media politics without developing certain personal and professional relationships which, at some level, if only unconsciously, color one's representation of reality. In my case, my task was further complicated by the fact that I was writing about a few people who had once published my work and upon whom my livelihood once depended. The reader is invited to draw his or her own conclusions about just how corruptive these personal and professional connections may have been, but I thought it would be wise to lay them out to be on the safe side. This is, after all, a book about personal and intellectual corruption.

None of the people discussed at length in this work are the kinds of friends whom I would call if my house were on fire or even if my car needed a jump start. A few, however, were "friends" in the Washington sense of the term. While living there, I would see them at parties, make lunch dates, gossip about other journalists and exchange pleasantries with their spouses. A small number of people quoted in the book or discussed regarding tangential matters are actual friends of mine, but they do not, by and large, figure significantly in my analysis.

Regarding the Root of All Evil, while working as a freelance journalist and think-tank consultant, I drew the occasional meager paycheck from the following media outlets mentioned or cited in the text: *The New Republic, The Nation, The Washington Post* Outlook section, op-ed page, and magazine, *The New York Times* op-ed page and magazine, *Harper's, Tikkun, World Policy Journal, Mother Jones, SPY, The Washingtonian, The Columbia Journalism Review, Newsday, New York Newsday, The Washington Monthly,* the Carnegie Endowment for International Peace, the Center for Strategic and International Studies, the World Policy Institute, and the United States Army. I also drew a few rather less meager paychecks from *Vanity Fair.* I have never been paid by *The Wall Street Journal* but I have been attacked there. After I completed the original manuscript, I entered into an informal consultative relationship with Bill Moyers's "Public Affairs Television" corporation.

As for political biases, I have none; what follows is a totally objective account.

I live in New York and I have not the vaguest idea what Brooklyn is interested in.

—*WALTER LIPPMANN,*
Liberty and the News (1920)

I can speak to almost anything with a lot of authority.

—*FRED BARNES ON*
"THE MCLAUGHLIN GROUP" (1992)

INTRODUCTION

On what forecasters like to call "an unseasonably warm" February 1990 morning, my friend Loring and I rode the subway to the Capitol, where Vaclav Havel, the new president of Czechoslovakia, was to address a joint session of Congress. Our friend George had secured two guest passes for the occasion but had misinformed me when I asked him if I needed to wear a tie. I was therefore barred at the door until I managed to convince the head of security that a sports jacket and a beat-up old wool scarf worn as an ascot represented "formal deeplomatic vear in mine country." Tragedy narrowly averted, we entered the chamber and took our seats with the senators and congressmen.

Havel entered the hall to a thunderous standing ovation. It was quite a moment and even the tough guys in the press gallery were fighting back tears. This modest, diminutive playwright, fresh from facing down the guns of the Soviet empire and leading his country in a democratic revolution, had been invited to share his wisdom in the hall that sits at the rhetorical center of what was now, undisputedly, the most powerful nation in the history of the world. Never in my adult life had I witnessed so unambiguous a victory for the forces of sweetness and light.

Yet for all the emotional power and moral uplift of the occasion, I still left the hall depressed. Havel was not exactly at his best but he was still Vaclav Havel. He explored many of the great themes of personal and political responsibility with uncommon wit and originality, and was certainly the only person in the chamber's history to offer even a brief plug for a

Hegelian interpretation of the dialectic of historical consciousness. But the sense of being addressed by a political leader who felt no compulsion to speak down to his audience, to insult its intellect with empty-headed rhetoric and pander to its egocentricity with kitschy encomiums, was almost wholly new to me. Seated above Havel's lectern, with that eerie, lost-in-space smile of his, was Vice President Dan Quayle. The hall exploded when Havel declared that the Marxists had been wrong, although the representatives did not bother to listen to the part of the sentence in which he explained just what they were wrong about. ("Consciousness precedes being and not the other way around.") How is it, I wondered, walking back toward Union Station to catch a train home, that the Czechs managed to elect this exquisitely eloquent, intellectually challenging moral champion as their president on their very first try, while more than two hundred years after *our* revolution, we remain mired in arguments about flag factories and Willie Horton. *

If ideas have consequences for society, then so, too, does their absence. Jay Leno and David Letterman get plenty of mileage out of George Bush's problem with the "vision thing" as well as the sectarian squabbling that characterizes the present-day Democratic party. But our lack of coherent political discourse is really quite a serious problem. Our politicians' rhetoric is so riddled with misinformation, mindless cliché, and meaningless spectacle that it has ceased to have any relevance to the problems it alleges to address. Even the candidates hardly pretend to believe themselves any longer. The forms of American political communication—nine-second television sound bites, negative advertisements, and ceaseless fundraising—have buried even the possibility of fruitful debate. And the political system has coasted so long on the fuel of its own irrelevance that the people who operate it have lost both the imagination and the inclination to rethink its premises. Meanwhile, back in the real world, our problems proliferate. Our economy declines, our cities collapse, our environment deteriorates, and Washington fiddles.

It is dangerous, Thucydides reminds us, to uncouple words from things. We begin by fooling others and end up fooling ourselves. Because American politicians' words are so thoroughly uncoupled from the things about which they speak, the role of setting the parameters of our national debate, of determining what problems require urgent attention and what issues may prove to be important to the national interest, must fall elsewhere. In our case, that means the media. Nothing else remains. As our political parties have transformed themselves into little more than glorified fundraising

---

*This being only 1990, Quayle had not yet had the opportunity to elevate political discourse sufficiently to focus the nation on the merits of Murphy Brown's lifestyle choices.

operations, and voluntary civic, ethnic, and labor-related organizations have either retreated into local politics or been shunted into the sidelines by megabuck special interests, the only place where national political communication and exchange can take place is within the elite television and print media outlets.

The problem here is that for a variety of reasons—some commercial, others cultural—the media is not up to its task. In the first place, there is the most obvious critique: the media is owned by international corporate conglomerates whose interests frequently conflict with those of the larger public. Equally troubling are a series of more subtle barriers to honest communication, such as the role of journalistic "objectivity." Almost everyone seems to agree that objective reporting is something to which journalists should aspire. Yet the rules of objective reporting often prevent the media from providing exactly the kinds of contextual information that would allow a reader to understand what is truly going on. This not only impedes our ability to judge a story's significance but it also gives politicians enormous latitude with the truth. Much of even the most conscientious objective journalism consists simply of the "misstatements" that politicians would prefer their constituents to believe.*

Because objectivity is the principle upon which virtually all important elite journalism defines itself, the only participants in the media's discourse licensed to provide sufficient context to allow people to form even a remotely well-informed political viewpoint are the pundits. Only the pundits are accorded both the authority and the audience necessary to explain, in language a concerned citizen is likely to understand, why such-and-such a proposal is either healthy or catastrophic for the future of the republic. Only the pundits are invested with responsibility to point out when a group of politicians are conspiring against the many on behalf of the few. Only the pundits are allowed to make the necessary connections between a scandalous

*A minor example in this case makes a major point. On March 24, 1990, *The New York Times* reported that President Bush had announced himself opposed to statehood for the District of Columbia because, the President said, "its funds come almost exclusively from the Federal government." Instead of seeking to discover whether the President's insistence was true or false, the report merely provided an opposing politician's quote, in this case Jesse Jackson, calling Mr. Bush "unfair" for his attempts to "disenfranchise 600,000 American citizens." The story wholly conformed to the *Times*'s demanding standards of objectivity but was nevertheless based on a falsehood. As *The Washington Post* did happen to mention in its story the same day, only 14% of the district's budget is provided by the federal government. Objectivity, in the unfortunately typical case of the *Times* report, had absolutely no relevance to truth. See Phillip Shenon, "Statehood for Capital Opposed by President," *The New York Times*, March 24, 1990, and Ann Devroy and R. H. Melton, "President Opposes Statehood," *The Washington Post*, March 24, 1990, p. 1.

rip-off of the public trust and a massive buyout of a political party. Alone within that section of the media where our political discourse takes place, the pundits have the power and the obligation to point to a naked emperor and observe that he has no clothes on—without first attributing it to "sources close to the alleged parade route."

It is the argument of this book that our economy, our security, and most particularly our democracy are imperiled by the decrepit state of our national political discourse. We lack the ability, as a nation, to conduct a simple, sensible, and civil conversation about the choices we face. Unless we diagnose the disease and begin to treat it, the sick state of the American body politic will certainly worsen. The net result will be not only the amplification of what George Will calls the "tawdry ferocity" of American debate but the increasing paralysis of our political system in the face of what is certainly the most daunting set of challenges America has faced since we slept through the birth of fascism more than a half century ago.

I do not argue that the dominance of our national political dialogue by political pundits is the only serious roadblock to the achievement of a vibrant political culture in the United States. Clearly, the power of money in American politics is an ongoing scandal. So is our inability, liberal and conservative, to deal honestly with the unspoken fissures in our society deriving from racial prejudice, religious conflict, and class-based stratification. Our shameful education system turns out so many illiterate citizens that intelligent political participation is all but impossible except for a decreasing minority. And political corruption, individual alienation, general laziness, and a pervasive sense that everything in America seems to be getting worse has led large numbers of Americans—perhaps even a majority—to remove themselves, en masse, from political life. Finally, the omnipresent influence of television, coupled with the increasingly short attention span of the viewing audience, has reduced much of the discourse to a kind of semiotic shorthand, designed to trigger the emotions without disturbing the mind. Many of these carefully constructed sound bites are nothing more than advertising slogans lifted directly from Hollywood or Madison Avenue.* Few last long enough to form even a coherent thought, much less outline a sensible political program.

Owing to the dominance of media forms over political content, the elevation of one issue or viewpoint over that of the competition is less the function of any real world concerns than of the twin dictates of television production values and the mores of Washington's insider political culture.

---

*"Where's the Beef?" "Make My Day," "Read My Lips," etc., etc.

Working together over the past couple of decades, these two forces have spawned something I call the "punditocracy." The punditocracy is a tiny group of highly visible political pontificators who make their living offering "inside political opinions and forecasts" in the elite national media. And it is their debate, rather than any semblance of a democratic one, that determines the parameters of political discourse in the nation today.*

Defining just who is and who is not a pundit at any given time can be a tricky matter. *Webster's New World Dictionary* informs us that a pundit is "a person of great learning." William Safire's *Political Dictionary* expands the definition to "a political analyst, usually associated with a sizable broadcasting outlet." Broadly speaking, pundits are the people anointed by the media to give their opinions on things. Political pundits give their opinions on things political. Whether these people can be expected to bring any special expertise to their subject matter is wholly at the discretion of those doing the anointing. The ability to call oneself an "expert" on a particular topic is a useful, but hardly necessary qualification.

Like what used to be the Soviet Politburo, the punditocracy has full-fledged members, candidate members, and membership hopefuls. Not all pundits are invited into the punditocracy and not all members of the punditocracy are professional pundits. As with the ex-Communists, relationships are in a state of constant flux and rarely conform to an easily discernible hierarchy.

A few extraordinarily visible perches within the insider media automatically confer upon their holders a seat at the punditocracy banquet table. These include the chairs on NBC's "The McLaughlin Group," CBS's "Inside Washington," ABC's "This Week with David Brinkley," and CNN's "The Capital Gang" and "Crossfire." The punditocracy's print portfolio consists of the op-ed columns of *The New York Times*, *The Washington Post*, *The Wall Street Journal*, the senior editorships of *The New Republic*, and the Washington-based columns in the newsweeklies. All told, there are barely

---

*Evidence of the American people's alienation from their political system is not exactly difficult to come by. The Times Mirror Corporation publishes a monthly poll of just how much attention Americans pay to the news. An extensive survey of the past three years of this data indicates that it is no exaggeration to say that it literally takes a major war (or a tax cut) to get more than half the country to sit up and pay attention to politics. At one point in 1990, more Americans were aware that George Bush hated broccoli than that he had ordered the invasion of Panama. See Times Mirror Corporation, "The American Media: Who Reads, Who Watches, Who Listens, Who Cares," July 15, 1990. This phenomenon has important implications for any consideration of the revival of American democracy, most of which are beyond the scope of this book. For an excellent discussion of many of them, however, see the Kettering Foundation's pamphlet *Citizens and Politics: A View from Main Street America* (1991), E. J. Dionne's thoughtful work, *Why Americans Hate Politics* (New York: Simon & Schuster, 1991), and William Greider's powerful *Who Will Tell the People?* (New York: Simon & Schuster, 1992).

more than a few dozen of these people at any one time. The most celebrated of them—super-pundits like George F. Will, William Safire, and Robert Novak—earn mountains of money and play a role in insider culture analogous to that of Kevin Costner or Warren Beatty in Hollywood. Their colossal incomes—Patrick J. Buchanan earned over $800,000 in eleven months in 1991—derive, however, not from their newspaper columns or their television commentaries, but from the inevitable celebrity appearances that these positions automatically generate. *

For those without access to the television personality/syndicated column route, admission into the punditocracy becomes largely a matter of conflating a career as former Secretary of Something or Other with a healthy dose of self-promotional talent. William Rogers and Henry Kissinger, for instance, were both Secretaries of State for Richard Nixon. Kissinger is a super-pundit; Rogers is history. In addition to his regular column syndicated by the *Los Angeles Times* and carried in *The Washington Post*, Kissinger is a regular "expert" on "Nightline," "The MacNeil/Lehrer Newshour," and many other network and public television outlets. He is also frequently given massive amounts of space to vent his feelings in both *Time* and *Newsweek*. Kissinger is the lodestar against which all former officials' pundit careers are measured. His closest competition comes from Zbigniew Brzezinski, Jimmy Carter's national security adviser, who has shadowed Kissinger for his entire professional life. Brzezinski has no syndicated column but he is a talk-show/ newsweekly/op-ed page fixture whenever a crisis materializes. It may be no coincidence that both men speak heavily accented English and therefore sound "intellectual" to American audiences. It is certainly no coincidence that Ted Koppel—a figure invested with nearly divine powers within the punditocracy realm—considers these two men to be perhaps the most intelligent political analysts in the United States.†

Beneath the Kissinger/Brzezinski stratosphere hovers a seemingly limitless—usually male—supply of former officials of past administrations ready and willing to share their expertise on today's issues with the larger public. Those who have successfully trained themselves to speak in short

---

*See Charles R. Babcock, "Buchanan's Income Exceeded $800,000 Last Year," *The Washington Post*, April 2, 1992, p. A13.

†Another exceptionally talented performer during the 1980s was Jeane Kirkpatrick, who managed despite the perceived disadvantages of being a Democrat, an academic, and a woman, to catapult into the first rank of ex-officialdom by any conceivable measure. In the spring of 1992, Maryland Public Television debuted "To the Contrary," a program devoted exclusively to the opinions of women pundits. Whether this new addition to the punditocracy's television line-up represents a significant improvement, however, remains an open question.

sentences and communicate in snappy slogans are rewarded with limited associate memberships in the punditocracy. When a crisis occurs in their "area," they are suddenly besieged with calls from bookers at "Nightline," "Crossfire," and MacNeil/Lehrer, editors from the major op-ed pages and newsweeklies, and reporters seeking a sound bite to confirm what they had already intended to say. The terms and duration of their memberships depend on a number of factors, including the length of the crisis and the pundit's ability to impress the gatekeepers who make the appointments. The Persian Gulf War was worth a lifetime of *New Republic* articles and strategically placed op-eds for those millitary experts appointed by the networks to walk the audience through the minefields of Kuwait. An invitation from MacNeil/Lehrer to discuss say, a U.S./EEC trade dispute, however, will result in little more than the fifteen minutes predicted by Andy Warhol and prescribed by the show's producers.*

The outer limits of the punditocracy are composed of a short list of televisually sophisticated academics. While these "experts" are not necessarily respected in their respective fields, they are without exception adept at responding to questions with a minimum of professional jargon and a maximum of clarity and brevity. The ability to begin sentences with a folksy "Well, Ted," or "That's an interesting point, Robin," is useful too. On *extremely* rare occasions it is possible for a single book or magazine article to propel a writer straight into the center of punditocracy debate. Just what confluence of events is necessary to accomplish this is not wholly clear, but academics Allen Bloom and Paul Kennedy, and political apparatchik/ academics Francis Fukuyama and Kevin Phillips, have all traveled this path in recent years. Of course it did no harm whatsoever that each of the works in question were championed *within* the punditocracy before the subsequent political explosion that opened the riches of temporary membership to their authors.

Whether the American people at large are decisively influenced by pundit pontification is not relevant here. The public at large does not possess the means, nor apparently the inclination, to interfere in Washington's policy

---

*For purposes of both illustration and disclosure, I should add that certain critics of my work have accused me of being a kind of mini- or metapundit on the subject of punditry itself. They have a point. Various op-ed page editors, reporters, magazine editors, and the occasional television producer have invited me over the past few years to share my limited wisdom on the subject of America's political dialogue with regard to whatever the issue of the moment might be. I usually do. On these occasions, I am playing the same game as the people whose work I critique. It is, after all, the only game in town.

apparatus in any but the most exceptional cases. This is particularly true in matters relating to foreign policy. It is not the populace whose views are defined by the pundits, but the Washington insiders—that informal aristocracy of the powerful, the influential, and the well-connected in whose hands either fate or a presidential appointment has placed the levers of national power.

The people who inhabit the insular world of insider Washington are largely divorced from the travails that can make everyday life in the United States such a struggle. They live in neighborhoods like Georgetown, Cleveland Park, and Chevy Chase, with green lawns, safe playgrounds, good schools, and an extra room for the maid. Their biggest problem in life, according to one *Washingtonian* magazine survey, is traffic.

Within insider culture, social status rests not so much on wealth as on proximity to power. How much money you earn is less important than whether you have been to Katherine Graham's (or even better, "Kay's") for dinner. Wisdom is judged not on the basis of depth of knowledge but the speed with which it is acquired. If you have to wait for the polls to close to hear who won an election somewhere, forget it. The only returns worth mentioning are those gleaned from exit polls. The only scandals worth raising an eyebrow over are those about to break. To know who is about to be appointed Assistant Secretary of State for Near Eastern and South Asian Affairs is a great deal more impressive than knowing where the hell either place is. Insiders intimidate outsiders in cocktail party conversation by implying that they know more about a particular policy than they can in good conscience say. (This has always been Henry Kissinger's secret.) Even worse, insiders possess the unspoken potential to end a conversation by responding, "Oh really; the Under Secretary and I just flew back on the Concorde together and he says you don't know what you're talking about." And it is this tiny but powerful universe where the intellectual sovereignty of pundit power reigns supreme.

The power of the punditocracy takes many forms. One can identify examples of political pundits entering the history books directly. There was the recently prominent example of Patrick J. Buchanan using his status as pundit as a platform to build what he hopes to be a second career as President of the United States. Buchanan was, of course, a special case and his decision to challenge George Bush appeared to have less to do with becoming President in 1992 than with building for 1996. But a pundit-presidential campaign at some point has been inevitable for more than a decade now, ever since the punditocracy achieved its prominence as the primary locus of our national political discourse. Upon announcing his candidacy in December 1991, Pat Buchanan could credibly brag that "No other American has spent as many hundreds of hours debating the great questions of our day, on national television." With seven weekly television appearances plus two regular columns and a popular newsletter, Buchanan was able to enlist the support of his conservative minions with infinitely greater access to the American people than any mere congressman or senator. As a result of his unmediated televisual relationship with his constituency, Buchanan was able to overcome accusations that he was both an anti-Semite and "pacifist isolationist" regarding the Gulf War—accusations that would likely have sunk the aspirations of any professional right-wing politician limited to the usual sound-bite responses. No less significant, moreover, was the decision of "Crossfire" to replace Buchanan during the campaign not with a journalist but with the ultimate political hatchetman, former White House Chief of Staff John Sununu.

On a less grandiose but equally significant scale, we have seen a number of direct pundit interventions into national and international politics. Ironically, we may have the punditocracy to thank for the man who currently sits just "a heartbeat" from the presidency. When Dan Quayle launched his aggressive insider campaign for the vice-presidency, he first conspired with his close friend, Washington Times pundit and former Reagan administration official Kenneth Adelman. "We should have a little boomlet over this," advised Adelman, sitting by the pool with the then-unknown senator. A few days later, on August 10, 1988, a column appeared under Adelman's name entitled "Why Not Dan Quayle?" George Bush apparently read and heavily underlined it. Days later, Quayle was asked to appear on ABC's "This Week with David Brinkley." James Baker III, the most powerful and influential figure in the Bush campaign save Bush himself, told Quayle not to do it. But George Will intervened and, in Quayle's view, outranked Baker. Quayle did the show and got the job.

Pundit interventions in international politics are rarely as heavy-handed, but politically no less significant. New York Times columnist William Safire, for instance, went on a rampage in 1989 against Germany's sale of poison gas to Libya, calling it "Auschwitz in the Sand" and comparing it to a "final solution" for the Jews. Chancellor Helmut Kohl complained to his visitors that "this Safire fellow has done more damage to German-American relations than any other individual." But Safire's story turned out to be true, and the Kohl government was forced to instigate a criminal investigation and change its export laws. When George Will challenged Ferdinand Marcos's democratic credentials on "This Week with David Brinkley," Marcos responded by calling a snap election on the air, setting in motion a process that yielded the "People Power" revolution of 1985. Lyndon Johnson once said that Washington Post op-ed page under editor Russell Wiggins was "worth two divisions" in Vietnam, while The Jerusalem

Post likened *New Republic* owner Martin Peretz to a similar percentage of the fighting force of the Israeli military. Punditocracy efforts, as will be discussed later in the book, were absolutely essential to President Bush's efforts to convince Congress to approve his decision to go to war in January 1991. When, in the war's bloody aftermath, White House Chief of Staff John Sununu quipped that the only pressure for the United States to intervene on behalf of the Kurds was "coming from columnists," those same columnists reminded him that six months earlier, they "were the only ones supporting the use of force to liberate Kuwait." Within two weeks the President had reversed himself and accepted an open-ended commitment to defending the lives of the Kurds.

But these, too, are rare cases. Usually, the punditocracy's influence is invisible and therefore unprovable. No politician can credit a television talk show or newspaper op-ed column with influencing his policies lest he compromise his own reputation for independence. Not a single political pundit earned a mention in Ronald Reagan's memoirs: not even Patrick Buchanan, who served as White House director of communications, or George Will, who coached the President's debating tactics, touched up his speeches, and frequently hosted dinner parties Reagan attended.

Nevertheless it is difficult to imagine a President who could pay more attention to political pundits than Ronald Wilson Reagan. In addition to hiring Buchanan and befriending Will, Reagan was a dedicated fan of "The McLaughlin Group" and was known to bang on the tables at Camp David when one of its members took issue with one of his policies. He appeared at the Group's birthday party, visited its host, John McLaughlin, at his home for dinner, and appointed McLaughlin's wife Secretary of Labor. Reagan was also known to call up members of "Agronsky and Company" after the show. The President took the editorial pages of Sun Myung Moon's *Washington Times* so seriously that when Buchanan entered the White House, he proceeded to allow his entire communications staff to languish in bureaucratic limbo while he devoted himself to the only work he thought truly mattered: planting articles and ideas in its Far Right "Commentary" section.

Today, Georges Bush and Will can't stand each other and apart from issuing the occasional invitation to state dinners, the President is not known to socialize with any major pundits.* Still, the political significance of Washington punditry has barely diminished. When Bush went looking for a

---

*Though Bush did earn himself considerable punditocracy goodwill early in his presidency by showing up at Al Hunt and Judy Woodruff's for a reporter's birthday party.

new top speechwriter in early 1991, he went back to Buchanan's old haunt and hired *Washington Times* editorial page editor Tony Snow. The 1990 mid-term congressional elections were conducted largely as a referendum on a punditocracy-inspired theme—Kevin Phillips's argument that the country's tax system had been tilted in favor of the rich. As the nation marched toward war during the same period, not only could most of Bush's articulate allies be found in the punditocracy, but so too could his most vociferous opponents, led by his soon-to-be Republican rival, Patrick Buchanan.

Even more important than the ability to influence the President's mind is the ability to fashion his intellectual environment. Walter Lippmann observed nearly fifty years ago that "he who captures the symbols by which the public feeling is for the moment contained, controls by that much the approaches of public policy." These approaches are exactly where the influence of the punditocracy is so powerfully pervasive. As the right-wing media critic Jude Wanniski observes, "If politicians are able to decide what the electorate wants, they have to have the parameters of the debate communicated to them by the scriveners." By determining these parameters, the punditocracy can create either a hostile or sympathetic context for a President to pursue his agenda. James Fallows, a speechwriter in the Carter White House, recalls that "what was on the op-ed pages provided the boundaries of what we were allowed to say in the speeches. Underlings in the government, like me, could move the ball up and down the playing field, but the columnists defined the field." Part of Fallows's job, therefore, was to contact op-ed writers to convince them to address areas into which the President was preparing to tread. In one particularly illustrative case, Fallows actually ghost-wrote a *New Republic* editorial himself in order to legitimate a discussion of its subject by his employer, the President of the United States.

The Carter presidency predated the explosion of pundit television, and the "punditocracy effect" had not yet reached its present proportions. The fruition of its influence can be seen a few years later in the 1985 invention of the "Reagan Doctrine" by *New Republic* editor, *Washington Post* and *Time* magazine columnist, and "Inside Washington" regular panelist Charles Krauthammer. On the basis of a few throwaway sentences in the President's State of the Union address, Krauthammer created a concept that brought coherence to what had previously been just an amalgam of rag-tag drug runners, terrorists, Islamic fundamentalists, Maoist revolutionaries, and a few hapless democrats pacing the Capitol hallways for taxpayer handouts. As "freedom fighters" for the Reagan Doctrine, these sorry fellows were transformed into romantic agents of the "restoration" of "democratic militance," fighting to turn back Soviet gains at "the limits of empire." In addition to considerably flattering Reagan's intelligence, Krauthammer's rhetorical umbrella vastly increased the limits of the ideological and financial tribute that high-powered Washington influence peddlers were able to wrangle out of Congress for them.

Similarly, when, in March 1983, Ronald Reagan unveiled his "dream" of a nuclear astrodome-protected United States rendering Moscow's nuclear missiles "impotent and obsolete," a healthy portion of the punditocracy underwent what one writer called "a mass conversion reminiscent of that decreed by King Ethelbert of Kent in the Sixth Century." Led by Kissinger and Brzezinski, the punditocracy created an ideologically inspired smoke screen on behalf of SDI that enabled the Reagan administration and its allies in Congress to soak up tens of billions of tax dollars on what was clear to all disinterested parties would be a perfectly pinheaded scheme.* The fact that 98 percent of the members of the National Academy of Sciences in relevant scientific fields believed that SDI would never "provide an effective defense of the entire U.S. civilian population," and only 4 percent expected such a system to be "survivable and cost-effective at the margin," did not carry much weight in Washington. Predictably, the program turned out to be a $25 billion boondoggle; a "still-expanding, high-risk, space-age national security pork barrel for contractors and top government managers," according to one Army scientist intimately involved with the program's development. The history of supply-side economics, moreover (discussed at length in chapter 8), can be charted along similar lines to those discussed above. Within the confines of Washington's punditocracy-driven insider debate, when reality and ideology come into conflict, it is the former, almost uniformly, that gives way.

For the first half century of its existence, political punditry was simply a branch of journalism. A newspaper column was considered the reward for a particularly distinguished career as a reporter or, in rare cases, of incipient political genius. The first Washington pundits arose in the decade between 1910 and 1920 as a complement to increasingly objective news reporting. During most of the previous century, journalists had few pretenses about their prejudices, and owners frequently used their newspapers as political

---

*Kissinger described SDI as "a major contribution to Western strategy . . . perhaps [Reagan's] greatest contribution to strategic theory." See Henry A. Kissinger, "How to Deal with Gorbachev," *Newsweek*, March 2, 1988, pp. 42, 47. Zbigniew Brzezinski, Robert Jastrow, and Max Kempleman chose the almost comically appropriate biblical incantation that "faith can move mountains," in support of their own version of the system. See "Defense in Space Is Not Star Wars," *The New York Times Magazine*, January 27, 1985, p. 47.

weapons. Neither had much incentive to divorce their opinions from the news and hence, equally little interest in explicitly labeled commentary. Washington was, for most of this period, just a backwater swamp compared to New York or Chicago, and journalists with literary pretensions wisely steered clear of it.

The first truly influential Washington pundit, Walter Lippmann, was in many ways the least typical. Lippmann had earned himself a national reputation as a New York editorial writer and columnist, as well as a best-selling author, when complications in his personal life led him to choose to relocate down South in 1936.* Lippmann's newspaper analyses were so vastly superior to those that had preceded them that he single-handedly raised both the social status and the professional standards of his chosen profession. His columns provided other journalists with an intellectual standard to which they might aspire and his readers with an education in the principles of foreign policy as the young republic grew to superpowerdom. Equally important, he offered high officials the opportunity to challenge, refine, and ultimately communicate their own ideas before attempting to chisel them in the stone of government edict.

But Lippmann was less a journalist than a public philosopher. The pundits who followed him did not have the option of simply applying their genius to the daily rush of events and knocking off something brilliant before lunch. They compensated by combining journalistic investigation with a bit of context, a few explicitly stated opinions, and the kinds of inside dirt that could not comfortably be included in a straight news story. Some, like James Reston of *The New York Times*, rested their reputations on their journalistic prowess. Others, like Joseph Alsop, earned reader loyalty through a combination of Lippmannian hauteur, Restonian legwork, and virulent anti-communism. As their influence grew steadily during the postwar era, a few pundits developed their own political constituencies and achieved the ability to throw their weight around Washington the way any senator or congressman might. In Lippmann's case, his endorsement of a presidential initiative was said to be roughly equal to the combined clout of either four U.S. senators or the Speaker of the House. But the numbers of the select few whose views mattered in terms of the success of a given government policy was truly minuscule. Beyond Lippmann, Reston, and Alsop, it is difficult to name more than a dozen pundits whose influence lasted for more than a single decade between 1930 and 1980.

---

*Lippmann fell in love with the wife of his best friend, Hamilton Fish Armstrong, and the two left their respective spouses in New York to begin a new life together.

The nature of the job and the power of its practitioners began to change during the 1970s as television discovered punditry and vice versa. Once again Lippmann was the pioneer, and once again his example spawned an offspring which bore him only passing resemblance. In the early sixties, CBS News took the extraordinary step of devoting a series of television interviews to a man whose only celebrity derived from his fame as a political columnist.* In the final year of that decade, *Post/Newsweek* stations took the equally remarkable step of devoting a weekly television show to the opinions of a group of journalists, none of whom was named Walter Lippmann. "Agronsky and Company" eventually spawned a series of imitators, opening the doors of stardom and riches to its beneficiaries, and vastly increasing both their visibility and ambitions.

Because of its tangled roots in personal journalism, political commentary, and television production values, the punditocracy never developed a recognizable code of ethics. This situation was further complicated by the entry into the profession in the early 1980s of large numbers of political operatives who could not even pretend to consider themselves journalists. No longer a means of rewarding the profession's most distinguished members, the job opened up to political dealmakers, speechwriters, press flaks, and professional ideologues. During this period, the political column came to be seen as the stepping stone to riches, fame, and kingmaker status all in one. Even better, there were almost no rules about how such success might be achieved. John McLaughlin, himself credibly accused of (and sued for) extremely offensive sexual harassment, feels free to attack the character and credibility of Anita Hill without so much as mentioning his own sordid history.† George Will feels free to coach the President's debating techniques and then judge his performance a few days later. Morton Kondracke and Fred Barnes of *The New Republic* and "The McLaughlin Group" sell their dinner conversation to wealthy American Express Platinum Card holders, "by invitation only." Kondracke, together with Robert Novak, happily accepts thousands of dollars in payments from the Republican party, ostensibly for sharing his political wisdom at a gathering of its governors. Novak and his partner, Rowland Evans, have created something approaching a mini-pundit conglomerate, hosting two television shows, publishing three newsletters, sponsoring pricey off-the-record briefings by cabinet officials for corporate fat cats and, like Barnes and Kondracke, auctioning off their dinner conversation to star-struck readers. Lest anyone object to the

*The first "Conversation with Walter Lippmann" aired on August 11, 1960.

†McLaughlin settled the case out of court for an undisclosed payment. See chapter 5 for details.

coziness of these arrangements, their beneficiaries are shocked, *shocked* that anyone would question their integrity.

Just why this class of commentators came to cohere as the most influential determinants of the shape of American political discourse in the early 1980s may be clearer to future historians than it is today. The most convincing explanation lies in the simultaneous collapse of what had been its competition coupled with the ever-expanding empire of media dominance in all aspects of American cultural life. In many ways, the pundits won the fight because they were simply the only guys left standing in the ring. The bull market in pundit influence coincided with the collapse of the bipartisan establishment that had guided American foreign policy for the previous five decades—as its august membership transformed themselves from the men who created NATO into those who fronted for BCCI. This process began in Vietnam, which sapped the self-confidence of the "Wise Men" and destroyed the trust the American political system had invested in them. It continued through Watergate, the 1970s' oil crises, and the debilitating stagflation of the same period. The rise of the New Right provided the final shove over the ledge. Political parties by and large disappeared during this period as well, in part because of internal divisions on both sides and in part because the onset of the electronic campaign made their infrastructure obsolete. The community of academic experts upon whom our national political discussion had previously relied took the same opportunity to withdraw back to the academy—partially as a result of Vietnam-related divisions and partially as a result of an increasing obsession with social scientific arcana. Independent intellectuals of the *Partisan Review* model also slipped off the public's screen during this period, falling victim to the balkanization of public culture and the collapse of the socioeconomic foundation that had supported their professional lives.

An equally important factor was the pundits' ability to hitch themselves successfully to Ronald Reagan's rising star. Whether it was right-wing pundits becoming influential during "the Reagan revolution" or influential pundits becoming right-wing is basically a chicken/egg proposition. Either way, the fact remains that owing to the wounds inflicted upon American society during the 1960s and 1970s, New Right and neoconservative partisans were able to exploit Americans' political confusion to transport what had been the Far Right borderline of political conversation directly into its center. Just as the Reagan crowd came to power, views that had been considered Cro-Magnon just months earlier became sophisticated. While a tiny cadre of stalwarts managed to hold fast to their liberal instincts during this period, most professed to see new wisdom in cutting taxes for the rich, threatening war with the Soviets, and cracking down on vodka-guzzling welfare queens. The punditocracy hardly required a weatherman to determine which way political winds were blowing.*

A final development completing the dominance of misinformation and misinterpretation in American political discourse was the punditocracy's ever-expanding pretension to expertise in areas its members could not really be fairly expected to master. This is less a reflection on the talents of the men and women who people the punditocracy than on the increasingly impossible demands of their jobs. In Lippmann's day, both the world and American role within it appeared a great deal simpler. When David Halberstam returned

---

*Several rightist organizations have spent a great deal of their funders' money convincing Americans that the media is biased on behalf of liberals. I would not argue that the media is not biased, nor that this bias does not manifest itself on certain issues—particularly abortion—in a politically liberal direction. But the bias is more cultural than political. It is urban, secularist, pseudo-sophisticated, wholly ahistorical, and tremendously cowardly in the face of concerted government or corporate pressure. Overall, conservatives benefit more from these biases than do liberals, but the point is arguable.

Whatever the case regarding the "objective" media, the right's argument has absolutely no relevance with regard to the punditocracy. According to Martin A. Lee and Norman Solomon's Unreliable Sources (New York: Lyle Stuart, 1990), exactly one Democratic candidate since 1932 has received the endorsement of a majority of newspaper publishers. I receive two collections of political punditry in the mail each week. The columnists carried in Conservative Chronicle can be found expounding their views on television approximately fourteen times each week (and this figure does not include John McLaughlin's seven weekly appearances). The writers carried by Liberal Opinion, many of whom are actually quite conservative, show up on average seven times. If we eliminate the two panelists on "Crossfire," CNN's one politically balanced program, the score falls back to nine to two, and the two crusading liberals are Carl Rowan and Jack Germond. (These figures derive from issues appearing the week of September 24, 1990.)

These numbers, meanwhile, do not speak to the deflationary impact that the 1980s has had on the word "liberal." Most of the "liberals" in Liberal Opinion are either humorists, apolitical beat columnists, or professional politicians. On "The McLaughlin Group," the "liberals" are the pro-Reagan Morton Kondracke and the anti-ideological, down-the-middle journalist Jack Germond. On Novak's "Capital Gang," they are former political consultant Mark Shields and Wall Street Journal bureau chief Al Hunt. Hodding Carter III, a former State Department spokesperson who is frequently called upon to play this role, complains, "It is a hell of a day for the Republic when I am offered up as the voice of the liberal left." (Author's interview with Hodding Carter III.)

Because right-wing columnists have so easy a time getting their views published, moreover, their ranks are populated with a great many more intellectual charlatans and self-evident fakers than are those of the center and the center-left. My favorite among these is Jeffrey Hart, a Dartmouth professor, who once composed an entire column on an allegedly famous meeting between George Bernard Shaw and Lyndon Baines Johnson. Hart had apparently read about the meeting in The New Yorker, wholly unaware, however, that the story was one of Veronica Geng's patented fictional parodies. See Jeffrey Hart, March 27, 1990, and Veronica Geng, "Settling an Old Score," The New Yorker, June 17, 1985, p. 36. (Thanks to Roy Rosensweig and Jean-Christophe Agnew.)

from spending two years in the Congo in the mid-1960s, his boss, James Reston, sent him over to see Lippmann. The pundit said to Halberstam, "When I understood Europe, they told me I needed to understand Asia. Now that I've been trying to get Asia, they tell me I need Africa. What can you tell me about Africa?" When Halberstam gave up daily reporting and was approached by a syndicate about beginning a regular column, he remembered this story and decided the entire idea was futile. Even in Lippmann's later days punditry was becoming increasingly difficult to defend as an intellectual enterprise.

Today, a good column has become harder than ever to write, not only because issues have proliferated and increased in complexity, but also because this has become increasingly obvious inside Washington owing to an explosion in the specialized fields of policy research and political consultancy. The most defensible columns are those that specialize on a beat, or those that speak with an intensely personal voice while addressing larger issues from something approaching a human scale. The problem with beat columns, however, is that they force pundits into the same hole into which reporters historically fall: they become prisoners of their sources. The latter, more personal form can have great value when done well, as Mary McGrory and Anna Quindlen continue to prove. But the tendency toward laziness, self-satisfaction, and plain old burnout are more than most pundits can resist. Only a negligible number of pundits manage to pull off the simultaneous feats of intellect, reporting, and integrity required to write an honest analytical column about the panoply of issues facing the country. At present this entire club would probably consist of William Safire of *The New York Times* and Michael Kinsley of *The New Republic*. The number who manage to present a coherent, contextual viewpoint on television is zero.*

As with virtually every aspect of life it touches, television has degraded the quality of political punditry, coarsening its language and destroying what remained of its Lippmann-era sophistication. The level of political analysis on even the best of these shows is usually a notch below that heard on "Cheers." Moreover, owing to the fact that virtually everyone in Washington journalism entertains at least the daydream of riches and fame that only television can bring, even good journalists are tempted to imitate the increasingly rich and famous performers, and so television's simpleton virus flows throughout the entire political discourse. Even in the unlikely event that a pundit has no wish to be television-rich and famous, he must nevertheless address himself to the particular pseudo-reality television has created. Consider the case of *The New Republic*. The magazine is widely

*This calculation includes Michael Kinsley, co-host of "Crossfire."

recognized on all sides of the political divide to be the most influential journal of political opinion in the country. But "the most important influence on *The New Republic* since Walter Lippmann, I fear," says its literary editor, Leon Wieseltier, is "The McLaughlin Group."

A community that lacks the means to detect lies, Walter Lippmann once noted, also lacks the means to preserve its own liberty. Lies of the Watergate/Iran-Contra variety are undoubtedly a problem for our political system. But even more threatening is the superfluousness of our political culture in the face of seismic shifts in our national and international balances of power. America in the 1990s is a nation undergoing an unacknowledged but wrenching transition. We have lost our role as the world's engine of economic growth and guarantor of financial stability, and replaced it with empty boasts of power and unity but nothing resembling a coherent vision of America's role in a reordered world. Our inability to put our financial house in order, to train and educate our workers, to protect our environment, and to provide for our children reveals an unspoken crisis of confidence beneath the surface of American public life. Our economic prosperity and environmental security are withering under sustained attack, and our political leadership—guided and tutored by the punditocracy's anachronistic ideology—has abdicated its responsibility even to think about, much less provide for, the common good. The result of this malign neglect has been the slow degradation of the economic, social, and political foundation for the sustenance of the American Dream.

These problems derive from a common foundation: the deadly combination of right-wing belligerence and intellectual irrelevance that dominates our political discourse. "Ignorance is correctable," notes the social critic Neil Postman, "but what shall we do if we take ignorance to be knowledge?" By allowing the punditocracy to determine the content of its political dialogue, the American political system has committed itself to a path that all but guarantees the acceleration of the destructive pathologies that threaten our common future. What follows is an examination of how this catastrophic situation came to pass.

SECTION I

THE BIRTH OF
A NOTION

"I wish we had never come to Washington. New York is so much nicer and the people there are much more amusing; they dance ever so much better and send one flowers all the time, and then they never talk about first principles."

—*SYBIL LEE, IN HENRY ADAMS'S*
Democracy (1880)

1

THE ROAD TO LIPPMANNDOM

The word "pundit" is a bastardization of the Hindi honorific *pandit*, which confers upon its holder the implication of great learning. *Pandit* derives from the Sanskrit *pandita*, meaning "scholar." Its metamorphosis into the American vernacular owes a great deal to the wives of a group of Rochester, New York, professional men who joined together in 1854 to found a club "devoted to the serious and conscientious investigation of the truth." Not much in the creativity department apparently, the men decided to call their club "The Club." Their wives, however, thinking all this high-mindedness to be a bit much, took to referring to the group as "The Pundit Club" in a facetious reference to the Eastern title. The members were well acquainted with the word's connotations, as one of its members, the Reverend Dr. McIlvaine, had given a report to the group entitled "Observations on the Sanskrit Language," and soon, in good spirits, they adopted the appellation as their own.

The term meandered into the American public dialogue via an article in *The Saturday Review*, dated 1862, in which the author noted a point upon which "the doctors of etiquette and the pundits of refinement" were likely to differ. The final stage of its etymological development seems to have come from the pen of Henry Luce. Having founded *Time* magazine in 1923, Luce adopted the term "pundit," which he derived, most likely, from another well-known club—this a group of Yale undergraduates—and applied it to the *New York World* editorial writer Walter Lippmann.

It is particularly fitting that Lippmann should have the honor of being the first journalist so zinged with the moniker, since the art form did not begin to approach its current level of pretension until he chose journalism as a profession upon graduating from Harvard in 1910. Pre-Lippmann, journalists had been considered an incompletely evolved life form on the American social scale. Reporting was seen as a job for winos, perverts, and those without sufficient imagination to become successful gangsters. The notion of a young man choosing to be a journalist rather than a professor of political philosophy at Harvard, as Lippmann had done, was akin to that of a guest at a society cocktail party refusing a glass of Dom Pérignon and inquiring, instead, if the hostess could come up with a cold Schlitz.

The emergence of Walter Lippmann as America's semi-official public philosopher in the 1920s and 1930s represented the fulfillment of a kind of circular journey for American journalism. In the days of the American revolutionary press, politicians, journalists, pundits, and pamphleteers were by and large the same people. Politicians owned and published newspapers and pamphlets, and probably no one even thought to separate "fact" from "opinion." The press played an absolutely essential role in the creation of a revolutionary consciousness among the colonists, stoking a vibrant public discourse in the late 1760s and early 1770s from resistance to rebellion. In order to achieve this transformation, it created an ideology that was both angry and inspirational. Firebrands Samuel Adams and Thomas Paine used the printing press to turn what were seen as simply a bunch of obnoxious restrictions sent over by the king into an irreconcilable conflict between freedom and slavery. The most important pundits of the time were therefore by definition the most important journalists and politicians as well.

With victory over the British assured, the pundit/politicians then turned their attention to the shaping of the new nation. Between 1787 and 1788, Alexander Hamilton, together with James Madison and John Jay, published the eighty-five essays that made up the *Federalist Papers* in the semi-weekly *New York Independent Journal* in support of the proposed Constitution under the nom de plume "Publius." Their opponents, less well remembered, though equally well regarded at the time, employed the names "Brutus," "The Federal Farmer," and "Cato," in response. In doing so, both sides provided a standard of scholarship and eloquence against which all subsequent political punditry would pale.

The American opinion magazine, where so much of the modern punditocracy is today housed, owes its pedigree in large measure to the wit and energy of Benjamin Franklin. A copy of the British *Spectator*, founded in 1711, landed in Franklin's hands when he was a young man, and he "bought it, read it over and over, and was much delighted with it." The sixteen-year-old Franklin then began his punditry career by stealth—slipping columns underneath the door at his brother's newspaper and signing them "Silence Dogood." Between April and October 1722, *The New England Courant* published fourteen such letters in which the fictional Mrs. Dogood complained of political and religious hypocrisy, championed feminist rights, and laughed at Harvard. James Franklin was so angry and embarrassed when the author's identity was revealed that he ran his precocious brother out of town. Young Benjamin was forced to move to Philadelphia, where he worked at various printing trades, finally founding his *General Magazine* in 1741. *

During the early life of the republic, newspapermen did the bidding of politicians and were rewarded in kind, with no questions as to whom any allegiance lay. Building on the success of his *Federalist* experience, Hamilton founded the *New York Evening Post* in 1801, where he frequently dictated the editorials verbatim. Ten years earlier, during the Washington presidency in Philadelphia, Thomas Jefferson promised the revolutionary poet Philip Freneau a $250-a-year clerkship at the State Department and complete access to all of his correspondence in return for establishing the pro-Jefferson *National Gazette*.

The cozy printing-contract-for-friendly-partisan arrangement continued through 1860, when the founding of the Government Printing Office put an end to the President's store of newspaper venture capital. Before that, Andrew Jackson set something of a record, carrying fifty-seven journalists on the public payroll. They were, according to John Quincy Adams, without exception "the vilest purveyors of slander during the last electioneering campaign," which, by the way, Adams lost. †

The carrying of newspapermen on the public payroll was no doubt helpful to the scribe's standard of living, but it was hardly necessary. James

---

*"Without Freedom of Thought," wrote Mrs. Dogood, "there can be no such Thing as Wisdom and no such Thing as Publick Liberty. . . . Whoever would overthrow the Liberty of a Nation, must begin by subduing the Freeness of Speech." See Karl E. Meyer, *Pundits, Poets and Wits* (New York: Oxford University Press, 1990), p. xvii. The letters themselves can be found in *Benjamin Franklin's Letters to the Press*, ed. Verner W. Crane (Chapel Hill, NC, 1950). The full name of Franklin's magazine was *The General Magazine and Historical Chronicle for All the British Plantations in America*. Unfortunately for Franklin's place in the record books, he went to press three days after his employee, Andrew Bradford, brought out his short-lived *American Magazine*.

†See John Tebbel and Sarah Miles Watts, *The Press and the Presidency* (New York: Oxford University Press, 1985), p. 78. Adams's quote may deserve greater credibility than his political interests might imply. These appointments were drawn from a pool described by fellow editor John Fenno as "the most ignorant, mercenary, and vulgar automatons that ever were moved by the constantly rusting wires of sordid mercantile averice." See Allen Nevins, *American Political Opinions, 1859–1922* (Port Washington, NY: Kinnikat Press, 1928), p. 7.

Gordon Bennett, the profession's first Washington correspondent, ably demonstrated the prevailing standards of fairness and objectivity in his first *New York Enquirer* dispatch, published on January 2, 1828, when he disclosed that "it will be found that the Jacksonian party are the truest friends of the country, and that they will encourage every interest but favor none." While wealthy publishers and their hired editors did enjoy the prerogative of purely editorial columns, these were often nothing more than a harmless vanity: the true editorializing was done in the news columns.

For the first twelve or so decades of the republic, the only generally recognized names in the journalism profession were those of the wealthy owner/publishers, crusading editors, and the syndicated feature writers, the vast majority of whom were humorists and satirists. Many belonging to the first category enjoyed a significant degree of influence over the opinions of their literate publics. The late *New York Times* pundit, Arthur Krock, saw the forerunners of his profession at work at the Cincinnati Liberal/Democratic Convention of 1872, at which publisher-journalist Horace Greeley was nominated for President. Scheming quite openly to deny their colleague his ambition were four powerful editors who called themselves the "Quadrilateral": Henry Watterson, the legendary publisher of the *Louisville Courier-Journal*; Murat Halstead of the *Cincinnati Commercial*; Sam Bowles of the *Springfield [Mass.] Republican*, and Horace White of the *Chicago Tribune*. The editors were so impressed with one another's wisdom that each printed the editorials of the other three in his paper.* The plot failed, due to the fact that Greeley's assistant, Whitelaw Reid, was inexplicably admitted to the inner councils of the cabal.

The incident may mark the beginnings of the all-important institution of the syndication of individual pundits. The technological phenomenon of newspaper syndication itself, the foundation upon which pre-electronic punditry rested, came on the heels of the invention of the telegraph, when, in May 1846, *The New York Tribune* and *The New York Herald* began running identical wire dispatches from Washington.† The most widely syndicated writers were, however, rarely political. *The New York Sun* syndicated the work of Henry James. The McClure's syndicate handled the work of Robert Louis Stevenson, Mark Twain, Henry Cabot Lodge, Rudyard Kipling, Jack London, and Arthur Conan Doyle. William Randolph

---

*Greeley was nominated on the Liberal Republican and Democratic tickets. He lost to Republican U. S. Grant, which was just as well, since he died before the Electoral College cast its ballots. See Arthur Krock, "The Early Personal Journalists," in Marquis Childs and James Reston, eds., *Walter Lippmann and His Times* (New York: Harcourt Brace Jovanovich, 1959), pp. 83–110.

†This development led to the formation of the Associated Press three years later.

Hearst's syndicate—the great-grandfather of today's King Features—featured the sardonic skepticism of Ambrose Bierce before he disappeared into the Mexican Civil War, and the prophetic satire of Chicago wit Finley Peter Dunne, whose barkeep, Mr. Martin J. Dooley, rivals Huckleberry Finn and Jay Gatsby as modern punditry's favorite fictional oracles.

Before punditry could come to play a significant role in political debate, however, "straight" American journalism first needed to rid itself of the opinionated arguments that were its foundation. The initial seeds of objective reporting appeared in New York in 1851, in part as a reaction to the perceived excesses of the crusaders. First and foremost among the guilty, no doubt, was Horace Greeley. Though not quite as vociferous as the *Liberator's* William Lloyd Garrison, Greeley hardly rested to take a breath as he and his newspaper, *The New York Tribune*, thundered against war, social inequality, and the South's peculiar institution. In addition to sponsoring the foreign-correspondent career of an unknown European journalist by the name of Marx, Greeley's *Tribune* can take credit for founding the institution of the modern editorial page.* The great American historian and former *New York World* editorial writer Allen Nevins described Greeley's creation as follows:

> a page treating a wide variety of topics in a variety of manners, though pursuing a consistent policy: achieving a level of genuine literary merit; produced by a body of editors, not by a single man and representing their united elevated judgment and information; and earnestly directed to the elevation and rectification of public opinion.

What Greeley did not do, or make any pretense of doing, however, was remove these same opinions from his news pages. His former managing

---

*Greeley's hiring of Karl Marx is a wonderfully ironic episode in the history of both the political philosopher and American journalism. Marx himself hated writing his columns, and complained to a friend that "this continual journalistic hack-work is getting on my nerves. It takes up a lot of time, destroys any continuity in my efforts and in the final analysis amounts to nothing at all." Judging by his published letters, however, it is hard to work up much sympathy. Unbeknownst to Greeley and his managing editor Charles Dana, Marx had subcontracted out at least nineteen of these London-based dispatches—those dealing with revolution and counterrevolution in Germany and published between October 1851 and October 1852—to his uncredited German partner, Friedrich Engels. The articles stopped arriving, however, because the paper cut the fee for them by 50 percent, from ten dollars to just five. With his family sick and hungry, the author "did not have the penny to go read newspapers." Why he needed to read newspapers when Engels was doing all the work, Marx does not explain. The "hack-work" quote appears in Neil A. Grauer, *Wits and Sages* (Baltimore: Johns Hopkins University Press, 1984), p. 7. The entire correspondence between Marx and Engels on the subject is reprinted in *Karl Marx–Friedrich Engels, Selected Letters: The Personal Correspondence, 1844–1877*, ed. Fritz J. Raddatz (Boston: Little, Brown, 1980), pp. 34–51. The "did not have a penny" quote appears on page 51.

editor, Henry J. Raymond, did not appreciate what he considered to be the overwrought prose of his ex-employer and on September 18, 1851, Raymond responded with the launching of *The New-York Times*. In a thinly veiled jibe at Greeley, he promised his readers on page one of the inaugural issue that "We do not mean to write as if we were in a passion unless that should really be the case; and we shall make a point to get into a passion as rarely as possible."

If one wished to chart the earliest antecedent of the search for the journalistic Holy Grail of "objectivity," one might do well to begin with Raymond's first issue. His paper was intended to emulate the *Times* of London in its aspirations toward a journalism of authority and completeness. Raymond's *Times* did introduce a new note of decency and restraint into political journalism, but a man who served as chairman of the Republican National Committee and managed Abraham Lincoln's second presidential campaign does not really provide an appropriate model for aspiring objectivists. Moreover, Raymond's impact was slight, and following his death in 1869, the profession came to be dominated by E. L. Godkin, the combative British aristocrat who campaigned against American imperialism, government corruption, and unsound money.

The editor of *The New York Evening Post* as well as *The Nation* magazine for nearly three decades, Godkin was said by William James to be the most influential writer of his generation. A combative generation it must have been. Godkin called President Cleveland an "international anarchist," and compared the modes of operation inside the nation's yellow journals to those of Hell, gambling houses, brothels, and brigands' caves, noting that judged purely on the basis of intellectual integrity, the newsrooms finished a poor fifth.* With the influence of Godkin and the continuing preeminence of old-time publisher/editors like Watterson of Louisville, Samuel Bowles I and II of Springfield, Massachusetts, and William Allen White of Emporia, Kansas, another serious stab at the virtues of newspaper objectivity would have to wait until nearly the end of the century.

In 1896, a Chattanooga publisher named Adolph Ochs purchased the ailing *New-York Times*. Ochs was a man with big plans. On August 19, 1896, the paper's readers awoke to a "business announcement" explaining that it would henceforth be the policy of the paper "to give the news, all the

---

*The Nation, America's oldest continuously publishing political magazine, was founded by the architect Frederick Law Olmsted in 1865. Godkin, its founding editor, sold it to his *New York Evening Post* in 1881, where it was issued as a weekly supplement for the next thirty-three years.

news, in concise and attractive form, in language that is parliamentary in good society," and "to give it impartially, without fear or favor, regardless of any party, sect, or interest involved." Adolph Ochs's *Times* would be an "independent newspaper" that would "tolerate no tampering with the news, no coloring, no deception." It would stand for "the fullness, trustworthiness and impartiality of its news service." Ochs's pronouncement was soon reprinted in papers across the country.

In addition to his grand public gesture, Ochs instituted a number of new features in the newspaper, all of which were directed toward attracting a new kind of readership. He began with a weekly financial review and followed up with a list of "Buyers in Town," lists of court cases and records, and a column called "The Merchants' Point of View." Most reporters expected these changes to make the *Times* duller than ever, but to their astonishment, it attracted thousands of new readers and fantastic increases in the flow of advertising. Soon enough, the paper that had been losing $1,000 a day when Ochs purchased it became the "Business Bible" of New York and a veritable money-printing machine for Mr. Ochs. Circulation skyrocketed from 9,000 in 1896 to more than 120,000 nine years later, and 343,000 by 1920.

The economic foundation for Ochs's success can be gleaned from the incredible urban growth statistics of the period.* New York was exploding with new wealth and a newly well-educated population. By providing commercially oriented information to consumers and removing the crusading tone opted for by Greeley and Godkin, as well as the sensationalist ravings of the yellow journals of the time, Ochs managed to invent a new and tremendously profitable form of American journalism and a status symbol for an emerging commercial class.

As Christopher Lasch observes, this new press attracted exactly the kinds of readers advertisers were eager to attain:

*The percentage of the American labor force engaged in nonagricultural work jumped from 41% in 1860 to 62% in 1900. Bank deposits tripled between 1865 and 1885, then quadrupled in the twenty years following that. The population of New York City jumped from 1 million to 1.5 million between 1880 and 1890. Meanwhile, illiteracy declined from 20% of the population to 10.7%. See Arthur M. Schlesinger, *Rise of the City, 1878–1898* (New York: Macmillan, 1932). For more recent data and interpretative material, see Sam Bass Warner, Jr., *The Urban Wilderness: A History of the American City* (New York: Harper & Row, 1972), and Charles N. Glaab and A. Theodore Brown, *A History of Urban America* (New York: Macmillan, 1976). The literacy figures in particular had enormous implications for politicians. When "Boss" William Macy Tweed instructed his henchmen to destroy copies of New York's anti-Tammany newspapers in the 1860s, he worried not about the editorials, but only their cartoons. "My constituents can't read," Tweed explained, "but damn it, they can see pictures." Tweed died in prison in 1878. See Stephen Hess, "The Ungentlemanly Art," in *Gannett Center Journal*, Spring 1989, p. 122.

well-heeled readers, most of whom probably thought of themselves as independent voters. . . . Responsibility came to be equated with the avoidance of controversy because advertisers were willing to pay for it. Some advertisers were also willing to pay for sensationalism, though on the whole, they preferred a respectable readership to sheer numbers. What they clearly did not prefer was "opinion." It did not guarantee the right audience. No doubt they also hoped that an aura of objectivity, the hallmark of responsible journalism, would also rub off on the advertisements that surrounded the increasingly slender columns of print.

Historians generally consider Ochs's *Times* to be the first example of a newspaper dedicated to objective journalism. But what Ochs and company wrought in the *Times* was less the goal of objective journalism than the goal of appearing to strive for it. As Godkin's successor, Oswald Garrison Villard, demonstrated in his 1933 book *Some Newspapers and Newspaper-Men*, the *Times* was still what Villard called "a class paper, pure and simple." Its dedication to impartiality fell by the wayside when it proved ideologically inconvenient. Vociferously opposed to the Russian Revolution, the *Times* reported that Petrograd had fallen six times, been on the verge of capture three more times, been burned to the ground twice, been in absolute panic twice and in revolt against the Bolsheviks on six different occasions, and insisted that the regime was on the verge of collapse over ninety times. None of these impending catastrophes, Charles Merz and Walter Lippmann pointed out in *The New Republic*, had much foundation in fact. But for the purposes of delineating the history of punditry, the *Times*'s failure to be "objective" in its news columns is less important than the impression it created: the impression that "objectivity" was possible and desirable, and that any "responsible" newspaper had better strive for it if its owners wanted to be rich, powerful, and admired like those of *The New-York Times*. As a result, during the next two decades, smaller-scale imitations sprouted up across America.

Though the professional developments it inspired were gradual ones, Ochs's departure was in fact quite a radical one. Without at least the pretense of objective news reports as a counterpoint, it is quite impossible to imagine punditry's playing anything like the political role into which it has grown in the past hundred years. Absent a professionally sacred faith in objective news gathering, there would be no call for political pundits to comment on it and interpret it. This relatively banal observation goes a long way toward explaining why the United States is the only Western country to enjoy (if that be the word) the presence of a pundit class: it is the only nation in which the aspiration toward objectivity dominates the profession of quality journalism.

Where journalism drops the pretense of reporting only fact, the need for "opinion writers," dedicated ideally to placing the news in a larger and more useful context for readers, diminishes accordingly.*

Around the same time that newspaper publishers were beginning to emulate Ochs, the young Walter Lippmann attempted in three remarkable studies of the American media—*Liberty and the News* (1920), *Public Opinion* (1922), and *The Phantom Public* (1924)—to grapple with some of the more complex interrelationships between imperfect journalism and the fragilities of modern democratic practice. Given the limits of even the best American journalism, combined with the inability of the average citizen to grasp even the most basic facts about its leaders and institutions, how, Lippmann asked, could a functional republic be forged?

Reality, to Lippmann (and to Ochs, no doubt) was something picturable, like a baseball box score or a stock market quotation. He titled the most impressive chapter in *Public Opinion*, the most demanding of his studies, "The World Outside and the Picture in Our Heads." The problem with journalism, according to Lippmann's critique, was its inability to focus the lens correctly on the more intricate manifestations of reality. "News comes from a distance," Lippmann complained, "it comes helter-skelter." Journalism works fine, Lippmann explains, "when it can report the score of a game, or a transatlantic flight, or the death of a monarch." But where the picture is more complex, "as for example, in the matter of a success of a policy, or the social conditions among a foreign people—where the real answer is neither yes or no, but subtle and a matter of balanced evidence," then journalism "causes no end of derangement, misunderstanding and even misrepresentation."

The inherent limitations upon journalists, moreover, are compounded by the inability of the general public to understand and assimilate the imperfect information it receives. The thirty-three-year-old public philosopher is rather harsh on his fellow citizens, but contemporary information surveys would seem to bear him out:

> The mass of absolutely illiterate, of feeble-minded, grossly neurotic, undernourished and frustrated individuals, is very considerable, much more considerable there is reason to think than we generally suppose. Thus a wide appeal is circulated among persons who are mentally children or barbarians, people whose vitality is exhausted, shut-in people

---

*Other Western nations have pundits, but they do not assume anything like the political significance they enjoy in the United States. For a discussion of the British and Canadian cases, see Lloyd Tataryn, *The Pundits: Power, Politics and the Press* (Toronto: Deneau Publishers, 1985), chapters 3 and 4.

and people whose experience has comprehended no factor in the problem under discussion. The stream of public opinion is stopped by them in little eddies of misunderstanding, where it is discolored with prejudice and far-fetched analogy.

The net result of imperfect journalism consumed by ignorant people is, in Lippmann's view, the creation of a "pseudo-environment" of the public mind, in which a perverse kind of democratic politics takes place.

Hardly the "omnicompetent" agrarian yeoman of Jeffersonian theory, the private citizen or "outsider," as Lippmann called him, had a vision of political realities no better than that of a deaf spectator in the back row of a sporting event. "He does not know what is happening, why it is happening, what ought to happen; he lives in a world which he cannot see, does not understand and is unable to direct." "We must assume," therefore, "that a public is inexpert in its curiosity, intermittent, that it discerns only gross distinctions, is slow to be aroused and quickly diverted; that, since it acts by aligning itself, it personalizes whatever it considers, and is interested only when events have been melodramatized as a conflict." The danger arises when the populace become the "inevitable victims of agitation and propaganda." The victors in such a system are "the quack, the charlatan, the jingo, and the terrorist." The result, both for democracy and for intelligent governance, is disaster.

At first, in the 1919 articles that became *Liberty and the News*, Lippmann suggested addressing the problem simply by improving the quality of the journalism Americans received. He complained that reporting was not a "dignified profession for which men will invest the time and cost of an education, but an underpaid, insecure, anonymous form of drudgery, constructed on catch-as-catch-can principles." Merely to value the reporter in terms of his "real importance to civilization" would go some distance in alleviating the problem.

By the time he published *Public Opinion* three years later, however, Lippmann had grown increasingly pessimistic. Journalism did not offer much hope. Even if undertaken relatively objectively, it could not create the "mystical force called Public Opinion" merely by "acting upon everybody for thirty minutes in twenty-four hours," when all other public institutions had failed to do so. Instead, in one of the strangest intellectual excursions of his career, Lippmann proposed the creation of "intelligence bureaus" made up of what he called "special men." These would be social scientists whose job it would be to model reality like a DNA molecule and explain it to the confused citizenry. His prototype was the government's Bureau of Standards. In Lippmann's plan, the group would act as a kind of social scientific House of Lords, which freed from the pseudo-realities of democratic politics would be able to inform and persuade in such a manner that citizens would be protected from their own ignorance and gullibility.

For all the brilliance and prophetic qualities of Lippmann's diagnosis, he never did come up with a sensible solution. He wisely abandoned his intelligence bureaus in *The Phantom Public*, but failed to replace them with a workable alternative. Fortunately for the history of punditry, however, Lippmann did offer a kind of stopgap answer to the problem: the services of one Walter Lippmann. Through his newspaper column, his books, and later his television appearances, Lippmann interposed himself between the inadequacies of incomplete, biased, and stereotyped "objective" journalism and the mass of confused, ignorant, and just plain lazy American citizens who were otherwise defenseless against the emotional pull of their pseudo-environments. In doing so he filled what was and remains an absolutely crucial vacuum in the functioning of American democracy.

While the governing elite—the "insiders," as Lippmann called them—sought to manipulate the news media in order to "manufacture the consent" of the governed, Lippmann worked diligently to inform himself on the great issues of the day and then educate his readers to the point where they might intelligently judge the actions of their leaders. "In this," Lippmann contended at the end of his career, he and other pundits performed an "essential service . . . to find out what is going on under the surface and beyond the horizon; to infer, to deduce, to imagine and to guess what is going on inside, what this meant yesterday and what it could mean tomorrow." In this selfless pursuit, political punditry would do "what every sovereign citizen is supposed to do but has not the time or the interest to do for himself."

The theory's fault line lies in its vulnerability to human idiosyncrasies. To work effectively, the theory required two enormous assumptions: First, that the pundit could accumulate the requisite "insider" information from those who control it via disinterested inquiry—rather than through some implicit quid pro quo of sympathy and support. Second, the notion assumes that the pundit will continue to identify with the interests of the outsider class vs. those of the insider elite. It does so despite the fact that virtually their entire profesional and social lives were likely to be dominated by interaction with that same ruling class. Should either of these two assumptions be undermined, the pundit becomes not an agent of democracy but an accomplice to its subversion.

It is right and proper that one of the richest American political biographies of the past generation had as its subject Walter Lippmann. Lippmann was born with the American Century, exactly one hundred years after the

Constitution, and spent his entire professional life seeking to educate his countrymen about the risks and responsibilities that its tremendous power entailed. From the time that Teddy Roosevelt called the twenty-six-year-old writer "the most brilliant man of his age in the United States," through the days that Lyndon Johnson drove him out of Washington, so angered by Lippmann's refusal to endorse his war in Vietnam that Johnson took to making bawdy jokes at Lippmann's expense in the presence of foreign dignitaries, no other private individual played so central a role in the shaping of the nation's political debate. Lippmann's own rise to preeminence coincided with America's rise from a massive, untamed industrial giant to the most influential power the world has ever seen. Given the relative ignorance that even the most sophisticated Americans exhibited about the foundations of international diplomacy, coupled with the vast ambitions of the emerging foreign policy elite, it seems fair to conclude that if Walter Lippmann had never existed, America would have had to invent him.

Lippmann was not the first full-fledged Washington pundit. David Lawrence, the founder of U.S. News & World Report, began adding a tag line of his pro-business, anti-labor opinions to his New York Post dispatches in 1915. When the Post began syndicating Lawrence a year later, he fulfilled the basic criteria for Washington punditry, nearly twenty-five years before Lippmann joined him: he wrote his column from Washington, he was nationally syndicated, and he had been given full authority by his superiors to vent his opinions.

Lawrence and his journalist colleagues, however, formed an intensely parochial and self-contained fellowship. When Arthur Krock first arrived in Washington in 1919, he found what he called "a small group of pompous frauds" dominating the press corps, "identifiable not only by their disinclination to do legwork, which was great, but in most cases by their attire. They habitually wore frock coats and silk hats, dropped big names in profession, carried canes and largely made contacts with their single news source in the noble saloons of the period." Before Lippmann came to the city in 1939, Washington punditry was important only to Washingtonians—and to them not terribly so.

Having already published two considerable works of political inquiry, Lippmann began his career as a regular political commentator in November 1914, when his name appeared on the masthead of the first issue of The New Republic. Herbert Croly, the magazine's editor-in-chief, and Willard and Dorothy Straight, its financiers, were deeply committed to Roosevelt's Bull Moose Progressivism. Lippmann, by his own account, was positively in love with the Moose himself. But the romance soured almost immediately when the magazine, opposing Woodrow Wilson's foray into Mexico in December

1914, gently chided Roosevelt for trying to goad the President into a full-scale invasion. Roosevelt went on a rampage, damning *The New Republic*'s editors as "three circumcised Jews and three anemic Christians."

With Teddy raging, Woodrow Wilson saw his opening and launched a personal lobbying campaign for the magazine's support, inviting Lippmann to his summer home in Shadow Lawn, New Jersey. There the President expertly massaged the young writer's ego, showing him secret cables and soliciting his advice. Probably no pundit has ever survived a personal session with a president and classified war cables without soon convincing himself of the merit of the man's viewpoint. When it was over, Lippmann returned to New York and convinced Croly as well. Shortly thereafter, he received his first invitation to dine at the White House.

From dinner at the Wilson White House through the days of his banishment from Lyndon Johnson's Oval Office more than half a century later, Lippmann dealt with the tension inherent in his business in a decidedly ambivalent fashion. He professed the need for an "airspace" between the worlds of power and punditry, but freely ignored his own advice. Time and again, Lippmann proved all too easily misled by powerful insiders, encouraging him to mislead his powerless outsiders with disastrous results. In the matter of the still unsolved 1948 murder of the journalist George Polk in war-torn Greece, Lippmann lent his name to a whitewashed investigation that dishonestly served the interests of U.S. Cold War diplomacy. Whether calling a 1933 speech by Hitler "genuinely statesmanlike" and "evidence of good faith," or accepting the Pentagon's 1965 assertion that the bombs it was dropping on North Vietnam did not "kill anybody" because "they're political bombings," Lippmann found himself being made to look ridiculous by history. On these occasions, as on many others, Lippmann simply accepted the word of power as sufficient evidence of its good faith.

Throughout his early life, Lippmann had benefited from the patronage of great and powerful men, to whom he attached himself with an enthusiasm that Michael Kinsley has named "the American sycophancy." From the time that he abandoned his radical Greenwich Village pretensions and moved metaphorically uptown to the luxurious and well-funded liberalism of *The New Republic*, Lippmann wedded himself to the views and interests of the American elite. Party meant nothing to Lippmann. His only loyalties were to the influence of his ideas and the idea of his influence.

As his friend James Reston observes, "One of the interesting things about Lippmann was that he did more to argue for the principle of detachment and was [himself] more attached" to politicians than any other columnist. Reston attributes Lippmann's weakness on the issue to his need for social status and his "fascination for the social whirl." Lippmann loved, according to Reston, "going to embassies and philosophizing after dinner and he liked to be asked to the White House. It's true that people talk about money as corruptive, but the social life is much more so than money."

Following the war and a short, unhappy return to *The New Republic*, Lippmann was recruited for what may have been the best job in the history of journalism: editorial writer for *The New York World*. Since the *World* turned out its final heartbreaking issue on February 27, 1931, America has yet to see a paper so literate, so exciting and faithful to the Front Page legends with which modern underappreciated journalists still console themselves. The *World* was a monument to the possibilities of drinking, lying, gambling, and relatively honest daily journalism.

Under editor Frank Cobb, the *World* invented the home and hearth of modern punditry, the op-ed page, and amassed a staff of writers that would make any modern editor cry. Heywood Broun, who began as a sportswriter, moved his pro-labor column to the op-ed page, where he fiercely defended its leadership from attacks by the Hearst chain and the Republican President. The rest of the constellation included Maxwell Anderson, the future playwright; James M. Cain, the future novelist; and Allen Nevins, the future historian.

Cobb was diagnosed with inoperable cancer in 1923 and left Lippmann as editorial editor-in-chief. Although his editorials were unsigned, Lippmann, by now the author of four celebrated books and countless magazine articles, had grown into a New York society celebrity. He found his counsel sought after from many quarters, including Calvin Coolidge's White House. Needless to say, he emerged from his meeting with renewed sympathy for the President's predicament.

The year 1923 was seminal in the history of political commentary for another important reason: the debut of *Time* magazine. Henry Luce's prospectus for his new magazine estimated that the number of American college graduates had reached a million by this time. Despite rising education levels in the country, the vast majority of people outside New York, Boston, and Washington had almost no access to quality information about the state of affairs in the world—with the exception of those who read Walter Lippmann. Television did not enter into most American lives until the 1950s, and commercial radio, which began in the twenties, was a medium devoted primarily to the insights of commentators like Jack Benny and George Burns. Few if any syndicated columnists paid much attention to foreign events and most local newspapers did not run the Washington columnists who did.

In the coming decades, Luce and *Time* would share with Lippmann the battleground for the college-educated mind in America. But in the twenties,

Time was still only the promise of power and influence. Its tiny New York staff clipped and pasted from other sources, throwing in generous helpings of American "corn" as demanded by Luce. The early twenties' *Time* was not terribly political, and it was not until the thirties that the voice of Luce, with its emphasis on small-town Presbyterian virtues, virulent anti-communism, and the U.S. imperial mission in Asia, came to dominate its news coverage.

When the *World* finally expired in 1931, Lippmann moved to the Republican *Herald-Tribune* and began writing his regular column, "Today and Tomorrow." Having turned down offers of a chair at Harvard, the presidency of the University of North Carolina, and journalism jobs at *The New York Times*, the *World Telegram*, and the Hearst chain, it was hardly an overstatement when *Time* announced that at age forty-one, its cover boy, Walter Lippmann, had become the "Moses," the "Prophet of Liberalism." The fact that a writer identified with daily journalism could be considered for so wide a range of honors, much less turn them down, bespoke a cultural revolution in society's perception of the profession for which Lippmann was almost singularly responsible. Before a distinguished crowd assembled by the Academy of Political Science at a dinner given in his honor, Lippmann defined what he considered to be the tenets of progressive politics, under fire from left and right during the dark days of the depression:

> Who but a political hack can believe [that] . . . the fate of the nation hangs upon the victory of either political party. . . . Who can believe that an orderly, secure and just economic order can be attained by the simple process of arousing the people against the corporations? . . . Is it vain to suppose that our problems can be dealt with by rallying the people to some crusade that can be expressed in a symbol, a phrase, a set of principles or a program? If that is what the progressives are looking for today, they are looking in vain.

Lippmann's liberalism had, by 1931, lost all vestiges of its former radicalism. He had long ago given up, as Reston notes, "bleeding for the poor." The problems faced by modern government, he recognized, were post-ideological and managerial in nature. Thirty years before Daniel Bell sounded his clarion call to the New Class/managerial elite, Lippmann enlisted liberalism in the search for a "more civilized and rational" organization of the corporate economy. While some of his former colleagues at *The New Republic* were calling for a vote for the Communists, Lippmann's liberalism was now completely self-identified with the exercise of power.

*   *   *

Thus did Walter Lippmann fulfill the role he had envisioned for his philosopher kings in *Public Opinion*. By convincing both the rulers and the ruled that his work was integral to their well-being, he created a central role for political pundits in the political power structure of the emerging superpower. The American people needed him to understand their world. The government depended upon him to explain its role, to the citizenry and to itself. Both political punditry and elite journalism grew in status as a result. As Lippmann negotiated these trends in the twenties and early thirties, the role of other pundits also expanded in the public's consciousness. Evidence of the increasing importance of pundits of all political stripes can be seen in the text of a prophetic resolution proposed but not passed at the 1938 convention of the American Society of Newspaper Editors (ASNE):

> This society sees in the increasing of the press of syndicated columns of opinions and interpretation—for which individual papers assume no responsibility—a threat to the independent thought of the newspaper public. It fears that predigested opinion, sweetened with rhetoric and garnished with Olympian pronouncements, may come to be accepted by too many readers as an easy substitute for fact and individual thought.

Among the beneficiaries of this growing influence were Dorothy Thompson, the fiery anti-Fascist, and Drew Pearson, the schmaltzy and sentimental liberal populist. On the right, know-nothing yahoos like Westbrook Pegler and pro-business, Chamber of Commerce voices like David Lawrence also grew in prominence.

Lippmann's most significant service during this period was the role he played in educating the young republic for its future as a superpower. Though it had grown to be the only nation powerful enough to frustrate the Nazi conquest of Europe, the United States was nevertheless still in its infancy in terms of the sophistication of its foreign policy. Franklin Roosevelt's 1933 inaugural address had contained exactly one paragraph about foreign affairs. When the war struck eight years later, the country was still obsessed with the domestic sources of economic depression, and even its ruling elite was relatively ignorant of both the international roots of the depression and the war. During the interventionist/isolationist debate that preceded Pearl Harbor, Americans began to get a taste of the kinds of questions that had riveted Europe since the Peace of Westphalia. Could alliance with warring countries prevent American entry into the war? Could a swift and early intervention prevent a long and bloody late one? Could America prosper with hostile nations and ideologies controlling Europe and the seas around it?

Public debate, however, remained mired in a Norman Rockwell

painting. Senator Harry Truman spoke for many when he explained, "if we see that Germany is winning, we ought to help Russia and if Russia is winning, we ought to help Germany and that way let them kill as many as possible." Wall Street by and large concurred. As the editors of *The Wall Street Journal* put it, "The American people know that the principal difference between Mr. Hitler and Mr. Stalin is the size of their respective mustaches."

But Walter Lippmann, together with the self-selected members of the infant foreign policy establishment, was laying the foundation for a far grander, and in many ways more ominous path. Lippmann saw, in the wake of Europe's exhaustion, a vision of a powerful and expansive American empire. As if intoxicated by this vision, Lippmann proclaimed, as war raged overseas, "What Rome was to the ancient world . . . America is to be to the world of tomorrow." The country, he worried, "cling[s] to the mentality of a little nation on the frontiers of the civilized world, though we have the opportunity, the power, and the responsibilities of a very great nation at the center of the civilized world." In a prophetic critique of this vision, the progressive historian Charles A. Beard took Lippmann to task for the "ornate, glistening, masculine" language he employed in this passage, without sufficiently considering the consequences that empire would bring. * But by the time the United States entered the war in December 1941, the die had been cast. Lippmann's side had emerged victorious in the war for the elite mind, and now needed only to enlist the blind, ignorant spectators onto the new playing field as well.

For a brief, thirty-year century, the United States would indeed become the new Rome: fighting wars and reordering the lives of people in countries whose names its citizens could not pronounce. An ambivalent general in this effort, Lippmann nevertheless enlisted countless majors and admirals, ensigns and privates, into the struggle to build a new empire. In the end it

---

*"Rome conquered, ruled and robbed other peoples from the frontier in Scotland to the sands of Arabia," wrote Beard, "from the Rhine to the Sahara, and then crumbled to ruins. Does anybody in his right mind really believe that the United States can or ought to play that role in the future, or anything akin to it? America is to be 'what Great Britain has been to the modern world.' Well, what has Great Britain been to the modern world? Many fine and good things, no doubt. But in terms of foreign policy, Britain swept the Spanish, the Dutch, the French and the Germans from the surface of the seven seas. During the past three hundred years Britain has waged numerous wars on the Continent to maintain, among other things, the balance of power. Britain has wrested colonies from the Spanish, the Dutch, the French, and the Germans, has conquered, ruled and dictated to a large part of the globe. Does anyone really believe that the United States can or ought to do all these things, or anything akin to them?" See Charles A. Beard, "Giddy Minds and Foreign Quarrels: An Estimate of American Foreign Policy," *Harper's*, September 1939, pp. 349–50.

proved a bitter, and in many respects, self-defeating effort. Most intoxicated journeys are. But through his remarkable talent for synthesis and persuasion, Walter Lippmann helped forge a new role in the American political dialogue for a tiny class of journalists and commentators who chose to emulate his example. If it was not exactly a road to an "omnicompetent" citizenry, it was at least a means of educating a new class of American leaders for the burdens that providence—together with Nazi Germany—had placed on our doorstep.

2

LIPPMANNDOM

In the spring of 1944 Henry Luce's *Life* magazine rejected an excerpt from Walter Lippmann's book *U.S. War Aims* because he found it "too anti-Russian." The problem was that Lippmann was simultaneously ahead of and behind his time. Had Lippmann offered the piece four years earlier, when Luce's *Time* was calling Joseph Stalin "the world's most hated man," he might have made a sale. Had he waited three more years, by which time Luce was calling Lippmann "naive" and *Life* was proclaiming that the Soviets were "intent upon bringing chaos, the collapse of civilization and the Communization of the European continent," then the piece might have gone over better too. But Lippmann had submitted an essay noting that the Soviet Union was a totalitarian country when Luce publications were calling Stalin "a great wartime leader," and the Russians "one hell of a people," who "look like Americans, dress like Americans and think like Americans." In the dawn's early light of the Cold War, the ideological constructs of American politics were in constant flux. As Lippmann learned to his dismay, timing was all.

The Cold War braced Washington like a gust of frigid wind. Two months into his presidency, in June 1945, Harry Truman, President of short memory, observed that Americans had no reason to be "afraid of Russia." "They've always been our friends," he insisted, "and I can't see any reason why they shouldn't always be." Truman certainly found his reasons. Like Luce and the rest of postwar Washington, he became increasingly frustrated with Stalin's truculence and the Soviet unwillingness to abide by U.S.

interpretations of wartime accords relating to Eastern Europe and the Middle East. U.S. politicians, led not infrequently by Truman, did their best to create a sense of permanent crisis, fanning the flames of Cold War hysteria to what his trusted adviser Clark Clifford accurately predicted would be "considerable political advantage." The city's temperature heated up so quickly that by March 1948, Joseph and Stewart Alsop reported, "The atmosphere in Washington today is no longer postwar, it is prewar."

The pundits played a key role in the creation and communication of America's new Cold War ethos. Even if they could not by themselves convince the majority of the American people of the righteousness of the enterprise, they could at least give the impression they were trying.* This was more than enough incentive for their recruitment. The new establishment's Wise Men, flush with victory over Germany and Japan, saw as their next task nothing less than the remaking of the world. For this they needed allies, and the printing press had proven itself to be every bit as mighty as the sword. The worldwide *Pax Americana* that men like Dean Acheson, George Marshall, Robert Lovett, and John J. McCloy planned to build was one that had precious little in common with prewar, isolationist America. If their vision were to have any hope of realization, it would require the energetic cooperation of those who had earned both the ear and the trust of the newspaper-consuming public. The pundits, pleased to learn of their new significance, were not exactly reticent about shouldering the Wise Men's burden. As both their ranks and appetites expanded, they stepped into their Cold War boots and marched lock-step into the brave new world of American empire.

Between Franklin Roosevelt's 1933 inauguration and the big victory party twelve years later, sleepy white Washington mushroomed into a full-blown American city, brimming with Ivy-educated bureaucrats and Wall Street lawyers. The new city manufactured only one thing, words on paper, and those with the ability to master this craft came to enjoy some of the same advantages of position and prestige enjoyed by Duke Snider in Brooklyn or Joe DiMaggio in the Bronx.

It may be useful to think of the city as a palace court where the pundits played multiple roles: they were courtiers, but they served as both advisers to and communicators for the Crown. Because the courtiers shared the basic assumptions of the court itself, but were ostensibly free to write whatever they pleased, the pundits were seen to be uniquely credible and hence well situated to parlay their positions into small fiefdoms of influence.†

---

*There is really no scientifically respectable measure of this.

†I am indebted to Marcus Raskin for this metaphor.

No longer treated by the truly powerful as mere newsmen, the most important pundits acquired some of the status of Washington's great families and most powerful political institutions. They had access to the highest reaches of the government, and in turn were expected to exercise good judgment about just how much truth was healthy for Americans to hear. By endorsing fundamental assumptions of the Cold War agenda and relaying its implications to their audiences, the pundits were able to perform two important functions on behalf of burgeoning empire: they carried on the political/cultural conversation of the capital with regard to this new endeavor, and they behaved as a politically articulate surrogate for the masses of uninformed and politically disinclined citizens for whom they alleged to speak. *

Excluding Lippmann much but not all of the time, the insider pundits depended heavily on their sources to provide information that would distinguish their columns from those of their competitors. While a certain degree of literacy was required, a fluid writing style was not really important. The necessary talents were, rather, the ability to get one's telephone calls answered and an aptitude for typing these answers up simply and quickly. A first-rate column depended on a steady stream of titillating tidbits that the writer could then spin into an 800-word morality play.

The extent of each insider pundit's dependence upon those in power varied from writer to writer. At one end of the spectrum was Lippmann; at the other stood those writers who consciously tailored their thinking to reflect the political fashions of the moment. They did so, ironically, in the hopes of being treated more like Lippmann: praised for their wisdom, invited to the best dinner parties, and called upon by the President for their advice.

Few pundits were actually able to achieve Lippmann's status of both adviser to and interpreter for the Crown. Most were dangled just close enough to keep them in the court but outside any circles where the truly powerful discussed business. Most went along for the ride quite willingly, happy just to be present somewhere near the creation. When necessary, top government officials had any number of pundit-manipulation tools available to them. There was personal flattery; there were confidential briefings; there were personal friendships, school ties, and institutional connections. Occasionally and most effectively, there was the whiff of raw power. In one especially chilling instance, one of the most influential pundits of the era found himself arrested in a Moscow bathroom for having made a homosexual pass. The Soviets agreed to hush up the incident once they discovered the writer's identity, but the CIA obtained its own confession. Allen Dulles, the agency's director, placed it inside his private safe and informed President

---

*In Washington then as now, *politics is* culture.

Eisenhower of its existence. The document was shown to people in the military, Congress, and the national security bureaucracy. Eisenhower apparently went to the trouble to make certain that a copy be made for President-elect Kennedy as well. The threat that lay behind this type of blackmail need never be explicitly carried out to achieve its desired effect. *

Frequently officials in power would take responsibility for satisfying the insider-tidbit-needs of individual pundits on a regular basis. Lippmann's voice was by far the most closely watched. But he was also the most difficult to control, so supremely confident was he in his own analytical powers. Still, he met regularly with the likes of George Kennan and Dean Acheson and found much in their plans he could endorse. Arthur Krock of The New York Times was perhaps the easiest fish to feed, and his tank was regularly sprinkled with classified data provided by his Princeton clubmate, James Forrestal. Joseph Alsop, who alternated with Lippmann in the Herald-Tribune and would soon come to rival him as the most influential voice inside the political establishment, regularly received thick folders from State Department Soviet specialist Charles Bohlen, a fellow alumnus of Harvard's Porcellian Club. Lippmann's protégé, the ace Times reporter and later columnist James Reston, it was widely noticed, would often publish important stories regarding "big planning at State" following the days he lunched with Dean Acheson at the Metropolitan Club. Bruce Cumings, the distinguished American historian of the Korean War, goes so far as to see "James Reston's lips moving, but Acheson speaking" in the series of columns Reston wrote explaining the changing bases of U.S. policy that led to the Truman administration's decision to defend South Korea in early 1950. †

---

*I have in my possession copies of six separate documents that refer to the confession, all signed by Lewis L. Straus, then head of the Atomic Energy Commission, containing lengthy discussions of this document, including the names of all parties involved and its possible use as an instrument of blackmail.

†Acheson's opponents, notes Cumings, especially Senator McCarthy, denounced his famous Janury 12 "Press Club" speech in which he explicitly excluded Korea from the U.S. defense umbrella, thereby allegedly giving the North Korean Communists "the green light" to attack. Many historians and political scientists, he notes, point to the speech as a classic example of the failure of deterrence. Though Acheson explicitly omitted it, Reston interpreted the speech to mean that Korea, like Japan, was now included in those areas where "the U.S. had direct responsibilities . . . and was in a position to do so." Cumings finds the weird accuracy of Reston's judgment fascinating, and wonders whether "Reston knew that Acheson privately backed containment in Korea" or whether he simply "got the speech wrong. . . . Since the North Koreans were still poring over Acheson's words," he notes, "they must have again scratched their heads about whatever it was Acheson had said in January." See Bruce Cumings, The Origins of the Korean War, Vol. II: The Roaring of the Cataract, 1947–1950 (Princeton, NJ: Princeton University Press, 1991), pp. 416–19 and 436–39.

Sometimes the pundit/power relationship became so confused it was impossible to tell who was manipulating whom. Perhaps the most illustrative example of this phenomenon can be found in the conversion to international-alism undergone by Senator Arthur Vandenberg, although the actual turn of events remains a matter of some controversy. Vandenberg, a frightfully vain and self-important man, planned to run for President in 1948. Ronald Steel, basing his account on an interview with Walter Lippmann, argues that Lippmann, together with Reston, convinced the senator in the summer of 1945 that no self-respecting presidential candidate could hope to lead this country without first jettisoning the immature vestiges of Republican isolationism. Together they wrote the senator's seminal speech, which praised the United Nations, abandoned isolationism, and decapitated the philosophy that had characterized the Republican party for decades.

Reston, however, remembers it differently. He cannot recall any involvement on Lippmann's part. His own role, he says, was limited to reading a speech Vandenberg was planning to give on the floor of the Senate denouncing the Soviets for their interference in Poland and suggesting that Vandenberg consider adding a section endorsing the continuation of the wartime alliance as a means of addressing Soviet paranoia about the security of its borders. "What changed his mind," argues Reston, "was not the speech, but the reaction to it. He became a hero to all the people who had thought he was just a big blowhard." Among those who lauded Vandenberg's heroism were Lippmann and Reston. The *Times* reporter noted a "brave and statesmanlike" address given by the senator. Whatever the exact inducement, Vandenberg's conversion all but crippled the once-proud tradition of main-street Republican isolationism.*

As Cold War tensions came increasingly to dominate public debate, Lippmann, as the perceived voice of history and reason, grew in stature. His first twenty-five years in the public arena had earned him enough political and intellectual capital that he came to be viewed as almost a separate branch of government. During the war, the British Embassy had appointed one official whose responsibility it was to keep His Majesty's Government apprised of the

---

*Vandenberg proved even more malleable in the future. When Reston outlined a $20 billion, four-year European recovery plan that would become the Marshall Plan in the summer of 1947, Vandenberg telephoned to tell him he was out of his senses, that "no administration would dare come to the Senate with a proposal like that," and that he himself would never support "any such goddamned foolishness." Nine months later, on March 1, 1948, Vandenberg himself rose in the Senate to begin debate on it. The Vandenberg quotes appeared in a sanitized version in James Reston, June 20, 1960, and later in Reston's memoir, *Deadline* (New York: Random House, 1991), p. 168. See also Patrick Lloyd Hatcher, *The Suicide of an Elite: American Internationalists and Vietnam* (Stanford, CA: Stanford University Press, 1990), p. 206.

great man's thoughts and vice versa. Lippmann had become better able to explain government policy to the American people and place it in a sensible political and historical context than was the government itself. When White House or State Department officials thought of seeking support in Congress for a new proposal for postwar reconstruction, they frequently floated it by Lippmann even before approaching the relevant committee chairman.

With the collapse of Henry Wallace's Progressive party in the 1948 election, the increasingly conservative Lippmann came to represent the liberal pole in the Cold War debate. His traditionalist balance-of-power orientation was as far as any insider pundit would go toward advocating the kind of foreign policy compromises that might catch the attention of some McCarthyite vigilante. On Lippmann's left, Drew Pearson continued to reach large numbers of people with his populist preaching and melodramatic scandal mongering. But Person's influence in insider circles derived primarily from the fact that every once in a while he put somebody in jail. *

---

*Pearson was not much on journalistic ethics. His motto was: "We will give immunity to a very good source as long as the information he offers is better than what we have on him." But if a man can be judged by the enemies he makes, Pearson might well have been a saint. The *Congressional Record* is filled with immunity-protected politicians reaching never-to-be-equaled heights of eloquence in their zeal to sully his name. Senator Kenneth McKellar of Tennessee once took the floor of the world's greatest deliberative body to call Pearson "an infamous liar, a revolting liar, a pusillanimous liar, a lying ass, a natural-born liar, a liar for living, a liar for daytime, a liar for nighttime, a dishonest ignorant corrupt and groveling crook. . . ." McKellar later fainted in the cloakroom. Not to be outdone, Senator Walter George of Georgia branded Pearson "an ordinary, congenital, deliberate and malicious liar." Representative Philip Bennett of Missouri labelled him "a dishonest, unreliable, vicious character assassin." Senator William Jenner of Indiana found him to be "a filthy brain-child conceived in ruthlessness and dedicated to the proposition that Judas Iscariot was a piker." And the infamous Theodore Bilbo of Mississippi said Pearson would "go down in history as 'Pearson-the-sponge' because he gathers slime, mud and slander from all parts of the earth and lets them ooze out through his radio broadcasts and through his daily contributions to a few newspapers that have not yet found him out." See Oliver Pilat, *Drew Pearson* (New York: Pocket Books, 1973).

Pearson's exploits on behalf of decency were of such force that Joseph McCarthy once felt compelled to sneak up on him in the men's room at the Sulgrave Club and either kick him in the groin or "belt the bloody and half-conscious Pearson in the mouth." According to the groin version, published in *Pilat*, the two men were separated by Richard Nixon before the fight could really get going. According to James Reston, however, an inebriated McCarthy beat up Pearson before he and Nixon stumbled around Washington for a half-hour trying to find McCarthy's car. (See *Deadline*, p. 226.) McCarthy had previously referred to the pundit as "the diabolically clever voice of international Communism . . . a Moscow-directed character assassin . . . a journalistic fake and a prostitute . . . a degenerate liar" and "a twisted perverted mentality." The *Pilat* version has McCarthy wondering aloud whether "to kill Pearson or just to maim him" as well. See also the wholly unreliable *Drew Pearson's Diaries 1949–1959*, ed. Tyler Abel (New York: Holt, Rinehart, Winston, 1974).

I. F. Stone, on the other hand, toiled alone with his wife, Esther, in northwest Washington on an extraordinarily learned and intellectually acute newsletter, combining the moral outrage of Jeremiah with the investigative skills of Philip Marlowe. But until the New Left adopted him as one of its patron saints during the anti-war movement in the late 1960s, Stone, a self-proclaimed "Jeffersonian Marxist," remained a virtually anonymous figure to the establishment and largely irrelevant to the shaping of the insider mind.

Because the owners of newspapers and newspaper chains were more likely to be sympathetic to the appeals of racism, Christian fundamentalism, and laissez-faire capitalism than they were to unions, health care, and democratic socialism, populists of the Far Right were far more common in the ranks of American punditry than the occasional Pearson or Stone. Westbrook Pegler was probably the most widely read of these. Pegler's ironically titled column, "Fair Enough," occasionally descended into what H. L. Mencken would term "Ku Kluxery," and his attacks on the Hearst family finally cost him his job in 1962. But by that time he had lost his thunder to an upstate Yalie named William F. Buckley, Jr.

If the left was largely irrelevant, however, the Far Right was important only insofar as it could make mischief. Joe McCarthy proved that this potential was considerable indeed and could be ignored only at the peril of one's career. But Pegler, Buckley, and his cohorts had no direct impact upon the shaping of the insider mind or the forging of its consensus. Though some of them may have lived or worked in Washington, they did not live and work at what Stewart Alsop called "the Center."

The Center, according to Alsop, was "the Washington which a political journalist sees with his tunnel vision." More than a place, it was a state of mind. The Center was where the action was. It was where men of goodwill met to hammer things out. "Extremists" and "ideologues" of all stripes abhorred the Center, but the truly Central knew that this was where political rhetoric on behalf of unarguable principles was turned into policies and sometimes wars. Defining these principles for the powerful people who made them and the powerless people who fought and sometimes died for them was the essential business of the Cold War–Washington pundit.

Postwar debate over the course of U.S.-Soviet relations peaked early. In July 1947, George Kennan published "The Sources of Soviet Conduct" in *Foreign Affairs* magazine, under the pseudonym "X." Soon afterward, Lippmann responded with a series of fourteen successive columns which, collected together in a small book, helped give the Cold War its name.

In his article and earlier "Long Telegram," where he first delineated the theoretical basis of his argument in a classified cable from Moscow, the not-so-anonymous Kennan argued on behalf of a U.S. "policy of firm containment, designed to confront the Russians with unalterable counter-force at every point where they show signs of encroaching" via "the adroit and vigilant application of counter-force at a series of constantly shifting geographical and political points." Arthur Krock, who had been shown an earlier version of the essay by Forrestal, cleverly promoted it in *The New York Times*, implying that the document was somehow far more significant than he could in good conscience say. Other pundits soon picked it up, and by the time the article snowballed into *Life* and *Reader's Digest*, it had been elevated, as Kennan notes, "to the status of a 'doctrine' which was then identified with the foreign policy of the administration."

Lippmann's brilliant critique of Kennan's argument stands today as a remarkable prophecy of the problems that "containment" presaged for U.S. foreign policy. Lippmann predicted that even if successful, the policy costs would outweigh its benefits. Merely to implement it would entail "recruiting, subsidizing, and supporting a heterogeneous array of satellites, clients, dependents and puppets." This would require a massive military apparatus with interventionary capabilities dwarfing anything the world had previously seen, and far beyond what was truly required to secure the safety of this nation and its vital interests. In addition to the expense, it would leave the United States vulnerable to those very puppets, who could fly the flag of "appeasement" in our faces to manipulate us into defending a murderous status quo on the basis of no stronger common interest than a shared antipathy for Communist revolution. "My strongest impression," Lippmann wrote, "is that the Russians have lost the Cold War and they know it." The task at hand was to "push toward a settlement which permits the recovery of Europe and the world, and to relax the tension, to subdue the anxiety, and to end the panic."

The "X" debate probably constitutes the apex of postwar punditry. Despite Kennan's ostensible anonymity, the argument itself was conducted publicly and served to focus attention on the American role in the world with considerable seriousness, integrity, and respect for the intelligence of the public mind. While Kennan has since come to agree with Lippmann's critique more than his own argument (just as Lippmann, toward the end of his career, would echo Charles A. Beard's critique of the 1939 version of Walter Lippmann), the two men conducted what amounted to a public seminar for an entire generation of American leaders previously unschooled in the discipline of international diplomacy and power politics. Writers and thinkers of all political stripes weighed in with their views, their minds more open to the various possibilities than would be possible again for the next forty years. The discussion was educative, to return to Lippmann's aspirations voiced in *Public Opinion*, as well as conducive to public inquiry and community conversation—as Dewey had hoped. The catch, however, was just how tiny this community had become. It would be tendentious to blame pundits for this, but just the same, it is impossible to ignore the fact that, aside from Lippmann's column or Kennan's "X" article, the greater American public enjoyed precious few opportunities to consider intelligently the arguments that would determine the course of the nation's foreign and domestic policies for the next half century. Containment developed its own momentum independent of the ostensible object of its affections, and none of the appointed agents of community conversation ever saw fit to question its fundamentals again. Still, one should not lose sight of the moment without tipping one's hat to Lippmann's prescience. Posterity has borne out his arguments, rather than those of Kennan, the lifelong scholar and Sovietologist; an astonishing accomplishment for a man in a business so fleeting as that of newspaper pundit.

Helpful in this debate, as well as many others, was an enviable talent for criticism that singed but did not burn. In addition, Lippmann had an exceptional ability to cast aside his sweeping principles on behalf of particulars when they had already become accomplished facts. Regardless of what he may have believed about the relative powers of nationalism and Communist subversion in the service of revolution, Lippmann nevertheless managed to find reasons to support military aid to the Greek colonels' regime, U.S. military intervention in Korea (though limited to air- and seapower), and even, briefly, French and U.S. military involvement in Vietnam. He went to great psychological lengths to convince himself that the makers of U.S. foreign policy shared his basic views and adhered to them with a similar dedication to honor and candor. As he wrote in 1952, "The real problem of our foreign policy is not in its objectives, on them there is fairly general agreement." The real problem, quite simply, lay with the "control and administration of the policy." The same year, when Communists accused the United States of engaging in germ warfare in Korea, Lippmann insisted that the accusations must certainly be false because "the two highest responsible men in the U.S. government—who would have to give the orders to conduct germ warfare—have said on their word of honor that there is no truth of any kind in the charges. Both of these men happen to be old personal friends and I believe them." This faith was absolutely essential to the job description of an aspiring Washington pundit and to all those who labored inside the Center. It was this faith, more than anything, that collapsed in the wake of Lyndon Johnson's war and ended Lippmann's career as Washington's ambassador from the world of history, philosophy, and context.

Lippmann once observed during the height of the Vietnam War that if Lyndon Johnson ever did become inclined to negotiate with Hanoi, "the most powerful voice against it would be that of Joseph Wright Alsop." A distant cousin of both Theodore and Franklin Roosevelt, Alsop was the only pundit in the Cold War debate whose political and intellectual influence could begin to approach that of Lippmann. * He cut his political teeth on the New Deal and maintained his column and his impressive influence for most of the next forty years.

Alsop arrived in Washington in 1935. He had been initially hired in New York, straight out of Harvard, by the *Herald-Tribune*, owing to his family's friendship with its owners. "Fat, soft, wholly untrained," and possessing what even he termed to be an "odd accent," Alsop recalled evoking reactions of "pessimism and horror" within the newsroom. City Editor Stanley Walker, "a great man and usually a great judge of human material," according to Alsop, described him as "a dreadful result of Republican inbreeding." But despite his aristocratic WASP lineage and Spenglerian demeanor, Alsop possessed a talent for reporting and, what's more, an unquenchable relish for the game of insider politics. He cut a distinctly odd figure on the Washington political circuit and his accent has been described alternately as "a clerk in a not-very-good London hotel trying to make people think he went to Harrow" and "Charles Laughton playing Oscar Wilde." But his Georgetown dinner parties were legendary, and Washington socialites still talk about them wistfully. Often on hand as a kind of living family heirloom was Alice Roosevelt Longworth, Uncle Teddy's daughter and a wonderfully tart-tongued old woman. Mrs. Longworth, who once congratulated Dorothy Thompson on having her "menopause in public and making it pay," admitted that she knew that "whenever I go over to Joe's house I am working for him. I don't mind a bit. I know Joe uses me. Good

---

*During the Cold War's early days, Alsop and his brother had launched a campaign to remove Truman Defense Secretary Louis Johnson from his job. Johnson had offended Alsop by observing that there was too much "fat" in the U.S. military budget, and Alsop considered him to be "a practiced liar, without a scruple," and "one of the two or three truly evil men I have encountered in American public life." The campaign was successful, as the Alsops almost single-handedly sent Johnson to the unemployment lines. But it disgusted Lippmann, who, in a rare personal rebuke, called the writers "little boys playing with matches." Alsop never forgot that, and according to one of his close friends, constantly made disparaging remarks about Lippmann and his wife thereafter. (The source for these remarks insists on remaining anonymous.)

heavens, he uses everyone." In between the exquisite food and wine, Alsop would ask his guests for a bit of "general conversation," before launching forth on his Subject, the American position in the world. Later in the week, the speech would appear, in slightly amended form, in Alsop's column.

Together with Robert E. Kinter from 1937 until the war, with his brother Stewart from 1946 to 1958, and alone thereafter until 1974, Alsop wrote a highly literate column that leaned, in equal parts, on his erudition, his ideological fixation, his dinner party guest lists, and his considerable legwork. On the night of June 24, 1950, Assistant Secretary of State Dean Rusk, Secretary of the Army Frank Pace, Under Secretary of the Air Force John McCone, State Department Director of Policy Planning George Kennan, and Justice Felix Frankfurter were all located by their underlings at Alsop's dinner table, to be informed that the North Korean Army had crossed the 38th parallel into the Southern zone. They had been discussing the Romanian threat to Yugoslavia, when the guests realized something was up. But no one, according to brother Stewart, "was tactless enough to ask what the something was—that is contrary to the Washington ground rules." At another party in October 1962, John F. Kennedy argued incessantly with his appointed ambassador to France, the Soviet-specialist/Wise Man Chip Bohlen, in order to try to convince him to delay his departure to Paris while the President grappled with the still secret information that the Soviets were placing nuclear-equipped missiles in Cuba. *

Alsop's influence during the fifties and sixties derived in part from his dinner parties but more importantly through the civilized manner in which he incorporated the foreign policy world view of the Far Right into polite society. Merle Miller once likened Alsop's views on communism to those of Pope Innocent III regarding the Children's Crusade: "While we sleep, they go forth and conquer the land." He was obsessed with what he saw as the nation's need to prove its collective manhood and was forever wondering whether this or that President was "man enough" to stop the Reds at some critical juncture.

Unlike many fervent anti-Communists at the time, however, Alsop's obsession stopped at the river's edge. His history during the depths of the 1950s Red Scare was a distinctly honorable one, particularly when compared to the relative silence of Lippmann and his peers. Alsop defended the patriotism of McCarthy's victims in the State Department's China bureau, despite the fact that he vehemently disagreed with their assessments of the relative merits of Chiang and Mao at the time they were proffered. He and his brother, Stewart, launched a crusade on behalf of J. Robert Oppenheimer, when Atomic Energy

---

*At another gathering in the Alsop dining room, the columnist's toucan spit a piece of chewed-up banana on the bald spot of Secretary of Defense Robert MacNamara.

Commissioner Lewis L. Strauss and the hawkish physicist Edward Teller were smearing the atomic scientist in an attempt to remove his security clearance. The Alsops wrote a book in defense of Oppenheimer that Strauss—whose influence rivaled that of J. Edgar Hoover at the time—worked hard to try to ensure would receive no reviews in any mainstream print forum. * Alsop also defended State Department official Owen Lattimore, whom he considered to be a "perfect fool" because, Alsop insisted, "There is a difference between foolishness and treason." In 1951, when Henry Wallace was called in to testify before McCarthy's Senate Subcommittee on Internal Security, Alsop spent all day on the phone trying to find a lawyer willing to defend the former Vice President. On domestic matters, Alsop showed a patrician's concern for middle-class problems and sensibilities that might be considered generous, given the limited contact he had with the common folk. "Joe was the kind of liberal," says his friend Tom Braden, "who thought it was a good idea for men of property—who wanted to remain men of property—to keep an eye on the social problems of the masses."

Alsop's clout was symbolized by the fact that on a cold and snowy January night in 1961, the President of the United States, just hours into the job, saw fit to interrupt his inauguration night festivities to shoot the breeze with Alsop and his guests. The two men had been great friends during Kennedy's service in the Senate, though Kennedy had generally declined the columnist's dinner invitations owing to the lack of "pretty young girls" on the guest list. † It was Alsop who convinced candidate Kennedy of the existence of a phantom "missile gap" with the Soviets, a notion he conjured up on the basis of wholly manufactured, or perhaps imaginary, evidence; and Alsop who, together with *Washington Post* publisher Phil Graham, convinced the Democratic nominee to offer the vice-presidency to his rival, Lyndon Johnson. Alsop also helped Kennedy choose his cabinet.‡ Moreover, the columnist lost none of his clout in the early Johnson administration. At one point during the war, the President was heard to accompany his decision to

---

*Joseph W. Alsop and Stewart Alsop, *We Accuse: The Story of the Miscarriage of American Justice in the Case of J. Robert Oppenheimer* (New York: Simon & Schuster, 1954).

†As President, however, Alsop insists, Kennedy would make it a point to come over for dinner at least once every six weeks. Perhaps most impressive to insiderdom was the rumor that alone within Camelot's court, Alsop was the sole close family friend spared the ritual of touch football. Alsop with Platt, *"I've Seen the Best of It,"* p. 411.

‡Alsop says he told the nominee at the convention that "You know damn well that Stu Symington [Johnson's competition] is too shallow a puddle for the U.S. to have to dive into." He also says he recommended to Kennedy that he choose Dean Rusk, Douglas Dillon, Averell Harriman, and George Kennan for their respective positions in the administration. See ibid., p. 427.

send another fifty thousand American boys to Vietnam with the quip, "There, that should keep Joe Alsop quiet for a while."

Alsop's myriad connections to those with their hands on the levers of power, coupled with his willingness to push and pull on them both publicly and privately, earned him considerable respect in important foreign capitals as well. The entire French cabinet—including the president—once appeared at a 1946 Paris luncheon given in his honor. In January 1957, on the occasion of an Alsop brother visit to Moscow, they were greeted with an article in *Komsomoskaya Pravda*, the organ of the Young Communist League, noting that "assassins, robbers, pirates and rapists of all flags and nations have been put to shame by the Alsops."

Although he was considerably less shy about using his influence behind the scenes to effect the policy results he desired, Alsop, like Lippmann, did much to elevate the level of public discourse and community conversation within Washington. Also like Lippmann, however, his effectiveness fell victim to the body counts in Vietnam. But while Lippmann was too well aware of the limitations of anti-Communist warfare for political comfort, Alsop was undermined by his inability to recognize these limits once the *Zeitgeist* reversed itself following the January 1968 Tet Offensive.

In his memoirs, published posthumously and written with a former employee of Sun Myung Moon's *Insight* magazine, Alsop recalled the most exciting adventure of his life as having been his experiences in China during World War II, where he first assisted General Claire Chennault and his "Flying Tigers," got himself interned by the Japanese as a journalist rather than the active soldier he was at the time, and returned to China to mastermind Chiang Kai-shek's ultimately successful offensive against the commander of American forces there, General Joseph Stilwell.* Alsop soon became obsessed with the Communist takeover there and professed to see the hand of Maoist manipulation behind every turn of events on the Asian mainland.† This was particularly true of Vietnam.

---

*In China, Alsop displayed, according to Barbara Tuchman, "a relentless animus to destroy the credibility of Chiang's detractors." In his memoirs Alsop admits that "with full conviction," he suggested to Chiang and his advisers that they "declare General Stilwell persona non grata and blame him, in large measure, for China's fearful situation." Alsop also suggested General Albert C. Wedermeyer as Stilwell's replacement and drafted the telegram Chiang sent to Roosevelt on behalf of these sentiments, along with another from Vice President Henry Wallace in support of the original from Chiang. See Barbara Tuchman, *Stilwell and the American Experience in China, 1911–1945* (New York: Macmillan, 1970), p. 358, and Alsop with Platt, *"I've Seen the Best of It,"* p. 242.

†Alsop's views on China were so extreme that he could not bear to discuss the issue with a reporter as famously moderate as Theodore H. White. As Alsop recalled in his memoirs, "In later years, Teddy and I had to agree not to discuss the China drama for fear

Alsop's Vietnamese obsession first became apparent during the Battle of Dienbienphu, where French imperial forces suffered a crippling defeat at the hands of Viet Minh guerrillas. A consistent critic of what he believed to be the unconscionable weakness of the Eisenhower administration in the face of an ever-growing Communist menace, Alsop demanded that U.S. forces be committed in support of the French. "A defeat at Dienbienphu," he insisted in January 1954, "or even a mild French reverse at Dienbienphu, will cause the same kind of reaction in Paris that Yorktown caused in London 171 years ago," adding that "the future of Asia may well be at stake in this remote and obscure engagement."

Once U.S. forces finally did enter the conflict, Alsop's inability to let go of his obsession eventually destroyed his effectiveness within the insider debate. His wildly optimistic reports of U.S. military progress there seemed ridiculous and pathetic in light of the gruesome reports of the reporters in the field. Alsop began predicting the enemy's imminent collapse as early as June 1964, and never let go. Following Tet, when much of the establishment was looking to extricate the nation from the Vietnam debacle, Alsop could only conclude that those who failed to support the war "had gone collectively insane." Should the United States withdraw, he promised, McCarthyism would run rampant and "the American future would hardly bear contemplation." The morning after his longtime friend Bobby Kennedy made a speech wondering whether the United States could ever win the war in Vietnam, Alsop left three messages with his receptionist to please tell his close friend, the Senator from New York, that he was a traitor to his country.* He also flew to Vietnam to lecture correspondents like David Halberstam and Neil Sheehan that "you'll be like those fools who lost their jobs in China. I tried to help them. I tried to warn them, but they never listened. I testified at their hearings, never fear, I shall testify for you as well." In the war's aftermath, Halberstam could write of the once respected columnist that he had been "wrong in almost everything he said or wrote."

Alsop continued writing his column through 1974, but by his fanatical devotion to the failed war effort and the men who lied about it he forfeited the fear and respect he had once engendered more than seven years earlier. He alienated many of his friends with his apocalyptic gloom, later admitting to having become an "old monster with a commitment." While Alsop never

---

one or the other of us would grow apoplectic and seek to do physical harm." See Alsop with Platt, "I've Seen the Best of It," pp. 229–30.

*Alsop later told Joan Braden that "the minute Robert Kennedy got to the White House, he would tear into Vietnam like a tiger. Robert Kennedy would not have permitted his country to lose a war." Quoted in Joan Braden, Just Enough Rope (New York: Villard Books, 1989), p. 151.

apologized for his obsession with Vietnam, and indeed, carried it with him to his grave, he did become aware in his later years that he "could no longer understand what was happening in America, perhaps because [he] had finally become an old man, frozen in the viewpoints of the past." It is safe to say, however, that for all of Alsop's arrogance and misguided passion, his mistakes were almost always honest ones; Washington is not likely to see another insider pundit with such dedication to his profession nor such verve and enthusiasm for his craft.

Of all the giants who walked the earth in punditry's golden age, by far the kindest, gentlest, and most inspirational of all was the chief Washington correspondent of *The New York Times*, James Barrett "Scotty" Reston. Arthur Krock had held the bureau's weighty title for two decades, but relinquished it to Reston in 1953 when he realized that it was the only way to keep the forty-three-year-old Reston from accepting an offer to be editor of *The Washington Post*. In all his years in punditry, stepping aside for Reston was probably the most graceful act Krock ever performed. It was certainly his greatest contribution to the quality of the profession.

The two men could not have been more different in demeanor. Tom Wicker remembers his first sighting of Krock in the Washington newsroom: "He would stalk through the office, carrying a statesman's girth with more aggressive dignity than anyone in Washington, his head cocked back to allow his gaze to play scornfully on the gods, a Churchillian cigar cocked toward his hat brim like a banner of war." Since Wicker was writing the foreword to a collection of Krock's columns, one can safely conclude that these were the most generous words he could bring himself to utter. Now here is Russell Baker on his first glimpse of Reston:

> There was an old-fashioned, boyish look about him. With black hair, slightly curly, and a wide mouth that smiled readily, and a brow so serene that it seemed never to have scowled, at first glance he looked as if he might have stepped down from an old photograph over the velveteen settee in a 1912 parlor. The eyes told a rather different story. He had the shrewdest, wisest, most disconcerting gaze I had ever seen on an honest man. Old fashioned or not, he was the most self-confident person I had ever met. . . . It was love at first sight.

Krock insisted that everyone who worked at the bureau call him "Mr. Krock." When a senior reporter asked him how long he was expected to keep up this ridiculous formality, Krock replied, "As long as you care to stay here." Later, even the delivery boys would call his successor "Scotty." Krock was a respectable journalist, though one wonders just how effective he would have been with a less august calling card. In his memoirs, he bragged of knowing eleven presidents, "one way or another." But Krock's reputation derived far more from his talent as a crony to great men than as reporter or commentator on them. He tended to seek favors of the wealthy, as when he borrowed Joseph Kennedy's (now infamous) Palm Beach winter home for vacations and proved more than willing to repay them in kind.* He wrote complicated, convoluted sentences that often obscured whatever meaning he might have intended. This impressed people but it did not guide their thinking much. While his sponsorship could be important, as in the case of Kennan's containment brief, the slightest trace of his influence on the period

---

*Krock had a particularly tortured relationship with Lippmann. Krock "envied and detested" Lippmann, according to Reston, and Lippmann's feelings toward Krock can probably be characterized as "detestation laced with contempt." (Author's interviews with Tom Braden and James Reston. The quotes are Braden's.) In *Walter Lippmann and His Times*, the collection of essays in honor of Lippmann edited by Reston and Marquis Childs, Krock managed to contribute an 18-page essay without ever mentioning the honoree's name. On another occasion, speaking of the close relationship developed by Lippmann with President Kennedy (whom Krock had once helped win his Pulitzer Prize for literature), Krock told a colleague, "I may be getting old and I may be getting senile but at least I don't fall in love with young boys like Walter Lippmann." See Halberstam, *The Powers That Be*, p. 546.

While the rivalry may have been in part professional, it was almost certainly cultural as well. Lippmann was born a wealthy, upper-crust German Jew. He attended the Sachs School and Harvard, where he later supported Jewish quotas as a means of limiting the population of Jews there. Krock, also Jewish, hailed from South Central Kentucky, and had to drop out of Princeton for lack of money, eventually earning only a junior college degree from the Lewis Institute in Chicago. When in 1937 Krock asked to be made editorial-page editor of the *Times*, he was told by C. L. Sulzberger that the sensitive German Jewish owners of the *Times* were not about "to put a Jew in the showcase." Krock protested that his mother, whom he liked, was not Jewish (actually, she was half-Jewish) while his father, whom he did not, was. According to Jewish law, he insisted, he was a Gentile. Sulzberger was not impressed. "Arthur," he replied, "how do you know all that if you aren't Jewish?" See Talese, *The Kingdom and the Power*, p. 232.

In addition to cultural and intellectual differences, the enmity between the two was sparked by an incident at the *World* back in the twenties in which Krock, who had been hired by Pulitzer to "ride herd" as a sort of ombudsman, was overheard by Lippmann talking on the phone to the investment firm of Dillon, Read & Co., where he moonlighted as a consultant. Lippmann, who was said to have a penchant for listening at doorways, became convinced upon overhearing a phone conversation that Krock was passing along inside dope on a future editorial likely to affect stock prices. He banished Krock from ever appearing on the *World* page again. Krock maintained that he was merely discussing a past editorial, but understood that as he was now known as an adversary of Lippmann's, his professional growth at the *World* was likely to be stunted. So he left for the *Times*. (Differing versions of this story can be found in Steel, *Walter Lippmann and the American Century*, pp. 200–201, and Arthur Krock, *Memoirs: My Sixty Years on the Firing Line* [New York: Funk and Wagnall's, 1968], pp. 61–63.) For Reston's characterization, see *Deadline*, p. 146.

is difficult to discern today. It was almost as if his entire Washington career had been a prelude to the era of Scotty Reston.

For Reston, almost as much as Lippmann, helped to define his profession by his example. When he took over the *Times* bureau and began his column in 1953, he was already recognized as the best reporter in Washington. He seemed to travel behind a kind of force field of good fortune, somehow marrying the high ideals of hard-charging reporter and Protestant clergyman. Reston was no philosopher. Neither was he much of an intellectual. But he was a brilliant reporter, with a genius for homespun American wisdom. Reston, as Murray Kempton once observed, was not a man of the left or right but of the *Times*. He was the perfect pundit for an America that saw itself living in a post-ideological age.

Born in Clydebank, Scotland, of poor, devout Presbyterian parents in a home where all the four Restons had to sleep in a single bed, young James grew to manhood in Dayton, Ohio, with an immigrant schoolboy's belief in the virtue of his adopted nation. He was a man who, as late as 1975, could say without irony, "This is a country in which good prevails over evil."

Reston was hired by the *Times*'s London bureau on September 1, 1939, the day Hitler invaded Poland. He took a brief leave of absence to work for the London-based Office of War Information, where he wrote his first book, *Prelude to Victory*. In the darkest days of the conflict Reston seemed able to breathe new life into shopworn American clichés. The author preached: "We cannot win this War until it ceases to be a struggle for personal aims and material things and becomes a national crusade for America and the American Dream. . . . We must strengthen the things that unite us and remove the things that divide us. We must look forward to the future with the faith in each other and in the rightness of the American Dream." A reviewer called it the work of a "valuable propagandist."

As a Washington reporter, Reston was in a class by himself. His success in persuading Chinese diplomats to leak him the details of four-power negotiations under way at Dumbarton Oaks in 1944 earned both a Pulitzer Prize and an FBI investigation.* Reston's energetic use of multiple sources, coupled with his subtle and unthreatening ability to exploit the power and influence of his employer, set a standard against which the Washington press corps still measures itself. Moreover, Reston benefited from the special cachet that derived from Lippmann's patronage. Lippmann was often willing to help young journalists up their respective ladders, but his mentoring

---

*Reston's conduit to the Chinese, he later revealed, was the former student intern at the *Times*, Joseph Ku. After he returned to China from the *Times*, Ku reappeared as member of China's delegation to the Dumbarton Oaks Conference. Author's interview.

relationship with Reston was understood by all to be one of unique respect and affection. Reston would work the town, finding everything out, and then Lippmann would sit Reston and the rest of Washington down to explain what it all meant. "He used my legs, and I used his brain," remembers Reston. "It was a wonderful relationship."

As a columnist, Reston was exceptional for his unexceptionableness. Earnest, moderate, and ostentatiously unpretentious, he was a kind of pundit's Ward Cleaver. Reston had, as David Halberstam notes, "a nice feel for the country," and he wrote in "wonderful quick, illuminating sentences." As a six-year-old boy, Reston explains in his memoirs, he used to respond to inquiries about his life's ambition by telling whoever asked that he would "preach the gospel to the heathen." Like many others, Joseph Alsop, who competed with Reston as a reporter in the same way that he competed with Lippmann the philosopher, found Reston a bit much on the inspiration front. He would frequently pick up the paper and complain, "There is one of Scotty's Sunday Presbyterian sermons again."

Inside the palace court Reston sought to soothe tempers and encourage everybody to just simmer down and work everything out. Outside the Beltway, Reston's task was to reassure a worried populace that things were not as bad as they seemed. In his valedictory column, published in August 1987, Reston wrote that "despite the recent silliness in Washington . . . things here are seldom as good or bad as most people think they are." An unkind Alexander Cockburn supposed that "There has not been a day in the past 2,000 years, that Reston would not have been capable of writing those words."

What distinguished Reston's column, aside from its author's infectious decency, was just how closely it mirrored "responsible" opinion within the councils of government. As he was the first to admit, Reston did not have Lippmann's intellectual self-confidence or Alsop's thirst for political combat. The combination of Reston's unquestioning belief in the ultimate good intentions of the American government and his ability to communicate his own uncynical patriotism led him to identify almost completely with the interests of the government as defined by the government. There was little that Americans could not accomplish, Reston seemed to reason, if we would just quit bickering and set our collective nose to the grindstone. Yes, "Life, tyranny and the pursuit of capitalists is the Russian way of life." Yes, the "underdeveloped world, still in the agony of transition, remains vulnerable to the sorcery, the subversion, and the techniques of Communist organization and conspiracy." But "one wonders whether Berlin would be divided if we further West had a little more faith in ourselves." All that was needed, Reston reasoned, was for "a patient, well-informed people, both attentive and unafraid, who know what this great country stands for and are willing to die for it if necessary."

This "good vs. evil" paradigm dominated Reston's ruminations from the early days of Hitler's rise throughout much of the Vietnam War. If Reston happened to hear reports of anti-American riots in Latin America, his immediate reaction would be to peg a story on Communist infiltration south of the border. His first move was to call the director of the CIA. Reston's deep, unyielding faith in America and its government made him all the more convincing as an advocate to the public at large, even when what he was advocating was transparent nonsense.

Reston's role in the pantheon of pundit history is partially distorted by the fact that his influence derived far less from his columns than from his stewardship of the *Times* bureau. The seminal moments in his career—convincing the *Times* to tone down its front-page story revealing the upcoming Bay of Pigs invasion in 1961, and standing foursquare behind the decision to publish the Pentagon Papers a decade later, were the actions not of a pundit but an executive. Young Washington reporters looked to Reston's example not because they were inspired by his column, but because they wanted to be *Times* men themselves. But the Presbyterian sermons, the columns about Washington's mood and its weather, and the occasions he would literally turn over his column to Dean Acheson or Henry Kissinger, became inseparable from the accomplishments of Reston the journalistic hero.* Reston once admitted to a reporter, "If you spend your life as a hatchet man—and there's something to be said for that—then eventually you find that everybody's out to lunch when you call. You're left with only your own opinion. I wouldn't like that, because my own opinions aren't that good." Instead, Reston relied on what he called "compulsory plagiarism" of "well-informed officials" in "high level quarters." This process appears to have worked in reverse as well. A 1960 *Time* cover story once noted that Reston "sometimes plants his own stories," calling sources with a policy idea, eliciting a commitment to consider it, and reporting that the idea was "under consideration."

Reston's modesty about his own considerable gifts makes it difficult not to like and admire the man, but his contribution to the development of Washington punditry remains problematic. By providing a model for virtually all aspiring Washington pundits—one that was far more accessible than the unapproachable genius of Walter Lippmann—Reston defined an essentially passive profession for his imitators. The pundit's job was less to

---

*Reston once titled a column "By Henry Kissinger with James Reston."

point out the foibles of a particular policy than to smooth over conflict and encourage bipartisanship. Altogether too eager to accept the government's word as truth, Reston acted, unwittingly, as a kind of advance man for U.S. government policy and a public relations executive for its favored supporters. No one, not even Acheson, exploited this vulnerability better than Kissinger. During Nixon and Kissinger's infamous 1972 Christmas bombing of Hanoi, Reston wrote that Kissinger "has said nothing in public about the bombing in North Vietnam, which he undoubtedly opposes. If the bombing goes on . . . Mr. Kissinger will be free to resign." The only problem with the story was that the bombings were Kissinger's idea.* He feigned anguish to Reston, on "deep background" no doubt, in order to deceive Congress and the country at large. In this deception, Reston was his invaluable accomplice, all the more helpful because he liked, admired, and needed to believe Kissinger himself.

The generation of Washington pundits that emerged in Lippmann's wake owed as much to Reston's example as to that of his mentor. Lippmann had single-handedly elevated the profession, socially and politically, to the point where it grew from undisguised flackery to a complicated amalgam of critical examination, community conversation, and somewhat better disguised flackery. Lippmann's example attracted a far better educated, ambitious, and socially well-born element into journalism, and the most ambitious of these often lusted for invitations into punditry's relatively exalted ranks. But his example was unapproachable, and in Scotty Reston, eager young reporters saw a model of both power and prestige to which they might reasonably aspire. The fact that his reputation sprang less from his original thoughts than from his dogged reporting further minimized the psychological space between his revered status and the unsung hacks who envisioned themselves in his place.

Lippmann's immediate successors, pundits like Marquis Childs, the 1960s version of Rowland Evans and Robert Novak, and David Broder—all men of the Center—earned their daily bread in Restonlike fashion: not through the acuity of their analysis but with the timeliness of their access. They were certainly better educated than their forebears, and their dinner parties were considered more desirable invitations. But Joseph Kraft, the

---

*Reston's column so infuriated Nixon that he had his staffers secure Kissinger's phone logs. These proved that Kissinger had spoken with Reston on the day he denied giving him "an interview." When Haldeman discovered this, he confronted Kissinger, insisting, "You told us you didn't give Reston an interview but in fact you did talk to him." Kissinger responded, "Yes, but that was only on the telephone." See Seymour Hersh, *The Price of Power: Kissinger in the Nixon White House* (New York: Summit Books, 1983), pp. 630–31.

main contender for Lippmann's abandoned crown, manifested his wisdom not by writing difficult philosophical tomes as Lippmann had, but by passing along the ministrations of kings, shahs, and prime ministers. *

Like Vladimir and Estragon, the Washington of the 1960s waited impatiently for the "next Lippmann" to appear on the scene. But the issues had become too diffuse and the pundit class too expansive for anyone to dominate the public dialogue quite as thoroughly as he had. No one inherited Lippmann's ability to define the political limits of the Center's debate. Instead, the post-Lippmann generation merely reinforced the borders set by others, attempting all the while to inject some drama and status into what otherwise would have been considered the most insignificant minutiae of insider politics. This was clearly a corruption of both the Lippmann and Dewey ideals, but it was not one worth getting terribly excited about; for excluding the notable exceptions discussed earlier, until the mid-to-late 1970s few pundits were influential at center stage. While the politicians attended to domestic policy, the bipartisan political establishment embodied by the likes of Acheson and McCloy managed, with Lippmann's assistance, to keep the portfolio of American foreign policy under control.

Beginning in the late sixties, however, the calculus of power and influence inside Washington began to change. The civil rights movement challenged the primacy of the politicians in the making of domestic policy, while the Vietnam quagmire proved the second generation of foreign policy "Wise Men" to be less masterful than their forebears in asserting control. In addition, the growth of television redefined the terms of the American political debate, and the rise of competing forces in the wake of the establishment's failures destroyed the Center's confidence as the leading political class. The net result was the slow formation of a restructured insider political constellation in which the role of the emerging pundit class would be enormously enhanced, just as its voice became simultaneously more vulgar and increasingly belligerent. Nothing symbolized this development better than the replacement on punditry's center stage of Lippmann, Alsop, and Reston by the deeply ideological and ceaselessly televised voices of George F. Will, Patrick J. Buchanan, and Rowland Evans and Robert Novak.

---

*In his article, "The Most Famous Journalist in the World," *Washington Monthly*, March 1975, p. 13, James Fallows quotes this story from an undated *Village Voice* column by rigid Marxist Alexander Cockburn. "Writing in the *New Yorker* about OPEC, Kraft is awfully above himself in this article. He meets the Secretary General of OPEC, Dr. Khene. 'When I greeted him in French,' reports Kraft, 'he was visibly pleased.' I should say so. If a fellow said to you, 'Bonjour, Monsieur, je suis Joseph Kraft, meilleur écrivain, homme le plus intelligent parmi tous les columnists du monde,' you might be pleased too."

3

POST-LIPPMANNDOM:
THE REST AND THE RIGHTEST

On the evening of August 11, 1960, CBS newsman Howard K. Smith turned to Walter Lippmann and asked the father of all softball questions: "Could you tell me why you felt that way then and why you feel the way you do now?" The nationwide, prime-time broadcast signaled the beginning of a new era in American politics: the marriage of television and political punditry. By creating an annual special broadcast devoted exclusively to Lippmann's opinions about the world, CBS had broken an old barrier. Never before had network television spent an entire one-hour program inquiring the views of someone who was neither an elected politician nor a Hollywood entertainer. Punditry, in its most exalted form, could now be called upon to stand in for both of them.

Before appearing on television, Lippmann had done little to disguise his contempt for the medium. "Television," he insisted, was the "prostitute of merchandising," whose primary influence had been to "poison the innocent" and "debase the public taste." But the camera was kind to Lippmann, and the first show met with virtually unanimous public acclaim. Lippmann soon upped his television fee to a remarkable $15,000 a year for one hour-long interview and $10,000 for each additional discussion.*

Looking back on Lippmann's annual televised appearances from the

---

*According to my friend Joel Friedman, who gets paid by the House Budget Committee to be able to figure these things out, Lippmann earned approximately $72,500 per hour for his first hour-long interview, and $48,500 for each additional interview, calculated in 1990 dollars.

vantage point of more than thirty years' hindsight, one can see in them the defining characteristics of the modern-day punditocracy. Lippmann brought prestige to television and television brought Lippmann riches. But the riches were not without a long-term cost. In Lippmann's last interview, conducted in February 1965, the pundit committed some of the most egregious errors of his career. (On Johnson's B-52 raids: "They're political bombings and . . . I don't think they kill anybody.") In the ensuing decades, the power of television, coupled with the right wing's post-Vietnam counterrevolution, would shape the American political dialogue in ways that could not but have depressed and disturbed the man who helped inaugurate them.

During the course of the August 11 interview, Lippmann outlined what he considered to be the most important qualities of presidential leadership. A great president, he explained, must have "the ability to see what matters in the excitement of daily events. He must be able to see through the latest headline to what is permanent and enduring." Just as important, moreover, was the President's ability to articulate:

> He must be able to talk in language which not the lowest common denominator understand, but the best—what you must lead in a country are the best of the country and they will carry it on down. There's no use of the president trying to talk down to a fellow who can just about read and write. Let somebody else do that. He must talk to the people who teach the man to read and write.

Both of Lippmann's criteria are consistent with the generally suspicious attitude he had demonstrated toward democratic governance four decades earlier. But they are also borne out by the quality of the American political dialogue as it developed over the course of those forty years. Daily American journalism, and its most prestigious tributary, Washington punditry, did not succeed in creating a vanguard of highly educated, sophisticated political consumers of the type Lippmann pined for in *Liberty and the News*. Instead, it helped to create a dichotomy of Washington "insiders," who had access to relatively unfiltered sources of information about the United States and the world, and the rest of us. Historically, Lippmann had concerned himself primarily with the former, despite the fact that the bulk of his readership could be found in the latter.

To television executives, who judged success or failure exclusively upon how many millions of people sat still for its commercials, the insider audience was meaningless. Television could not cordon off an op-ed page for its highbrow customers. The medium addressed itself exclusively to the masses. If elite audiences found something they enjoyed in the wasteland, well, that was unobjectionable. But it was also irrelevant. The numbers, and therefore the money, were in stupidity. Network executives liked to congratulate one another about their commitment to the "public interest," but they had a curious definition of the word. In one of the great moments in the history of inadvertent truth telling, then-CBS President Frank Stanton once explained: "A program in which a large part of the audience is interested is by that very fact . . . in the public interest."

When Lippmann delineated the foundation of presidential leadership to Howard K. Smith in the summer of 1960, he hit on precisely the two qualities in a political figure for which television had the least interest: invisible, subterranean, long-term forces and the need for a sophisticated, relatively well-educated, elite to elevate national political discussion.* To ask a television audience to think about something it cannot see is folly; the medium is entirely visual. Similarly, while television executives might have been willing to relinquish most of their audience in order to bask in Lippmann's reflected glow once a year, the heart and soul of the industry clearly belonged to poison and prostitution. Since no other pundits commanded the degree of deference enjoyed by the great man, if they wanted a piece of television's phenomenally remunerative action as well, stupid or not, they had better learn to play by television's rules.

Lippmann's 1960 appearance may have marked the beginnings of political punditry's passage into the phosphorescent universe, but the true origins of highbrow television punditry lie not with Lippmann but with Edward R. Murrow. Murrow vaulted into the American consciousness during the wartime raids on London. He was a radio reporter then, leaving the job of commentary to the likes of Raymond Gram Swing, a moderate liberal with a spooky voice, and Elmer Davis, whose voice so engaged the President that Roosevelt called upon him to run the Office of War Information.† These radio pundits were popular, but could not hope to match the drama of Murrow's dispatches. When CBS radio anchor H. V. Kaltenborn came on the radio "calling Ed Murrow, calling Ed Murrow," an entire nation sat

*One is today depressed, though hardly surprised, to note that the strongest criticism Lippmann voiced for the Eisenhower administration was for its refusal to demand sufficient taxes to pay for an adequate education system for America's children. ("And once you've failed to educate a child, you've failed, and you can't make that up later.") *Conversations with Walter Lippmann*, pp. 8–11.

†"You know the one I mean," said the President, "the one with the funny voice." See Barnet, *The Rocket's Red Glare*, p. 224.

transfixed, as Murrow's dramatic baritone brought them the story of the century, with full special effects courtesy of the Luftwaffe. Through his radio broadcasts, Murrow became a national hero, single-handedly demonstrating the journalistic possibilities of the medium. Amid the drama of the gunfire, however, Murrow and his staff did not concern themselves with the niceties of objective journalism. Nobody would have stood for it. This was the Good War with all of the good guys on the same side, and the rules of objectivity simply did not apply. As in the early stages of print journalism, the punditry and the reporting were one and the same.

Following the war, television gradually replaced radio as the primary news and entertainment medium in the United States and Ed Murrow made the transition with little difficulty. Murrow's CBS television career is most notable for his famous piercing of the armor of Senator Joseph McCarthy. The fact that Murrow is remembered as the White Knight of the McCarthy era is less a tribute to his foresight or bravery, however, than to the increasing primacy of television in the American cultural universe. The February 1954 broadcast that helped end the McCarthyite scare came four years after McCarthy began his noxious campaign and long after the Alsops, Reston, and Martin Agronsky had begun to attack him. But because McCarthy was a heartland rather than a Beltway phenomenon, the influence of these condemnations was minimal. And if Truman or Eisenhower did not have the courage to denounce his antics, then by 1954, only one political institution had the power to do so.

Murrow's dramatic program provided the cross that pierced the vampire's heart, but it also signaled the beginning of the end of Murrow's own effectiveness within the profession he helped build. Destroying McCarthy somehow stained Murrow in the eyes of his employer. Shortly afterward, CBS began to move the show around the schedule and restrict the extent of Murrow's broadcast time. In 1955, he was further weakened when the Alcoa Corporation discontinued its support of the program after Murrow featured a lengthy interview with J. Robert Oppenheimer and an unflattering report on Texas real estate in the same program. Oppenheimer was still damaged goods despite McCarthy's self-immolation and Alcoa had been planning to increase its investments in Texas. CBS began to limit Murrow to an occasional documentary series, referred to contemptuously on Madison Avenue as "See It Now and Then." Within four years of Murrow's 1954 McCarthy triumph, his show was history. Two years after that, so was Murrow, having been systematically emasculated by the network that to this day never ceases to invoke his name.

In retrospect, Murrow's sins were two. He appeared overly intellectual and he was not sufficiently anti-Communist. This remained the case despite the fact that Murrow had gone to great lengths to inoculate himself against exactly these charges. His celebrity interview program, "Person to Person," was a deliberate attempt to convince Americans (and CBS corporate executives) that Murrow was a member in good standing of the apolitical celebrity aristocracy that ruled the American entertainment industry.

On the anti-Communist front, Murrow had also done his utmost to protect himself. In March of 1947, Murrow failed to come to the aid of his friend and colleague, William Shirer, whom he had hired in Berlin in 1938. Shirer's radio program was unceremoniously canceled by William Paley when its commercial sponsor, a shaving-soap manufacturer, found Shirer's name on a blacklist of accused Communist sympathizers. The sponsor soon reversed itself in the face of a massive public outcry, but Paley refused to budge. Murrow, according to Shirer, declined to expend any of his professional capital on the matter and immediately distanced himself from his old friend. Shirer, of course, was not a Communist, but this was hardly the point. He was an unapologetic liberal, and in March 1947, that was just as bad. As Irving Kristol would explain six years later, "there is one thing the American people know about Senator McCarthy; he, like them, is unequivocally anti-Communist. About the spokesmen for American liberalism, they feel they know no such thing. And with some justification."

Although Murrow had helped destroy McCarthy, television executives were nowhere near ready to bask in the glow of their newfound political power. But by allowing McCarthy to self-destruct on his program, Murrow had in fact appeared to cross the invisible barrier that journalism had set up between "fact" and "opinion." Objective journalism had given free rein to McCarthy's antics, and so the unmasking of them was by definition not objective. Murrow's opinions were not an issue during the war, for they generated no controversy. But no matter how much McCarthy had done to discredit witch-hunting, handing him the pistol with which to shoot himself appeared to be an act of political bias. So nervous were CBS executives about challenging any aspect of political power, even in this backhanded fashion, that William Paley suggested offering McCarthy thirty minutes of unrestricted air time for a rebuttal.

After Murrow, television commentary was returned to its respectful norm, offering politicians a platform from which to pontificate without much interference from the men behind the cameras. Until the CBS Lippmann broadcast, explicit political opinions on television remained the exclusive property of politicians, starlets, and the ubiquitous man on the street.

Non-Lippmann punditry did not make a significant impression on television again until 1968, when ABC News, trailing in the ratings and constantly strapped for funds, introduced the notion of regular commentaries on its

nightly broadcast. (ABC expanded its newscasts from fifteen minutes to thirty in late 1967; CBS and NBC had done so in September 1963.) The stable of commentators included Bill Moyers, James J. Kilpatrick, and Gore Vidal. The network's intention was to provide an inexpensive way to help flesh out the program and give it a unique identity. Private polling indicated that viewers liked the commentaries, but thought they lacked star quality. The constant rotation prevented the audience from making an emotional investment in any one of the commentators. The obvious answer was for the network to concentrate on just one or two personalities. Howard K. Smith, the conservative, and Frank Reynolds, the liberal, thus became television's first daily pundits, paid not only to tell you the news but also what to think about it. Soon Eric Sevareid was added to Walter Cronkite's broadcast to offer political commentary as well. But executives at both CBS and ABC grew uncomfortable with the phenomenon of commentary on the evening news. The commentators themselves proved uncontrollable and unpredictable. More serious, however, was the fact that Washington pundits had so successfully defined the parameters of thoughtful analysis that TV news executives had come to associate "responsible" commentary with "access to information on a 'background' or off the record basis." Because their New York–based anchors were excluded from "the main business of gathering information—across a lunch table or on the cocktail circuit in Washington," television commentary struck them as "bland and predictable." That a person could simply be expected to comment intelligently on national affairs without having achieved the status of a Washington insider was considered by these executives to be beyond the pale. *
Quickly banished in large measure from the network news programs, political commentary soon became the sole purview of the Sunday morning talk-show ghetto.

The fickle romance between television and punditry was finally consummated when the Washington Post Company discovered a format which answered the needs of both sides: the Pundit Sitcom. The idea was that instead of merely relaying information, each pundit would portray himself as a stock character, thereby giving viewers a chance to identify, either positively or negatively, with an entertainment "personality" rather than just a boring journalist. The show that discovered this formula, "Agronsky and Company" was launched in December 1969. Here, for the first time, were print pundits not named Walter Lippmann being asked to give their opinions on the news without bothering to invite the politicians along. Host Martin

---

*In the 1980s, George Will, Bill Moyers, and John Chancellor were given a chance to reinvent political commentary on the evening news on each of the respective networks. All but Chancellor's regular appearances were dropped, however, and his political influence has always been difficult to gauge.

Agronsky borrowed the format from Public Television's "Washington Week in Review," founded in February 1967. But the PBS show simply asked straight reporters who covered a beat to explain their stories in a bit more detail, with the other members of the roundtable occasionally chiming in with a question. Had anyone offered an opinion without first attributing it to a major political figure, he would likely have been hooted off the air. The Agronsky show improved the entertainment quotient of this formula by inviting pundits and encouraging them to argue. The "facts," so well respected on PBS, were disputed on "Agronsky and Company," and its members were encouraged to develop distinct characters.

The show's secret weapon for many years was the late Peter Lisagor, the gregarious Washington correspondent for the *Chicago Daily News* and a living relic of the Ring Lardner/Front Page days when men were men and reporters were broke. Lisagor used to delight in "sticking little needles into [Southern conservative] James J. Kilpatrick," as Jack Germond recalls, "and watching all the hot air come out of him."

It was on Agronsky, following the death of Lisagor, that George Will honed his act before taking it on the road. Will's withering witticisms dominated the dialogue on any given program, but not quite to the point where each of the other regulars was prevented from defining a personality of his or her own. Martin Agronsky was a grandfatherly presence of the liberal, anti-Communist Center. Hugh Sidey, *Time's* White House correspondent and perhaps the most determinedly sycophantic newsman ever to grace the profession, was Mr. Samgrass, journalistic valet to presidents great and small. * Carl Rowan, among the only prominent African-Americans to give public voice to J. Edgar Hoover's concern about subversives in Dr. King's

---

*Sidey's musings provided countless presidents with a direct conduit to *Time's* 4 million readers with minimal journalistic interference. Reminiscing on the first part of his career, Sidey observed that, yes, as he looked back, "We were too easy on Eisenhower. . . . We were too easy on Kennedy. . . . I might also say we were too easy on Nixon. . . ." Even Ronald Reagan would look to Sidey with the knowledge that as late as December 1986 the pundit would literally turn his weekly column over to the Communicator in Chief, offering the beleaguered President the opportunity to sound off against his enemies in the Iran-Contra affair unimpeded by commentary or context. President Bush's reputation for extreme caution was not endangered in the slightest when *Newsweek* reported that he expected Sidey to "treat him favorably" during his presidency. Sidey was also the only pundit invited by the Bushes to attend the official state dinner in honor of Mikhail Gorbachev at the spring 1990 summit. His hard-hitting report: "In the White House, candlelight and the aura of history soften the edges, bringing everyone closer together. That magic was at work Thursday night." See Jonathan Atler, "Bush's Media Tastes," *Newsweek*, April 9, 1990, p. 6, and Hugh Sidey, "Capitalists over Corn Bread," *Time*, June 11, 1990. Sidey's self-criticism appeared in *The Presidency and the Press*, The LBJ School of Public Affairs, University of Texas at Austin, Conference Report, 1977, p. 80.

entourage during the 1960s, held fast to his Great Society heritage.* James J. Kilpatrick, the former segregationist firebrand, jettisoned his separate-but-equal shtick, but held fast to his courtly Southern gentleman/proud-to-be-a-Confederate routine in order to harrumph at Rowan. *The New Yorker's* Elizabeth Drew evoked a censorious new England schoolteacher, one who told us that the homework she was giving us was for our own good and one day we would thank her for it. To anyone not caught up in the rhythms of Capitol life, either personally or vicariously, the show was about as much fun as a proctology exam. But over time, "Agronsky and Company" developed a strong following in the Center. Power Washington would catch glimpses of it while getting dressed for cocktail parties and honorary dinners, only to recap the arguments of its favorite players over the hors d'oeuvres.

From the standpoint of pundit history, the primary function of the Agronsky show was the creation of a new kind of stardom for its participants. Certainly no certified players in the insider game could admit to allowing so mass-directed a vehicle to influence their thinking on the Important Issues of the Day. Rather, it allowed a few chosen pundits to develop television personalities identifiable to a mass viewership. This led to enormously lucrative speaking engagements, along with the kind of recognition inside Washington that usually attends only to the starting five of a small-town varsity basketball team. Neither would go ignored within the journalism profession.

The successful marriage of television and punditry was just one aspect of the black box's increasingly dictatorial power over American politics. Television's transformation of American cultural life is beyond the scope of this book. (It may be beyond the scope of human analysis.) In many ways, television has simply replaced our lives with itself. In Mark Crispin Miller's haunting phrase, "Big Brother Is You, Watching." The average American family keeps its television humming for more than seven hours per day. Since 1961, majorities of Americans surveyed have deemed it their most believable news

---

*When, in March 1967, Martin Luther King, Jr., called the Vietnam War "a blasphemy against all that America stands for," Rowan wrote that "King was listening most to one man [Stanley Levinson] who is clearly more interested in embarrassing the U.S than in the plight of the Negro or the war-weary people of Vietnam." The following Sunday he insisted that the civil rights leader had an "exaggerated appraisal of how much he and his crisis techniques were responsible for the race-relations progress that has been made." Rowan also raised the specter of "Communists influencing the actions and words of the young minister," although he insisted that he personally did not "endorse what King and many others consider a 'guilty by association smear.' " See Grauer, *Wits and Sages*, pp. 204–6.

source, with a more than two-to-one margin over newspapers since 1968. As Richard Schickel observes, "Television has come to provide the only meaningful context for that speculative enterprise: the idea of America; the only external reality that matters."

Print may have looked down its nose at television, but once Lippmann joined in, even its most revered insiders had no choice but to follow suit. The suggestive power of television is such that a raised eyebrow or a feigned expression of surprise could be subliminally more convincing to the unschooled viewer than a year's worth of well-reasoned columns. Politicians and pundits alike were therefore forced to remain exceedingly respectful of the medium's distorting and trivializing potentialities. Nowhere was this more evident than in the twisted history of the domestic politics of the Vietnam War.

Vietnam, David Halberstam has observed, was the first war in American history whose end was declared by an anchorman. When, on February 27, 1968, Walter Cronkite decided to shed his Olympian objectivity and explain in plain language on a special CBS News broadcast that the war simply did not work, Lyndon Johnson turned to his press secretary, George Christian, and admitted that it was all over: If he had lost Walter Cronkite, he had lost Mr. Average Citizen.

There were 10,000 television sets in America when the Japanese bombed Pearl Harbor and 10 million by the time the North Korean troops crossed the Yalu River. The night that Cronkite came before the cameras to denounce the war effort in 1968, that number had reached 100 million. The U.S. Air Force could bomb every outhouse in Indochina to ashes, but if it could not convince the most trusted man in America that it was winning, then it might well not have bothered. When Cronkite closed his broadcast with the tag line, "And that's the way it is," that was the way it was for all practical purposes in the minds of tens of millions of Americans. Whether Cronkite was correct in his assessment made little difference; he was Walter Cronkite; that's the way it was.*

Cronkite was anchorman, not a pundit. But on that historic broadcast, Cronkite combined television's persuasive powers into the most powerful pundit portfolio in the history of the business. Cronkite's status as an impeccably objective anchor certified his opinion with a kind of irresistible force. That "objectivity" could be enlisted on behalf of a political opinion

---

*During the Nixon administration, the President's political advisers briefly considered attacking Cronkite for his alleged bias. But staffer Dwight Chapin told his colleague Lyn Nofziger, in a memo dated February 15, 1971, that "taking on Walter Cronkite can not do us any good whatsoever. It is like taking on the Lord himself." See Bruce Oudes, ed., *From the President: Richard Nixon's Secret Files* (New York: Harper & Row, 1989), p. 218.

was well known to the governing establishment. Its manipulation had become an essential ingredient in creating what the theologian Reinhold Niebuhr called the "necessary illusion" providing "emotionally potent simplifications" required to win the support of the average American voter. Lippmann had a similar concern in mind when, in *Liberty and the News*, he spoke of the "manufacture of consent." But the fact that these manipulations could be used to overturn the policies of the government, and that television now felt sufficiently confident to try it; this was something new—something revolutionary, something dangerous.

A second important result of the Cronkite broadcast was its confirmation that on matters of both war and peace, the government itself was no longer to be trusted. The war had been a lie from start to finish and it contaminated the credibility of almost everyone who touched it. Americans were slow to digest the fact that their leaders had misled them, but soon all of the institutions that had invested themselves in Vietnam began to suffer similarly, from loss of internal self-confidence as well as a decline in their public trust. Congress did not have the courage to put an end to the war either by cutting off its funding or to go the distance with the President in seeking to prosecute to an ever more grisly end. Meanwhile, the civil rights and anti-war movements were creating what appeared to be a crisis atmosphere in the country, in the face of which Washington's pontification seemed impotent and pathetic.

Equally significant was the deterioration of the Center, whose best and brightest had nurtured the political illusions that sustained the war for so long. With their children denouncing them as war criminals and their former academic colleagues signing petitions to bar them from setting foot on campuses, the men who so proudly had guided the nation's struggle against the dark forces of communism lost the will to continue. As America confronted collapse in Vietnam, the entire establishment seemed to enter into a period of extended nervous breakdown. While some of the war's architects continued to put on a brave front, most simply faded back into the oak-paneled woodwork from whence they came. Meanwhile academia became so thoroughly divided and disgusted by the war effort that it, too, began a process of withdrawal from the political dialogue. Back at the vortex of foreign policy and national politics, the only remaining political institution to emerge strengthened by the debacle was the one that had been instrumental in unmasking its deceptions: the news media. By the end of the sixties, however, bruised and battered by the war and their role in promoting it, they alone, it seemed, were left standing in the mud-splattered ring of the American public dialogue. And it was left to the pundits, the media's most prestigious component, to forge a new American consensus.

Owing to their multifaceted political, ideological, and social connections to the men who conducted the war, the insider pundits were not among the first to comprehend the bankruptcy of America's Indochina policies. One pundit who did not shrink back from the war and its complications, however, was James Reston. This was true, in part, because Reston's immunity to Johnson's bellicose rhetoric had been strengthened by his close relationship with Lippmann. Lippmann had insisted all along that the United States was essentially an air and sea power. Vietnam offended Lippmann's sense of proportion as well as his conception of the country's natural advantages. Johnson's conceit, he argued, "was based on a totally vain notion that if we do not set the world in order, no matter what the price, we cannot live in the world safely. If we examine the idea thoroughly, we shall see that it is nothing more but the old isolationism of our innocence in a new form." Until Lyndon Johnson escalated his pursuit of the Vietnam War beyond what Lippmann considered all reason, however, he had never burned his bridges to an administration nor questioned anything more fundamental than the "control and administration" of its policies. With Johnson, however, Lippmann's treasured lines of comity were broken by a man whose pride and stubbornness were unmatched.

Lippmann had initially gone out of his way to be friendly to Johnson, and muted his criticism of Vietnam during the early part of the American commitment. But as the President allowed himself to be drawn deeper into the Indochinese mud, the two men grew obsessed with what each saw to be the other's duplicity. Johnson used to tell Vietnam dissenters in Congress to "go ask Walter Lippmann" next time they wanted a dam built in their districts, and delighted in making off-color remarks about Lippmann at diplomatic gatherings. Lippmann, meanwhile, gradually withdrew from the very insider contacts with which he had defined the profession. Shortly before he went into unhappy exile back in Manhattan in May of 1967, Lippmann was using language he had not had occasion to employ since he stopped hanging around with John Reed at The Masses. Johnson's America, he wrote, "was no longer the historic America," but a "bastard empire which relies on superior force to achieve its purposes."

When the course of Johnson's conduct of the war seemed to bear out Lippmann's prognosis, Reston proved readier than most to entertain its implications. He supported his Vietnam correspondents down the line and indulged in not a whit of the grumbling about their having "gone native" that characterized the conversations of so many Washington insiders. Moreover, in part because he had children of counterculture age, Reston did not axiomatically reject its political analysis, though he was at great pains to understand its vehemence.

Thus Reston came to view Vietnam with what was an extraordinarily open mind for a Washington insider. In January 1968, the U.S. District Attorney approved indictments against five individuals, including the baby doctor Benjamin Spock and Yale chaplain William Sloane Coffin, Jr., for counseling young men to resist the draft. Exactly a day after the indictments were handed down, Reston invited one of the defendants, Marcus Raskin of the Institute for Policy Studies, to lunch at the Metropolitan Club. The symbolism of the engagement spoke volumes both about Reston and the new legitimacy the anti-war movement was acquiring in the mind of the establishment. "Maybe it is a good thing," Reston wrote of the resisters' decision to seek arrest:

The country has been arguing for months now about a great many other things: Is bombing effective or not? Should we negotiate with the Vietcong and the National Liberation Front or not? But this case of Coffin and Spock has raised even more fundamental questions: Is the policy of the United States in Vietnam morally right or wrong? Who is "committing offenses against the United States"—the people who oppose the war or the people who want to continue it and expand it?

It was not only Vietnam, however, that led Reston to reassess the panoply of beliefs that had sustained the Washington consensus of the postwar years. The war had merely lifted a scab on the nation's conscience and left in its place a visible, festering wound. Reston did not shrink back from this wound. Rather, carefully, tentatively, he examined it, in the hopes of determining just how infected the body had become. The deeper Reston looked, the more troubled he became. Of Martin Luther King, Jr.,'s assassination, he wrote, "The nation is appalled by the murder of Martin Luther King, but it is not appalled by the conditions of his people. It grieves for the man, but not for his cause. This is the curse and tragedy of America. This is the real crime of which the assassination of Dr. King is but a hideous symbol."

The year 1968 would prove a traumatic one for the United States; a year of political assassination, orgiastic violence, and immense psycho-political tension. But it was not merely the counterculture that had stressed the system toward its breaking point. A significant proportion of the voters who shocked Lyndon Johnson into early retirement by supporting McCarthy's peace crusade in New Hampshire voted for George Wallace in the general election. The discovery of the "Silent Majority"—the 56 percent of those polled who thought that Mayor Daley's cops had used an appropriate level of force in senselessly beating both student protesters and members of the visiting news media before national television cameras—threw what remained of the Center into a state of confusion. About all that Washington pundits could agree upon, as Joseph Kraft admitted, was that "most of us . . . are not rooted in the great mass of ordinary Americans."

With Richard Nixon's election in 1968, the competing ideological currents within the insider dialogue came to a head. In the first place, Nixon was faced with something with which no Cold War president had ever had to deal: an unapologetic intellectual opposition. In Anthony Lewis, who began appearing on its op-ed page in June 1969, The New York Times had given voice to a writer who, alone among influential commentators, was willing and able to articulate the moral outrage against the American government that characterized the anti-war movement.* The war, he thundered, constituted "a crime against humanity," causing "the most terrible destruction in the history of man." Today Lewis tends to see the war as less a "conscious evil" than just a "combination of miscalculation and ignorance." Yet his language, published day after day on the Times op-ed page, was probably the most powerful that had ever been used to criticize an American president in so prestigious a forum.

Significantly, Lewis did not write his column from Washington. He had intended to, and had found a house in the capital, but when he went to his new office, he decided almost immediately to move out of town. "I realized," Lewis recalls, "that I could not live [there] because I could not write about public figures the way I wanted to. . . . When I see people regularly I find it very hard to be unabashedly critical." But even in Washington itself, voices were cropping up that appeared to embrace a rejection not only of the war but of the entire Cold War ideology that had produced it. Ignored for more than three decades, I. F. Stone suddenly became a celebrity as over 70,000 subscribers read his radical newsletter. Tom Wicker, the former Times bureau chief, joined Lewis on the op-ed page and adopted a similarly anti-war perspective. The Washington Post hired former community organizer Nicholas Von Hoffman and gave him a column (albeit in the Style section) with which to vent some old-fashioned left-wing moral outrage. And The Washington Star found a deceptively polite, well-mannered New England lady named Mary McGrory who, once she got interested in Vietnam, found she could write about nothing else. As what McGrory termed the "infectious choler that is rising from the city" under Lyndon Johnson gave way to the "continuing spiral of obliviousness from the White

*Ironically, Lewis was offered the role because publisher Punch Sulzberger had asked him to fly back from London to discuss a new job, which was filled by the time he arrived. Sulzberger felt guilty, and Lewis got his column. Author's interview.

House" under Richard Nixon, her rage grew in scope and intensity, but it never overpowered the wonderfully measured tone of her carefully constructed prose. "Senators used to tell me," explains McGrory, "you're not funny anymore. Why aren't you ever funny anymore? What they meant was, 'Please shut up about Vietnam.'"

Even Reston, though still a hopeless sucker for Kissinger, was sufficiently shocked by the lies and mendacity of the Nixon administration to adopt an entirely new vocabulary with regard to the symbols of American power and prestige. In response to Nixon's initial defense of his lawlessness, that his subterfuge was undertaken in the name of "national security," Reston wrote, "And the tragedy is that more crimes and brutalities have been done in the name of 'national security' in this country than in the name of anything else. . . ." This was indeed an amazing moment. Here was the most important political commentator of the day—the man who had written, during the Bay of Pigs crisis, that "overriding questions of national security are involved in Cuba," and that, "in these days of subversion and indirect aggression, these things justify the pursuit of national security without regard to national laws or international treaties," debunking this most sacred mantra of his generation as not merely a sham but a mask for "crimes and brutalities."*

But in politics, unlike science, not every action causes an equal and opposite reaction. Some actions cause reactions that far exceed the power and scope of their initial inspiration. The insinuation of "movement" values into the thinking and writing patterns of insider pundits, however tentatively, created a reaction that, over time, would sweep away not only the emerging left but also the cinders of the old establishment, leaving in its wake a new political/intellectual formation that would cripple liberal and moderate political culture for decades to come.

The rise of the New Right began almost immediately with the collapse of the Center. Richard Nixon was a man with an almost bottomless capacity for resentment, and he resented nothing and no one so much as the men and women who wrote about him each day in the great newspapers of the country. †
As he explained to Patrick Buchanan: "If you consider the real ideological bent

---

*Reston later qualified this by adding: "The statement that 'more crimes have been committed with the excuse of national security' is absolutely right. But it doesn't follow from that that any time they proclaim that national security is at stake, you reject it. It may be true. It was true during the missile crisis." Author's interview. The initial quote appeared on April 12, 1961.

†William Safire now says that his biggest misjudgment of Nixon's character resulted from his underestimation of the President's hatred and contempt for the press, which he had previously interpreted to be Nixon's respect for personal privacy. Author's interview with William Safire.

of the *New York Times*, the *Washington Post, Time, Newsweek*, and the three television networks, you will find overwhelmingly that their editorial bias comes down on the side of amnesty, pot, abortion, confiscation of wealth (unless it is theirs), massive increases in welfare, unilateral disarmament, reduction of their defenses and surrender in Vietnam."

Nixon was certain that he, not these self-selected Ivy League smarties, understood what the American people wanted from their president, and whatever criticism he received from them he filed under the category of hostile conspiracy. Spiro Agnew spoke for his boss in a series of November 1969 speeches when he attacked the national news media for "giving the American people a highly selective and often biased presentation of the news," and blamed it for the continuing salience of the anti-war movement, singling out for special contempt "the effete corps of impudent snobs who characterized themselves as intellectuals."

Insider punditry continued to grow in influence as Nixon's stature fell, but it was a nervous growth, unsettled by the fact that Nixon was playing a new kind of extra-constitutional hardball. Reporters' phone lines were tapped, the FBI unleashed against them, and the White House even hired a private investigator to search the home of *Post* pundit Joseph Kraft. The Agnew attacks, moreover, proved a brilliant tactic in creating a political atmosphere more palatable to Nixonian conservatism. Newspaper publishers worried that their high-minded commentators were out of touch with American values, and Nixon's visible hostility gave them great incentive to address this. Actually finding pundits whose views were "rooted in the great mass of ordinary Americans" may have been beyond the capacities of the media barons, but responding to direct political pressure—that was something they understood.

The distinguished careers of William Safire and George F. Will owe a great deal to this historical moment. Safire, a Nixon speechwriter, was brought on the staff of the *Times* amid great controversy in 1973. David Halberstam spoke for many when he wrote the publisher that Safire "was not a Conservative . . . but a paid manipulator. He is not a man of ideas or politics but a man of tricks." Safire did not do much to assuage the fears of his colleagues when, in his earliest columns, he suggested that Nixon "reestablish the confidentiality of the presidency" by setting off "a public bonfire of the tapes on the White House lawn."

The Washington Post op-ed page was also in the market for an insider pundit to take up the Conservative banner. Alsop was no longer effective, having discredited himself over Vietnam, and editor Philip Geyelin could not afford to match Sulzberger's offer to Safire, though he "struggled like hell" to try. As a consolation prize, Geyelin settled on a young ex-professor and

Republican speechwriter whom his deputy, Meg Greenfield, had recommended. George Will was brought onto the page on a trial basis, where he quickly developed a flair for enlisting the likes of Edmund Burke and G. K. Chesterton on behalf of his hawkish sentiments. But as Geyelin recalls, Will had not as yet developed even an "elementary sense of journalistic propriety." When Geyelin told Will that his trial period had ended and the Washington Post Writers Group was ready to syndicate him nationally, Will asked, "Does this mean I have to stop writing speeches for Jesse Helms?"

The fact that neither Safire nor Will were journalists in their pre-pundit lives explained much about the post-Lippmann direction the profession had taken. Most of the journalists who could have been expected to be nominated as columnists and commentators came to be classified as "liberal" during this period. Like Reston, their work had led them to the conclusion that the United States required a period of quiet soul-searching to deal with its own seething internal tensions. A few hard-liners remained committed to Cold War contests and Vietnamlike wars, but by and large, the nonpolitical response to Vietnam, and later Watergate, was to try to think more modestly about the nation's ambitions in the future. In order to find pundits who could convincingly argue the opposite—that what the United States and the world required was an even greater dose of military adventure—publishers had to turn outside the profession to professional ideologues like Will and Safire.

Like Nixon, the Far Right had always suspected a liberal (and usually Jewish) conspiracy to dominate the media, but because the movement had traditionally been in thrall to its lunatic fringe, it had trouble distinguishing its crazier notions from those with which a significant portion of Americans could be expected to identify. In William F. Buckley, Jr., however, the right found itself an amazingly fortuitous spokesperson. Although his influence on the political mainstream was initially negligible, Buckley's achievements were nevertheless significant. First his magazine, *National Review*, founded in November 1955, managed to unify conservatism's politically palatable elements into the beginnings of a cooperative movement. Before the days of Buckley's journal, organicist, religious conservatives who traced their lineage to Burke and the American philosopher Russell Kirk did not feel they had much to say to economic conservatives, who looked to Adam Smith and the Austrian economist Friedrich A. Hayak as their lodestars. The former viewed capitalism with considerable suspicion, entailing, as it did, the Shumpeterian "creative destruction" of the class-based order on which the organicists placed so much emphasis. *National Review* pioneered what it called a "fusionist movement," which, according to Buckley, offered necessary "godfatherly moral attention" to the "concrete and observable services" rendered by capitalism.

Buckley's second crucial contribution consisted of his successful expunging of some of the movement's loonier elements. According to Marvin Liebman, one of Buckley's most stalwart foot soldiers, in the "dark ages" before *National Review* was formed, the Conservative movement was predominantly an "ooze . . . made up of bigots, anti-Semites, anti-Catholics, the KKK, rednecks, Know-Nothings, a sorry lot of public hucksters and religious medicine men."*

Third, and no doubt far the most pleasurable for him, Buckley was able to present himself to literary tastemaking society as a perfectly dashing sort of fellow, a conservative without fangs, without a tail, and congenitally incapable of sipping his vichyssoise with the wrong spoon. As children, the Buckleys had been tutored in: apologetics, art, ballroom dancing, banjo, birdwatching, building boats in bottles, calligraphy, canoeing, carpentry, cooking, driving, trotting horses, French, folk dancing, golf, guitar (Hawaiian and Spanish), harmony, herb gardening, horsemanship, history of architecture, ice skating, mandolin, marimba, music appreciation, organ, painting, piano, playing popular music, rumba, sailing, skiing, Spanish, speech, stenography, swimming, tap dancing, tennis, typing, and wood carving. As an adult, Buckley's famous charm and ever-growing celebrity status offered uncounted avenues for him to insinuate his political philosophy into mainstream forums, particularly in the omnipresent universe of television celebrities. In the days when Ronald Reagan was still a B-movie actor, Buckley proved the movement's most effective ambassador.

Buckley began a syndicated column in 1962, and 1966 introduced "Firing Line," a television show that provided a boon both to the movement and to Buckley's personal stock within mainstream culture. His half-serious 1965 New York City mayoral campaign also earned him considerable capital as a social commentator, so much so that by 1968, Richard Nixon felt he needed to court Buckley's support in order to shore up his right flank. With Nixon in the White House, Buckley and his lieutenants set about building a movement that would be capable, some day, of electing its own presidents, rather than merely attaching itself to the lesser of two evils.

Like Moses (and Mikhail Gorbachev), Buckley would eventually be able to lead his people out of the land of Canaan, but not quite so far as the promised land. In the 1970s Buckley's celebrity as a television host, a spy novelist, and a jet-set bon vivant displaced his image as a Far Right

---

*See Phil McCombs, "Revelation from a Right-Winger," *The Washington Post*, Style section, July 9, 1990, p. 1. Buckley says his friend exaggerated a bit. Author's interview.

ideologue. With his patrician instincts and countless liberal admirers, he ultimately lost touch with the middle-American grass-roots conservatism of Nixon's silent majority and the New Right movement leaders building upon it.* Before *National Review*, Buckley recalls, "conservatism was considered philistinia," and he found "obsequy to populism" to be "unnecessary and demeaning." But the New Right minions were nothing if not proud Philistines. Like WFB II, they hated Communists; but they hated liberals even more. The movement that Buckley and his magazine had helped create and effectively fronted for, was, by the late 1970s, ready to be taken to places where he himself could not comfortably go.

The New Right was a movement built on middle-class grievance. The reaction to the events of 1968 had demonstrated an American middle class that was made distinctly uncomfortable by what it considered to be the increasing influence and lurch leftward of much of the national media that accompanied Vietnam and Watergate. These anxieties, along with the fires of class and racial resentment, were consistently stoked by the Nixon administration and its supporters in the New Right. Moreover, the stagflationary macroeconomic impact of the war followed by the oil shocks of the 1970s was shrinking people's disposable incomes. This put further stress on the values of progressive tax rates and welfare for the poor. Conservative social movements, moreover, sprouted in response to unpopular Supreme Court decisions relating to abortion, school prayer, and racial integration. Finally, Americans felt helpless observing the military adventurism embarked upon by the Soviet Union coupled with the explosion of anti-American nationalism throughout the Third World. Together with the humiliation and denial that comes with losing a war, and the collapse of the Cold War foreign policy elite, these forces gave aid and comfort to ideas that just a decade earlier had been the exclusive province of the Westbrook Pegler end of the spectrum. They also swept away the tentative (and often misguided) efforts liberals were making to scale down America's global ambitions and redistribute some of its wealth and power.

In the conservative ideological attack of the early seventies, all the uncomfortable changes the country was undergoing were welded together into a single critique of "liberal elite culture." Like the vulgar Marxists a number of them had once been, the right-wingers saw an unspoken conspiracy ruling American political and cultural life, in which everyone and everything was connected to everyone and everything else. It was a kind of bargain-basement

---

*Not all liberals found Buckley's charms irresistible. *New York Daily News* columnist Lars-Erik Nelson says, "Buckley exists to wrap up people's base, greedy, bigoted, low-life, mean, and nasty views into high-faluting language so that they don't have to go around thinking that they are just mean, stupid, and nasty, but instead have a philosophy like Buckley's." Author's interview with Lars-Erik Nelson.

Hegelianism: the entire American culture moved as if guided by a single dialectical spirit. Harvard and Yale, feminism and taxes, school prayer and Soviet power: all of these social problems and more stemmed from the same source of political/cultural malaise, namely, the post-Vietnam victory of the "New Class" and the "permissive" culture it has foisted upon the nation.*

The New Class, according to neoconservative godfather Irving Kristol, was made up of "scientists, teachers, and educational administrators, journalists and others." They had somehow manipulated Americans to believe that they were an evil people who rained death and destruction on Vietnam to feed their own sick compulsions. As for Watergate, where the liberal press had carried out a successful "coup d'etat" (in Norman Podhoretz's judgment) to please its own vanity, it succeeded only in increasing its own appetite. In the aftermath of Vietnam and the establishment's failure of will, 'the New Class radicals had swallowed the entire establishment and annexed the Supreme Court. Among the most dangerous aspects of the tactics of these people, moreover, was the stealth with which they went about their ideological mission. While they spoke of social justice, what the New Class was really after was the Triumph of Socialism.

The ranks of the neoconservatives were largely composed of former sectarian Marxists of mostly Jewish academic origin, who transferred their intellectual allegiance to capitalism and American military power but retained their obsession with theological disputation and political purity. The impresario at the center of this attack was Irving Kristol, a onetime Trotskyist who had since become a passionate defender of capitalism.† The job of the neoconservative intellectual, Kristol once remarked, was "to explain to the American people why they are right and to the intellectuals why they are wrong." Beginning with the early days of the Nixon administration, this is just what they began to do. Spreading the Word was a costly proposition in America, however. There were think tanks to be started, journals to be founded, scholarships to be offered, and university chairs to be endowed. Like Willie Sutton, Kristol had to go where the money was—in this case, downtown about thirty blocks to the once-forbidden Philistine city of Wall Street.

The money tree did not bear immediate fruit. Historically, as Kristol observed, business wanted "intellectuals to go out and justify profits and

---

*My favorite example of this dialectical pattern came in George Will's 1991 equation of the dangers faced by the United States in the Persian Gulf War with those embodied by the threat of multiculturalism. Runner up would be Norman Podhoretz's 1986 equation of New York City's anti-sex discrimination law with support for the Sandinistas. See George F. Will, Newsweek, April 22, 1991, and Norman Podhoretz, March 20, 1986.

†And whose son, William, is generally considered to be the puppeteer behind Dan Quayle and his anti–Murphy Brown offensive.

explain to people why corporations make a lot of money." Kristol had a far more ambitious agenda in mind, but first he needed to convince the businessmen that they needed him. In this effort he could not conceivably have cultivated a more valuable ally than Robert Bartley, the editorial-page editor of *The Wall Street Journal*. Both men were already fierce Cold Warriors, but Bartley, tutored by Kristol, soon enlisted in the New Class war as well. The ideology of the New Class, according to Bartley, was fomenting "something that looks suspiciously like a concerted attack on business." In order to thrive and prosper in the upcoming battle for control of the American economy, businessmen and their allies needed to publish or perish. The *Journal* editorial pages soon became a hotbed of neocon counterrevolution, and Kristol a regular contributor.

Once business began to pony up the kind of cash necessary to fight a media class war, the terms of Washington's insider debate began to change. With tens of millions of dollars solicited from conservative corporations, foundations, and zillionaire ideologues like Nelson and Bunker Hunt, Richard Mellon Scaife, Joseph Coors, and the Reverend Sun Myung Moon, the new Conservative Counter-establishment (so named by journalist Sidney Blumenthal) did a masterly job at aping the institutions on the establishment's Washington and replacing them with its own. Unable to transform (or blow up) the liberal think tank, the Brookings Institution, the conservatives created the American Enterprise Institute (AEI), the Center for Strategic and International Studies (CSIS), the Heritage Foundation, and a host of small ideological shops to drown out the liberals and moderates with their own analyses. * In need of a newspaper to run its second-string pundits and give jobs to its wives and children, they embraced the Moonie-financed *Washington Times*, which came to serve as a daily crib sheet through which right-wing insiders could keep tabs on their ideological stock exchange. †

*These foundations did more than just promote the spread of conservative ideas. According to Sidney Blumenthal, the Heritage Foundation, at the suggestion of Robert McFarlane and Oliver North, transferred $100,000 to a front group controlled by partners of Iran-Contra moneyman Spitz Channell. Heritage president Edward Feulner wrote, "My colleagues and I have discussed your proposal in some detail and we are pleased to respond in a positive way." When this was discovered by the congressional investigative committees, Congressman Richard Cheney quashed the investigation by threatening to call up the records of every nonconservative think tank in Washington. See Sidney Blumenthal, *Pledging Allegiance: The Last Campaign of the Cold War* (New York: Harper & Row, 1990), pp. 29–30.

†Among the neocon brethren whose sons, daughters, or wives enjoyed regular Moonie-financed paychecks were Norman Podhoretz, Ben Wattenberg, Irving Kristol, Richard Grenier, and honorary neocon and Contra front-person Arturo Cruz. Young Podhoretz, affectionately known around the office as "John P. Normanson" for the way his editor introduced him, became enough of a *Moonie macher* to achieve a status akin

Having made insufficient progress colonizing the Council on Foreign Relations, the conservatives founded the Committee on the Present Danger (CPD), a Cold War-obsessed cadre of disaffected hawkish Wise Men and newly respectable neoconservative intellectuals. The group, which would eventually furnish fifty-nine members of the Reagan national security team, including the President himself, dedicated itself to the notion that "the principal threat to our nation, to world peace, and to the cause of human freedom is the Soviet drive for dominance" and its "long-held goal of a world dominated from a single center—Moscow.*

The newly sophisticated right-wingers recognized that they required a combination of political and cultural strategies to transform the American political debate. Had they relied on a strictly insider-based battle plan, the old Center could have ignored them at relatively little cost. And if the right had kept to an exclusively grass-roots organizing model, they would likely have seen their champions co-opted. But together, the two strategies worked synergistically to create a momentum that seemed, by the election of 1980, to sweep away virtually all traces of the old-guard elite.

It is impossible to determine whether the pundits provided the cannon shots that softened up the underbelly of respectable Centrism or the cavalry that broke through the final line to victory. Certainly no soldier in the conflict was given a more prominent position from which to declare victory. And none seemed to relish the fight more than the Mutt 'n' Jeff combination of Rowland Evans and Robert Novak.

The dynamic duo had begun writing their column back in 1963 as strictly a news-gathering enterprise. Evans, a Main-Line Philadelphian who wears custom-made suits and throws Alsoplike dinner parties, took care of the diplomatic beat. Novak, a beer-bellied tough guy who buys his suits off the rack, wore out the shoe leather in the Capitol. The column was ideologically balanced, treating insider politics the way *Popular Mechanics* treats cars and *Stereo Review* treats tape decks. Novak may have slugged a *New York Times* reporter at the 1964 Republican Convention, but he also slugged a Goldwater Republican for balance.

---

to that of a poor man's Abe Rosenthal. His atrocious, self-infatuated prose style, according to one staffer, was regularly read aloud at the *Post*, "to the accompaniment of gales of laughter." Charlotte Allen, a staff writer for the Moonie-funded magazine *Insight*, which young Podhoretz edited, coined the term *"podenfreude"* to describe the enjoyable sensation one experienced when reading awful writing. See Charlotte Hays, "Moondoggled," *The New Republic*, February 17, 1992, pp. 17–18.

*Note the inverted historical parallel between the CPD and William Allen White's Committee to Defend America in the pre–World War II period. See "Common Sense and the Common Danger," Policy Statement of The Committee on the Present Danger, *Alerting America* (Washington, DC: Pergamon/Brassey, 1984), p. 3.

As with the neocons, the duo's flight to the hard right was a reaction to the incipient leftward forces which they termed "McGovernism." In the three months just before the 1972 election, thirty-seven of their ninety-three pre-election columns assaulted either McGovern or his political views, accusing him, among other things, of consorting with "zealots with long hair, bizarre costumes and peace signs." This strategy coincided perfectly with the political direction mapped out personally by Nixon to destroy the McGovern campaign, by associating him with "Abby [sic] Hoffman, Jerry Rubin, Angela Davis, among others," whose support of McGovern "should be widely publicized and used at every point."

Owing to their excellent sourcing inside the political establishments of both parties, the columnists' anti-McGovern rampages had a considerable effect on the coverage of the 1972 election. In one of the most influential columns ever to be written during a presidential election, Evans and Novak helped coin the famous phrase, "acid, amnesty and abortion," to describe McGovern's political positions. The quote was attributed to "a liberal senator whose voting record differs little from McGovern." The speaker warned that "Once middle America—Catholic middle America in particular—finds this out, he's dead." The "Triple As" slogan, as it came to be called, was picked up by Reston and given much wider circulation as a slogan for McGovern opponents.* With the McGovern campaign, Evans and Novak leaped over the line that allegedly distinguished straight reporting from avowed partisanship. In the admiring words of the rigidly Marxist Alexander Cockburn, the journalists took Mao's advice and "put politics in command."

The same tendencies that helped create the "Triple A" political firestorm were also at work in a column that would have an equally important effect on the election of 1976. In the sequel, the authors wrote a blistering attack on a Kissinger aide named Helmut Sonnenfeldt. According to an Evans and Novak report of March 22, "Intense debate was set off when Secretary of State Henry Kissinger's right-hand man declared in a secret briefing that permanent 'organic' union between the Soviet Union and Western Europe is necessary to avoid World War III." The column, based on a leak of Sonnenfeldt's speech to a group of U.S. diplomats in London, set off a political crisis for Kissinger both in Congress and inside the ethnic communities that President Ford needed to sway to win the 1976 election. "Of all my columns," Novak insists thirteen years later, "that is the one I am most proud of. It really showed the hypocrisy of the Kissinger State Department and it really nailed them."

---

*According to McGovern, the column was a "dishonest one, which distorted my position in a way I could never catch up to." Author's interview with George McGovern.

Of course, Sonnenfeldt did not see it that way. His concept of an "organic relationship," he says, was diametrically opposed to the notion that the columnists sought to portray with the phrase "permanent 'organic' union"—one he never used. Sonnenfelt's speech implied a greater Soviet tolerance for diversity in Eastern Europe, rather than reliance upon the use of force.

As a result of the column, Sonnenfeldt and his patrons Gerald Ford and Henry Kissinger were called before congressional panels, attacked in the Eastern European ethnic media, and even manipulated by the KGB, which sought to demonstrate to the Romanians and Poles that the United States supported their subjugation. Candidate Ronald Reagan also attacked Ford relentlessly for his support of Eastern Europe's "permanent enslavement." Finally, Ford was asked at his second debate with Jimmy Carter if he accepted the permanent domination of Eastern Europe by the Soviet Union. "There is no Soviet domination of Eastern Europe," replied the soon-to-be ex-President.

Aside from its arguable electoral impact, the defection of Evans and Novak to the Far Right end of the spectrum was crucial in the shaping of insider political dialogue for a number of reasons. The fact that they were so powerfully wired into the main currents of the Republican party and the national security bureaucracy made their column impossible to ignore for inside dope purposes. Its appearance three times a week on *The Washington Post* op-ed page gave its Far Right ideological interpretations the establishment seal of approval. Moreover, their breathless, Pearsonlike prose, coupled with Novak's well-rehearsed Joe Sixpack television persona, gave Washington insiders the impression that Evans and Novak spoke for (and with) that elusive silent majority for whom everyone in Washington always seemed to be looking. The fusion had the effect of softening up the right-wing borders of polite insider society, and creating an opening for their intellectual betters to exploit and expand.

Ready and willing were Will and Safire, who together set the standard for political punditry in the late seventies as Lippmann and Reston had done two decades earlier. When both men began their columns, each had something to prove. Safire needed to show that he was more than just a Nixon flack, and Will, that he was more than a nerd with a copy of *Bartlett's*. Will's opportunity came when he joined Buckley's brother and conservative New York senator, James, in calling for Nixon's impeachment back in 1973, rather early in the impeachment-calling game. Safire never fully emerged from Nixon's shadow during the Watergate period, but demonstrated a bit of previously undetected moxie when he found out that his friend Henry

Kissinger had been bugging his calls and lying to him about it.* Safire had made his journalistic reputation during the Carter years, when he tirelessly pounded away at the unorthodox financing techniques of Carter's budget chief, Bert Lance. His congenial personality had already won over many of his enemies at the *Times* Washington bureau, and his energetic, though biased, reporting struck many liberals and conservatives as model punditry for an ideological era, however marred by his incessant hammering at such memorable scandals as "Koreagate," "Oilgate," "Peanutgate," "Angolagate," "Lancegate" and "Billygate," and Safire's own personal favorite, "Double Billingsgate."†

Both Will and Safire shared almost all the basic tenets of the Counter-establishment thesis, including its critique of the New Class and its permissive culture, but were most effective in using the Vietnam stick to beat liberals into submission and to destroy the ideological underpinnings of the Carter presidency. "The real lesson of Vietnam," wrote Safire in January 1979, "is that the perception of America's weakness of will invites aggression; that Moscow is willing to use its client states to bring about a Pax Sovietica; and that there is no turning away from our allies anywhere without a cost in lives and human freedom everywhere." Similarly, Will was angered to learn that, as late as 1978, Carter still considered the civil war in Vietnam to be an "internal affair." The reason Carter deserved to be dumped onto the ash heap of history, argued Will, was his inability to see that the "Western democracies are, whether they know it or not, in the fifth decade of a war with totalitarians." Fortunately, "today the Soviet regime is so grotesquely ignorant and arrogant, so boorish and bullying, that its cruelty and recklessness may awaken Americans from their dogmatic slumber."

The difference between the Lippmann/Reston regime and that of Will/Safire is instructive. Lippmann and Reston had allied themselves with the establishment. By the time of the Will/Safire regime, the old establishment was disintegrating, and the new power pundits threw their lot in with the nascent Counter-establishment. Their constant stream of ideological

---

*When Safire originally wrote about the incident, in *Harper's*, Kissinger called it a "fairy tale" riddled with errors resulting from "a desire to claim inside information he in fact never possessed." Safire, in turn, assailed this "blustering deceit on Kissinger's part." The two have since made up, as Safire says that "the statute of limitations on Henry has run its course." Author's interview with William Safire. The quotes appear in Charles Michener, with Philip S. Cook and Thomas M. DeFrank, "Puppet and Puppet Master," *Newsweek*, May 3, 1975, p. 71.

†Safire today admits that, yes, psychologically, he may have been seeking to minimize the relative importance of the crimes committed by his former boss with this silliness. Author's interview.

invective toward the Carter presidency helped to destroy the insider political foundation upon which it had tenuously rested. It is impossible to separate these efforts from those undertaken in the heartland by the Moral Majority, California's tax revolters, and the New Right's direct-mail maestros. But within Washington, where the tone and parameters of the national political dialogue were determined, punditry was clearly king.

The remarkable rise in the fortunes of Washington pundits that accompanied their destruction of the Carter administration could be seen through the prism of the city's social life. In December 1977, Barbara Walters held a dinner party in honor of the newly cordial Egyptian and Israeli ambassadors. The real news of the evening, however, had nothing to do with the headliners. Aside from Carter aide Hamilton Jordan's oafish comments to the wife of one of the dignitaries, the most significant aspect of the dinner was the social pecking order it bespoke. It was Walters, not Henry Kissinger or Zbigniew Brzezinski, who elicited from Anwar Sadat the prime-time pledge to visit Jerusalem. In his opening toast, Art Buchwald fêted the hostess for "bringing together two men who have been ideologically miles apart, who fought each other over the years—Hamilton Jordan and Bill Safire." Reports of this historic moment appeared later in Safire's column.

The Washington represented in this room was, for most practical purposes, the only Washington that mattered. There was television, in the regal form of Ms. Walters, staging the entire event. There was the editor of *The Washington Post*, Ben Bradlee, and *The New York Times* Most Important Pundit William Safire, listening to off-the-record speeches by pundit Buchwald and proto-pundit Kissinger on the subjects of Safire and Kissinger. Jordan, who had been given honorary status as Safire's equal by virtue of his relationship with the President, cracked under the pressure and reverted to his Georgia frat-boy origins.* At the end of the evening, when Safire went home to write his column, it was clear to everyone where lasting power in Washington genuinely lay.†

In the Carter years, dinner parties like Walters's expressed a world in

*While gazing down the Egyptian ambassador's wife's cleavage, Jordan pulled on her elasticized bodice and loudly declared that he "always wanted to see the pyramids." A little later, he stood up and announced, "This administration has to piss." For the gory details, see Sally Quinn, "Where Did All the Good Times Go? Where Have All the Good Times Gone: The Trials and Separations of the Carter Crowd and the Washingtonians," *The Washington Post*, Style section, December 18, 1977, p. G1.

†When Jordan's sidekick Jody Powell left the White House to try his hand at columnizing, Safire penned him a note reading, "No more the trappings of power, just the real thing." See Eleanor Randolph, "William Safire, Right to the Core: The Columnist and His Novel Look at Abraham Lincoln," *The Washington Post*, Style section, August 24, 1987, p. 1.

which the pundit, Safire, slightly outranked the President's most trusted adviser, Jordan. Immediately after the 1980 election, however, punditry ascended still further. Even before Ronald Reagan had a chance to get his presidential seat warm, George Will threw a series of dinner parties at which the host outranked everyone but the guest of honor. The pundit who hosted the Reagans and the rest of power Washington at these dinners was a different animal than that Lippmann had envisioned when he invented the business more than four decades earlier. In the first place, Will had become no less a television star than a revered newspaper pundit. In contrast to Lippmann's reluctant annual appearances, Will expounded from the black box twice a week. Lippmann was a failure at maintaining his distance from high public officials, but he did profess to try. Will, on the other hand, flaunted his political friendships and made no apologies for them. While Lippmann did his best to moderate the military appetites of his countrymen, Will encouraged them, siding in almost all disputes with those who argued for war. Lippmann did not have much journalistic training: a few months as a cub reporter and a sting as an assistant to Lincoln Steffens. But Will had none at all. A former professor and Republican aide, Will saw himself not as practicing a higher form of journalism, but a new kind of political partisanship: one in which the weapons of choice were television stardom, presidential access, and a regular newspaper column, in declining order of significance.

Perhaps the most important difference between Lippmann and Will was the fact that in Lippmann's day, there had only been Lippmann. By the time that bow ties and steel-rimmed glasses became fashionable among young conservative operatives, Will was simply at the head of an ever-expanding pundit class. The numbers were still tiny, but the job had become at least a reasonable ambition for well-educated, socially ambitious young men who, fifty years earlier, would not have allowed a journalist into their living rooms. No longer was it astonishing to find a newspaper commentator who had studied political philosophy at Oxford and Princeton. No longer was it amazing to find one who earned more than the President. And it seemed hardly worth noting that however many papers may have carried Will's column, he was better known for what he looked like than what he wrote.

When Lippmann, Reston, and Alsop ruled the day, the political spectrum they embodied was not much narrower than that defined by the Reagan-era pundit class. But it was less self-consciously militant, and had a far healthier respect for the complexity of world affairs and the difficulties most Americans had incorporating the details of politics and policy into their busy lives. But by the end of the 1970s, a complex array of reactionary and revisionist political forces had succeeded in redirecting the American political conversation away from past concerns with the expansion of political rights, racial tolerance, fairness and equity into angry new territory that denied not only the possibility but even the desirability of the liberal center's agenda. Americans were confused by the events of the 1960s and 1970s, as our time-honored traditions and seeming invulnerabilities suffered one buffeting attack after another. They demanded answers from their political leaders, and the liberal center, exhausted and dispirited, failed to provide them.

Into this void, and supported by hundreds of millions of right-wing dollars along with the natural biases of most of the media-owning corporations of America, stepped New Right and neoconservative pundits. They offered simple, self-congratulatory answers that not only flattered American egos but released them from the painful uncertainty and introspection that the events of the past two decades had inspired. In the age of the Reagan punditocracy, politics had once again become quite simple. All that was required for peace and prosperity was for America to start acting more American: to be tougher, stronger, and to feel better about itself. Women, the poor, and the minorities needed to quit whining and get with the program. The rich needed to forget about their guilt and start enjoying themselves again. And perhaps most important, the media needed to stop telling Americans everything that was wrong with the country and start celebrating our power, our bravery, and our genius. With their political opposition defeated and their remaining competitors for what Lippmann called "the approaches of public policy" ejected from the playing field, the pundits suddenly had the game all to themselves.

The net effect of these changes laid the groundwork for untold political damage to the American people and the political system during the decade of the 1980s. For Lippmann, however loftily, had envisioned a group of pundits like himself who would shield the republic from the force of its emotion and arm it with the means to defend itself intellectually against the charlatan, the terrorist, and the jingo. The punditocracy that he indirectly spawned, however, worked hand in glove with these same forces. For its access to information and social status, it attached itself to the very rulers against whom it was supposed to be guarding. And for its income, it relied upon a medium dedicated to "poisoning the innocent" and "debasing the public taste." Lippmann may not have intended to plant these seeds, but it was clear that by the dawn of the Reagan era, his inheritors would gladly reap their harvest.

SECTION II

THE REAGAN PUNDITOCRACY

Now judge, judge I got debts no honest man could pay.
The bank was holdin' my mortgage and they was takin' my house away.
Now I ain't sayin' that makes me an innocent man.
But it was more 'n all this, judge, that put that gun in my hand.

—BRUCE SPRINGSTEEN, "JOHNNY 99" (1982)

4

THE TRIUMPH OF GEORGE WILL

It is a strange observation to make about a man who has—and has done—virtually everything, but William F. Buckley, Jr., never has lived up to his potential. Buckley is a pioneer of conservative political organization as well as of public affairs television. But by the time the two came to rule American public discourse in tandem, the Israelite himself had become something of a museum piece. When his friend, charter *National Review* subscriber Ronald Reagan, was elected President in 1980, George Will, William Safire, Patrick Buchanan, and Robert Novak had long surpassed Buckley's influence within both insider and conservative movement audiences. On "Firing Line" in particular, Buckley was badly dated by his good manners. While occasionally high on genuine intellectual fireworks, the show was notoriously lacking in sitcom fundamentals. Yes there was Buckley playing the old Mr. Chips role, but beyond that, it was all so . . . civilized.

But Buckley's television career did leave one extremely important legacy to the punditocracy. It derived, not from "Firing Line," but from his short-lived career as Gore Vidal's partner as an ABC commentator during the 1968 Republican and Democratic conventions. It was during that engagement that the two pundits set a standard for intelligent political dialogue against which future political commentators would one day be measured.

A generation ago, ABC was something of a semi-pro news organization. Its executives' desperation to attract viewers overrode their desire to be taken seriously as a "credible" and "responsible" voice in the political dialogue.

While planning their 1968 election coverage, these executives were searching for something that would truly distinguish their coverage from that of Walter Cronkite and company on CBS or Huntley and Brinkley on NBC. The idea for pairing Buckley and the unpredictable Vidal had come from Buckley himself, albeit in a backhanded manner. The network had asked him to name a liberal with whom he could profitably spar during the convention coverage, and Buckley replied that he would appear with any non-Communist, but he would prefer it not be that "philosophical degenerate," Gore Vidal. "Bingo," said the men at ABC.

The network's reporting of the 1968 Republican gathering—like the convention itself—passed without incident. The Miami gathering was marred only, in Buckley's view, by Vidal's insistence, during their debates, that he had based the "entire style" of the transsexual hero of his novel *Myra Breckinridge* on Buckley. Buckley replied that Vidal was "immoral" and held American culture in "disdain," but there the colloquy ended. Buckley tried to convince the producers to allow the two commentators to make their presentations separately for the ensuing Democratic Convention, but it was no go: A star had been born.

Amid the violent chaos that was the 1968 Chicago Democratic Convention, however, Buckley and Vidal began to argue over the relative provocational potential of the student protesters' raising of a Viet Cong flag the night before. Buckley compared it to the raising of a hypothetical Nazi flag during World War II. Vidal then insisted that "as far as I'm concerned, the only sort of pro- or crypto-Nazi is yourself." "Now listen, you queer," retorted the conservative elder statesman, "stop calling me a crypto-Nazi or I'll sock you in the goddam face and you'll stay plastered." The evening degenerated from there.

The incident drew itself out in a long and fruitless exchange in *Esquire* where Vidal implied that Buckley was not only a homosexual but also an anti-Semite.* Buckley considered a lawsuit, eventually concluding a complex legal agreement with *Esquire* instead. Of greater significance than the legal machinations, however, were the prescient observations of Buckley's friend, the conservative literary critic Hugh Kenner. Kenner admonished his friend for sacrificing the seriousness of his intended purpose upon the altar of celebrityhood. "What you have in fact done is accept a role as a Celebrity. You will be playing William F. Buckley, Old Antagonist of Gore Vidal." Buckley may have regretted his exchange with Vidal, but once again, he was merely embodying the *Zeitgeist* before its time. Calling one's opponent a

---

*For an illustration of things going around and coming around, see Buckley's discussion of Vidal's alleged anti-Semitism in William F. Buckley, "In Search of Anti-Semitism," *National Review*, December 30, 1991.

queer and threatening, if only metaphorically, to plaster him so that he stayed plastered, would have been considered the height of good manners in the punditocracy of the 1980s.

The pundit who best embodied the remarkable increase in the power, prestige, and prosperity the profession enjoyed in the Reagan era was not Buckley, but a man he had hired briefly to be *National Review* Washington correspondent and book editor. Riding the crest of a harmonic convergence between the rise of the television-based punditocracy and the victorious revolt of the New Right, George Will achieved, in the Washington of the early 1980s, a cultural presence among insiders akin to that of patron saint of a small Sicilian village. Completely unknown when Nixon won his second term in 1972, Will saw his shadow loom larger over Ronald Reagan's Washington than the monument at 17th Street. That barely one in ten "real" Americans recognized his face was irrelevant. In the media's most influential outlets, Will's bow-tied, bespectacled visage was everywhere: in *The Washington Post,* in *Newsweek,* on "Agronsky and Company," on "This Week with David Brinkley," on "The ABC Evening News," on "Nightline," in the ad copy for *Newsweek,* for "Agronsky and Company," "This Week with David Brinkley," "The ABC Evening News," etc. To earn so much free and favorable media attention in most provincial capitals, one generally has to overthrow a regime and name oneself Emperor for Life.

Will's star rose so quickly there is almost no charting it. When discovered by the deputy *Post* editorial-page editor in 1973, Meg Greenfield, Will was just, according to Greenfield, "a snotty-nosed little kid" showing up a roomful of politicos at a conference at Kenyon College. (Actually, he had, at age twenty-five, already been hired at *National Review.*) One writer described him as looking like an usher at a Whiffenpoofs' concert. Born in suburban Illinois of mildly Socialist parents, Will served as senior-class president and captain of the track team before earning degrees from Trinity College, Oxford, and Princeton. He taught political philosophy at Michigan State and the University of Toronto before joining the staff of Republican Senator Gordon Allott in 1970. Allott's defeat two years later left Will unemployed, until Buckley discovered in him a kindred soul and user of large words. "He came along at a time when there was a seismic change in American politics," observed NBC Vice-President Tim Russert. "Someone had to explain why Ronald Reagan's conservatism was sweeping the country and he filled the vacuum."

Will filled the vacuum so powerfully that by the mid-1980s, a front-page *Wall Street Journal* story would call Will "perhaps the most powerful journalist in America—rivaling—and some say surpassing—such famed pundits of previous decades as the late Walter Lippmann." But Philip Geyelin, a Lippmann protégé who, as *Post* editorial-page editor at the time, had made the final decision in January 1974 to go ahead with Will's column, considers his work "demeaning to the profession." However one judged the quality of Will's criticism, there could be no mistaking the power and influence his unofficial status as first pundit seemed to carry. Just in case anyone had missed the point about his unparalleled access to the new President, Will opened his first column of the Reagan era approximately six inches from the era's new desk: "the one under which John-John played hide and seek."* When Will irritated Reagan by calling him "incontinently eager" to placate the Soviets, the President immediately called Will in for a thirty-minute conference. He was received, according to one journalist, "like some head of state." And when Will was forced to defend his coaching of Reagan in the presidential debates one Saturday evening on "Agronsky and Company," the President phoned him at home immediately after the show aired, just in time for Will to mention it to 6 million people on the David Brinkley show the next morning.

Before he began filing from the Oval Office, Will had spent the second half of the seventies on the front lines of the New Right Panzer divisions, relentlessly attacking what he calls "the infantilism; impatience; hedonism; inability to defer gratification that produced the cultural dissolution of the sixties." His July 1973 call for Nixon's impeachment gave his right-wing politics the special oomph required to distinguish him from the typical Kilpatrick/Buckley fare then available, and his 1977 Pulitzer Prize for commentary sanctified his growing reputation as the Counter-establishment's boy wonder. But it was his television performance, coupled with his remarkably nondeferential friendship with the newly elected Ronald Reagan, that marked Will as the avatar of the emerging punditocracy.

Just as Lippmann had defined the pundit profession in the thirties and forties, so Will redefined it at the dawn of the Reagan era, thanks to his unique ability to master every level of the pundit business simultaneously. A useful way to think about the just-emerging punditocracy is to envision three concentric rings conforming (coincidentally) to the inner circles of Dante's *Inferno*. Each circle feeds into the next smaller one and each represents a different degree of a single political/philosophical continuum. At the center of it all lies George Will: television commentator, syndicated columnist, occasional political philosopher, and close personal friend of Ron and Nancy.

*Will also felt compelled to note that his buddy, the President, was "wearing a suit of blue-plaid that is . . . bold enough by Washington standards to set off an alarm." George F. Will, *Newsweek*, February 2, 1981.

Together with Will in the center ring are his fellow cast members on the various pundit network sitcoms, each conforming to a personality type with whom viewers can be expected to identify.* The epicenter of the punditocracy includes only those shows on which journalists and commentators are invited to be pundits—to pontificate regardless of expertise. Old-fashioned-politician-meets-the-old-fashioned-press programs do not qualify. If the politician wants to be invited to the party, as happens on CNN's "The Capital Gang" or Fox's "Off the Record," it is with the express condition that he or she be prepared to behave like a pundit.†

To argue that few people outside the Washington Beltway watch these shows is to misunderstand the nature of punditocracy's power and influence. Washington watches them, and that's what matters. Those pundits who make the final cut are its most admired stars. Those who decide who will be the regulars and what topics will be discussed are among its most powerful moguls. But there's a catch: despite their ostensible freedom to discuss almost anything, virtually all the pundits' discussions are devoted to the same issues, and most of these, with helpful White House guidance, are framed to coincide with the sympathies of the Reagan/Bush agenda.‡

The second ring, surrounding that of television, is newspaper and newsweekly syndication. The reach of a syndicated column is not nearly as wide as that of a regular television spot, but for most pundits it is a necessary foundation upon which to build an empire. The column attracts the attention of television producers and talk-show hosts. Columns are also taken

---

*For example, one reason for the successful reinvention of David Brinkley's career in the early 1980s appears to have been his talent for filling the gaping hole in the "National Grandpa" role left by Walter Cronkite's retirement. The show's producers reinforced his image by casting the Eddie Haskell-like Sam Donaldson opposite Brinkley, no doubt to highlight his reassuring calm and sardonic wit.

†"Meet the Press" and "Face the Nation" do not qualify. "This Week with David Brinkley" does because it gives the pundits a chance to schmooze in its final segment.

‡Drawn from *The Washington Post* television listings, these were the topics covered on the weekend of December 2, 1989:

"Evans and Novak," live from Malta;
"Newsmaker Saturday," live from Malta;
"Inside Washington," topics include the summit . . . ;
"The Capital Gang," topics include the summit . . . ;
"The McLaughlin Group," issues are the summit . . . ;
"Journalists Roundtable," topics are the Soviet-U.S. summit;
"Sunday Today," live reports on the Malta summit;
"CBS News Sunday Morning," live coverage of the summit;
"This Week with David Brinkley," the Malta summit;
"Newsmaker Sunday," live from Malta, the Summit at Sea;
"Face the Nation," The U.S. Soviet Summit.

(Thanks to Jack Shafer)

quite seriously inside the government's massive public relations apparatus, which works in a kind of parallel universe with that of the punditocracy, trying to shape opinion by virtue of its ability to control the national agenda and its ability to reward those pundits who support it with increased access to the President's inner sanctum. The only columnists who qualify for this ring, however, are those who either work or are read in Washington, preferably both. Garry Wills, William Pfaff, and Murray Kempton may be great columnists, but they might as well be writing in Albania from the standpoint of insider influence. With syndication in nearly five hundred subscribing papers and semi-permanent ownership of one of only two bimonthly columns in *Newsweek*, Will has few rivals as king of the highbrow syndicated pundits as well.

The punditocracy's third ring is made up of the smaller, limited-circulation periodicals in which mainstream political ideas are discussed and—defining the term quite loosely—debated, along with those television shows and op-ed pages where "experts" are given the opportunity to sell their views to a larger audience. The membership of this ring fluctuates seasonally with the insider *Zeitgeist*. One week, terrorism experts are all the rage on "Nightline"; the next, one would have to blow up a failing S&L to be called. There are two explicit punditocracy categories here, although each performs roughly the same function of injecting ideas into the two smaller, more influential rings. The print section of the third ring is made up of regular contributors to *The New Republic* and the *Post* Outlook section, with regular input from *National Review*, *Commentary*, *The National Interest*, *The Public Interest*, *Foreign Affairs*, *Foreign Policy*, and every once in a while, special contributors to op-ed pages of *The New York Times*, *The Washington Post*, and *The Wall Street Journal*. Historically, insiders have taken note of articles appearing on the op-ed page of the *Christian Science Monitor* or the *Los Angeles Times*, but hard-and-fast examples of these phenomenon are difficult to come by. Perhaps three times a decade, an article in a source with no direct ties to Washington insiderdom will also have an impact. This happens occasionally with *The New Yorker*, *The New York Review of Books*, *The Atlantic*, and more recently, *Daedalus*. The best recent example of the phenomenon may have been *The New Yorker*'s 1982 serialization of Jonathan Schell's *The Fate of the Earth*, which almost single-handedly challenged the primacy of the Reaganite nuclear agenda. Will got his start in this subsection of the ring when he was appointed Washington correspondent of *National Review*. Since then, however, his presence here has been a kind of ghostly one, hovering over the "ideas" discussion without actually entering it.

The television subsection of ring three is made up of those academic experts and former government officials who are sufficiently expert in the medium to be able to speak in short, uncomplicated sentences. The divisions here can be a bit confusing. When Harvard Sovietologist Marshall Goldman came on "The MacNeil/Lehrer Newshour" to predict the imminent overthrow of Mikhail Gorbachev—as he appeared to do every few months from the moment Gorbachev came to power—he was working the third ring of the punditocracy. But when David Gergen and Mark Shields appeared on the same show on the same evening to argue about whether Gorbachev liked broccoli, they were back in the center. This televised segment of the third ring had been the exclusive province of Harvard liberals John Kenneth Galbraith and Arthur Schlesinger, Jr., until Milton Friedman and his conservative legions came along in the mid-seventies. Today, its much larger, though constantly fluctuating, membership is largely determined by the young, overworked bookers on "Nightline" and "The MacNeil/Lehrer Newshour," with considerable input from that morning's op-ed pages.* Ironically, though his dominance of the first one would seem to disqualify him, Will is even a player in this ring. He has been designated an all-around Wise Man by the producers at ABC News—the only full-time commentator the network employed during the Reagan years. Thus Will is frequently invited on "Nightline" as an expert on matters from homeless to violence in the cinema, about which he does not even pretend to have any specialized knowledge. This last category—the designated public philosopher—is perhaps the most exclusive insider club of all.

Once again, the contrast with Lippmann is instructive. Lippmann made his initial reputation as a thinker by writing lengthy philosophical treatises—the most significant being *Public Opinion*. The columns were a product of the intellectual capital acquired in writing them. But George Will did not even attempt to write a serious book until his *Statecraft as Soulcraft* in 1983, and the work proved to be an embarrassment. ("Reads in long stretches like Monty Python's shooting script of Bartlett's," wrote Sidney Blumenthal in *The Washington Monthly*.) For Will, whose pretensions to be taken seriously as a political philosopher were no less serious than Lippmann's, the television screen and the 750-word column proved the entire basis of his claim. His appeal, as his published oeuvre made clearer and clearer, rested not on thoughtfulness but on cleverness. But for the purposes of achieving

---

*National Public Radio, which invites a wider spectrum of commentators than do television public affairs programs and succeeds occasionally in offering offbeat perspectives, is nevertheless guided by similar principles.

Lippmannlike brightness in the pundit constellation of the 1980s, cleverness was more than sufficient.*

Of course one might argue in Will's defense that, by the time he achieved Lippmannlike prominence, the reading and writing of books had become largely irrelevant to the American political dialogue. This is only partially true. Books cast an evanescent shadow on the insider dialogue. Power Washington does not generally read books. But its inhabitants like to sound well read anyway and are therefore required to refer to them occasionally. Sometimes a book is referred to so frequently within the punditocracy that people feel compelled to buy and thumb through it—just to see what all the fuss is about. (This is particularly true in the ever-burgeoning genre of former White House aide confessionals.) Usually, however, insiders keep up exclusively by reading reviews. For most functional purposes, in these cases, the review becomes the book. A good review can provide the ticket to "Nightline" or "MacNeil/Lehrer" for the author, and the reviewer generally benefits by making new friends.

Though generally just collections of his columns, Will's books sell well and are almost always respectfully reviewed. Writing in *The New Republic* in early 1982, soon to be a famous pundit and soon also to be a close friend of Will's, Charles Krauthammer called Will "the undisputed leader of [con-

---

*A second characteristic shared by Lippmann and his heir is the embarrassingly gossiped-about relationship with a woman. Rumors about the self-declared "thoroughly married" George Will and Lally Weymouth, globetrotting daughter of *Post* owner Katharine Graham, and former main squeeze of rigidly Marxist reporter and left executioner Alexander Cockburn, were initially dismissed by Washington wags as Too Good To Be True, but then Will left his wife and children to buy a $990,000 house a few blocks away from his family in Chevy Chase, only to see, according to *The Washingtonian* magazine, his office furniture left on his front lawn with a note reading: "Take it somewhere else, Buster." The cocktail party circuit exploded. Will and Weymouth both denied that the relationship had been romantic and threatened to sue *The Washingtonian*. The magazine offered to write a correction if it would be allowed to investigate the matter and interview Will's friends. The matter was dropped there.

Will's ex-wife Madeleine, whose father owned the diner that Will patronized as a liberal Trinity College undergraduate, had formerly been employed as the treasurer-secretary of GFW Inc. at a salary of $30,000 annually. As part of their May 4, 1989, divorce settlement, she was awarded $460,021 from the "defined benefit plan" that GFW Inc. maintains at Alex Brown & Sons, a brokerage firm. She also received the Will house, worth over $1 million, and an undisclosed amount of child support. Following her stint at the Will corporation, she worked as Ronald Reagan's director of the Office of Special Education and Rehabilitative Services (OSERS) in the Department of Education from 1983 to 1989. According to a November 28, 1989, General Accounting Office audit, 79% of her employees thought she had "negatively influenced the management of their organizational units."

Since breaking off with Weymouth, Will apparently found love again with former White House communications worker Mari Maseng, thirteen years his junior. The couple was married at Will's home on October 12, 1991.

servatism's] House of Lords." Will repaid the favor by devoting an entire column to Krauthammer's first collection, published four years later, comparing the writer to the distinctly un-Krauthammerian strikeout king, Dwight Gooden, and observing that it had become "widely recognized" that his new friend was now "the best new, young writer on public affairs."

In examining the relationship of the punditocracy's three rings to one another and to the shape and scope of the insider dialogue, it would be tempting to argue that television has come to dominate our political dialogue so forcefully that it is really the only forum that matters today. It would be tempting, but as Richard Nixon might say, it would be wrong. Television is a vacuum that sucks in everything in its path, but like the bag on the vacuum cleaner handle, it changes its shape with the content of whatever is filling it. This is not to say that the form of the medium is not the overriding determinant of its content. It is. But the process is a dialectical one. The derivative ideas that are bandied about on the average pundit talk show derive from somewhere. Television is certainly the dominant medium in the punditocracy, and for most Americans, it is the only visible part. But like the captain of the *Titanic*, we ignore the rest of the iceberg at our own peril.

Because television is the only medium that can simultaneously make a pundit fabulously wealthy, impress one's parents and high school rivals, and still leave the rest of the day free for putzing around, it is the focal point of most pundit ambitions. *The New York Times* forbids its employees from appearing regularly on any pundit shows. It can do so, because it is perhaps the only print institution whose power and prestige can offset the loss of money and fame that television offers. Still, its employees gripe about the policy a great deal and a handful have moved to less fastidious outlets in pursuit of television's riches. *

Most papers, unlike the *Times*, are pleased to see their reporters on television, preferring not to think about the journalistic difficulties this creates. The attraction of television for the journalist is not merely fame, but also money—a great deal of it—and it is the easiest money imaginable. With the right kind of television exposure, political biases, and an energetic speaking agent, a pundit can earn an extra $10,000 or $20,000 a week at lunch and still keep most of his day free for golf.

Again, the pioneer here is not so much Lippmann or Buckley, both of

---

*The *Times* management considers it demeaning for its reporters to accept regular stints as television commentators and forbids them from doing so more than once a month. The *Los Angeles Times* is also said to have a policy that discourages its reporters from appearing regularly on any program. But given the fact that Washington bureau chief Jack Nelson's weekly appearances on "Washington Week in Review" comply with the policy, it is difficult to imagine just what the restrictions might be.

whom indulged their fondness for money quite unabashedly, but Will. Back in 1975, when the Agronsky show was still the only ticket to sitcom stardom, Will explained to Henry Fairlie the secret of his success: "He said that his column was important to him because it got him on TV. And the Agronsky show was important because it got him on the lecture circuit. He told me I should be doing the same thing, because, if you choose your audiences right, you could give the same speech every time." In the Reagan era, despite fees that hovered in the vicinity of $20,000 a pop, Will had more invitations than he could possibly accept. Nancy Reagan recalls in her memoirs that after her operation for breast cancer, Will came to see her one morning in the hospital, "just back from one speaking engagement and then on to another at noon."

To begin to approach the $10,000-per-hour neighborhood, a pundit needs to be a certified superstar. But any major figure can expect a minimum hourly income of $7,500 just for showing up and pretending to have a good time. The only rules, explains Joe Cosby, a Washington-area booker, are "be conservative" and "be on television." I once saw Jeane Kirkpatrick deliver to a conservative conference a speech that appeared verbatim in her *Washington Post* column four days later. She would not even stay for dinner. Kirkpatrick's usual fee is $25,000.

The appearance of greater influence that accompanies television stardom is part of an endless cycle that leads to even greater television stardom. Of *The Washingtonian* magazine's fifty "most influential journalists" in the capital in 1989, only nine were print reporters who did not appear on television.* When one combines regular speaking fees with six-figure television consultancies, not to mention the psychic gratification that comes with pontificating before millions of people, the price of being recognized in airports and fancy Washington restaurants does not sound terribly onerous. † The complications that arise from trying to think in television terms—the denigration of linear intellectual progressions; the dominance of superficial form over content; the inability to communicate nuance, paradox, and cultural relativism—these are difficult drawbacks to get overly excited about in comparison.

Much of insider Washington did make a show of getting quite exercised when *New Republic* editor-in-chief Michael Kinsley, widely recognized as

---

*Jack Germond and Jules Whitcover co-author a column together for the *Baltimore Sun*. Germond appears on television each week; Whitcover does not. Germond appeared on *The Washingtonian*'s list; Whitcover did not.

†Morton Kondracke once explained to the wife of another *New Republic* editor that his life's ambition was to walk into a room and see people whisper to one another, "There goes Mort Kondracke." Author's interview with Philip Terzian.

the sharpest liberal mind of his generation, opted to step down from his influential perch at the magazine to accept a lucrative job fighting with Pat Buchanan on CNN's "Crossfire" every night. Yes, Kinsley allows, he fears the job may, over time, make him "dumber." It is, oftentimes, an extraordinarily dumb show.* But Kinsley's "main feeling is that life ought to be an adventure, and what the heck." Few beneficiaries of television's largesse are even this self-critical. McLaughlin Group member Jack Germond justifies his television appearances with the quip, "It is a half-hour of being a dancing bear to make a better living. . . ." Will, on the other hand, becomes indignant at the suggestion that too much television may be bad for his brain. "Anyone who goes to reread the stuff, as I have, will agree with me. I think this rubbish about my doing too much is mostly jealousy, and the rest is not understanding my lifestyle."

Will's "lifestyle" was one of the important new wrinkles he brought to the job of power pundit. Will's publicly affectionate relationship with the First Couple flew in the face of all known journalistic ground rules and certainly conflicted with the idealized notions of which Lippmann had spoken half a century earlier. By coaching, socializing with, and generally cavorting around with the men who ran the country and making no apologies for it, Will trampled upon the constitutional provision embodied in the First Amendment that entrusts the press to guard against the illegal and unwise exercise of power. Whether he actually did favors for his powerful friends was almost less important than the fact that he saw no reason to justify his appearances of having done so. For if fame, riches, and plenty of time to go to baseball games were the primary penalties for throwing most of journalism's principles out the window, then its less exalted practitioners might quite understandably become a good deal more cynical about trying to live up to them in the first place. That Will took refuge in his status as a columnist, argued that, unlike a typical reporter, his political prejudices were secret to no one, did not really clarify matters. Rightly or wrongly, punditry is still considered to be merely the most prestigious sinecure in the journalism business. None of the pundit shows that ruled the dialogue bothered to distinguish between those cast members who were bona fide pundits, those who were simply journalists who hoped to be pundits, and those who behaved like pundits even though they were forced to masquerade during the week as old-fashioned journalists. Because the rules of punditry had never been codified or even much discussed in the profession, Will's behavior infected nearly all aspects of the journalism profession. In the past, punditry had offered merely greater freedom to journalists to escape the stultifying rules

*No less so the time I appeared on it.

of objectivity. But in Will's case, it seemed to cloud the basic issue of which side punditry—and by extension, high-powered Washington journalism—was really on: Were they the politicians or were they the rest of us?

Will defended himself in part by minimizing the intimacy of his friend-ship with the President. Though the Reagans were frequent guests at Will's Chevy Chase dinner table, Will explained, "When Ronald Reagan comes to my house, I say, 'Hi. Here are my guests,' and then my wife takes him, sits down at the table with him. I mean it's not a close personal relationship." But the First Lady and First Pundit could often be spied lunching at the Jockey Club together, and Nancy named Will, along with Meg Greenfield and Katharine Graham, as one of her "pals," who called her with support and encouragement during the "dark and hurtful time" of the Iran-Contra affair. When Will received an invitation to a White House Christmas party, he refused on the grounds that other journalists were to be invited as well.

Of even greater notoriety than Will's personal relationship with the First Couple were his professional ties to its "more colorful" half. Privately, Will seemed to concur with Clark Clifford's characterization of Ronald Reagan as something of an "amiable dunce." Before Reagan won the Republican nomination, Will called him "The unsurpassed master of Jeremiads." Reagan biographer Lou Cannon reports that Will "wondered how anyone so uninformed could reach the top of the American political system." Will was "particularly annoyed," Cannon noted, by Reagan's "substitution of anec-dotes for analysis." He considered the President's thinking to be "terribly banal . . . Durango, Colorado, Rotary thought." But these reservations did not appear to interfere with either Will's social relationship with the Reagans, or his political championing of the President once he landed the job. Will helped write a 1982 speech that Reagan gave before the British House of Commons.* He accepted a nonpaying appointment to the Board of Visitors of the U.S. Naval Academy and openly politicked to get super-hawk John Lehman appointed Secretary of the Navy. These machinations also coin-cided with his (now-ex) wife's high-level appointment in the Department of Education. Phil Geyelin, Will's editor at the *Post* op-ed page during the seventies, recalls telling Will that he should not have been sitting in the Reagan family box at the 1976 Republican Convention and that he should have resisted the temptation to write Reagan's speeches for him, as well. Will apparently disregarded Geyelin's advice, and in the summer of 1983, Will's conduct itself became a political issue. During the 1980 election season, Will spied a copy of a purloined Carter briefing book in David Stockman's

---

*Will defends this by insisting that "it was not a partisan speech, it was a great state occasion—I was asked some thoughts and I gave some thoughts." Quoted in Tataryn, *The Pundits*, p. 81.

kitchen and failed to inform his readers, editors, or producers. Even more egregiously, Will had helped coach Reagan in his debate with President Carter and then, presenting himself on "Nightline" as an impartial observer, credited his student with a "thoroughbred performance."

The "Debategate" issue brought to the forefront all the issues that had troubled other journalists about Will. Previously he had been able to ascribe such criticism to the fact that "journalists are spurning choices not really open to them." Finally, as the denunciations grew in vehemence, and the *New York Daily News* publicly expunged him from its editorial pages, Will was forced to respond. He argued that the Carter papers looked unimportant to him, and so far as coaching Reagan, all he had done was to ask Reagan "a recondite question bristling with references to Resolution 242 and 'the green line,' regarding the Arab-Israeli peace process." Reagan, he felt compelled to add, "did not distinguish himself." Will insisted that he was correct to accept the invitation to help prepare the President for his debate as a columnist, rather than as a journalist, and argued that Lippmann, Krock, Alsop "and others have had various relationships with presidents from Woodrow Wilson on."*

Debategate divided the ranks of the punditocracy. Lining up against Will was most of the journalistic establishment. A *Los Angeles Times* media critic called Will "a political shill." Chicago tough-guy columnist Mike Royko called him a "lap-dog." Arguing that it was fine for Will to coach Reagan one minute and set himself up as an allegedly impartial judge of his performance the next were Hugh Sidey and his occasional ventriloquist, Ronald Reagan. Ben Bradlee later complained that if it had been up to him, "I would have canned him on the spot."

But far from resulting in Will's losing his job, the controversy only added to the Willian lore, further blurring the lines between the watchdogs and the watched. The *Daily News* reinstated him, and soon Will's kingdom was bigger than ever. It is ironic that Will was professionally beyond the reach of Bradlee, the editor of his flagship newspaper, and then the nation's most respected newspaperman. By the end of the controversy, Will's political status was so great he was also beyond virtually all accepted journalistic rules and practices. When it was all over, a *Wall Street Journal* reporter asked Will just where he drew the line between personal and professional relationships. "I don't," he replied.

*　　*　　*

*Moreover, Will could not resist mentioning, he was frequently invited to dinner with Reagan and other celebrities and they all had a marvelous time together. There was, for instance, that "small dinner" the previous winter "with Reagan, who enjoyed himself enormously—which is easy to do when Lee Iacocca is present and feeling feisty." George F. Will, July 10, 1983.

The talents that made Will a ubiquitous presence in the Washington media of the 1980s and the supremely powerful and influential television pundit of his era bore precious little relevance to those embodied by any journalist before him, Lippmann and Reston included. When former *Washington Post* Moscow correspondent Robert Kaiser returned home from his Soviet assignment, he called George Will on the recommendation of a mutual friend. The two men had dinner and Kaiser said to Will, "You know, George, you really ought to go to the Soviet Union. It's different than you imagine it." Will's face looked, Kaiser recalls, as if the suggestion had been made by someone who had recently returned from a stay in an insane asylum. That Kaiser seemed to believe that a pundit's ability to pontificate about a place could in some way benefit from his having observed it firsthand was an indication of just how long he had been away from Washington.

The Pulitzer Prize–winning pundit and close friend of Will's, Charles Krauthammer, has rightly praised his comrade for single-handedly injecting a Burkean sensibility into the American political consciousness. Indeed, as Krauthammer points out, Will is in many ways at philosophical odds with the phenomenon known as "Reaganism." Almost alone among prominent American conservative pundits, Will confronts head on the philosophical contradiction between simultaneous loyalty to Adam Smith and Edmund Burke. "Capitalism," Will worries, "undermines traditional social structures and values: it is a relentless engine of change, a revolutionary inflamer of appetites, enlarger of expectations, diminisher of patience." Will is contemptuous of "the most familiar and fashionable" conservatives who, "complacently . . . define the public good as whatever results from the unfettered pursuit of private ends." It is foolish, he insists, "to treat laissez-faire economic theory as a substitute for political philosophy. . . ." It is for statements like these that some of the vociferous conservatives in the movement consider Will an unserious parvenu. *National Review* writer Joseph Sobran calls Will's conservatism "a toothless, coffee-table Toryism, nicely calculated for liberal consumption."

At the core of Will's philosophical project is his distinction between "statecraft" and "soulcraft." Like most Marxists, Will insists that the state has a positive role to play in the shaping of its citizens' cultural consciousness. What distinguishes Will from the Marxists are the values he seeks to inculcate. "The United States acutely needs," Will argues, "a real conservatism, characterized by a concern to cultivate the best persons and the best in persons. It should express renewed appreciation for the ennobling functions of government." Singularly, among his peers on the right, Will supports increased taxation and additional government spending on such projects as child nutrition, prenatal care, and aid to dependent children. These communitarian functions are not only morally sound, he argues, but they contribute to the civility of the American polity, a value Will prizes almost above all.

That Will has managed to navigate a coherent philosophical position within the swamps of American political discourse is no mean achievement. But the achievement, however impressive, is undermined by the manner in which it has been achieved. Will does not earn his reported $1.5 million a year on the basis of his refined Tory sensibility. Rather, Will achieved his unique perch in American political culture—a perch the writer William Henry III has called "a national version of the smartest boy in the class"—on the strength of his television persona and the bellicosity of his foreign policy views. While Will does have a smooth pen and an enviable ability to speak precisely and concisely on television, the seriousness of his purpose is marred by a terminal addiction to intellectual name dropping, a writing style that veritably drips cuteness, and a shameless fealty to his social set in the pages of his columns.

Bathed in the phosphorescent glow of the cathode rays, George Will was glibness itself. Bon mot after mot seemed to spin off the Will tongue as if placed there by the ghosts of Burke and Chesterton. Aside from his eccentric Tory demeanor and shameless Anglophilia, Will was most revered for his pioneering work in the art of the sneer, both literal and figurative. The Will sneer took many forms. He would quiz Jesse Jackson on international monetary policy in a manner intended to make the presidential candidate look foolish. He would deliberately oversimplify the writings of Jean-Paul Sartre to the point, literally, of absurdity. ("Existentialism seems to be the belief that because life is absurd, so philosophy should be too.") And quite frequently, Will would deploy obscure historical references to illustrate the fact that he was smarter and better read than the person about whom he was writing, particularly if that person was the leader of a rival superpower. In this last strategy, one begins to sense considerable insecurity. Will once bragged in an interview, positing no evidence, that when he goes "to hear old Gorbachev, I've read more Marx than he has." In a 1979 column on Soviet expansionism, he observed, "It is not that Brezhnev reads Marx before bedtime (anymore than Richard Coeur de Lion went around constantly reciting the Athanasian Creed). . . ." Will liked this argument so well that, eight years later, he observed of Gorbachev, "The problem is not that Gorbachev reads Lenin nightly, anymore than Richard Coeur de Lion went around reciting the Athanasian Creed."

Will's ability to fashion a compact alliterative putdown of almost any occasion further added to his fame. When, in January 1982, Will observed on the Brinkley show that President Reagan "loved commerce more than he loathed Communism," the city reacted as if Will had written a sequel to *Remembrance of Things Past*. Will himself was forced to admit that he had come up with "the most quoted . . . sentence yet written about the Reagan administration," drawing on his sound bites the way Lippmann drew on *A Preface to Morals.*

Having been chastened in the most painful and public manner conceivable—the revelation from a Mr. Timothy Dickinson that he, in fact, was supplying Will with his simulated erudition followed by a full week of Doonesbury variations on this theme—Will began in the late 1980s to lay off a bit on the quotes. But the early Will years contained some pretty hard going for those seeking to discern a consistent intellectual theme amid the maddening crowd. In a 1973 column on Hubert Humphrey, Will found occasion to call into service the thoughts and reputations of: Robert Kennedy, Eugene McCarthy, Roger Branigin, Lyndon Johnson, Barry Goldwater, Alexander Bickel, Ambrose Bierce, Samuel Johnson, James Boswell, and Charles Maurice de Talleyrand. In a 1976 discussion of what ails the English ("Englishness does"), Will enlisted: George Santayana, Muriel Spark, Peter Drucker, *The Economist,* Randolph Churchill, Napoleon, Henry James (twice), and Arthur Koestler. In his 1978 encomium to the reactionary Russian mysticism of Alexander Solzhenitsyn, Will augmented his argument by recruiting: Augustine, Aquinas, Richard Hooker, Pascal, Thomas More (twice), Edmund Burke, G. W. F. Hegel, Alexis de Tocqueville, Henry Adams, Irving Babbitt, Paul Elmer, Peter Viereck, and "others" (twice) whom Will believed to constitute a "submerged but continuous tradition that shares Solzhenitsyn's anxiety about American premises and the culture they produce."*

To atone for his intellectual pretensions, Will likes to show his readers

---

*George F. Will, June 18, 1978. By the end of the 1980s, Will had grown strangely lackadaisical about his quotemongering. In a 1989 column about the rejuvenated German Question, Will wrote, "Someone—Clemenceau perhaps—said he loved Germany so much he wanted there always to be more than one." The quip in truth belonged to François Mauriac, who noted, "I love Germany so much that I am happy there are two of them." When I wrote to Will, wondering about his source, I received the following reply, dated August 11, 1989, signed by a Mr. James Martignon, "Assistant to Mr. Will":

Dear Mr. Alterman,
    Thank you for your enquirery [*sic*] and information concerning columns that Mr. Will has written. The Francois Mauriac quote will make a fine addition to our files. It is quite possible that this is the quote that Mr. Will was referring to in his May 7th column. It is difficult to tell, for Mr. Will reads a great deal of information. His memory is excellent, but it would be impossible to find the exact source of every quote and meet deadlines. That is the reason for "Someone—Clemenceau perhaps—said . . . ," and not a direct quotation credited to Clemenceau. It is possible that either both (and possibly others) have made this statement concerning Germany. Whatever the case, Mr. Will appreciates that you were concerned enough to provide additional sources of information to our office. They will indeed make a fine addition to our files.

and viewers that he too can be a regular guy. In print he most often does this by inserting dialogue from "Dennis the Menace" into his arguments. Here is Will on the 1980 election: "Gadzooks! If a Republican majority emerges, it may do so wearing galoshes." Here is Will at the foot of Reagan's desk once more, worrying about presidential panic: "Gadzooks! Is there a panic detector, akin to a smoke detector, that sniffs anxiety in the air?" Here is Will defending himself against charges that he should not have coached Reagan in his debate: "Nobody says 'Gadzooks! George Will favored Ronald Reagan.' "

A second favorite trick of Will's is the insertion of a contemporary American city or political issue within a well-known classical quotation. Here is Will on Topeka: "Et tu, Topeka?" On Iowa: "Et tu, Iowa?" On Indiana: "Et tu, Indiana?" On Nicaragua: "Et tu . . ."

A third foundation upon which the Will stylistic edifice rests is the clever, almost offhand plug of the author's friends in politics and the media. John Danforth, Will observes, is "one of the most judicious and least flamboyant members" of the Senate as well as "the only person ever to receive degrees from the Yale Law School and the Yale Divinity School on the same day." An equally accurate description might read, "Senator Jack Danforth, the godfather of my daughter Victoria . . ." Will devoted ten full columns to Robert Bork's brilliance during his 1987 Supreme Court nomination battle and threw in a full-page plug in *Newsweek* for Bork's "masterpiece of American reflection," *The Tempting of America*, published on the heels of Bork's Senate rejection. Nowhere in this avalanche of verbiage did Will find the space to mention that he had been an usher at his subject's wedding.* Sometimes Will had trouble juggling all these plugs. Will friends and political allies Richard Scammon and Ben Wattenberg were touted as "the Butch Cassidy and Sundance Kid of electoral analysis," while just three months later, David Stockman and Martin Anderson were said to be the "Butch Cassidy and Sundance Kid" of budgetary politics.

The chief beneficiary of Will's encomiums was his friend the President, a man whose foremost achievement, according to Will, "has been in convincing the country not that he knows the future, but that he knows his own mind." The only times when Will truly seemed to lose patience with his advisee were those when he thought Reagan was letting his wishy-washy advisers tone down his hawkish instincts. The communitarian values Will paraded on domestic policy bore no relevance to Will's foreign policy. When it came to foreign nationals, Will—who sat out Vietnam with a married student deferment—was spoiling for a fight.

---

*It did, however, contain the following prediction: "The bad news for Biden is that . . . the confirmation process [for Bork] will be easy." George F. Will, July 2, 1987.

From the beginning of the Reagan era, Will was on the lookout for a conflict somewhere where the United States might win a proxy war against the Soviets. It would be necessary "during our watch," he wrote, to "take one of their pieces of the board." The notion that, above all, Americans needed to win a war—any war—led Will to celebrate the use of force at virtually every opportunity. His harshest attacks on the administration came when its leaders opted for a policy of relative restraint. When American Marines were killed in Beirut, Will called for an attack on Syria. This act of war was necessary because "terrorism serve Syrian interests," and "such attacks could probably not have occurred without the knowledge of Syria, which controls the road by which the truck had to approach to attack sites; Syrian occupation is a necessary precondition for such attacks." During the Beirut crisis, Will found hysterically funny the notion put forth by Senate Majority Leader Howard Baker that the United States should use retaliatory military force if and only if the attackers could be identified "with precision and exactness." "What is this," he guffawed, "the Warren Court conducting foreign policy? Who will read the suspects their Miranda Rights?"*

In an almost perfect repudiation of Lippmann's credo, Will argues that, in moments of diplomatic tension, politicians should do their utmost to inflame popular passions in support of the escalation of violence. "Intelligent behavior," Will explained to Peter Jennings during the 1985 TWA hostage crisis, "flows not from keeping one's passional and rational capacities separated, but from reasonably relating a proper passion—in this case, cold fury—to action." When the Soviets shot down the KAL-007 jetliner over the Sea of Japan in 1983, Will likened the public mind to wax, noting that "it is easiest to shape when hot." Here Will is stepping down from his customary elitist disdain for the popular will for the purposes of manufacturing the consent necessary to carry out a policy of force and violence. Will's hatred for the Soviets and those nations he deems to be "terrorist" overrides virtually all

*George F. Will, November 10, 1983. Will takes an interesting leap of logic here, for among the bloodiest terrorist attacks of the 1980s was that unleashed by Sikh militants upon the 1985 Air India 747 bound from Montreal to London, killing 329 people. The perpetrators learned their craft at a private paramilitary camp in Dolomite, Alabama, where U.S.-supplied mercenaries were trained for military action in Central America and elsewhere by an American citizen named Frank Camper. The United States government must certainly have known of the existence of the camp, yet did nothing to shut it down. By Will's rules of great power machismo, both Canada and India would have been justified in bombing Alabama. "Great nations," after all, Will teaches, do not concern themselves with the measurement of justice to "persons who are instruments of other nations' interests." If Americans complained, Canada could always read us our Miranda rights. For details about the camp and Camper's role in training the terrorists, see Leslie Cockburn, *Out of Control* (New York: Atlantic Monthly Books, 1987), p. 26. For the "Great nations" quote, see George F. Will, February 10, 1983.

of the elegant moral distinctions upon which he prides himself when writing of the American (or West European) polity. But in some cases this proclivity spills over into his domestic analysis, leading the armchair psychologist to conclude that Will appears to have a problem with the "other," whether at home or abroad.

Will's difficulty in emphathizing with society's victims can lead to comical results. The most notorious of these was the September 1984 evening that Will and his family were given tickets to a Bruce Springsteen concert by E Street Band drummer Max Weinberg. Dressed in full bow-tie regalia with cotton pads stuffed in his ears, Will somehow heard in Springsteen's "Born in the USA" "a grand, cheerful affirmation," of American life. * The song in question is a story of a working-class youth in trouble with the law and forced by the courts to go to Vietnam "to kill the yellow man." In Vietnam, he loses his brother, only to return to his hometown where his factory job has been eliminated. This is a "grand, cheerful affirmation" of American life in much the same way that Alexander Solzhenitsyn's *The Gulag Archipelago* is a grand, cheerful affirmation of the Stalinist penal code.

Will's America is a country that was "born on the farm and moved to town, leaving behind the Jeffersonian vision." This is a country, needless to say, of upstanding white Christian folk. Consider George Will on the homeless. The most conspicuous aspect of the problem to Will is the "simple matter of public order and hygiene . . . getting these people off the streets." "The community," he argues, "has some rights here. If it is illegal—and it is and ought to be illegal—to litter the streets, frankly, it ought to be illegal for people who must survive on panhandling, among other things, to sleep on the streets." The homeless are explicitly excluded from the Will "community" in this analysis, and their stubborn demand to sleep on the streets in full view of Will and his friends should be punished. "Should society arrest them?" Will was asked. "Not arrest them," came the response, "but move them off to some place where they are simply out of sight and no longer a visible . . . public nuisance."

Will's reputation as a thoughtful, communitarian conservative, his support for child-welfare programs, and his concern for the effect of state "soulcraft" had the result, during the Reagan years, of increasing the

---

*George F. Will, September 13, 1984. The Will column led to a wonderful comedy of errors when the politicos in the Reagan campaign read it and tried to secure Springsteen's endorsement. Springsteen told all the president's men to get lost. Reagan had to make do with quoting Springsteen in his New Jersey campaign appearances, and went on to enlist the celluloid psychotic killer, Rambo, the summer of 1984's other cultural icon, for his campaign. Walter Mondale's campaign also tried, unsuccessfully, to claim Springsteen's endorsement, based on the fact that he had refused it to Reagan. In fact, the last presidential candidate the great man had voted for was George McGovern.

credibility—and therefore influence—of his less generous impulses. It was so much more impressive for Will to call for random retaliation upon the Lebanese or Syrian population, as well as the internal exile of the homeless, regardless of constitutional liberties, because he had earned his moral capital, so to speak, by virtue of his support for higher taxes. Because of the civilizing veneer of his elegant philosophical distinctions, Will could not simply be dismissed with much of the Reagan coalition as morally retarded or ideologically obsessed. Yet the snideness of his tone seemed to brook no principled opposition regardless of the relative soundness of his analyses.* Owing to Americans' notoriously short memories. This proved an enor-mously effective combination throughout the decade, as Will maintained his status as Lippmann's rightful heir without doing any of the difficult philosophical explication that marked Lippmann's career and precious little of the kind of interpretive work that had characterized Lippmann's idealized notions of the educative function of punditry.

Instead of setting himself above the battle with Lippmann, or astride it with Reston, Will threw himself into combat on behalf of the winning side while at the same time posing as its most distinguished arbitrator. In this regard, his position in the public dialogue had less in common with that of Lippmann than with one of Lippmann's early patrons, President Woodrow Wilson, during the early stages of the Great War. Wilson, too, had pretended to mediate a conflict from above while simultaneously scheming to support those he expected would be its victors. The result was American entry into the war and the disastrously misguided peace settlement that Wilson later engineered. Without stretching the metaphor overly much, one could say that Will's hypocrisy in this regard accomplished for honest political punditry approximately as much as Wilson's chicanery did for the notion of disinterested peaceful mediation.

Toward the end of the Reagan era, Will decided for reasons still unknown to foreswear his executive privileges. Offended by George Bush's supplications to the party's Far Right in early 1986, he launched a premeditated attack on George Bush, whose self-effacing efforts to secure his right flank Will found distasteful. The columnist insisted that "the unpleasant sound Bush is

---

*Will's timing of these brook-no-opposition pronouncements was often unfortunate; examples dealing with the Berlin Wall in 1989 and the fate of Mikhail Gorbachev in 1991 are detailed in later chapters. Readers enjoyed a kind of sneak preview, however, in Will's *Newsweek* column dated April 2, 1979. In it, he berated the makers of the film *The China Syndrome* for "manipulat[ing] audiences into anti-nuclear hysteria" and "falsely suggest-ing that nuclear-power companies [would] carelessly risk destroying their billion-dollar investments." As the magazine hit the stands, the Three Mile Island nuclear power plant began its partial meltdown.

emitting as he traipses from one conservative gathering to another is the thin, tinny 'arf,' the sound of the lapdog." The day before it appeared, Will told a Florida audience, "if he [Bush] survives it, the power of the written word is gone."

Washington was scandalized. Here it was, only 1986, and George Bush had already lost the Will Primary. Bush called a meeting of his staff and urged them not to get too depressed over the Will thing. Will insisted that he meant the column as a kind of "shot across Bush's bow." Why, for goodness' sake, asked Will-watchers, would the First Pundit have wished to shoot across the bow of the one man who could keep him within spitting distance of John-John's favorite desk? Could it be that Will felt his journalistic manhood threatened by his close association with the increasingly befuddled First Lame Ducks? Would that have anything to do with Will's decision to write a baseball book as well?

Shortly after publishing the "lapdog" column, Will sent Bush a handwritten note suggesting that the two Firsts hold a summit conference to discuss their differences. "Thanks, but I'm booked up," replied the grudge-holding Skull and Bones Man. "Criticism is one thing, personal attack another."

Will has since been seen on a number of occasions grimacing through lunch with Dan Quayle. In the meantime, the baseball book, *Men at Work*, proved to be so meticulously reported and sparely written that it has occasioned many observers to wonder just what this brilliant sportswriter could do if he ever turned his attention to politics.

5

"O.K., LET'S GET OUT"

First aired in April 1982, "The McLaughlin Group" proved a breakthrough in the history of pundit television. Only two shows before it had eliminated the politician and allowed journalists to question one another, and both were boring. "The McLaughlin Group" may have been simultaneously annoying, irritating, aggravating, grating, and galling. But boring, it wasn't.

In achieving its landmark status, the show broke a number of once-sacred pundit barriers. In the first place, some panelists were only nominally journalists. John McLaughlin was himself a journalist in the sense that somebody who takes his car into the shop to get it fixed a great deal is a mechanic. He had always kept the company of journalists—leaked to them, perhaps, and gone to their dinner parties. But he had hardly been spending his time wearing out shoe leather. During the period from 1983 to 1988 when McLaughlin held the title of "Washington Editor" of *National Review*, his column was regularly ghost-written by his assistants. "Sometimes he would change it," recalls one former ghost, "sometimes it would sail right through." Among the other panelists, meanwhile, Patrick Buchanan spent a grand total of two months as a reporter before becoming an editorial writer and beginning his distinguished career as a conservative polemicist, part-time government official, and presidential aspirant. Robert Novak had, during the 1960s, been among the most respected and hardworking journalists in Washington, but in the decade preceding the launching of "The McLaughlin Group," Novak's intense conservative bias had overtaken his reputation as a straight-shooting journalist.

The regular cast had no blacks or women. The atmosphere was soaked in the same country-club locker-room machismo that drifted out of the White House in the Reagan years. *Rolling Stone* national affairs editor William Greider, an occasional substitute, recalls a pre-show runthrough in its early days at which McLaughlin, Novak, and panelist Morton Kondracke spent the whole time telling "incredibly crude and sexist jokes" about prostitutes in Bangkok. When the Group discussed a Texas gubernatorial candidate's insistence that Mexican brothels were the only place a young man could "get serviced" in West Texas, Jack Germond noted that this comment was offensive to West Texan sheep.

The show's success derived from McLaughlin's ability to conduct it in a fashion that owed more to roller derby than to public affairs television. The discussions were fast-paced and extremely short on both attributed information and contextual nuance. Few topics lasted more than seven or eight minutes and some were abruptly ended in less than thirty seconds, depending on McLaughlin's moods. Panelists were quick to personalize their criticism of one another and insult each other's manhood whenever the opportunity arose.

As in any good sitcom, each of the regular panelists played a stock character. McLaughlin was the ringleader—a combination Catholic school headmaster and circus announcer. Patrick Buchanan played the tough Irish cop with twinkly eyes and a heart of granite. Robert Novak portrayed a beer-guzzling, middle-class construction worker whose idea of a good time was to sic his German Shepherd on welfare queens and pinko student demonstrators. Morton Kondracke, with his much-abused yuppie steel glasses and his altar-boy haircut, was the guy who always sat in the front of the class, waving his arms in front of the teacher, only to forget the answer once he was finally called on. His waffling responses almost always gave Novak the opportunity to call him a weenie and to threaten to take away his lunch. The balding, proudly overweight Jack Germond—by far the most attractive character of the lot—was the sort of pundit Fred Mertz would have been had Ethel ever let him out of the house, willing, just barely, to undergo the torture long enough to pick up his check each week.

"The McLaughlin Group" advertised itself not as a group of Lippmann-like sages or Seymour Hersh-type investigators but as a collection of "Federal Authorities," giving "inside opinions and forecasts." Excluding Germond, the words "I don't know" or even "I think" or "I believe" were not to be found in any of the panelists' vocabulary. Whether it was the guerrilla strategy of Afghan *Mujahedeen* or the next open-market operation by the Federal Reserve Board, the members always seemed to have just gotten off the phone with the guy in charge.

Judged strictly on its entertainment value, the show worked just fine. Germond harrumphed. Buchanan huffed and puffed. Kondracke hemmed and hawed until Novak pounced. McLaughlin would then close out the discussion by saying something like: *Okay, let's get out. On a scale of one to ten, one being Adolf Hitler's* Mein Kampf, *ten being the Ten Commandments, George Shultz's Middle East peace plan rates what on the scale of divine inspiration, Mor-TAHN?*

Washington loved to hate it. "The McLaughlin Group" quickly surpassed "Agronsky and Company" as *the* pundit show to watch. Journalists and pundits alike vied with one another for the ever-important rotating seat. (*New Republic* editor Michael Kinsley lost his spot in the rotation, however, when his magazine carried testimony of McLaughlin's reliance upon ghostwriters.) Occasionally a mere politician would be granted the honor of sitting in. But it had to be a politician with special qualities; somebody with the modesty and charm of, say, Ed Koch.

The Reagan White House understood just how important television punditry had become in political tastemaking and displayed a nice touch for symbolism when it arranged for special pundit briefings to be conducted in the Reagan family theater for members of the Group and the rest of the network's weekend pundit line-up. At these Friday-morning briefings, White House officials would come by and give "not for attribution" information to the lucky few. The boys would then hustle straight to their tapings, when the tidbits and leaks were repeated verbatim, either in the form of predictions or inside scoops.

These predictions, ironically, were among the best researched and well grounded of all those offered by the show's guests. A series of tracking polls by *Regardie's* magazine showed the average Group member's accuracy to hover between 12 and 25 percent. Oftentimes, when McLaughlin would find himself approaching a taping without any inside kitty, he would turn to one of his young assistants for help. The assistants, sensing the opportunity to begin a politically useful rumor, would literally fabricate one. In one instance, recalls former issues consultant Tom Miller, he told McLaughlin that Assistant Secretary of State Chester Crocker was in trouble for his insufficient dedication to Reagan Doctrine causes in Southern Africa. McLaughlin then went on the air to predict that Crocker might soon be removed. Crocker, according to Miller, was forced to deny the story, and was undoubtedly a bit wary of raising his profile on issues dear to the heart of the Reaganites for a while thereafter.

Inside the Beltway, Group members were Washington's New Kids on the Block. Reagan would watch the show at Camp David and bang his fists on the table when a panel member failed to take his side. At one McLaughlin party, Reagan dropped by and read a speech about the Group written for him by his new director of communications, former and future panelist Patrick Buchanan.* The historically right-wing General Electric Corporation, which took over the show's sponsorship from the Edison Electric Institute, soon began to spend many millions of dollars to advertise the show and to give it free to any PBS station. "Don't miss it. The people who run this country never do," warned the Orwellian advertising copy. "Listen to the voices of authority."

McLaughlin reveled in his increasingly powerful role as a media kingpin. He soon adopted GE chief executive officer Jack Welch on the Washington social circuit, inviting him over for dinner with his wife's new boss, Ronald Reagan. Ann Dore McLaughlin, who engineered his resounding Senate defeat and had been public relations director for a small Catholic college before that, managed to get herself named Secretary of Labor. In between she had worked for Donald Regan in the White House, for Union Carbide, and for Nixon's infamous Committee to Re-elect the President (CREEP). Whether her position in the cabinet was likely to influence McLaughlin's own treatment of the President on the show was a question so déclassé that no one even thought to raise it publicly.

While not as thoughtful as Will, nor as feared and respected as Safire, John McLaughlin nevertheless appeared in the early 1980s as the living Zeitgeist of American politics—the Frankenstein of the Buckley/Vidal experiment run amuck. A pure creation of the nexus of media power, corporate money, and the conservative insider boys club, McLaughlin had no discernible political beliefs. A man of tremendous appetite for power, riches, and control over the lives of those around him, McLaughlin was a modern-day Citizen Kane, building a television empire of media hot air on the basis of a quick wit and a talent for ideological body-surfing. Having lived his adult life on the fringes of political power and ideological obsession, McLaughlin found himself at the height of the Reagan era with three television shows and between six and eight hours of air time each week, depending on the market. In terms of frequency of television appearances, his only real competition was Lucy and Ricky Ricardo. An ex-Jesuit, ex-anti-Nixon, dovish Senate candidate, as well as an ex-pro-Nixon, hawkish "Watergate priest," the story of McLaughlin's rise, fall, and rise again rivals that of the man from Whittier for self-reinvention in the service of political opportunism.

*"The McLaughlin Group serves as a most tasteful television program alternative to professional wrestling, live from Madison Square Garden," read the President. "Thank you for making that half hour every weekend something very special to look forward to. I wouldn't miss it; I can't afford to."

McLaughlin's achievement was tainted, however, not only by the damage inflicted to American politics by the deification of his brand of lightning-fast, quarter-inch-deep political analysis, but also by personal flaws that his celebrators and sponsors were willing to ignore in the face of his success. To the youthful underlings who worked in his office, McLaughlin was a petty tyrant, and according to the testimony of at least three women, an insatiable sexual harasser. McLaughlin settled one lawsuit over his sexual harassment tactics and faced the possibility of at least two others.* That he

---

*On petty tyranny: Former Marine officer and McLaughlin employee Tom Liddy regards McLaughlin as a "brilliant" and "inspiring" boss. Once, when Liddy came back to his old haunt for a visit during a three-week vacation from the Marines, McLaughlin took him into the office, shut the door, and said, "I understand you're free for three weeks. I want you to work here." When Liddy protested that it was his only vacation and that he would like to be able to spend some time with his family, McLaughlin replied, "Look, I really need you." Three weeks later, Liddy left the office, picked up his mortar platoon, and flew to Okinawa. The young man's characterization of McLaughlin as "demanding, but not overly demanding" would appear to be ludicrously generous, until Liddy himself raises the truly excellent point: "Don't forget, I was raised by Gordon Liddy."

On alleged sexual harassment: These stories do not have such endearing punchlines. According to several former employees, some still friendly with McLaughlin, he would personally insult a number of his female underlings, telling them that they were "fat" or "stupid" and that they "would be out on the street were it not for him." It was the responsibility of one staffer to cut the pieces of his chicken sandwich into the right sizes and shapes. Kara Swisher, now at *The Washington Post*, was once buzzed into McLaughlin's office and told to make her boss toast. When she refused, McLaughlin called it "a very serious toast situation," and threatened—seriously according to Swisher—"If I ask you to make toast and you don't do it, I can fire you."

One McLaughlin staffer had the task of arranging the pens and pads in McLaughlin's suitcase to be exactly in the order he preferred. "If one of the pens was out of place," the staffer noted, "it was a national security emergency." All were expected to run, literally, into McLaughlin's office whenever he buzzed them. (McLaughlin loved his buzzer.) There they were told where to stand, like chess pieces, until dismissed.

The staff's basic attitude, says Anne Rumsey, a former employee, was that "Yes, he was a lunatic but he has this, this, and this going for him, so I'll try to stick it out." Rumsey quit after only six weeks at the job, after McLaughlin asked her to walk him to the elevator, only to thunder, "I've been told that you spend a lot of time on the phone with your friends. Do you value your job?" While McLaughlin was reading Rumsey's resignation letter, she was out collecting his laundry.

When Linda Dean, a former office manager, promulgated her lawsuit alleging sexual harassment by McLaughlin, she swore that McLaughlin told her that "he needed a lot of sex" and that if she would stick by him, "he would take care of every material desire she had." McLaughlin, according to Dean, insisted that he "owned" her and on several occasions touched her "intimately and against her will." She was eventually fired, but since has settled her lawsuit and refuses to discuss the matter with reporters.

The complaint also discussed the case of another female receptionist who, according to Dean's sworn testimony, complained in a letter to her employment agency that McLaughlin had "behaved improperly toward her by committing acts which the receptionist perceived to be sexual harassment." The receptionist, when reached by telephone, refused to discuss the incident.

could rise to where he was in American political culture with only quiet whispers of resentment is an indication of just how successful success had become in Ronald Reagan's Washington. That McLaughlin would still feel free to pass judgment on the propriety of Chuck Robb, Pee-wee Herman, and other people's sex lives on his show—to say nothing of his tasteless and unseemly attack on Ms. Anita Hill's testimony regarding her alleged harassment at the hands of Clarence Thomas—says something even uglier.

A third female McLaughlin employee, Sharon T. Wulbern, also appears in the court record. Having read of Dean's suit in *The Washington Post*, Wulbern (her name is spelled three different ways in the documents) told Dean's lawyer that Dean's accusations mirrored "quite a bit of my experience," containing "all the things I had been experiencing." Wulbern was terminated by McLaughlin in January 1989. These accusations appear in her own deposition, parts of which were printed in the court records.

A fourth female former employee also confirms that McLaughlin made unwanted sexual advances toward her on more than one occasion, including once on a business trip to Mexico. Both Kara Swisher and Tom Miller, a former issues consultant to McLaughlin, recall instances of McLaughlin "leering" at the fourth woman, and making suggestive sexual comments to her. McLaughlin, according to the recollections of these same two employees, occasionally put his arm around the woman in a way that struck both of them as surprising and undesired.

McLaughlin also liked to make personal comments about his young female employees. Anne Rumsey recalls him telling her one day that her sweater was too tight. "He was very touchy," recalls Swisher. "I think that sexual harassment is like pornography. You know it when you see it. People can tell you you look nice and there will be no menace to it. With John McLaughlin, there was menace." Miller recalls McLaughlin asking an employee whether she liked her sex rough. McLaughlin's own court filings contain references to a conversation with Dean about having sex in an airplane. When a Supreme Court decision on sexual harassment was handed down during Miller's tenure on the job, he showed it to a Beverly Larson, a high-level staffer, to give to McLaughlin as a warning. Swisher, too, says she met with McLaughlin "Executive Director" Margaret Suzor, to complain of McLaughlin's alleged sexual harassment, with no results.

McLaughlin's interviews are littered with strange ruminations about the relationship between power and sex. He told one reporter, "Power as an experience is as intense as sex. Power is more pervasive and unremitting. Sex has periods of remission." But he has refused to discuss any and all accusations about sexual harassment, except to deny those laid out in Dean's lawsuit, including the fact that anyone in his office ever complained to him about alleged sexual harassment. A spokesman for GE, who continues to fund McLaughlin, calls it "a private matter." Because the suit has been settled, it is unlikely that the accusations will ever be given a public airing. (The above is based on the documents relating to District of Columbia Court Case, 1 88-CV-02185, *Dean* vs. *McLaughlin et al.*, filed on August 4, 1989, as well as the author's interviews with Tom Miller, Tom Liddy, Kara Swisher, Anne Rumsey, and a female former McLaughlin staffer who wishes to remain anonymous for fear of retaliation.)

Final note: John McLaughlin and Ann Dore McLaughlin announced their separation in late October 1991. According to Mrs. McLaughlin's lawyer, Peter Sherman, however, they continued to live in the same house as they sought to "resolve financial and other issues." When asked how this amounted to a separation, Sherman replied, "They are leading separate lives—they are not living as spouses." The couple finally separated in March 1992 as Mrs. McLaughlin vacated the premises, divorce settlement in hand.

As a young Jesuit seminarian, John McLaughlin was expected to weave small whips with thongs on the end and, occasionally, engage in self-flagellation. He was also expected to wear a chain made of barbed wire around the upper thigh, the better to battle feelings of sexual arousal. The pain was prescribed to remind the young men that the "flesh has an inclination toward evil." Following the seminary, McLaughlin went on to earn three graduate degrees before becoming an editor at *America* magazine, the Jesuit weekly. There McLaughlin began to develop his unique public persona, traveling the country giving lectures on such subjects as "Intimacy Outside Marriage" and "Intimacy Before Marriage and the Swedish Experience (Parts I, II, III and IV)."

In 1970, the Jesuit sex expert shocked virtually everyone who knew him when he announced that he would switch parties to challenge Rhode Island Democrat John Pastore for the U.S. Senate. McLaughlin campaigned as a high-profile Republican dove, calling for an even quicker withdrawal of U.S. troops from Vietnam than George McGovern was pushing for at the time, and supporting a rapprochement with both Cuba and China. He lost big, but his candidacy somehow won him an appointment in the Nixon White House.*

McLaughlin began his tenure as a relatively low-level speechwriter and special assistant to Nixon on refugees and other such matters that Nixon didn't care too much about. But as the Nixon ship began to sink from the weight of its Watergate baggage, McLaughlin made his break for the captain's bridge. Larry Speakes, who was working in the Nixon press office during the Watergate crisis, was having trouble getting any White House staffers to show their faces to the television cameras on the lawn. McLaughlin volunteered one afternoon, gave a boffo performance, and a day later, four network crews showed up in his office. A staffer turned to Speakes and warned, "My God, he's a monster and I've created him."

McLaughlin called Nixon "the greatest moral leader of the last third of this century." He defended the President's 1972 Christmas bombing of Hanoi, mining of Haiphong Harbor, and frequent use of the Lord's name in vain. He called the latter "a form of emotional drainage . . . a form of release, almost therapy." As late as May 9, 1974, barely ninety days before Nixon finally ended our Long National Nightmare, McLaughlin was still insisting that Nixon was a "moral man thirsting for truth." The accusations

---

*In a typically accurate Evans and Novak column entitled "The Vetoed-Writer Priest," the dynamic duo reported that "combined pressure from the Republican right, Capitol Hill Democrats and even the White House itself has just about killed a unique scheme to install a left-of-center Roman Catholic priest as presidential speech-writer." Evans and Novak, June 13, 1971.

leveled against him were "erroneous, unjust, and contain elements of hypocrisy," he asserted, predicting that Watergate would be a mere "footnote to a glorious administration."

The press had quite a good time with McLaughlin's rather atypical Jesuit lifestyle. McLaughlin lived in the Watergate and earned $33,000 a year, while publicly defending a man whose presidency seemed to have decidedly little in common with the teachings of Jesus Christ. McLaughlin made no pretense of donating his salary to the Jesuit community as is customary, and his attempts to justify his lifestyle on theological grounds had a decided lack of conviction. He told friends that yes, while he did live in the luxurious Watergate, his apartment faced a gas station and he only rode the trash elevator. His friend and former campaign manager Ann Dore, not yet Ann Dore McLaughlin, was a frequent hostess at McLaughlin's parties, leading many in the order to wonder just how faithfully McLaughlin was executing his vows of celibacy. Having extricated himself from a high-profile censure by the Jesuit authorities with an agreement to leave the White House, McLaughlin then did everything but chain himself to his White House desk when Nixon finally fled for San Clemente. As late as September 30, Evans and Novak were still able to report that "the notorious Father John McLaughlin" was still on the job. Seventy-two hours later, McLaughlin was eligible for unemployment.

After leaving the order and marrying the previously wed Ms. Dore in a 1975 civil (not Catholic) ceremony, McLaughlin gradually worked his way back into the media limelight. He was hired in 1980 by a local Washington radio station to co-host a talk show, but was fired a year later for talking too much. Soon, however, McLaughlin was frying even bigger fish. He had convinced his wealthy friend Richard Moore (now George Bush's ambassador to Ireland) to pony up the funds to create a new kind of public affairs program. The pilot for "The McLaughlin Group," featuring Jack Germond, Robert Novak, the distinguished black journalist Chuck Stone of the *Philadelphia Daily News*, and Judith Miller of *The New York Times*, was hardly promising. Miller lectured, Elizabeth Drew-style, and Stone was stone silent. But it did attract the corporate sponsorship of an electric utility trade association, the Edison Electric Institute. When McLaughlin replaced his black and woman panelists with Patrick Buchanan and Morton Kondracke, the juggernaut was launched.

The show's chief strength was its weird personal chemistry. McLaughlin's chief adversary in the group was Robert Novak. The two men started out the program in 1982 as close friends and political allies. But McLaughlin became upset with Novak's monopolizing of the show's air time and tried to force him to shut up. He did so by refusing to tell Novak what days he would be invited and by literally thumbing his nose at Novak when the time came to cue him. Novak endured, but the animosity welling up in each man, coupled with their naturally theatrical tendencies, made for surprisingly interesting theater. When they finally did blow up, it was McLaughlin who exploded; but in the interim, each man would needle the other, and the viewer was left to wonder what was real and what was not.* Both men were frequently approached in airports and asked how they could stand the other. Other Group members were asked how they could stand either one.

Unlike McLaughlin, Novak was well liked by his peers and it was generally understood that politics aside, he was a pretty harmless fellow. On the tube, however, the only clear difference between Robert Novak and Archie Bunker was that the former got more air time. Despite—or perhaps because of—its bellicosity, the Novak character seemed to go over well in the heartland, earning Novak in the area of $7,500 a lecture. But the reason insiders continued to read his column was not the television shtick but his continued devotion to the kind of inside dope that political junkies mainline.

The Evans and Novak column played a crucial role in helping to form and execute what it called the "Reagan revolution." As "pragmatist" battled "ideologue" for the limited attention span of the President, the column worked as a kind of tribal drum for the warrior faction. From David Stockman to Ollie North, important administration principals could read the column in the *Post* three mornings a week and determine their own standing in the Grand Struggle. Stockman told stories of posting notices on what he called the "Bob Novak Bulletin Board" in order to manufacture the appearance of a "David Stockman for OMB Director" movement. "At the time Mr. Novak wrote it, it was a movement of three or four people, if you include the minority of my staff that favored the idea," wrote Stockman. By the time it was over, Stockman had the job and went on to become the most influential member of the Reagan cabinet.

*In the summer of 1988, McLaughlin spontaneously combusted. Needling McLaughlin about his chameleonlike political views, Novak accused him on the air of tailoring his views to fit the contours of what might be a Democratic administration, given Michael Dukakis's then strong standing in the polls. At the commercial break, McLaughlin exploded, turning "beet-red in the face" and screaming at the top of his lungs, "VILE! VILE! VILE!" Novak said he expected McLaughlin to have a heart attack any minute. Germond, who is a longtime friend of Novak's, said to his buddy, "If you want to tell this guy to go fuck himself and walk, I'm with you." McLaughlin managed to compose himself by the time the commercial break ended. Novak gratefully declined Germond's offer but left the Group to form his McLaughlinlike show on CNN—hosted by the ubiquitous Buchanan. (Author's interviews with Novak, Germond, Buchanan, and Kondracke.)

Congressional bomb-throwers like Phil Graham, Malcolm Wallop, Jack Kemp, and Newt Gingrich received millions worth of free public relations from the column. Barely a week went by without some "brave," "tough," "canny," or "strong" action by one of these men, usually accompanied by some previously unrevealed tidbit designed to portray them in as favorable a light as was humanly conceivable. Among the most historically significant of these morality plays was a column published in May 1986, in which a hitherto unknown "star player in the long, hard fight to keep alive the Nicaraguan contras" found himself endangered by "the gray and faceless officials" of the Reagan National Security Council staff. Oliver North, about to be reassigned back to the Marine Corps by his gray, faceless, and certainly luckless boss, John Poindexter, managed to retain his job in large measure as a result of the Evans and Novak column (along with another by Suzanne Garment of *The Wall Street Journal*). There, he could continue his sideline business of selling arms to the Ayatollah and funneling the profits to the Nicaraguan Contras undisturbed.

In most cases, Novak and his partner went to the trouble of getting most of their facts down right, only to explode them in a wildly imaginative interpretation. But they could be mighty careless at times. An unsuspecting reader who accepted everything Evans and Novak have reported in recent years would find himself believing, as Michael Massing once demonstrated, in the reality of a "direct Soviet intervention in Poland" during the 1981 Solidarity crisis; an "imminent move by the Soviets from Afghanistan into Pakistan" in September 1984; and the sad fact that as of January 1985, "Mikhail Gorbachev is no longer considered the heir apparent" in the Kremlin. Somehow, Novak's popularity and influence only seemed to increase with the outlandishness of his views and reporting.

Seated across from Novak in McLaughlin's studio was the cherubic Catholic crusader and recent presidential candidate, Patrick J. Buchanan. Buchanan's decision to announce for the presidency in December 1991 came as no surprise to anyone who had closely observed his career in the punditocracy. He carefully considered the idea four years earlier, but demurred in favor of the more conventional politician, Representative Jack Kemp. By the time Buchanan reversed himself, however, the displacement of "real" politicians at the center of the political dialogue was considerably further advanced. All of a sudden, in 1991, there was nothing ridiculous about the idea of the move from the small screen to the White House without having earned any interim qualifications in between.

Before his ambitions got the worst of him, Pat Buchanan was a popular and much-admired character in Ronald Reagan's Washington. (George

Bush is so far the only Republican president since Eisenhower who has managed to survive a presidency without Buchanan by his side.)* On television, throughout the eighties, Buchanan was no less ubiquitous than Novak. He was widely syndicated columnist, the co-host of "Crossfire" each night, a regular on McLaughlin, and the host of Novak's own pundit CNN roundtable, "The Capital Gang." (Novak thought he could not be nasty enough if he had to act as a fair-minded host as well.) Because of his extensive government experience, moreover, Buchanan was also treated as an honored former official. During one Middle East hostage crisis, Ted Koppel found it necessary to book him on "Nightline" twice in three days.

Buchanan may have had his own column, but unlike Novak, or even Will, he made no pretense of being a reporter. Rather, he was a professional right-winger. As Reagan's White House director of communications, Buchanan was the only member of the President's inner circle to speak favorably, at least in the abstract, of treason. During the Iran-Contra scandal, when the Buchanan for President boomlet first began, its standardbearer gave inflammatory speeches, insisting, "If Colonel North ripped off the Ayatollah and took $30 million and gave it to the contras, then God bless Colonel North." During a particularly tense congressional debate on Contra aid, Buchanan drew the lines as follows: "With this vote on contra aid, the Democratic Party will reveal whether it stands with Ronald Reagan and the Resistance or with Daniel Ortega and the Communists." When the AIDS virus first hit the national news, Buchanan pooh-poohed the national trauma. "The poor homosexuals," he wrote, "they have declared war upon nature and now nature is exacting an awful retribution." Buchanan regularly refers to gay men as "perpetrators" and argues that "by buggering one another" and "committing promiscuous sodomy," they "threaten doctors, dentists, health workers, hemophiliacs and the rest of society by their refusal to curb their lascivious appetites." It is a measure of Buchanan's own inimitable style that both his almost-presidential campaign and his 1988 memoirs began with the same cri de coeur: "Let the bloodbath begin."

Despite what appears even to most conservatives to be a deeply extremist world view, Buchanan sits comfortably at the hub of punditocracy life. An October 1991 charity roast of Buchanan featured tributes from two Republican ex-presidents, one Democratic presidential candidate, two almost-Democratic presidential candidates, the House Minority Whip, and leaders

*And look what that got him.

from every wing of both parties.* The evening testified to Buchanan's role in polite Washington society as a kind of white man's Louis Farrakhan.† Just as intelligent blacks would ignore the weird, nonsensical, and often hateful pronouncements the Black Muslim leader makes on the grounds that he peppers them with statements that appear sensible and well conceived, so, too, Patrick Buchanan was embraced in the bosom of insider Washington despite views that fall somewhere in the twilight zone between Goldwater and McCarthy—that is, between conservatism and hatemongering. ("McCarthy was cheered because for four years he was daily kicking the living hell out of people most Americans concluded ought to have the living hell kicked out of them," wrote Buchanan of his hero.)

But despite his engaging manners and charming persona, Buchanan is a man at war with his surroundings. The secret to his success—aside from his considerable talent as a writer and debater—is his ability to conduct this holy war in a huggable fashion. Buchanan comes from a deeply religious Irish Catholic family that prized loyalty and discipline above all. To impress upon Buchanan what the loss of the soul through mortal sin meant, Buchanan's father would light a match, grab his son's hands, and hold them briefly over the flame, saying, "See how that feels: now imagine that for all eternity." It was in this atmosphere that Buchanan imbibed the religious dogma that he has so effectively preached in American political life. It was in his lower-middle-class, Scotch-Irish Catholic household that Buchanan came to his most important political understanding: "Before we believe, we know."

The Buchanan family's disillusionment with contemporary life dates from the day Pope John XXIII opened Vatican II, liberalizing canon law and sanctioning all kinds of behavior that the family had been taught to consider deviant and dissolute. "Our political and social quarrels now partake in the savagery of religious wars because they are, at bottom, religious wars," Buchanan writes. The cultural civil war, with which Reagan dealt "in a very gentle fashion," according to Buchanan, "is a conflict between what might be called the Right which proceeds from Christian beliefs and values and the counterculture which proceeds out of secularist beliefs and values. Its

---

*"Compassion. Warmheartedness. Generosity of Spirit," said Richard Nixon, "the last words that come into my head when I think of Pat Buchanan." See Lloyd Grove, "Fresh Roasted Conservative," *The Washington Post*, Style section, October 17, 1991, p. C7.

†I asked Buchanan what he thought of Farrakhan, and he was surprisingly generous. He said Farrakhan was "part healthy and part-unhealthy. He has turned the worst people in prisons away from crime, drugs, and alcohol, but what is bad about it is the hatred of whites. Conversion is important, however, and both Farrakhan and [Charles] Colson believe in it." Author's interview.

manifestations can be seen in the move to equate homosexuality with normal heterosexual activity, tolerance of pornography, [the belief that] anything goes so long as it doesn't hurt another individual." Buchanan proudly observes that he comes "from the tradition that my great grandfathers tried to overthrow the government of the United States. . . . The idea of standing up to an establishment is a great tradition."

To Buchanan, the "establishment" is the same radical-thinking and Socialist-inspired monolith that destroyed Nixon and McCarthy. Its institutions, like the pro-Contra, pro–MX missile *Washington Post*, appear to him as "the untethered attack dog of the American left." Congress, to Buchanan, is guilty of "complicity in permitting the enemies of the U.S to consolidate a military beachhead on the mainland of North America." Buchanan delights in upsetting the sensibilities of respectable Washington by championing the cause of accused Nazi war criminals and paying no heed to the sensitivities of the American Jewish establishment. Some of the Nazis, he claims, may be innocent; others may not. But Buchanan insists, "There is political cowardice so thick you can cut it with a knife. If these guys were accused of being communist spies on behalf of the Soviet Union in World War II, you wouldn't have to ask me, there would be ten thousand reporters working on their behalf demanding a hearing."*

Add to this strange mixture of intolerance and good-heartedness, of religious certitude and political savvy, of blind idolatry of anti-communism and Catholic conservatism, a street fighter expelled from Georgetown University for punching out *two* DC policemen, and you have an enormously effective spokesman for a radical, reactionary minority. Buchanan imagines that he speaks for approximately a third of the country, "people to the right of Ronald Reagan."

The triumph of Buchanan over Buckley as the unadulterated voice of the Conservative movement is a significant one. While the political philosophies expressed by the two men were quite similar, their cultural differences spoke volumes about the transformation of American politics

*The "attack dog" quote, given to a rally of the faithful in Lafayette Park across the street from the White House, is reprinted in *Newsweek*, January 19, 1987, p. 18. The "Congress" quote comes from Patrick J. Buchanan, "Whom Will History Indict?" *Newsweek*, July 7, 1987, p. 21. The "Nazi" quote is from the author's interview. I am deliberately avoiding the question as to whether Buchanan's thirst for combat with the Jewish establishment crosses over into anti-Semitism because the issue is too complex and too sensitive to do justice to in this context, and anyway, has been the subject of oceans of verbiage already. For the record, I have discussed the issue at some length in the November 5, 1990, issue of *The Nation* and generally find persuasive William Buckley's far longer dissection of it in his essay on anti-Semitism in the December 30, 1991, *National Review*.

between the late 1950s and the early 1980s, as well as the changes in the role of the punditocracy. Buckley, the grandson of a Texas sheriff, was a self-styled aristocrat. Though he hoped to reconfigure and repopulate the important elite institutions in America, his bottom line was protecting the privileges of the privileged. The movement Buckley headed was as much about skiing in Gstaad or yachting in the Caribbean as killing Commies. Buchanan's politics, however, were steeped in the cultural resentment of the New Right. The working-class Catholic boys of Washington's Gonzaga High School were not recruited by Yale and could not have afforded the tuition anyway. Buchanan's Conservative movement was not about teaching the liberals at Yale to repent; it was about dynamiting the place to Kingdom Come. It was an angrier, less sophisticated movement than Buckley's, but one that had learned the lessons of mass political organizing and political intimidation from its enemies in the anti-war, feminist, and civil rights movements. It was one, moreover, whose spokesman in the punditocracy participated in politics not at its periphery, as Buckley had, but at its center, literally displacing the politicians whom Buckley had sought only to influence. It is a measure of the punditocracy's denial of its own power, as well as its ultimate priorities, that few of Buchanan's pro-Fascist sentiments raised any eyebrows until he began directing his mortar fire at Israel, its supporters, and George Bush. *

Sociologically speaking, the most interesting member of the McLaughlin roundtable may be *New Republic* senior editor Morton Kondracke. Like Novak, Kondracke grew up in Joliet, Illinois. He earned his spot on "The McLaughlin Group" after a career as a straight reporter of moderately liberal leanings at the *Chicago Sun Times* before being hired by *The New Republic* in the mid-seventies. On "The McLaughlin Group," however, under pressure from his fellow Jolietite, Kondracke soon began to change his stripes. On issue after issue, he developed greater sympathy for the line of reasoning coming out of the Reagan White House. Instead of fighting back when Novak would impugn his manhood on the issue of this or that proposed nuclear attack somewhere, Kondracke would insist that he could be every bit as mean and nasty as his tormentor. Just point out the enemy and

*Both Jacob Weisberg and the author called Buchanan pro-Fascist in print in the fall of 1990. The view did not gain much currency until Charles Krauthammer used it during the 1992 primary campaign. Krauthammer's use was immediately seized upon by A. M. Rosenthal as an example of the nation's "political disease" and "current sorrow of American life." Krauthammer called Rosenthal "courageous," while the latter settled for referring to his fellow neocon as a "cool and clear-minded thinker." See Charles Krauthammer, March 1, 1992, and A. M. Rosenthal, March 7, 1992.

Kondracke, too, would support the funds for others to fight and die for the cause.

The easiest explanation for Kondracke's shift across the spectrum was simply gullibility. Despite his veneer of insider sophistication, the man was a journalistic yokel. His hero in life had been James Reston, whose photo, for a brief time, he carried around in his wallet. Like Reston, Kondracke generally believed what his sources inside the government were telling him. But while Reston may have been a bit easy to mislead, he was at least dealing with a group of men whom he knew extremely well and about whose characters he could form independent judgments. Kondracke seemed incapable of distinguishing the lies and the liars. During the Carter years, it was the liberals who were doing the lying, and so he was a liberal. During the Reagan years, he became a conservative.

Early in the new era, Kondracke saw in Reagan a man who had "cast a kind of golden glow over the past four and a half years," his programs representing a return to bedrock American values and optimism, shielding the country from bitter realities such as burdensome debt, social inequity, and international challenge. "Reagan," Kondracke wrote, "is a kind of magic totem against the cold future." When Kondracke's "magic totem" was later revealed to have sold weapons to the Ayatollah and lied about it, while funneling the profits to illegally arm the Contras in Nicaragua, Kondracke was reluctant to give the story much weight. "As scandals go," he wrote, "the Iran mess wasn't much . . . the Administration did wrong but in defensible causes."* Kondracke did admit that Reagan's decline restored what he called "the reality principle. He has been a good leader and a political genius," said the critic Buchanan called his "Left-Wing comrade," and "he was on the right track for his time. . . . But he is, after all, an ordinary mortal in need of criticism. It's good to know that, but the truth still hurts."†

Unlike the rest of the Group, who reveled in argument like pigs in a manure pile, Kondracke seemed adrift when asked to think on his feet. Sometimes this led him to positions that were entirely nonsensical, even by the considerable standards of "The McLaughlin Group." When McLaughlin made the prediction that, in fact, Mikhail Gorbachev's politics would

---

*Kondracke later retracted this statement. Author's interview.

†The first half of the quote appears in James Fallows, "Washington's New Celebrities," New York Review of Books, June 12, 1986. The Iran-Contra quotes come from Morton Kondracke, "Reagan Stumbles and Can't Recover—A Sad Spectacle," Los Angeles Times, January 15, 1987, Part II, p. 5. Note: When the scandal initially broke and McLaughlin surveyed his panelists, asking whether they believed Ronald Reagan knew about the transfer, Kondracke replied, "I hope he didn't know." Pressed for his evasion, Kondracke replied, "If he did know, he's a liar . . . I'll say he didn't know." This segment was rebroadcast on October 13, 1991.

turn out to be similar to those of Olaf Palme, the late Social Democratic leader of Sweden, Kondracke replied, "Yeah, what happened to Palme? He got shot." Did Kondracke mean to imply that Palme was shot for his political views? Was he saying that Gorbachev faced similar dangers to those faced by the president of one of the world's wealthiest, most stable democracies on his way home from the movies? When I asked him, he had no idea.

Like many apostate liberals, Kondracke dates his loss of faith to the Vietnam War. Kondracke explains that the "arrogance of the journalistic profession reached its height" with the Tet Offensive. "The same people who are now heroes, Halberstam, Sheehan, they should have written the goddam story and just shut up about whatever the solution was. They stopped being reporters and started being pundits . . . and they killed Diem."* The quote is instructive. Ngo Dinh Diem was killed by his own troops with no objections from the American Embassy. Halberstam and Sheehan undertook some of the most distinguished reporting in the history of the profession, forcing John Kennedy to exclaim at one point, "Why can I get this stuff from Halberstam when I can't get it from my own people?" One need not be a Freudian psychiatrist to marvel at the sight of a comfortable, well-remunerated Washington pundit blaming heroic war reporting for "killing" the president of South Vietnam. †

In addition to his duties at *The New Republic* and "The McLaughlin Group," Kondracke is also a frequent guest commentator on "This Week with David Brinkley," and the sole host and interviewer on PBS's weekly foreign policy show, "American Interests." (The latter is funded by Counter-establishment cash deriving from the Far Right Olin and Smith-Richardson foundations, along with the Maytag Corporation.) He was a tri-weekly columnist for *The Wall Street Journal*, and later, the Washington bureau chief of *Newsweek*. (The latter job did not work out, as Kondracke assumed as one of the prerogatives of his job to assign staff to research his children's homework assignments.) Kondracke has also recently been named a senior editor of *Roll Call*, a Capitol Hill weekly, and a national editor for *The*

---

*Author's interview. Halberstam calls Kondracke's quote "ridiculous. We were reporters for print organizations and we were going against the conventional wisdom of the time. It was real reporting. Mort is dumb and lazy and this kind of reporting is alien to him. Perhaps one day Kondracke will write a book as brilliant as Neil Sheehan's A Bright Shining Lie but I doubt it." Regarding Kondracke's assertion that the reporters "killed Diem," Halberstam notes, "I doubt Morton would be willing to say that to my face." Author's interview with David Halberstam.

†The irony thickens when one recalls that both Halberstam and Sheehan were forced to hide out in the home of the U.S. Embassy press attaché owing to death threats from Diem's security forces. See William Prochnau, "Halberstam's War," *Gannett Center Journal*, Fall 1989, pp. 25 and 28.

Washingtonian. In the latter capacity, he listed one "Morton Kondracke" beneath the headline "Top Foreign Affairs and Defense Journalists" in an article he authored.

One searches in vain for an explanation as to exactly what professional quality propelled Kondracke to his exalted status within the punditocracy. He is not an engaging sitcom character like Buchanan, nor a likable buffoon like McLaughlin, nor an easily hatable Novakian villain. Unlike Will, who has made a career of being a know-it-all, Kondracke plays the part of a man without a clue. Neal Freeman, the producer of "American Interests," says he chose Kondracke to be the host because "Mort is conducting his education in public," and on television, "that earnestness comes through."

What Freeman is saying, but would never admit, is that the Kondracke persona is effective explicitly because of its owner's mediocrity as both a thinker and a reporter. Why did Richard Nixon choose Kondracke as the sole interviewer for his May 1990 comeback interview? Was Nixon worried about the tough going-over he might receive from Kondracke, or was he confident of questions like "How do you feel toward [George Bush]? Do you feel toward him as though he's your kid brother . . . ?" Might the man Kondracke called a "rehabilitated senior statesman" have been in the market for a journalist willing to ask him if he had yet made peace with "the enemies who brought down his presidency: the liberals, the media and the bureaucrats" while leaving out Nixon's most important enemy, the United States Constitution? How about an interviewer who would be willing to assert, offering no proof whatsoever, that "it has been fairly established that anything your adminis-tration did during Watergate had been done by the Johnson administration and by the Kennedy administration," and then follow it up with: "Why do you think the system conspired to get you?"

With Hugh Sidey getting on in years, the system needs a reporter who is wholly incapable of embarrassment while prostrating himself before whatever powers might happen to be. The value of this kind of "reporting" and "analysis" is obvious from the perspective of Nixon and the others who sit under the glaring light of Kondracke's grueling technique. But why do editors and producers seek him out? What lies at the bottom of what John Gregory Dunne would call the "Kondrackoid" phenomenon? Herein lies the true mystery.

One of the few—if not the only—lasting contribution Ayn Rand made to the history of literature was her creation of the character Lancelot Clokey in her novel, *The Fountainhead.* Clokey was the author of *The Gallant Gallstone* and according to the town's powerful critic, Elsworth Toohey, "a worse piece of trash was never put down on paper." But Toohey, and his equally cynical and manipulative critic friends, praised *The Gallant*

Gallstone to the sky in their newspaper columns, because they believed that "the little people" needed role models like themselves in order to continue to justify their small-minded, bourgeois lives. Soon, 200,000 copies had been sold and *Gallstone* was on the lips of all the town's glitterati. Clokey, "a total nonentity who'd done nothing more outstanding than eating, sleeping and chatting with neighbors," soon lost all perspective and began, quite understandably, to believe that he was in fact a brilliant social critic and public philosopher. Like the Clokey-reading public, he was deluded but he was happy. But Rand completed *The Fountainhead* in 1943, and so Clokey never made it onto "The McLaughlin Group."

After Robert Novak left to form "The Capital Gang" on CNN in 1988, McLaughlin added a combination of *Newsweek* reporter Eleanor Clift, *Chicago Tribune* columnist Clarence Page, and *New Republic* White House reporter Fred Barnes to the line-up. Both engaging and attractive personalities with mildly liberal politics, Clift and Page helped McLaughlin answer the frequent criticism that the show ignored women and blacks. Barnes, a preppy pro-Bush Republican, melded perfectly with the Group's collective persona. When asked by McLaughlin whether he could discuss the question of silicon breast implants "with authority," he replied—perfectly straight-faced—"I can speak to almost anything with a lot of authority."

Baltimore Sun veteran Jack Germond rounded out the Group, rolling his eyes upward and gently subverting the gravitas with which the others called for an immediate declaration of war over this Outrage Against the Common Decency or that Insult to All Americans. Germond played along with the rest of the boys when the subject was politics. He remains the kind of reporter Novak once was, devoting himself to the minutiae of the political system. Germond's distaste for ideological politics, coupled with Kondracke's conversion, has allowed the others to cast him as the "liberal" in the discussion, when in fact he is no such thing. Germond is a pure pragmatist. He may have some sympathy for old-style liberal programs, but he is much more likely to look at things as they are and ask "why?" than to look at them as they never were and ask "why not?"

The value of casting an apolitical fixer as the show's liberal during the Reagan era was considerable, as it severed the legs of any truly liberal alternative without any further discussion. Few developments were more helpful to Ronald Reagan's effort to de-legitimize liberal solutions to America's problems than the growth of conservative-dominated television punditocracy. With Novak, Buchanan, and later Barnes attacking from the right, and Kondracke agreeing from the so-called left, Ronald Reagan's brand of genial reaction came to appear downright reasonable. Centrist solutions became liberal by virtue of the show's skewed political geography, and truly liberal ideas were marginalized entirely.

Unapologetic liberals were occasionally trotted out as guests, but they often sounded as if they were filing from another planet. What was the reasoned reply to a panel member insisting that black teenagers were unemployed because "these kids don't want to work"; or that the only way to deal with Muamar Khadaffi was to "slit his throat with no fingerprints"; or that the reason the National Organization for Women (NOW) differed so strongly with the administration was because the group was "twenty-five percent lesbian"? To even engage these issues on such far-out ideological territory is to admit defeat. Christopher Hitchens, columnist for *The Nation* and Socialist bon vivant, managed one McLaughlin invitation. Seconds before the show ended, Novak referred to Cuban drug runners as Hitchens's "friends." (Hitchens later retorted by calling Novak a "polecat" and a "McCarthyite bum," on "Crossfire.") When historians one day seek to understand how George Bush and Lee Atwater succeeded in making "liberalism" a dirty political word in 1988, they will need to look no further than the tapes of five upper-middle-class white guys sitting around a TV studio talking about how black families "are just going to have to stop relying on government and politics to solve [their] problems."

In addition to its decimating effects on liberal participation in the insider dialogue, one of the most damaging legacies of "The McLaughlin Group" was its implied notion that any idea, no matter how complex or enormous, could be boiled down to a yes or no question or a letter grade on a sliding scale. On one show, McLaughlin asked his fellow panelists to give "a grade on the planet Earth." McLaughlin gave it a "B," and I quote his rather amazing justification in its entirety: "Overcoming nationalism and a general spirit of internationalism."

As was frequently the case, in addition to having little discernible relationship to reality, his response was also thick with irony. Of all the offenses that can be laid at the feet of McLaughlin, and the politics that he and the Group represent, the most galling is their smug ethnocentrism and paternalistic hubris. On the very same show on which McLaughlin gave his generous grading to the planet and the century for its "internationalism," Group members had gone on record voicing some of the most distasteful xenophobic statements ever heard in punditocracy debates. We learned from Fred Barnes that "The United States is the center of the world. . . . All the smart people and entrepreneurs are winding up in the US," he noted, whereas "it is the Europeans that are going to be in trouble and to a lesser extent, the Japanese in the 1990s." Morton Kondracke observed that "the more we know about the Japanese ways of living and Chinese and Korean, the less we like them. I mean, they're rigid, they're nasty, you know, they're still Confucian and all that." These statements recalled a CNBC McLaughlin show, where the host flew into an uncontrollable fury over the refusal of the president of Mexico to speak English on his program. While discussing the subject of bilingualism with the Hispanic politician Linda Chavez, McLaughlin became suddenly enraged by the fact that two presidents of Mexico had been graciously invited to be interviewed by McLaughlin and both proceeded to speak in their native language. Their insistence, he raged, necessitated an "elaborate simultaneous translation which is a yawn as far as the audience is concerned." "When are they going to get into the twentieth century down there?" he demanded of his befuddled guest. "When is someone going to show some leadership and say to the Mexicans, 'Look, it's good for us that I speak English. . . . Somebody should tell the president of Mexico that when he appears on American television, he should speak English."

Perhaps the most intriguing fact about John McLaughlin was his own self-awareness. During one hectic afternoon when all of Washington seemed to be calling, McLaughlin explained himself. His assistant Kara Swisher asked him, "Why do so many people kowtow to you?" McLaughlin "got down really low on his desk, almost like he was a lizard," recalls Swisher, looked up at her, and replied, "They're all whores. Every one of them, they're all whores. And so am I. But I've got the TV show."

6

ALL THE VIEWS FIT TO PRINT

Heartless and dumb," "vicious and unbelievable," "scathing and cruel." These are the adjectives Nancy Reagan chose to describe not her biographer Kitty Kelley but *New York Times* super-pundit William Safire.* In his March 2, 1987, column, when Nancy was still in charge of the White House and riding high in the punditocracy, Safire pounced on the First Lady for making her husband "appear wimpish and helpless." Complaining of her "political interference," Safire accused Mrs. Reagan of "extraordinary vindictiveness," and called her "power-hungry," and "an incipient Edith Wilson, unelected and unaccountable, presuming to control the actions and appointments of the executive branch."

The Safire attack on Nancy Reagan was the stuff of Washington legend. Not only did a perceived presidential ally go after the one sacred personage in Reagan's White House, but he challenged conventional wisdom in doing so. It was Nancy, after all, who had only just engineered the replacement of evil, incompetent Chief of Staff Don Regan with likable, effective Howard Baker, thereby allowing the President to cut his Iran-Contra losses and save Washington from much hand-wringing about whether to consider impeachment. A close personal friend not only to George Will but also to Katherine Graham and Meg Greenfield, Nancy had overcome her early PR difficulties and blossomed into insider Washington's local hero, maneuvering to try to

---

*Ever the chivalrist, Ronald Reagan—said Nancy—felt Safire's column "was a terrible thing for a man to do to another man's wife." See Nancy Reagan, *My Turn*, pp. 333–34.

win her husband the Nobel Peace Prize and perhaps prevent nuclear war as an unintended bonus. Moreover, immediately following that morning's blitzkrieg, Safire refused all television invitations in which he had been asked to discuss his column. The latter move was, if anything, even more shocking than the column itself.

Word for word, William Safire was the most influential newsman in Ronald Reagan's Washington, and remains so today. Any number of writers could have given voice to nasty accusations about Nancy Reagan's behavior, and quite a few had the power and influence to wound the First Lady mortally if they got the inkling. William Safire, however, was the only pundit in Washington who not only could do it, but would. Well connected, principled, extremely hawkish, and politically fearless, William Safire was, like Lippmann, an institution unto himself.

The name Safire (originally spelled Safir, but too often mispronounced "Say-fur," and since changed) derives from the Yiddish *soifer* meaning "scribe." The power to make the Nancy Reagans of the world livid derives less from Safire's reputation as a *soifer* than as a *macher*. The journalese translation of *macher* is "bigfoot": the kind of writer political Washington regards as able to leave footprints on the issues he covers. Some journalists confess to liking this power. None exercise it with greater frequency than William Safire.

Appearing twice weekly on the op-ed page of *The New York Times*, Safire was the only cleanup hitter in the Reagan-era punditocracy whose home-run swing rested solely on the power of his reporting and the force of his argument. Alone among the punditocracy's high rollers, he did no regular television. Though he attended his share of dinner parties, he was never accused of trading on his friendships. In fact, some of Safire's toughest attacks were reserved for those with whom he had the longest histories. Not only Nancy Reagan, but USIA Director Charles Z. Wick, Attorney General William French Smith, Reagan adviser turned influence peddler Michael Deaver, and former friend and business partner CIA Director William Casey, all came under the Safire scalpel during the Reagan years and emerged considerably worse for the operation. When Casey experienced a fatal cerebral hemorrhage on the day that Safire had accused him of being "corrupted by power and secrecy" (despite the fact that Casey had called him three times on a Sunday to try to prevent it), a mutual acquaintance called the pundit and told him not to worry: Casey's seizure came "at least an hour" after reading the column.*

*   *   *

---

*Safire confessed to "pulling his punches" a little as a result of the calls. See Eleanor Randolph, "William Safire, Right to the Core; The Columnist and His Novel Look at Abraham Lincoln," *The Washington Post*, Style section, August 24, 1987, p. 1.

The New York Times is credited with having invented the modern op-ed page, but this is only partially true. In September 1970, after much institutional soul-searching, editorial-page editor John Oakes and publisher Punch Sulzberger decided to clear out the old obituary page and make room for an expanded opinion section to "afford greater opportunity for exploration of issues, and presentation of new insights and new ideas by writers and thinkers with no institutional connection with the *Times*." The innovation was a subtle one. Though the first op-ed page began with Frank Cobb and Herbert Swope at the *World* in the early 1920s, its opinions rarely conflicted with those of the publisher. Nonstaff editorials had also been running on the editorial page of *The New York Herald-Tribune* for years before it folded in April 1966, but they, too, rarely disagreed with its editorial policy and were published on a largely ad hoc basis. What Oakes and Sulzberger invented was the notion of a separate page pairing guest editorials, some contrary to the paper's own editorials, with its regular rotating columnists on a daily basis. Edited initially by Harrison Salisbury, the page inspired many imitators and soon developed into the most prestigious print forum available anywhere.

Although the *Times* remained the world's most influential newspaper by virtue of its readership and the thoroughness of its coverage, in the decade when Reaganism ruled Washington, Safire's column constituted pretty much the sum total of all of *The New York Times* op-ed page insider influence.* The guest spots on the op-ed page remained the zenith of the now crowded op-ed page field, but such contributions rarely had much lasting effect. For reasons geographical, stylistic, political, and journalistic, no other regular *Times* columnist enjoyed a fraction of Safire's regularly deployable power, and none were important players on the insider battle-ground where the wars of the Reagan years were fought.

The exile of Safire's op-ed page colleagues at the *Times* from the dinner tables and policy planning sessions of Ronald Reagan's Washington was apparent almost immediately after Reagan's election. James Reston, approaching his fourth decade as a columnist, was initially put off by the oversimplifications and chauvinism of the Reagan campaign. He worried on the day after the victory that "it had not clarified the nation's problems, but deepened them, not unified the people but divided them." Within just four days, however, the

---

*The influence of the *Times*'s unsigned editorials across the page is difficult to gauge, lacking as it does a physical presence in the city or a recognizable face within the punditocracy. For most of the Reagan era, however, its careful, balanced centrism was considered *way* too liberal within the administration to matter much, except to land certain cabinet members in hot water with the fire-breathing crowd when it appeared to approve of them.

forces within Reston that sent him like a homing pigeon to the center of debate—regardless of how far over to the right that center had moved—were already working their way through his typing fingers. Reston latched onto Reagan's superficial rhetorical nod in the direction of a "bipartisan foreign policy," celebrating the fact that "in the foreign policy field, he has indicated quite clearly that he wants a national partnership." On what basis such a partnership might be forged did not concern Reston so much as the partnership itself. "It has long been recognized here that there is a difference between campaign rhetoric and the more realistic policies that follow an election," he wrote. In other words, like much of what remained of the old establishment, Reston was willing to embrace Reagan so long as he promised not to act on any of those foolish promises he had made during the campaign. When it became clear that Reagan truly meant what he had been saying—that he really did intend to try to translate his anti-Soviet rhetoric into policy, to fight a few proxy wars regardless of their constitutionality, and gamble the nation's economic future on his untested theories, Reston lost his intellectual footing. He remained with Safire at the *Times* Washington Bureau filing his column for much of the next decade, but he lost most of his clout.

Of the other three political columnists who surrounded Safire on the *Times* op-ed page, none wrote regularly from Washington, and none made much of an impact on the forming of insider opinion. Flora Lewis, the first woman to be given her own column on the page, filed from Paris what was quite possibly the most boring regular column in the history of journalism. It certainly contained no hint that it had been written by a woman. Lewis wrote like Reston, but without his charm, his history, or the implicit indulgence on the part of the reader he inspired. Her gray, leaden prose had a deadening effect on the reader, to the point where it was often a challenge to wade deep enough into her column to determine what her point might have been. When *The New Republic* held a "world's most boring headline" contest, its inspiration was a Lewis column entitled "Worthwhile Canadian Initiative." (This was not even a particularly boring day for her.) Shot through with cautious, carefully weighted *Times*-style centrism, Lewis's soul was at one with the Council on Foreign Relations, which she somehow considered to be a beleaguered organization, under threat from "isolationism, know-nothingism and freaky suspicion. . . ."* Without being unnecessarily

---

*For some reason, in December 1989 Lewis felt compelled to defend the Council from an attack by the nearly moribund John Birch Society. Her final sentence could in truth be attached to any one of her columns, regardless of subject: "There has scarcely been a time when American interests more urgently needed the sober, informed thought about foreign affairs the Council promotes." Flora Lewis, December 13, 1989.

unkind about a person with sound instincts and sensible political judgments, one might say that Lewis was to columnists what Michael Dukakis was to presidential candidates.

The two liberals on the page, Tom Wicker and Anthony Lewis, who had appeared so important during the brief late-Vietnam-era interregnum, also entered the decade on a collision course with insider irrelevance. Wicker, whom Reston had groomed to replace him as Washington bureau chief, ran out of steam during the late seventies. Like his mentor, he kept pitching too long after his curveball started to hang. Wicker greeted Reagan's election by pointing out the intellectual and ideological inconsistencies in the candidate's record, then waited patiently for the common sense of the American people to prevail. On the major issues that dominated the Washington debate during the 1980s through his retirement at the end of 1991, Wicker was predictably pacific, tolerant, and racially sensitive. While these qualities make for a fine human being, they were not enough to power interesting columns. "I think after Vietnam people just got tired," he explained in an interview, speaking of his colleagues, and inadvertently of himself.

In the case of Anthony Lewis, insider irrelevance was a clearly defined political and intellectual choice. Lewis had never had any intention of being a Washington pundit. He spoke throughout the eighties as the voice of disinterested morality, of the Constitution, and of the victims of American foreign policy. While he did not have occasion to use the kind of prophetic rage he employed during the Christmas bombings of 1972, Lewis still has enough fire in his belly to light up a corner of the *Times* op-ed page with the kind of political passion that, for most of the Reagan era, was roped off in Washington at marches and rallies.

Michael Kinsley, a liberal who did become quite influential, said he admired Lewis for choosing not to be. "He is not a Washington journalist on purpose," notes Kinsley. "He wasn't marginalized by anybody else. Tony speaks for liberals who want to be told about how they feel about things. And his views percolate back." By refusing to countenance the assumptions of the Reagan and Bush rhetoric, Lewis willfully forfeited whatever direct influence over policy his influential perch in the *Times* might have accorded him. Instead, he played the role ostensibly mapped out in the 1920s by Walter Lippmann; to educate the public in the hopes that they would make more intelligent choices about their leaders.

An intense conversationalist with an easygoing manner and an unwieldy curly pate, Lewis laughs at the notion that he is the most radical of left-wing political commentators in the American mainstream. "It's absolutely hilarious to me," he admits. "I mean, I'm a pro-capitalist, middle-of-the-road, tepid centrist. I mean, is it left to insist that presidents and CIA directors adhere to the law? I don't think so. I think it's American." Indeed, to truly balance the likes of Safire, the *Times* would have to offer its column space to Alexander Cockburn, Chistopher Hitchens, Gore Vidal, or Noam Chomsky. * For all his commitment to human rights and conflict avoidance, Lewis never called into question the fundamental precepts of the American establishment during the Cold War except to denounce what he viewed as the self-destructive manner in which it was conducted. He thinks it unfair to expect an organization like the *Times* or the *Post* to reflect anything but the view of the establishment. "All of the people we're talking about," he notes, "are upper-middle-class and establishment figures who tend to share in the selfishness that afflicts the political system. . . . It is hard to escape the economic structure that you live in, and we're not radical in nature. We're not like some outsider journalists in some Third World country. We are part of the system."

Safire meanwhile was less a part of *the* system than of his own mini-system, mucking up the larger one. He began the Reagan era triumphant. "The silent majority, like a great soaking-wet shaggy dog [or a once-ostracized political columnist], banished from the house during the Watergate storms," he announced two days after the 1980 election, "romped back into the nation's parlor and shook itself vigorously." Safire graded Reagan's inaugural address "a respectable seven," one point below the one he had helped write for Richard Nixon in 1969 but a point above the one he had pounded out in 1973. That Safire could, by 1980, have recovered from Nixon and the innumerable strikes against him and develop into not only a powerful pundit but also a respected journalist was one of the most remarkable ironies of the making of the Reagan punditocracy.

Having grown up fatherless and near poverty in New York and California, Safire won a scholarship to Syracuse University. After two years, however, during the summer of 1949, he landed a job with Tex McCrary and Jinx Falkenberg, whose many ventures included a personalities column for the *Herald-Tribune*. Safire found that he enjoyed interviewing famous writers and politicians rather more than he did reading about them in school. The nineteen-year-old college drop-out did not return to Syracuse until he gave the commencement address there almost forty years later.

Working for McCrary, Safire drifted into public relations, for which he

---

*The *Times* editors' February 1992 decision to publish Mikhail Gorbachev's columns written for the Turin, Italy, newspaper *La Stampa* does not really qualify as a good faith effort to redress this balance. The punditocracy has long relied on Russians to give socialism a sinister tinge. And although Gorbachev may be one of the great figures of twentieth-century history, when it comes to punditry, he's no William Safire.

demonstrated a singular professional genius. At the 1959 American National Exhibition in Moscow, he achieved one of the biggest coups in advertising history when he maneuvered Vice President Richard Nixon and Soviet Premier Nikita Khrushchev into his client's mock kitchen for their historic "kitchen debate." Safire then blocked the exits so that the two blowhards would have to blow at each other, and finally took the picture himself that ran on the AP wires.

Safire quickly became a name in the public relations world, hiring eager young assistants like Barbara Walters and working for clients that ranged from Nelson Rockefeller to Ex-Lax. When the "new Nixon" ran for President in 1968, the increasingly conservative Safire went to work on the selling of the President. Hired as a speechwriter in the Nixon White House, Safire likes to joke that his real job was to walk into the empty Oval Office and call out, "Do the popular thing, Mr. President. Take the easy way out." Then he would walk back into his own cubby hole and write into Nixon's speech, "My advisers counsel me to do the popular thing, to take the easy way out. . . ."

As a political wordsmith Safire was a whiz, but he is best remembered as an accessory to the Nixon administration's crimes against the English language. By far the worst of these occurred when Spiro Agnew asked him for a colorful epithet for media gloomsters. Safire "went overboard," he says, offering the incipient language felon a choice between "hopeless, hysterical hypochondriacs of history" and "nattering nabobs of negativism." Agnew replied, "Hell, let's use both."*

Safire's career hit bottom when, after retiring from the White House in 1973 to write a memoir of the Nixon years, he saw his president self-destruct and his massive memoir rejected by his publisher, with a demand for the return of its advance. The book was eventually published, and when both the *Times* and the *Post* began beating on his doors with the request that he please say whatever he wished for their op-ed pages twice a week, his life took on a sunnier cast. †

"There was lots of outrage," recalled *Times* editorial-page editor Jack Rosenthal of Safire's hiring. "Not so much because he was a conservative

---

*Safire credits Patrick Buchanan with coming up with "pusillanimous pussyfooters," but accepts the blame for the above, along with Agnew's earlier "vicars of vacillation." McGovern denounced Agnew's "foaming fusillades," author unknown. See William Safire, *Before the Fall: An Inside View of the Pre-Watergate White House* (Garden City, NY: Doubleday & Co., 1975), p. 323.

†When Arthur Krock, *The New York Times*'s conservative Washington columnist, began to falter in the mid-sixties, Punch Sulzberger attempted unsuccessfully to recruit William F. Buckley, Jr. After this proved unworkable for contractual reasons, the *Times* publishers waited more than seven years until Safire, an acceptable conservative, became available. Author's interview with Harrison Salisbury.

voice in this temple of the eastern liberal establishment, but that he had been a hired gun for the Nixon administration. They thought he was just a shill." All of the *Times* editors polled advised the publisher against the move. As Safire recalls it, "When I walked through the city room of the Washington bureau, silence fell. My new colleagues were unfailingly civil, a few even friendly, but my written opinions were ill-received; some *Times* reporters took pride in the paper's willingness to publish the unpopular views of 'a Nixon apologist,' but most felt the publisher had been suckered." Feelings were so strong that only one member of the Washington bureau, his boyhood friend Martin Tolchin, would even eat lunch with Safire.

Life inside the office began to improve after a summer office party when Safire ruined a good suit fishing a drowning child out of a swimming pool; but the column floundered. Safire had begun inauspiciously, accusing Nixon's critics of being McCarthyites and calling on the President to burn the White House tapes. At the end of his first two-year contract, Sulzberger summoned him to New York and told him it just wasn't working out. Unless the column improved, Safire would be out of work. "Bill had not learned to be a columnist yet," recalls his editor, Harrison Salisbury. "He was still writing like a PR flack for the Republican right wing." When Safire left the publisher's office, he was completely despondent. "He didn't want anything but to be a *New York Times* columnist," says Salisbury, "and he was blowing it." Safire went back to his office, sat down at his desk, put his head in his hands, and wondered how the hell he was going to save his job. Then he looked up and, lo and behold, saw his salvation: the telephone. Safire knew everybody in Washington and he knew how everything worked. So he made a few calls. Soon Washington had its most effective pundit in a generation.

Safire's influence as a pundit during the Reagan years derived from many sources. He combined Far Right political principles with a distrust of the Far Right itself. He demonstrated an investigator's bloodlust for the powerful and arrogant, but blunted it with an admirable sense of humor and a felicitous sense of style. If you threw in the fact that he happened to be writing in the most influential print organ in the world, you would have a recipe for a pundit with unique credibility and respect across the political spectrum.

Safire is feared by the German government, beloved by the Israelis, and viewed with affection but not trust by the conservatives of the past five American administrations. On the wall of his Chevy Chase home is a framed Safire column vigorously annotated by the current President of the United States. Washington political consultants read him the way swamis read tea leaves, grilling their candidates twice a week on Safire's pet issues and daily obsessions in order to head off the predictable Safire-inspired questions from the traveling press. Unlike most pundits who take a coach-tour attitude toward issues ("If this is Tuesday, it must be nuclear proliferation"), Safire has no qualms about returning day in and day out to the same subject if he thinks doing so will raise the hackles of those he suspects. Bert Lance lost his job this way, winning Safire a Pulitzer in the process. So, in some measure, did Jimmy Carter.

Perhaps most alarming from the perspective of his opponents, Safire is, almost alone in the contemporary punditocracy, a wonderful writer. While he may be the most feared and respected media presence in Washington, Safire is known to the majority of *Times* readers as the paper's Sunday language columnist, where his pieces draw an incredible eighteen thousand letters a year. An inveterate punster, he is responsible for a healthy percentage of the wit allowed to bypass the *Times*'s Wit Police over the past two decades, as well as some of the worst puns in pundit history. *

Not above making himself tremendously rich, Safire also gives speeches at a hefty $20,000 per. When questioned about his fee in his Century Clublike office in Washington, Safire pooh-poohs the money. His fee, he says, is based on what it costs him to park at the *Times*'s garage on Washington's I Street. "Every time parking goes up a quarter," he explains, "my speaking fee rises a thousand bucks." Whatever the money goes toward, it certainly is not his own wardrobe, which could double for that of some of the city's more sartorially careless plumbers. In addition to his talents as a linguist, a columnist, and a journalist, Safire has proven himself to be a more than passable historical novelist and an ambitious biblical scholar as well. †

If all the Washington news media shared Safire's love of combat, his intellectual seriousness, and a fraction of his wit and brilliance, this book would not be necessary. But because there is only one William Safire, his shortcomings are magnified within the punditocracy by the lack of any equally powerful opposition. The straitjacketed rules of objective journalism exist because reporters are not trusted to leave their own personal and professional agendas out of the story they are covering. Columnists are

---

*Among those unearthed by Victor Navasky were: porn-free, tongue-in-chic, radical-sheik, columny, pressycophants, trendustry, journafiction, ukasy char, Spock-marked generation, the President's populism and the First Lady's momulism, Peking-too-soon, Hiza-yatollah, sycophancy network, and Haigemony. The classic Safirism of all time appeared atop a column on the Saudi Arabian oil minister Sheikh Ahmed Zaki Yamani. Safire called it, "Yamani or Ya Life." See Victor Navasky, "Safire Appraised," *Esquire*, January 1982.

†His massive 1987 novel, *Freedom*, received respectful reviews, though the author of this book decided that, for purely research purposes, it was roughly a thousand pages beyond the call of duty. In the fall of 1992, Random House published *The First Dissident*, Safire's Midrashic ruminations on the Book of Job—a work alleged by its publicist to "put the Bible back on the front page."

exempt from these rules, excluding libel and slander laws, and are subject only to the sanctions of their paper and the value of their reputations. When the paper is the *Times*—which does not interfere at all with the content of its columnists' columns—and their reputations are as imposing as Safire's, the sanctions are strictly internal.

One problem with Safire is political. However engaging and talented the man may be, he has developed over the years into a political extremist by virtually every measure save that employed in contemporary Washington. On occasion this has tended to cloud his journalistic judgment.

Safire was thrilled with Reagan's first term, reveling in what he called its "years of stable growth," while either ignoring or failing to understand the long-term costs to the economy that precisely such a facade involved. At the heart of Safire's world view, moreover, was the same impossibly myopic vision that gave the Soviets credit for everything deemed unpleasant by American right-wingers from Managua to Mars. Safire bought into Claire Sterling's misrepresentations of a fabricated "KGB/Bulgarian connection" to the Pope's attempted assassination, and then misrepresented even her own specious claims.* On a larger scale, he celebrated Reagan's Star Wars fantasy without ever addressing the question of its obvious technical limitations. He admitted to being "elated" over Reagan's "evil empire" rhetoric because this pointless posturing somehow "brought moral pressure to bear on international mischief-making in Afghanistan, Nicaragua, Angola, and the Middle East," as if Oliver North and his cronies were setting up Peace Corps offices in these same places.

The Reagan administration disappointed Safire precisely when it behaved most responsibly. Safire likened Reagan's belated effort to join Mikhail Gorbachev in winding down the Cold War to "the failing Roosevelt with 'Uncle Joe' Stalin at Yalta." He cried "appeasement" at the announcement of every negotiating success. On issues related to Israeli security, Safire was frequently holier than Jerusalem itself, often siding with the revanchist Ariel Sharon against the rest of the civilized world.†

---

*In addition to Sterling's incredible imputations, Safire may have fallen victim to Robert Gates's "doctored assessments" of the likelihood of KGB involvement in the plot. These allegations were being trumpeted at the time by Safire's old friend, William Casey. For a thorough explanation of the CIA's role in this pretense, see the Select Committee on Intelligence, U.S. Senate, "Nomination of Robert M. Gates to be Director of Central Intelligence," 102nd Congress, 1st session, October 24, 1991, pp. 111–16.

†Safire's devotion to Israel has led to two of his most serious mistakes in the column. In 1981, when the Israelis destroyed Iraq's nuclear reactor, Safire quoted "Baghdad's official newspaper" insisting that the reactor was "not intended to be used against Iran but against the Zionist enemy." The quote, however, was an invention of the Israeli Foreign Ministry and Safire was forced to issue a personalized correction at the bottom of a later

Safire's ethics as a journalist have also been the subject of some speculation. Michael Kinsley called Safire a "bully" with the soul of a PR man when Safire beat up on the hapless USIA director, Charles Z. Wick ("by all accounts, a jackass," said Kinsley), for tapping his phone calls without telling people. Kinsley then damned Safire for printing the contents of Wick's taped conversations, thereby vastly magnifying the invasion of privacy which so upset the bigfoot-pundit in the first place. Safire's series of patented insinuating interrogatories, imputing corrupt fund-raising practices to Wick (which were later picked up by Mary McGrory and The Washington Post editorial page), also peeved Kinsley, as they rested on what then appeared to be the slenderest shred of evidence. Wick survived the ensuing investigation with the help of a considerable number of $250 hours contributed by Washington superlawyer Leonard Garment—like Safire a Nixonian who had managed to spin Watergate dross into Reaganite gold—but Kinsley pronounced Safire guilty of "misusing the power of his august office."*(The fact that Kinsley was defending the Reagan administration while Safire was bashing it goes some distance toward explaining why these two remain the most interesting pundits in Washington.)

Another problem with Safire's modus operandi is the liberties he grants himself with regard to the deployment of his own power. According to sources quoted in The Washington Post, Safire once had trouble getting Under Secretary of State William Clark to call him back. Furious, he allegedly told Caspar Weinberger that he was "going after" Clark, which he did—calling him "miscast," "inexperienced," and "a living example that still waters could run shallow." Safire calls the incident a "Rashomon thing," where many people have differing recollections of the same event. In another variation on the same theme, during the 1984 campaign Safire lobbed a

---

column. More recently, in 1990, when a group of Israeli tourists were slain in Egypt, Safire wrote that the PLO had "condoned last week's slaughter of Israeli tourists in Egypt." Yet according to four separate stories in the Times and Post, PLO spokespeople had "denounced the attack," "strongly condemned the assault," "denounced the attack" (again), and "formally distanced [themselves] from the assault." This time no corrections ran. See Victor Navasky, "Safire Appraised," Esquire, January, 1982, p. 50, and William Safire, February 12, 1990. The PLO quotes noted above appeared in: Joel Brinkley, "A Grieving Israel Pushes Politics Aside," The New York Times, February 5, 1990; Alan Cowell, "Attack on Israelis Upsets Palestinians in Egypt," The New York Times, February 7, 1990; Caryle Murphy, "Egypt Pledges to Pursue Talks," and Jackson Diehl, "Israel Postpones Peace Moves After Attack," both in The Washington Post, February 6, 1990, p. 16.

*Wick later invited Kinsley to lunch. When Kinsley said he was surprised by this, given that he had called Wick a jackass, Wick replied, "I don't mind criticism from the press, as long as it's accurate." See Kinsley, The New Republic, January 30, 1984, p. 4, and Michael Kinsley, Curse of the Giant Muffins (New York: Summit Books, 1987), p. 10.

verbal hand grenade at Vice President George Bush for "ducking questions" and campaigning in a "media-free cocoon" when Bush declined to return Safire's call regarding the administration's position on the ill-fated merger of Libya and Morocco. The fact that the Vice President was en route from Paducah to Houston when Safire called did not impress the columnist. He told a staff member to have the Vice President use the Secret Service telephone at the bottom of the ramp and call him immediately after landing.

"There is no doubt that not returning calls in my mind is evidence of being either fearful of calling back or contemptuous," argues Safire. "I don't buy that they're too busy."

Those are awfully imposing words for a mere columnist, but they are probably true. Few insiders doubt that William Safire is the most influential and respected pundit alive. When the point is made to Safire himself, he does not dispute it. During the opening days of the Bush administration, Chief of Staff John Sununu went through the elaborate charade of pretending to refuse a call from the President so as not to interrupt a Safire interview. When Safire felt like going to Riga to interview Latvian independence fighters, the Latvian Thomas Jefferson put down the draft of the Latvian Declaration of Independence he was writing to spend a few hours talking with him. When Safire traveled to Bir Zeit University on the occupied West Bank to meet Palestinian nationalists there, he simply knocked on a door, called out, "Safire, from the *Times*," and was treated to a first-class tour of Palestinian misery. This was regardless of the fact that he, as much as any American pundit, has been responsible for supporting Israel in its imposition of that misery on his hosts. From Riga to Nablus, from Pennsylvania Avenue to South Capitol Street, William Safire is known to everyone whose name might one day appear in a newspaper as one tough SOB. When asked if he would one day like to be Secretary of State, Safire responds, "Why step down?"

Safire admits that he has gone beyond the bounds of fairness on a few occasions, and says he feels particularly bad about a "cheap poke" he once took at Ted Kennedy. He also confesses to pulling his punches occasionally, but "perhaps not often enough. In this business," he philosophizes, "it's okay to take a hard shot if you show your hand when you do it." The power, however, he recognizes, is real and considerable. "This is *The New York Times*. It's powerful. If you abuse or misuse it, it's like abusing power in the White House, so you've got to be careful. . . . You can't just take a pop at a little guy."

The contrast with George Will here is particularly telling. Safire turned down the request from the Reagan debate team in 1980 that caused Will so much heartache. During the period when Safire was relentlessly beating up on Nancy Reagan in his column, she could be frequently spied at the Jockey Club, consoling herself with Will. Safire, also unlike Will, is a brilliant reporter. Liberal *Washington Post* columnist Richard Cohen recently wrote, "Most opinion columnists cannot be relied upon for breaking news. That, by common agreement, we leave to William Safire." Is it any wonder that Ben Bradlee, who said he would have fired Will if given the chance during Debategate, and who once denounced Safire as a "master of the cheap shot" who "automatically impugns the motives of everybody he thinks is against him," recently named Safire as the only pundit he would have liked to steal for the *Post*?

Philosophically, Safire came to conservatism from almost a diametrically opposite position from that of Will. On foreign policy, both men are uncompromising hawks. But with regard to the proper role of government in society, where Will sees the sate as the moral tutor of the masses, Safire calls himself a "libertarian conservative" and says his "political mind-set resists the intrusion of government into the individual's moral decisions." This libertarianism has led him to attack the arrogance of "the Christian Republican party," who, led by "Reverend Reagan," committed the "Constitutional sin" of refusing to distinguish between politics and morality. Safire's endorsements of gay rights, abortion rights, pot-smoking rights, and a whole host of other rights during the Reagan administration had the dual effect of driving social conservatives in the Reagan coalition to distraction while earning Safire the respect and admiration of those who rarely agree with him. This, in turn, made him all the more valuable to these same right-wingers when he deployed his hard-earned mantle of thoughtful iconoclasm on behalf of the administration's militant foreign policy.

Politics aside, the obvious question to be asked about William Safire's column is why the *Times* has only one of him. An important reason may be the fact that while the job of columnist for the *Times* op-ed page is difficult to attain, it is even harder to lose. As former *Times* op-ed page editor and current foreign policy columnist Leslie H. Gelb explains, "The publisher chooses people who they think have something to say and stands by them for their journalistic careers. The column itself goes up and down." The only way to lose one's appointment is to reach retirement age, as Reston and Flora Lewis have, or to use one's column to attack the *Times* itself, as former metro columnist Sydney Schanberg did.* Moreover, the publisher's efforts to

*The hero of the film *The Killing Fields*, Schanberg refused to cozy up to his publisher's pals and rather amazingly did not even exempt the *Times* itself from criticism. Shortly before he went on vacation in July 1985, Schanberg wrote three columns in a row

improve the page during the 1980s were sidetracked by the decision to give a column to his forcibly retired editor-in-chief, Abe Rosenthal, a man whose newsroom during his later years was casually likened to Stalinist Russia and Castro's Cuba.

On January 6, 1987, Rosenthal's first column ran under his own headline, "Please Read This Column." If it struck readers as a mite pathetic, it in no way prepared them for the masochistic experiences they would endure were they to accede to Rosenthal's plea on a regular basis. Rarely in the history of any industry has a man once so powerful humiliated himself so publicly as Abe Rosenthal has done with "On My Mind" (nicknamed "Out of My Mind" by *Times* staffers) on the *Times* op-ed page.

The *Times* advertising copy promised its readers, "Whatever it is that's on Mr. Rosenthal's mind, it's going to be interesting." That may or may not have been true on any given day. One had difficulty judging, because Rosenthal hides his thoughts behind a writing style made up of short staccato outbursts that resemble sentences only at great distances. In praising his friends in the media and hires at *The New York Times*, Rosenthal once committed the following paragraph: "Even Barbara Walters could not have done better—no higher compliment. And Larry Tisch once more is a hero at CBS." Another

---

on subjects of particular sensitivity to the *Times* management. In the final one, he attacked the paper's news judgment in ignoring a series of scandals involving the construction of the Westway superhighway on Manhattan's West Side at the same time that it devoted fawning coverage to the chef of a popular new Cajun restaurant facing licensing problems. The *Times* editorial page, along with most of the city's power structure, was committed to Westway. That "the city's newspapers, like the big politicians," had "ignored most of the scandal" was part, in Schanberg's view, "of the shame of Westway." When Schanberg returned from his fishing trip in upstate New York, he was summoned to the office of publisher Punch Sulzberger's assistant, Sidney Gruson. There he was given the bad news: There would be no Sydney Schanberg column the next day. Shocked and angered, Schanberg wanted to fight. He told Gruson, "You cannot keep your trust by killing a voice. An op-ed page is dedicated to diversity," he insisted. "You have put a taint on the *Times*." Gruson remembers telling Schanberg that he and the publisher "found the tone of the column to be too shrill." Nor did Gruson or Sulzberger approve of the way Schanberg returned to the question of New York real estate developers "day after day." Finally to imply, as Schanberg had, "venality on the part of the *Times* with regard to Westway, that was more than we could accept." When Schanberg asked just how the paper planned to announce this, Schanberg says Gruson replied, "I'm not going to tell anyone. Are you going to tell anyone?"

This account is based on the author's interviews with Sydney Schanberg and Sidney Gruson. It is not inconsistent with the version published in Joseph Goulden, *Fit to Print: Abe Rosenthal and His Times* (Secaucus, NJ: Lyle Stuart, 1988), pp. 243–48, which relies primarily on Gruson. Schanberg nevertheless insists that "I am ashamed of Sidney Gruson for all the lies he told to Joseph Goulden about me and my departure from the *Times*." Gruson says he cannot reply to Schanberg's charge without knowing what he is alleged to have lied about, but he denies telling any lies, either to Schanberg or to Goulden or to the author. See also Sydney Schanberg, July 27, 1985.

four-month period saw three Rosenthal columns entitled, respectively, "How to Be Stupid in New York," "How to Be Crazy in New York," and "How to Love New York." All three were sentimental paeans to the outgoing mayor, Ed Koch. Like Rosenthal, Koch was an insecure Jewish neoconservative, obsessed with critics of Israel and intensely critical of civil rights leaders and other outspoken liberals and people of color. To Rosenthal, Koch was "the saint of Gracie Mansion" and "the best mayor" New York ever had.

To say that Abe Rosenthal had an exalted sense of the importance of his own judgments is to utter one of the great understatements of our age. Some Rosenthal columns have sought to hook readers with this opening: "The City of Washington is quite interesting," or this headline quoted in its entirety: "Something Is Happening." Shortly after the column began, *Village Voice* writer Geoffrey Stokes counted up thirty-nine uses of the personal pronoun in a single Rosenthal column. Later in his career, Rosenthal began one using it three times in the first sentence. In yet another historic column, he achieved the hitherto unimagined literary feat of quoting himself quoting himself.*

Under most circumstances, Rosenthal might inspire a degree of pity among the kind-hearted. Not only was he booted from the job he loved so dearly, but it was given to his rival, Max Frankel. At the end of Rosenthal's brilliant but erratic reign as editor of the paper, he was greeted with the publication of a trashy biography, which drew heavily upon the intimate recollections of his longtime mistress, whom he jilted after allegedly promising marriage. When Rosenthal did finally divorce his first wife and remarry, his new romance coincided with the appearance of the satirical New York monthly magazine, SPY. There, Rosenthal's enemies have chronicled the adventures of "Abe 'I'm Writing as Bad as I Can' Rosenthal" and his wife, Shirley "bosomy dirty-book writer" Lord to a degree that is painful to read. SPY's spies regularly report on the columnist's unpopularity with his colleagues, his exacting interior-decorating standards, his inexplicably emotional behavior at society dinner parties—even the poor man's renting of adult videos.

Rosenthal did earn and retain the respect of many in the human rights community for his relentless coverage of the plight of various political prisoners rotting away in the world's jails, excluding those held by Israel. But

---

*See Jonathan Alter, "Abe Speaks His Mind," *Newsweek*, March 9, 1987, p. 54; A. M. Rosenthal, "On My Mind," March 17, 1989; and Eric Alterman, "The Pat and Abe Show," *The Nation*, November 5, 1990. For the three "I"s, see A. M. Rosenthal, March 19, 1991. In early 1992, Rosenthal began yet another column with three "I"s in the opening two lines, but this time he had the grace to divide them between two short sentences. The surprise subject: "Decent," "democratic" Israel vs. "Israel-hating, Jew-hating" Arab "dictatorships" and "tyrannies." See A. M. Rosenthal, February 25, 1992.

any sympathy Rosenthal might have earned based upon SPY's treatment, the awful biography, and his human rights advocacy was soon squandered by his uncompromising self-righteousness and inability to countenance differences of political opinion. When Rosenthal began the column, well-wishers had hopes that he would develop along the lines that Safire had: a conservative with contacts who would ask tough questions and dig out the answers. Instead, he metamorphosed into a twice-weekly version of Norman Podhoretz—only without the self-deprecating wit and charm. By far the most exasperating aspect of Rosenthal's bloated sense of self derives from his apparent belief that he has been anointed by American Jewry as the official ambassador of its angst. Rosenthal lectures the goyim incessantly on the importance of Jewish sensitivities, almost always mixing up his own personal paranoia with the fate of millions of Americans and Israelis. In his hysterical haranguing of those he deems to be either anti-Semitic or anti-Israel—there is no distinction to be made here—Rosenthal's column frequently puts one in mind of a character in Franz Lidz's memoir about growing up in postwar New York with his four daffy Jewish uncles, *Unstrung Heroes.* Attending his first baseball game, one uncle sees a line drive careen off Mickey Mantle's bat in the direction of his seat and starts screaming that Mantle, together with Yankee manager Casey Stengel, is planning a pogrom.

Thus, owing to his confusing writing style, self-important pronouncements, and social embarrassments, Rosenthal's influence within the punditocracy was virtually nil.* The main beneficiaries of the introduction of Rosenthal's column have been the op-ed pages of *The Washington Post* and *The Wall Street Journal,* whose relative improvement, through no fault of their own, appears unarguable on the days when Rosenthal appears in the *Times.* The main losers have been Rosenthal, the *Times,* and the business of columnizing itself. Says Lars-Erik Nelson, Washington columnist for the blue-collar *New York Daily News,* "Rosenthal is an embarrassment to the *Times* and an insult to all columnists. The idea that he was given the job as a sort of going out to pasture. . . . It shows a basic contempt for informed commentary."

During the Bush presidency, the *Times* began to rebuild its op-ed page by appointing to it Leslie H. Gelb and Anna Quindlen. Gelb, a former Carter administration official, national security correspondent, and op-ed page editor, is one of the subtlest and most complex foreign policy minds anywhere.

*When I asked Ben Bradlee whether he thought Rosenthal—whom he did not admire as an editor—was any improvement as a columnist, he started to laugh so hard I feared he would fall off his chair. Finally, he managed to sputter, "No!"

As editor of the op-ed page, he had made a major commitment to removing it from the staid, formulaic commentators of the Metroliner crowd and bringing in the voices of a vastly wider spectrum of writers, reaching out to rap singers, punk rockers, poets, and artists. It was a slow process, and white male establishment voices still dominate.* But the overall effect Gelb sought to build was one approaching the ideal of the social histories of a Fernand Braudel rather than the old-style Louis Namier–diplomatic history to which the page had always devoted itself. The transition from Flora Lewis to Gelb, despite a slow start on the latter's part, did much to rejuvenate the page and increase its political relevance. Arthur Sulzberger's decision to hire Anna Quindlen to join Russell Baker twice a week in writing a social, rather than explicitly political, column proved to be a stroke of genius. A former yuppie/metro/women's columnist at the paper, just thirty-seven when given the column, Quindlen spoke to issues and emotions that do not fall neatly into the political debate, but nevertheless help shape and underlie it. Her ability to bring her honest emotional reactions and psychological insights to the Great Issues of the Day had the effect of undercutting the oh-so-serious tone of the rest of the page, while making it far more relevant to the average *Times* reader. Though one could not discern any impact of Quindlen's on the insider debate—except perhaps on the question of abortion—she nevertheless achieved remarkable results in humanizing the language behind which politicians and political pundits hid. It may sound like a weird compliment, but despite the antics of William Safire's power wielding, Anthony Lewis's steadfast morality, and Abe Rosenthal's twice-weekly primal scream, the most attractive quality of the post-Reagan-era *Times* op-ed page was that it learned not to take itself too seriously.

---

*During the first six months of 1989, a mere 13% of the 309 guest editorials carried on the page were written by women. See Marion Goldin, "Father *Times*: Who's on the Op-ed Page?" *Mother Jones*, January 1990, p. 51.

7

GLASS HOUSES AND
REVOLVING DOORS

When Donald Graham ascended to the job of publisher of *The Washington Post*—a position for which he had trained for much of his life—his first major initiative was to replace editorial-page editor Philip Geyelin with his deputy, Meg Greenfield. That move, taken in August 1979, would provide a strong foundation for the ideological shifts within the punditocracy that would characterize the Reagan era.

The decision was a painful one for both Graham and Geyelin, and neither one will discuss it. Chalmers Roberts's semi-official history of the *Post* quotes Katharine Graham, Donald's mother and still a major power behind the paper, complaining that the page had become "too gelatinous, too much of 'on the one hand . . . on the other.' " Unlike Geyelin, a Lippmann protégé drafted in large measure to lead the *Post* away from its misconceived support of Lyndon Johnson's war, Greenfield was expected to take a harder line on foreign policy issues than her predecessor. A Seattle native, Greenfield had worked for eleven years at Dow Jones's *National Observer* magazine, a snappy, liberal, anti-Communist magazine, before coming to the *Post*.

Donald Graham says he picked Meg Greenfield for her "wide-ranging, free-thinking, and interesting mind," and indeed, she had won the Pulitzer Prize for editorial writing a year earlier. A close confidante of both Grahams, Greenfield rules the editorial and op-ed pages of *The Washington Post* with a degree of freedom enjoyed by few of her peers. A thoughtful neoconservative on foreign policy issues and a chastened liberal domestically, Greenfield describes herself as being "at the right-ish edge of each of the arguments" of the Reagan era.

While Greenfield herself is no ideologue, the page over which she presided during the 1980s nevertheless came to be dominated by its voices of the right. The shift occurred because the page's liberals were either confused or uninspired, and its centrists unwilling to challenge the Reaganites' assumptions. Greenfield has written that "true audacity is having the daring to question the tired assumptions in which most politicians nest." But for virtually the entire decade, the only direction from which her columnists' audacity seemed to derive was the Far Right. Many of the ideas that originated from that direction, however, turned out to be awful ones. Supply-side economics, Star Wars, the deregulation of the S&L industry: all of these disastrous Reaganite innovations received considerable support from the most influential denizens of the *Post* page. In some cases, merely by publishing its regular right-wing columnists, the *Post* helped legitimate views that, before Ronald Reagan came to town, were considered just this side of lunacy. The mere appearance of Evans and Novak in so prestigious a forum, for instance, invested them with instant and wholly undeserved credibility. *

The paper's unsigned editorials, meanwhile, also overseen by Greenfield, enjoyed extraordinary influence among insiders and in Congress. (Fully aware of their power, the writers would frequently direct their arguments at wavering senators and congressmen.) The influence derived in part from Greenfield's own extraordinary reputation within the punditocracy, and in part from her close personal and intellectual relationship with Mrs. Graham. The latter remained chairwoman and CEO of the permanent Washington power elite throughout the eighties and into the nineties.

Owing largely to the old-fashioned liberalism of Herb Block's editorial cartoons, which appeared beside the lead editorial, as well as the conservative political tactic of labeling moderates "liberals" in order to decertify their true opposition, the paper managed to retain its reputation as a bastion of the liberal establishment throughout the Reagan years. Donald Graham makes a persuasive case that the *Post* deserved its reputation, at least on domestic matters. The *Post*, argues the publisher, endorsed both of Ronald Reagan's opponents, consistently called for tax increases, opposed the death penalty, supported increased funding for social programs, and remained committed to civil rights legislation. But on the crucial foreign policy issues of the decade—Nicaragua and the MX missile, for instance—*Post* editorial policy

---

*In their April 25, 1991, column, for instance, the boys argued that the federal trial of junk bond swindler Michael Milken demonstrated that America, "while far from totalitarian, is only semi-free."

led to the sawing of one leg after another out from under the foundation upon which establishment liberalism had once rested.

Racially and sexually the op-ed page remained a relic of an earlier America. Of the twenty-six regular contributors to the *Post* page, three were women and two were black. But even this was deceptive. Of the women, Greenfield published bimonthly, while Ellen Goodman and Jeane Kirkpatrick wrote weekly. Of the two blacks, Carl Rowan was also only sporadically published. Thus, over an eleven-week period surveyed, one could find approximately 8 percent of regular *Post* columns authored by a woman and fewer than 12 percent authored by a black. Zero percent in this city of black and female majorities were written by a black woman. *

But the racial and sexual makeup of the *Post* op-ed page is of less intrinsic interest than its ideological composition. The ability of the right to dominate the politics of the *Post* editorial pages was not a matter of majority rule. Ever since *The Washington Star* folded in the summer of 1981, the *Post* has carried so many regular columnists that any attempt to map out a coherent theme amongst them would come to despair. Among the page's contributors during the eighties were: pacifist vegetarian Colman McCarthy and radical civil libertarian Nat Hentoff (both on Saturdays only); liberals Hobart Rowen, Mark Shields, Michael Kinsley, Bob Kuttner, Richard Cohen, and Mark Alan Stamaty; main-line establishmentarians James Hoagland, Philip Geyelin, Edwin Yoder, Stephan S. Rosenfeld, David Broder, and Robert Samuelson; the moderately conservative African-American William Raspberry; neoconservatives Jeane Kirkpatrick, Charles Krauthammer, Henry Kissinger, and Greenfield herself; and Goldwater-style right-wingers George Will, Evans and Novak, James J. Kilpatrick, William F. Buckley, Jr., and W. Emmett Tyrell. In the fall of 1991, Lally Weymouth, Mrs. Graham's daughter, who specializes in politically charged but pro-Israel Evans and Novak–style foreign reporting, was also awarded a column.

If the right succeeded in dominating the politics of the *Post* page during the 1980s, it was because only writers who appeared on television (Safire excepted) and who shared the general principles of the Reagan administration

---

*In fairness, Donald Graham points out that at least three other black staff writers—Courtland Milloy, Dorothy Gilliam, and Juan Williams—are given the opportunity to vent their opinions in the newspaper, although none of them appears regularly on the op-ed page. "The *Post* has a number of very fine black columnists," Graham notes, "and I'm very proud to put their views in the paper." Author's interview. Also in fairness, these statistics would probably read quite similarly if either the *Times* or *The Wall Street Journal* were the subject of analysis. The calculations derive from data contained in Christopher Simpson, "Content Analysis and Commentary of the Op-ed Page of *The Washington Post*," unpublished manuscript, December 1988. It is based on the op-ed pages of September 1, 1988, through November 15, 1988.

were considered relevant by the city's movers and shakers. George Will, the king of the television hill, was obviously important. So were Evans and Novak. So, particularly, was Charles Krauthammer, who began his column in 1984, invented the Reagan Doctrine in 1985, won the Pulitzer Prize in 1986, and soon thereafter replaced Will as the cast intellectual on "Inside Washington."

The quality of the page during the Reagan era was wildly uneven. Its most consistently original contributions, Michael Kinsley's TRB column and Mark Alan Stamaty's brilliant "Washingtoon" saga, were reprinted from other sources, though Greenfield does deserve credit for recognizing their talent and, in Stamaty's case, for inspiring his idea. Will and Krauthammer wrote elegantly and often thoughtfully on the conservative side. Of the page's own liberals, however, only Richard Cohen maintained the capacity to surprise. But Cohen suffered for much of the decade from a professional identity crisis. Having been moved by Donald Graham from the metro page onto the op-ed page against the wishes of Greenfield, Cohen sacrificed the engaging nebbishness of his earlier voice in an ill-fated attempt to achieve what he apparently considered to be a more serious tone befitting an Important Political Pundit. By the time he regained the disarmingly self-effacing tone that had made him a star on the Metro page, the eighties had pretty much come and gone. Mary McGrory, perhaps the most charming writer and sharpest wit on the entire Post staff, filed her liberal opinions and reportage by her own choice on page two.

A few of the pundits carrying on the Post's centrist traditions would occasionally demonstrate the ability to see some operational defect of a Reagan policy in a fresh light. James Hoagland's columns out of Paris, though no less doggedly moderate than those of Flora Lewis, were nevertheless vastly superior, because he supplemented his consensual political instincts with some excellent reporting. Rosenfeld, Geyelin, and Yoder had their good days as well. But by and large, the Post op-ed page began the 1980s in a slump and remained in one for most of the decade. This was all the more unfortunate since, along with The New Republic, it provided the punditocracy with the lion's share of its most influential members.

The decline in the page's quality could be traced to three factors. The first was economic. As columnists grew increasingly wealthy from television and corporate appearances, they found themselves with less time and energy to devote to producing a well-reported or originally conceived column. Second, too many of the Post regulars were so powerfully tied to the mind-set of the government that they effectively conceded the ability to critique it. Finally, and most damagingly, Greenfield opened up the paper's pages to professional Reaganite politicians, such as Henry Kissinger and Jeane

Kirkpatrick. Unlike Safire, these operatives had no intention of making their careers as journalists or pundits, but merely saw their columns as an additional means to rewrite the historical records of their performance in office and to retain the public eye. The result was a further diminution of the perceived integrity of the pundit profession, with absolutely no consequential improvement in the quality of the page's analysis.

Because the insider community is itself so small and geographically concentrated, its television stars cut far more imposing figures in the city's social hierarchy than their equivalents do in Manhattan or even Hollywood. In a town whose social structure is not unlike that of a suburban high school, they are, as James Fallows points out, the varsity.

Owing to the stern *Times* television prohibitions, a regular column in the *Post* has become the most effective blast-off platform for the television/ lecture circuit financial stratosphere. Its denizens can often be viewed at various transit points between the punditocracy's three rings. *New Republic* editors Charles Krauthammer and Michael Kinsley saw their columns in the *Post* lead to regular television appearances, thereby transversing all three rings simultaneously. (Both writers are also enormously well-paid monthly contributors to *Time*.) A particular advantage for *Post* writers in this regard is the company's ownership of the Agronsky/Inside Washington show. Among current *Post* contributors, Krauthammer, George Will, James J. Kilpatrick, Carl Rowan, and former editorial writer Juan Williams have all been tapped for that particular starmaking institution. Other *Post* writers with regular television gigs include: Mark Shields on MacNeil/Lehrer and "The Capital Gang"; Will, formerly of "Nightline," ABC Evening News, and "Agronsky and Company," and still of "This Week with David Brinkley"; and Novak, formerly of McLaughlin fame and the short-lived "Money Politics," now consigned to "The Capital Gang," and "The Evans and Novak Report," where he appears with his *Post* partner, Rowland Evans, Kinsley of "Crossfire" and "Firing Line," and Buckley of "Firing Line." Writing in August 1983, Tory curmudgeon Henry Fairlie observed:

> The repetitiveness and predictability of most of the op-ed page of *The Washington Post* are directly related to their unimportance in the eyes of their authors. They are hackwork, which, if their authors were not media stars, any self-respecting editor would drop. . . . They have become mere adjuncts to the paper's main interest in them, that they are written by media names.

Television, however, is only the half of it. Evans and Novak, as has been noted, are less a journalistic enterprise than a small multinational conglomerate. As Fairlie observed, the effect of this corporate expansion has been devastating for the quality of the *Post*'s page. It is television, and television alone, that lays the groundwork for $20,000 speaking engagements. Time wasted writing interesting or unorthodox columns detracts from speaking engagements. Or worse, such a column might offend some potential conventioneer somewhere and thus stand in the way of an offer. Richard Cohen shed some light upon this phenomenon when he grappled with a hypothetical speech offer from a group whose position he was about to bash:

> But wait! Will this column endanger my speech engagement? I think. I ponder. I check my bank account and, with a ruler, measure the pile of bills on my desk. I decide: It's time to write about the glories of spring in Washington.

Cohen argues that this situation corrupts high-powered punditry, and he is right. He also argues that "the public, my readers, will perceive nothing," since columnists always kill a few days a year with rhapsodies about cherry blossoms and so forth. In the short term, he has a point. But over the long run, readers will likely perceive an increase in exactly the kind of toothless, Milquetoast punditry that characterized many *Washington Post* pundits during the Reagan era and beyond.

To the degree that a newspaper can be said to have a soul, that of *The Washington Post* can be found in the columns of its venerable political reporter and pundit, David Broder. The dean of the Washington press corps, Broder carries on the Reston tradition with a degree of spunk and verve that belies his three decades in the business.

Consensual, generous, and moderate to an almost Confucian degree, Broder expresses an unflagging enthusiasm for political reporting that is widely recognized as a model for young reporters in journalism schools across the nation. A 1973 Pulitzer Prize winner, with his unfailing integrity and willingness to admit error, Broder is viewed across the political spectrum as a guardian of journalistic ethics and traditions. According to a 1990 *Washington Journalism Review* poll, Broder was the most admired political reporter in the city, with a six-to-one margin over the nearest competition. The fact that he is both a reporter and a pundit does not seem to confuse anyone, since most of his columns are so politically balanced and consciously anti-ideological that they could run just as easily in the news section.

The son of a dentist, Broder grew up in Chicago in a family of FDR Democrats who talked politics constantly at the dinner table. As a teenager, he published a weekly political newspaper and peddled it around the neighborhood. When he attended the University of Chicago, he led the Liberals to victory over the Communists and gained control of the campus newspaper. Broder trained at the *Bloomington* (Ill.) *Pantograph*, coming to work for *Congressional Quarterly* in 1955 and later *The Washington Star*. He was hired at *The New York Times* in 1965 but resigned a year and a half later to go to work at the *Post*. For this act alone he is revered by his colleagues.

Numerous journalistic legends have arisen regarding Broder's political acumen. During the 1972 campaign for President, Broder bet gonzo journalist and McCarthy partisan Hunter Thompson $100 that Hubert Humphrey would win a crucial Democratic primary. Thompson kept the bet a secret, however, for fear that if Broder's judgment became known within the traveling press corps, it would tilt their reporting of the race in favor of Humphrey. Broder's greatest moment as a journalist came when he walked out on an interview with Henry Kissinger, then Secretary of State, because the latter insisted that their discussion be considered off the record.

A famously honest and hardworking reporter, pundit Broder nevertheless operates from an alarmingly romantic notion of how power in Washington is exercised. As what his colleague Richard Cohen calls "the Olympian voice of the mainstream political community," Broder holds an almost religious devotion to the notion that the salvation of the American political system lies in the rejuvenation of America's two political parties. Like Reston, he sometimes seems to revere the successful manipulation of the process irrespective of the content of the legislation for which it is being manipulated. A man of the floating center, Broder considers all ideologies (save the unspoken ideology of the pragmatist) to be anathema. He finds accusation of bias, either left or right, on the part of the media to be "laughable. There just isn't enough ideology in the average reporter," he insists, "to fill a thimble."

Despite the political upheavals of the sixties and seventies, Broder remains wedded to a narrow vision of political participation, which results in an inability to appreciate the significance of forces that fall outside the purview of traditional party politics. His manner of dealing with maverick politicians and political movements usually involves a mixture of scorn and denial. Upon the launching of Eugene McCarthy's insurgent effort to dethrone Lyndon Johnson in 1967, Broder harrumphed that "the frenzy of the anti-Johnson Democrats has now reached the point where it degrades the Democratic Party and those involved in the mutiny as much as it hurts the President himself." The fact that the mutineers felt they had an unconstitutional war to end apparently did not impress Broder. "Those Democrats," he lectured, "ought to realize that their own reputations are being affected by their behavior." Seventeen years and thousands of political interviews later, Broder took much the same tack during the brief 1984 candidacy of George McGovern, who, at the time, was suggesting that Walter Mondale's calls for higher taxes to pay for essentially Republican goals was not the best direction for his party to take. When McGovern distinguished himself, before withdrawing, by forcing the rest of the candidates to direct themselves to a panoply of issues they would have preferred to ignore, Broder demonstrated the personal and professional class for which he is rightly famous by issuing an apology in his syndicated column.* But the tendency remains in the DNA structure of Broder's reporting.

An even more troubling problem for the Broder brand of punditry is its frequent inability to distinguish between the surface and reality of political maneuver. Like most successful insiders, Broder is a sucker for a smooth-talking political operator. This makes him notoriously easy to manipulate, even when he is upholding the highest standards of his profession. It is not that Broder was unaware of the lengths to which the Reagan administration was willing to go to mislead the public; it's just that he never mentioned it when it was taking place. Consider *The Washington Post* Outlook section of March 22, 1987. On page one, the newspaper carried a thoughtful rumination by one David Broder on the dangers of White House manipulation, drawn from his book *Beyond the Front Page*:

> The White House propaganda machine has . . . enhanced the power of the communicator-in-chief. And it has raised to even greater importance the unmet challenge for the press to provide an alternative, non-propagandistic view of the presidency. This is a challenge we in the Washington press corps—and our editors and bosses—cannot afford to ignore.

Yet on the last page of the same section, Broder found himself helpless before this exact challenge. Of Reagan's speech earlier that week, during which the President continued to adhere to his preposterous notion that he had not intended to trade arms for hostages, nor to encourage his administration to contravene any laws on behalf of the Contras, Broder commented:

> The White House has repaired the damage from the Iran affair explosion and reopened for business. President Reagan's news conference on Thursday night provided the strongest evidence yet that the proprietor of the shop has regained a good measure of his emotional balance and is

---

*McGovern framed it and hung it on the wall of his dingy campaign office above a Dupont Circle Greek deli.

ready to reclaim his role at the center of government. The president did not change his story—or add much to it. But he showed the steadfastness and confidence that had been so conspicuously missing in the final months of 1986. Now Reagan can begin refocusing the nation's attention on his policy agenda without being accused of trying to avoid That Painful Subject.

What is Broder actually saying here? He does not claim that Reagan offered any coherent explanation for the Iran-Contra debacle nor for his own role in it. Neither does he explain what has changed inside the White House to prevent such occurrences from taking place in the future. Instead, he appears to be endorsing Reagan's attempt to downgrade the importance of the administration's willful subversion of the Constitution and its conduct of an illegal proxy war against Nicaragua. All Reagan truly demonstrated to Broder was the fact that, after five months of hiding, he could collect himself sufficiently to play the role of president for approximately forty minutes without lapsing into gibberish. Broder considered the Iran-Contra revelations to be not just a well-deserved comeuppance for a group of politicians who behaved contemptuously toward the Constitution, but a "disaster . . . and calamity for the nation." Thus he was particularly eager to grant the President, on the basis of this pathetic scale of performance, a pass for all of his dissimulations during the entire Iran-Contra affair and encourage him to "reclaim his role at the center of government."*

Similarly, during the trial of Oliver North, Broder wondered why "we are going through this expensive legal exercise" when "clearly the courts do not lack work." Ignoring the importance of completing the historical record on Iran-Contra as well as any "debt to society" owed by North for his crimes, Broder wondered "what more could be gained by sending [North] to Allenwood or one of the other federal prisons for white-collar prisoners?" Historians might wish to examine that statement when searching for reasons why Ronald Reagan and George Bush consistently managed to evade responsibility for the actions of their own administration.

Broder's inability to examine the forces underlying political behavior virtually paralyzes his analytical abilities, leaving him in thrall to the strictly

---

*More worrisome, perhaps, is the fact that Broder's statements were not defensible even in the limited sense he intended them. Reagan's public approval ratings remained, at the time, twenty points lower than they had been before the scandal. For the political elites to which Broder was addressing himself, Reagan's political reputation was thoroughly destroyed. See Robert N. Entman, *Democracy Without Citizens* (New York: Oxford University Press, 1989), pp. 70–71. See also Broder's attack on Kinsley and Buchanan for enjoying Iran-Contra too much, quoted in *The New York Times*, December 29, 1986.

show business elements of American politics. Broder was unimpressed by George Bush's 1988 presidential campaign until Bush gave what Broder thought was a good speech at the New Orleans convention. With this single speech (and, lest we forget, his appointment of Dan Quayle to be his running mate), Bush succeeded, in Broder's eyes, in dispelling his image as "the 'wimp' of the Doonesbury cartoons. Republican Senate Minority Leader [and failed presidential candidate] Bob Dole called him a 'tough, aggressive' candidate." Few, argued Broder, "would disagree."

That Broder thought it noteworthy that Dole should praise his party's presidential nominee is astonishing. Every loser in every presidential campaign has made the same gesture. Given the historic standards for this type of insincere flattery, Dole's limited concession constituted faint praise indeed. That Broder could be so impressed by a single speech—a speech, after all, that was written by Peggy Noonan under the direction of James Baker—is depressing. It indicates just how powerfully surface-level television images have replaced a politician's record as the ultimate arbiter of character and competence, even in the eyes of the most experienced and high-minded critics of the process.*

No one can doubt that David Broder is sincerely devoted to reversing the deteriorating foundations of American democracy. But by offering the politicians themselves such an overpowering degree of sympathy, however pure his motives, Broder contributes to that deterioration by playing the role of a toothless watchdog. Moreover, because Broder is generally considered to be the very archetype of a responsible liberal pundit in Washington, his failings have consequences far beyond the shortcomings of his own reportage. In addition to his prominence at the *Post*, his syndication in over three hundred papers means that Broder is the only non-right-wing pundit who begins to challenge the circulation numbers of the likes of Will, Kilpatrick, and Buchanan. Setting aside the inanity of television, the "responsible" political dialogue on the Great Issues of the Day is thus often perceived to fall between Will on the one hand and Broder on the other. Nowhere in this constricted conversation—at least until the Attorney General explains it himself—is there room for the possibility that the President is conducting a secret war, selling missiles to our sworn enemies. American politicians, it is assumed by all sides, are simply too honest, too committed, and too sensible

---

*When I raised this issue with Broder, he tried to point out how foolish I was being, without hurting my feelings. "There is no way to be polite about this," he told me. "To say that somebody is simply reciting a speech that somebody else writes is to totally misunderstand the process by which a speech gets put together. It suggests that there is only one speech, that it is handed to him, that he is passive about it. . . . I have to say respectfully that that is a simple-minded view of American politics." Author's interview.

to play such childish games. And certainly, even if such shenanigans were conceivable, none of them would dare lie to David Broder about it.

Broder's saving grace, finally, is his complete lack of pretense. If Washington insiders wish to take his ruminations overly seriously, that is their fault, not Broder's. He is just a reporter with a column. "I am not a terribly interesting or fluid writer and I don't have any deep philosophical thoughts . . . so if I didn't do the reporting," Broder claims, "I couldn't do the column."

Given Broder's untouchable reputation for judiciousness, modesty, and moderation, it came as a shock to insider Washington when, in November 1988, the usually soft-spoken, mild-mannered reporter emerged from his phone booth of the soul to launch a decidedly immoderate attack upon the ethics of a number of his colleagues. At a black-tie dinner in his honor given by the National Press Club, Broder took to the podium and lashed out at "a new hybrid creature, an androgynous binding of politician and journalist called The Washington Insider. One day, he or she is a public official or political operative; the next, a journalist or television commentator." Broder worried that if "the people . . . see us as part of a power-wielding clique of Insiders, they're going to be resentful as hell that they have no way to call us to account." Broder concluded his speech with the observation that he could not fathom why journalists would *want* to become insiders when "it's so damn much fun to be outsiders—irreverent, inquisitive, impudent, incorrigibly independent outsiders—thumbing our nose at authority and going our own way."

Broder was no doubt operating from a frightfully exaggerated notion of just how impudent he and his incorrigibly independent colleagues had been during the previous decade. After all, it was at the very same dinner that Secretary of State-designate James Baker III read a note from the President-elect noting that Broder had "come a long way" since the Bushes, the Broders, the Bakers, and others spent weeks touring China together in 1977 "as a kind of private, bonding experience. Read my lips," concluded Bush, employing the phrase that during the presidential campaign signaled an approaching falsehood, "David, you're a pro."

However black his own pot may have been, Broder put his finger on one of the hottest kettles in the ongoing degradation of American political commentary: the plethora of professional politicians who have been able to negotiate themselves into the punditocracy without first renouncing any further political ambitions.

In the old days, when high officials lost their posts, they retired to the relative obscurity of a Wall Street law firm or a university institute. The Wise

Man model, Dean Rusk, withdrew to a foreign policy institute somewhere in Georgia and was not heard from again for a quarter century. Even Clark Clifford, who remained a lifetime player at a K Street law firm, still had the good taste to devote himself to making money the old-fashioned and—until BCCI—much quieter way.

But beginning with the Nixon administration, losers gave up the graceful habit of slinking quietly into the night and began to offer their services as pundits. Some of them—Safire being the obvious case—turned out to be terrific. But most did not. Few were able to write without an eye over their shoulder toward their boss's (and often their own) place in history. Fewer still were trained as journalists or displayed any respect for the honest conventions of the trade. Moreover, one could not be certain that these ex-officials were not temporizing their judgments in the hopes of an even higher-level reappointment some day. Journalist/pundits had never been immune to these dangers, but the politician/pundits represented a completely higher order of corruption.

This trend, manageable under the Nixon, Ford, and Carter administrations, exploded beyond reasonable proportions during the Reagan years. Kenneth Adelman, Richard Perle, Mona Charen, David Gergen, Caspar Weinberger, Edwin Meese, Patrick Buchanan, Jeane Kirkpatrick, and Henry Kissinger (briefly) were all Reagan administration officials who came to enjoy the fruits of syndicated pontification. Kirkpatrick and Kissinger, however, are the only two who enjoy it in the *Post*. Their results ranged from merely bad to fundamentally corrupt.

As an ostensibly honest pundit, Jeane Kirkpatrick was so inept, her work was actually instructive. No pundit cliché was safe in her presence. Concerned about the post-Cold War evolution of the German psyche? Don't worry. "A Berlin taxi driver assured [her], 'we have learned that the civilized way to express power is in the economy.' " Curious how the entire continent of Europe is "feeling" about German reunification? Ask Dr. Kirkpatrick. "Europe is feeling ambivalent." Kirkpatrick's column manifested some of the same problems as Abe Rosenthal's, but she lacked his engaging flair for self-dramatization. Like Rosenthal, Kirkpatrick had a schoolchild's fondness for inconsequential, insignificant, unessential adjectives coupled with a poor poet's attraction to alliteration. The result, as when Kirkpatrick described young Chinese demonstrators as "hunted, haunted *and* hollow-eyed," recalled no one so much as Eliza Doolittle.

Laziness was also a problem. In attempting to offer Margaret Thatcher some strangely racially exclusive encouragement, Kirkpatrick called her "the only woman to achieve the position of Prime Minister or President of an Anglo-Saxon or European democracy." This led one *Post* reader to wonder if, in Kirkpatrick's judgment, "a) Norway is not in Europe or b) Norway is not a democracy or c) Norwegian Prime Minister Gro. Harlem Brundtland is not a woman."

More serious was Kirkpatrick's habit of attempting to rewrite reality to fit the political and ideological contours of her past and future political career. In March 1986, following a dishonest Philippine election stolen by forces loyal to Ferdinand Marcos, a typically attractive "authoritarian" government according to the Kirkpatrick doctrine, the former UN Representative accused "American liberals" of orchestrating a "campaign . . . to suggest the existence of an anti-Marcos 'consensus' inside the United States government." The effect of such "meddling" was "interference in Philippine politics." Americans should "cease" their "interference," she insisted, or could expect to suffer the fate of the explorer Magellan, who was "hacked to death" by "the Philippine tribes." The day before the column appeared, however, Reagan administration officials began edging away from their embrace of Marcos on the Sunday-morning talk shows. Kirkpatrick, out on a shaky limb, quickly sent out a revised version of the column in which she observed that "charges of fraud destroyed [the] perception" of "a creditable election." The two columns appeared simultaneously the next day in various newspapers. In another column, this one on El Salvador, Kirkpatrick promised her readers that "there was no question" that President Jose Napoleon Duarte would do any of the things with regard to the upcoming Salvadoran elections that he had, unbeknownst to her, announced he *would* do the previous evening. In this case, however, there was no time even to attempt a rewrite.

Henry Kissinger, as always, presented a unique set of problems. Standards had become so lax within the punditocracy by the 1980s that the fact that Kissinger lied to reporters and placed wiretaps on his staff's discussions with them while in office did not appear to disqualify him as an ostensibly honest pundit. Nor did Kissinger's service on Ronald Reagan's Foreign Intelligence Advisory Board, which offered him full access to the nation's most sensitive secrets simultaneous to the launching of his column. When a Kissinger controversy finally did erupt in the spring of 1989, it was not over these issues, nor even that during the Reagan administration he had served as its Central American adviser, but rather over his reaction to the Tiananmen Square massacre in China.

Following the massacre, Kissinger wrote that "no government in the world would have tolerated having the main square of its capital occupied for eight weeks" and that "a crackdown was therefore inevitable." America's ability to ignore the murderous force with which the "inevitable" took place, keeping in mind "the extraordinary sensitivity of any Chinese leader to what appears to be foreign intervention," became, in Kissinger's eyes, "a test of our political maturity." China, according to Kissinger, remained "too important for American national security to risk the relationship on the emotions of the moment."

Three aspects of Kissinger's analysis stood out immediately. First, he hoped to whitewash the mass murder of a people by its government with an appeal to alleged American geopolitical interests. Lives sacrificed upon the altar of "national security" were nothing new for Henry Kissinger, but it had become an increasingly tired excuse in the aftermath of Mikhail Gorbachev's dismantling of the Soviet military empire. Second, Kissinger proved to be demonstrably wrong. The governments of Czechoslovakia, East Germany, Bulgaria, Nepal, and even Gorbachev's Soviet Union all witnessed massive demonstrations in their public squares in the aftermath of the Tiananmen crackdown. These resulted in forced concessions and a transition to a more democratic rule. Even the neo-Fascist government of Augusto Pinochet in Chile—whose existence owed so much to Kissingerian diplomacy—saw the wisdom, in 1989, of handing over the reins of power to its opposition in the streets. Only in Romania did the dictators adhere to Kissingerian principles, and the decision set off a brief civil war.

What damaged Kissinger, however, was not the substance of his analysis but the atmospherics that surrounded it. The Wall Street Journal revealed that as he was apologizing for the Chinese butchers, Kissinger was sitting on an announcement of a limited partnership called "China Ventures," to pool $75 million raised from U.S. investors for joint ventures with the China International Trust and Investment Corp. While Kissinger said he had put the initiative on hold following the bloody events of June 6, the timing smelled bad to everyone. As head of the super-secret consulting firm bearing his name, Kissinger had long given super-secret advice to foreign corporations for hundreds of thousands of dollars in super-secret fees. * But this time his timing was so egregious and his words so offensive to Americans who had seen the young heroes killed live on their television sets that, for the first time in decades, Kissinger felt compelled to defend himself in public. Kissinger called the story "outrageous" and blamed the charges on those who sought to "blacken" his reputation. He described as "McCarthyism" any attempt to link his views on China to his business interests. Journal Washington bureau chief Al Hunt said later that he had "never seen the kind of reaction that he saw with Henry." No one, including Kissinger, Hunt points out, suggested the story was inaccurate. "What they basically said was that we didn't have the right to address the issue." Soon the entire punditocracy lit up with angry denunciations of the Journal's

---

*Kissinger did this, though, not because he liked to, but because he had to. "Making money is actually boring," he complained in his final words to diplomatic adversary Andrei Gromyko, "even if it is necessary." See Andrei Gromyko, Memoirs (Garden City, NY: Doubleday, 1989), p. 394.

temerity. Former Kissinger aide Winston Lord rose to his friend's defense with a ringing statement of the decidedly unobvious, insisting: "No one can question his motives." As always, the controversy petered out and Kissinger came out on top. Just five months after the massacre, Kissinger accompanied his client, Maurice Greenberg, chairman of the American International Group (AIG), to Beijing, where the two men met with Deng Xiaoping and secured an agreement, according to CBS's "60 Minutes," to expand AIG's business there. At the time, Deng was "unavailable" for meetings with U.S. Ambassador James Lilly. (For a lengthy discussion of complications arising from Kissinger's business ties to firms engaged in working with Saddam Hussein's Iraqi regime, see chapter 12, pages 256–257.)

When asked, in the aftermath of the China episode, how he felt about the fact that Henry Kissinger was now published regularly in what was then his newspaper, Ben Bradlee sighed, looked up at the ceiling, and slowly replied, "I feel badly about it." He should have, but the appearance of Kissinger and Kirkpatrick in *The Washington Post* was not Bradlee's decision but Greenfield's. Geyelin, Greenfield's predecessor, accuses both Kirkpatrick and Kissinger of "recycling old ideas and tending toward their place in history." In some ways, though, both columns are useful. As with caricature and portraiture, sometimes only by thorough exaggeration are the features of an object made sufficiently clear to see its essence. Kirkpatrick and Kissinger may provide the clearest example of the most egregious violations of the ethics journalists profess to live by. But *The Washington Post* op-ed page is filled with writers and political operatives who transgress these rules on a less grandiose scale virtually every day.

Broder's noble efforts notwithstanding, *The Washington Post* op-ed page is literally the worst place in the world from which to launch a campaign against insiders. No institution did more during the Reagan era to invest insiderdom with a false authority that derived simply from its proximity to power. None did more to legitimize notions of governance that were not merely untested but in many instances contrary to common sense. It is significant that Broder worries that people will start to see the media as a "power-wielding clique of Insiders." What would be truly dangerous would be if the Washington media—specifically the punditocracy—really did constitute a "power-wielding clique of Insiders" and the public, still in thrall to the myths of a politically and intellectually independent Fourth Estate, failed to perceive it.

8

"WE ARE THE WILD MEN"

Ray Shaw, the onetime president and director of Dow Jones & Company, may or may not have had strong feelings about the complex and convoluted lines that divide punditry from politicking. But when he found himself on a New Jersey commuter train platform one balmy June evening in 1978, confronted by a *Wall Street Journal* editorial writer handing out campaign literature for a Republican senatorial candidate, he knew instinctively that something was amiss. Jude Wanniski, the writer in question, had allowed himself to become so convinced by the righteousness of his cause—that of the nascent economic philosophy labeled "supply side"—that he had jettisoned all journalistic decorum. Wanniski was, in fact, writing speeches, brokering political deals, and reportedly throwing the paper's weight around quite crudely in Washington.* On the leafleting matter, Wanniski recalls that it took place during what he remembers to be "my most manic phase. The only way I could see to elevate the supply-side idea was in the political realm. Without it, the United States would not find a path back to economic growth and the whole world would implode. You know, war and depression, the whole thing." Of course, supply side did eventually triumph

---

*The *Journal's* Washington bureau complained to their boss of Wanniski's preaching to the congressmen they were trying to cover. Some congressmen reportedly insisted that Wanniski had twisted their arms with threats of favorable or unfavorable publicity. At the 1976 Republican Convention, Wanniski wrote Jack Kemp's floor speech and did his utmost to broker a deal between the Kemp and Reagan forces. According to Kemp, however, it was done without his permission.

and, as readers will be aware, war and depression were by and large avoided. But this did not save Wanniski's job; he left the paper to form a consulting firm shortly thereafter.

The story of *The Wall Street Journal*'s editorial page ability to reverse decades of official U.S. economic doctrine in the late 1970s and early 1980s has few historic precedents. According to the economic historian Wayne Parsons, the *Journal* "had an absolutely vital role to play in disseminating and legitimating the ideas which became associated with Ronald Reagan and without its support it is difficult to see how the supply-side argument could possibly have achieved such a leading position in the economic policy debates." The closest parallel, the victory of John Maynard Keynes over classical economics in the late 1930s and early 1940s, had been decades in the making. Moreover, Keynesianism entered the political lexicon the hard way: by breaking through the walls of orthodoxy at the Harvard economics department. It received important but hardly decisive support in the public arena from young Walter Lippmann in *The New Republic* as well, but it was not until after the Great Depression—and the complete ruination of the old system—that Keynesian assumptions began to supplant the ruling elite's conventional economic wisdom.

Wanniski and the supply-siders at the *Journal* editorial page played a completely different ball game. They bypassed academia entirely, propagating their ideas only via regular contributors to their own page and at seminars with tiny groups of like-minded politicians and Counter-establishment think-tank analysts, particularly those at the Heritage Foundation and the Hoover Institute. And while the 1970s did see the first prolonged period of stagflation— what one economist called the "diabolic double helix" of rising unemployment coupled with rising inflation—this can hardly be compared to the political and intellectual wreckage that lay strewn on the road to the New Deal. Few events in recent American history demonstrate more succinctly the new power of the punditocracy than the replacement, in the 1980s, of Harvard, Brookings, and Keynes as the nation's traditional guardians of economic policy by Jude Wanniski, Robert Bartley, and *The Wall Street Journal*.

The *Journal*'s role within the punditocracy is a paradoxical one. According to a Brookings Institution study, the *Journal* is read daily by approximately half the Washington press corps and 60 percent of "high federal officials."*

---

*The numbers for the *Journal* are 51% for journalists and 62% for officials. For *The Washington Post*, they are 89% for reporters and 90% for officials. *The New York Times* is read daily by 73% of those journalists questioned but only 45% of the federal officials. No other paper has remotely as wide a readership. The *Los Angeles Times*, for instance, is read by 5% of journalists and 4% of high federal officials. See Stephen Hess, *The Washington Reporters* (Washington, DC: The Brookings Institution, 1981), p. 25.

Nationally, fewer than 30 percent of the paper's readers pay regular attention to the editorials, less than half the number who say they buy it for its business news. Among Washington insiders, however, these numbers are quite probably reversed. Business news is important in Washington largely to the degree it affects politics. At least until the recession of 1991, the insider Washington economy had been almost fully insulated from that of the rest of the nation.

The prestige of the *Journal*'s Washington bureau has grown enormously under the direction of its extremely competent, high-profile chief, Al Hunt. But ironically, it is Hunt's own avocation as a pundit on "Washington Week" and "The Capital Gang," coupled with his power marriage to anchorwoman Judy Woodruff, that propels him to the punditocracy stratosphere. As for the *Journal* itself, against all the rules of insiderdom, the unsigned opinions of its editorial page have, under Bartley, carved out a tremendously influential perch in the insider dialogue without so much as a Washington office or even a widely recognized face. Bartley himself tends quietly to business in his spacious, oak-filled office atop the World Financial Center in Battery Park City, Manhattan. He does not appear on television and is amazed, he says, at just how "dumb" his friends like Mark Shields and Robert Novak sound when they do. Indeed, it is difficult to imagine Bartley, a soft-spoken man with a patrician's gentle demeanor, managing even to complete a sentence on "The McLaughlin Group."

But Bartley's manner has little in common with his politics, or for that matter, his style of argument. "We are the wild men," said his comrade, Wanniski, of the supply-siders centered at the *Journal*, and he wasn't kidding. Beginning in 1972, when the midwestern conservative firebrand was given de facto control over them (the title "editor" did not follow until 1979), the *Journal*'s editorials have had a harsh and unforgiving tone. Throughout the Bartley era, *Journal* editorials have been among the most dependable allies of the Far Right elements of the Republican party on both foreign and economic issues in the entire punditocracy, going so far as to attack other journalists in advance of their published works when they fail to hew to the administration line.*

Quite frequently, ideology drove Bartley's page so relentlessly that it appeared to blind him to the facts published in his own paper. In 1980, a *Journal* reporter broke a story proving that an alleged $100 million administration cost offered up by a group of California oil firms protesting a new

---

*Donald Graham says he enjoys reading Bartley's editorials but he would be "very uncomfortable if the tone of the *Post* editorial page was as harsh and intolerant as the typical *Journal* editorial." Author's interview.

state tax was, in fact, a wildly exaggerated estimate of the expense of administering the tax. Two days later, the editorial page noted that "according to one estimate, enforcement of the tax would cost taxpayers $100 million. . . ." The pattern repeated itself in 1984, when Washington reporter David Rogers discovered that the CIA had been illegally mining Nicaragua's harbors. The story ran on page six and was picked up by *The Washington Post*. Six days later, the editorial page, standing foursquare behind the Contra war, criticized members of Congress for leaking the information to the *Post*.

Ben Bagdikian, former dean of the journalism school at the University of California, Berkeley, explained the dichotomy between the editorial page and the news pages as follows:

> Executives and stockholders really do want to know the unpleasant truth about corporate life when it affects their careers or incomes. At the same time, however, most of them are true believers in the rhetoric of free enterprise, whose imperfections and contradictions are standard content in *The Wall Street Journal*. By reporting critical stories about realities in particular industries in the news columns, but singing the grand old hymns of unfettered laissez-faire on the editorial pages, the *Journal* has it both ways.

Bartley himself attributes the occasional conflicts to the fact that "the front page has its own sources and we have ours. We do our own reporting, and I have never quite figured out how the reader suffers by having access to two sets of sources."

As is typical of most neoconservatives, Bartley stuck to the straight and narrow on most Reaganite matters, excluding those issues with the significant exception of those involving the Religious Right. The paper strongly supported the various Reagan Doctrine counterinsurgencies of the 1980s and plowed considerable ground beneath the construction of Reagan's SDI program. "Mutual Assured Destruction is immoral," Bartley insisted, "and we tried to keep the issue alive until Reagan proposed SDI." Wanniski attributes what he terms Bartley's "softness on social issues like abortion" to the editor's desire to "take some of the 'throw the orphans into the snow' pressure off the right wing." In Wanniski's view, however, this was eventually accomplished far more effectively by his ex-boss's embrace of supply-side economics.

Determining the influence exercised by financial punditry within insider Washington is an even murkier matter than determining that of the political punditocracy. Most insiders, like most people, understand little about economics. Editors, moreover, can't seem to make up their mind about whether economic news is of special or general interest to their readership. The *Times* consigns its financial pundits to the paper's Business section, where they have little impact on the high politics of the Washington insider debate. The *Post* does publish Hobart Rowen, Robert Samuelson, and now Bob Kuttner, on the op-ed page, but they are not considered to be among the page's heavy hitters.

Newsweek probably did more for the institution of economic punditry than any other publication when, in September 1966, it invited Milton Friedman and Paul Samuelson to contribute regular tri-weekly columns. Samuelson stuck to Keynesian assumptions, but tended to explain rather than preach. He was Restonian in his prejudice in favor of good sense over bad. His ideological predilections generally tended in the direction of: "This is not a time for taking chances or laissez-faire. It is a time for prudent action."

Milton Friedman could not have been more different, either by temperament, ambition, or intellectual inclination. Through his *Newsweek* column, along with his best-selling books and a few strategically scheduled television series, Friedman established himself during the 1970s as perhaps the single most influential American economist in history.

Friedman was a Keynesian in the sense that he believed in the power of ideas to move society. He hurled himself into the Keynesian conventional wisdom with popular tracts relentlessly attacking the notion of positive government interference in the economy, beginning with *Capitalism and Freedom* in 1962, and sustaining this consistent line through the best-selling election-year tracts *Free to Choose* (1980) and *The Tyranny of the Status Quo* (1984), both co-authored with his wife, Rose. Friedman's ideas were generally considered beyond the pale of reason when he began his attack on the Keynesian orthodoxy; he was the only member of the profession to advise Barry Goldwater in 1964. But through *Newsweek*, the books, his television series, and his association with Counter-establishment think tanks, particularly AEI and the Hoover Institution, this bald, diminutive professor managed to reeducate a nation on the principles of economics. As his intellectual adversary, John Kenneth Galbraith, observed, "the age of John Maynard Keynes gave way to the age of Milton Friedman."

Friedman's academic delineation of what he termed "Monetarism," in which the health of the economy rested on the government's ability to provide a stable, tightly controlled money supply, eventually divided the profession between various factions of Monetarists and Keynesians (with occasional Marxist outliers in selected institutions) and earned Friedman the economists' equivalent of the 1976 Nobel Prize. But Friedman's most important contributions came in the political arena. Most significant was his sustained attack on the efficacy of government intervention in the economy. "I know hardly any do-gooder legislation . . . which on examination of its full consequences, does not do more harm than good," he told readers. "We have heard much these past few years about using the government to protect the consumer," he explained. "A far more urgent problem is to protect the consumer from the government."

Previous to the Reagan administration's walk on the supply side, Friedmanite experiments had been undertaken by three different national governments. All vastly increased, at least in the short and medium term, the economic misery of the masses.* "It is possible," worried William F. Buckley, Jr., at the time, that Friedmanite theories "suffer from the overriding disqualification that they simply cannot get a sufficient exercise in democratic situations—because it takes longer for them to produce results than the public is prepared to wait."

To the growing number of conservatives in Friedman's corner, Buckley's diagnosis underscored a particularly serious problem for a nation addicted to instant gratification. Before Friedman's Monetarist prescription could be considered politically palatable in the United States once again, it would require a kind of sugar coating; one that would offset its harsh side effects long enough to allow the medicine to take hold.

Supply-side economics, as preached by its evangelists at the *Journal*, was not simply sugar-coated; it was the sweet gooey essence of the stuff. As outlined in the *Journal* editorial pages by Wanniski, Bartley, Arthur Laffer, Paul Craig Roberts, Norman Ture, and George Gilder, supply side seemed a money tree. The less the government taxed, the more money it received.† Counterintuitive, perhaps, to those educated in the shadow of Lord Keynes,

---

*The three experiments were conducted by Richard Nixon, Augusto Pinochet, and Margaret Thatcher.

†Wanniski and other supply-side partisans will argue that this is a caricature of their ideas. It isn't. The argument of the Laffer curve is that high taxes are a disincentive to work. At two points on a curve plotted with taxes on one axis and government revenues on the other, the latter will equal zero: that of zero taxes and that of 100% taxes. The goal for policymakers is to locate the point on the curve where sufficiently low taxes provide the greatest level of revenue. If the nation is already above that point, as the supply-siders clearly argued the United States was in 1980, than the entrepreneurial forces unleashed by a tax cut would indeed raise government revenues. In the spring of 1981, Laffer wrote of the proposed Reagan tax cuts that "it is reasonable to conclude that each of the proposed reductions in tax rates would, in terms of overall revenues, be self-financing in less than two years. Thereafter, each installment would provide a positive contribution to overall tax receipts." See Arthur Laffer, "Government Exactions and Revenue Deficiencies," *Cato Journal*, Spring 1981, p. 21.

yet in truth the idea was one of the oldest in economics. (Indeed, it was taught as gospel to all students who, like Ronald Reagan, passed through Eureka College between the years 1928 and 1932.) Deriving from the writings of Jean-Baptiste Say, a French follower of Adam Smith, supply side reintroduced the classical notion known as Say's Law: Supply creates its own demand. Keynes had buried Say under an avalanche of counterexamples drawn from the Great Depression in his *General Theory of Employment, Interest and Money* (1936), but the supply-siders were able to resurrect him amidst the stagflation of the seventies.

The story of how supply-side economics came to be the official doctrine of the government of the United States of America with virtually no support from the economics profession has already been documented. What is important to understand about the doctrine is its Holy Grail aspect. After half a century of orthodoxy in which it had always been assumed that fiscal and monetary policy was a Hobson's choice on the Phillip's curve between inflation and unemployment, the hard-headed captains of industry at the *Journal* were suddenly promising painless gain. Philosophically, this was as un-Friedmanite as it was anti-Keynesian. But politically, it turned out to be irresistible. For, whatever its murky intellectual justification, supply side promised an end run around the primary dilemma that had plagued the American government since the "escalation without taxation" policies of the Johnson administration: how to provide a level of services and military forces far beyond that for which Americans were willing to pay.

The new theory offered the new Counter-establishment something for everyone. During the post-Vietnam/pre-Reagan interregnum, the insider mind had often appeared to be drowning in a sea of jeremiads, from Christopher Lasch's *The Culture of Narcissism* to Lester Thurow's *The Zero-Sum Society*, the Club of Rome's infamous *Limits to Growth*, and Jimmy Carter's all-purpose malaise. Supply side provided the equivalent of a psychological lifeboat.* For Freidmanites, it promised a close watch on the money supply to control inflation and keep interest rates low. For conservative politicians, it provided an irresistible election issue: lower taxes. For wealthy voters and campaign contributors, it promised free money. For Bartley and *The Wall Street Journal* editorial page, supply side provided a stick with which to beat its enemies and the vehicle by which it could

---

*Supply-side mania, hardly coincidentally, corresponded almost exactly with the reheated Cold War of the neoconservatives and the social offensive of the Christian New Right as a means of redefining the political dialogue on the basis of "traditional American values." In this case, the values were laissez-faire economics and unquenchable Yankee optimism.

distinguish itself as the most influential economic voice in the national political dialogue.

Under the previous editorial regime, headed for decades by two-time Pulitzer-winner Vermont Royster, the page had been a dependable respository of conservative conventional wisdom. In economics, that meant unlimited support for free enterprise and opposition to government interference. Monetary policy was broadly Friedmanite. When Robert Bartley took over the editorial page in 1974, he was consciously searching for a way to shake up his readership. Under Irving Kristol's tutelage, Bartley wanted the page to adopt a more combative tone toward what he considered to be the liberal establishment—to "capture some of the intellectual appeal traditionally associated with liberalism." To this end, he recruited a bevy of prestigious regular contributors. They included Kristol, economists Walter Heller, Paul McCracken, Herbert Stein, Martin Feldstein, Charles L. Schultze, and the liberal historian Arthur Schlesinger, Jr. Later to this list were added whipping boys Hodding Carter, Michael Kinsley, and most astoundingly, Alexander Cockburn.* These additions had the effect of livening a page that had been drifting like deadwood for decades. Instead of being merely America's best business newspaper, the *Journal* became the Counter-establishment's newspaper of ideas.

Bartley's very first move, he recalls, was to try to hire as an editorial writer "a young assistant to Senator Gordon Allott by the name of George Will." When Will demurred, wishing to remain closer to the seat of national power, Bartley went after Jude Wanniski. The son of a Pennsylvania coal miner and raised on the streets of Brooklyn, Wanniski came to the *Journal* by way of newspapers in Alaska, Las Vegas, and finally Dow Jones's own *National Observer.*† He had gone off in search of journalistic fortune, hoping to emulate his hero, the mild-mannered centrist pundit James Reston. But he returned from his sojourn with the fiery eyes of a zealot

*The appointment of the rigidly Marxist lady's man as a regular columnist aroused feverish opposition on the part of many of the paper's readers and Bartley's ideological allies. For a brief time, Bartley even printed up "Alex Cockburn complaint cards" to give to the complainers. Cockburn's romance with Lally Weymouth, daughter of Katherine and Philip Graham, and his marriage to the novelist Katherine Kilgore, the granddaughter of Barney Kilgore, the famous *Journal* editor of the forties and fifties, inspired what must be the cleverest observation Joseph Sobran ever made: "Alex Cockburn's scorn for the men who created the wealth of America is exceeded only by his admiration for the women who inherited it." Quoted in Charlotte Hays, "Alex Cockburn's Popular Front: The Nation's Wittiest Soviet Apologist Has an Eye for Rich Men's Daughters," *Policy Review,* Summer 1984, p. 60. In a 1989 interview, Bartley allowed that, personally, he found the column to be "not as interesting as [it] used to be." He discontinued Cockburn's column, along with that of his irregular colleagues, in January 1991, whereupon it was picked up by the *Los Angeles Times.*

†Dow Jones published the weekly *National Observer* from February 1962 through July 1977.

without a cause. Initially, when Bartley made the offer, Wanniski protested that he knew nothing of editorial writing. "All it takes is arrogance," replied Bartley. That, all agree, the good Lord had given Jude Wanniski in generous measure. George Will, no slouch in the confidence department himself, once said of his competition, "I wish I were as confident of something as he is of everything."

An ebullient character of almost limitless enthusiasms, Wanniski taught Bartley what the latter calls "the power of the outrageous." Nowhere was this more apparent than in the area of monetary and fiscal policy. Wanniski had no formal economic training himself, but upon arriving in Washington, had found himself a willing tutor by the name of Arthur Laffer. Laffer had served under George Shultz in Richard Nixon's Office of Management and Budget, where his unorthodox forecasting method had made him a brief laughing-stock.* He returned to the University of Chicago, where his life went from terrible to much worse. Compulsively overeating from nervousness, Laffer ballooned in size. As a welcome-home greeting, his department sponsored a lecture by Paul Samuelson entitled "Why They Are Laughing at Laffer."

Soon afterward the department leaders decided that Laffer, who had been the youngest member of the Chicago economics faculty to be given tenure, had misled them about the completion of his doctorate. "It was horrible," Laffer wrote. "I knew there was no way on God's earth that I could make it in the profession. So, I went other routes—the press, the political process, consulting." Fortunately for Laffer's national reputation, Jude Wanniski, ostensibly just an editorial writer at the *Journal*, had a talent for all three.

By the time Bartley hired Wanniski at the *Journal*, he had become more than just a supply-side convert: he was a dedicated disciple in the fully religious sense of the word. Laffer, building on the teachings of his Canadian mentor, Robert Mundell, was pushing a policy mix that called for a simultaneous (Friedmanite) contraction on the money supply and an enormous (Keynesian) reduction in the rate of personal income taxes on the wealthy. The former method was intended to control inflation; the latter to spur investment. The combination of lower taxes plus a stable money supply would, insisted the supply-sider, unleash a flood of pent-up entrepreneurship, displacing inefficient government spending with an explosion of growth in the private sector.

It took Bartley nearly two years to convince himself of the wisdom of Wanniski's new vision. But once Bartley was in for his own dime, the page

---

*The predictions that caused Laffer so much heartache—those for the 1971 GNP—turned out to be far closer to the mark than did those of any of his competitors at the time.

was in for all of the *Journal's* dollars. The page's economics columns soon became a kind of tribal drum for the businessman's new theology. Wanniski would call Laffer every morning, and with Bartley's guidance, write supply-side editorials on the basis of their conversations. "It was our story," recalls Bartley with undue modesty, "and we ran with it."

The first full revelation of the supply-side Word, Wanniski's "The Mundell-Laffer Hypothesis: A New View of the World Economy," appeared, quite appropriately, in Kristol's neoconservative policy journal, *The Public Interest*, in 1975. Before Wanniski's article, neither of the two economists knew they had fashioned a hypothesis, and in any case, the piece met with a yawn within the academic community, given its lack of a rigorous theoretical basis or mathematical modeling. Conventional wisdom at the time—as embodied by the Brookings Institution—attributed the breakdown of traditional Keynesian relationships to "outside shocks" to the system. The most prominent of these were the impact of the trebling of oil prices in 1973 and 1979, as well as the delayed inflationary impact of the surreptitious funding of the Vietnam War. But Wanniski and Bartley soon won over a small cadre of Washington politicians, a group whom Wanniski would call "the cabal." In time, this cabal would conquer the most important intellectual territory in the land: the "mind" of the 1980 Republican presidential candidate.

Within the upper reaches of the Republican party, supply side was not exactly a difficult sell. Potential presidential candidates looking for an issue with which to defeat Jimmy Carter were not terribly skittish about embracing the notion of an enormous tax cut as a campaign plank. The success of the 1978 tax revolt initiative in California, Proposition 13, implied almost revolutionary potential for the issue. Quarterback-turned-conservative Republican Congressman Jack Kemp had picked up the tax-cutting ball and begun to run with the issue with Nagurskilike abandon—soon moving it to the top of his party's agenda. What the politicians lacked, however, was a respectable economic theory to justify their political intuition.

Political prayers were answered in the form of a chance meeting between Wanniski and Kemp. Irving Kristol had suggested that Wanniski stop in and see Kemp, whom the editorial writer had previously considered to be little more than "a right-wing football player." Wanniski stopped into Kemp's office while researching another story at 10:00 A.M. one morning, spent the rest of the day with Kemp, and later went home to the congressman's house for macaroni and cheese. "I think I've just fallen in love," Wanniski told a friend that night. Before Jack Kemp, "I was just ammunition in search of a weapon." Kemp assumed the role of an all-but-caped Supply-Side Crusader, with his staff members, economists

Paul Craig Roberts (soon to be Wanniski's replacement at the *Journal*) and Norman Ture, sharing the role of Robin. Soon all three began preaching the gospel on the campaign trail and throughout the halls of Congress.

Following the conversion of Bartley and Kemp, the road to Reagan proved a relatively straightforward one. The candidate himself was an easy mark. He had never learned Keynesian economics and experienced extreme emotional discomfort at the thought of taxing a rich person. The underlying psychology of supply side resonated perfectly with the mythology of a once potent, self-sufficient capitalist class in America that had been tied by the tenterhooks of intrusive government interference. This was Cowboy Capitalism with a vengeance.

Moreover, in order to keep Kemp from challenging him, Reagan and his handlers had straightforward political incentives to hitch their wagons to the supply-side star. There was some confusion in the Reagan camp, but as David Stockman later recalled, once Kemp, Laffer, and Wanniski had "thoroughly hosed [Reagan] down with supply-side doctrines . . . it set off a symphony in his ears. He knew instantly that it was true and would never doubt it a moment thereafter."

From 1974 through much of the 1980 presidential campaign the *Journal* held a near monopoly on the supply-side discourse. Professional economists simply refused to take the notion seriously, and the nation's other op-ed writers, with the significant exception of the fire-breathing Evans and Novak, saw no reason to do so, either.

One could argue, quite convincingly, that the economics profession's decision to ignore supply side was both arrogant and short-sighted. However unscientific it may have seemed, particularly with regard to the dense econometric modeling that dominated economic discourse in Cambridge and New Haven, supply side was the only train leaving the station. Keynesian explanations no longer sufficed. It was up to the professionals to either derail it or jump on board; instead, they could not even bring themselves to look up from their computer models and wave. As a result, nowhere was the theory subjected to anything like the rigorous testing one would expect before the world's largest economy literally bets its future savings on it. For the better part of the half-decade that the assault was under way, the *Journal* editorial pages provided virtually entire public discourse on the doctrine that would soon govern the organization of the American economy. In fact, the only serious academic discussion of the model during this period appeared in an article by Kemp aide Paul Craig Roberts, in the Summer 1978 issue of Irving Kristol's *The Public Interest*. It should surprise no one that the author provided an altogether favorable view.

Liberal economists involved in the political process viewed Reagan's supply-side rhetoric with undisguised contempt. Speaking to *The Wash-*

ington Journalism Review in the spring of 1980, Lester Thurow, now dean of MIT's business school, called the Reagan economic plan "absolute nonsense" and observed that its policies "don't make any sense from the point of view of conservative economists, much less anybody else." But like most observers, Thurow probably expected Reagan to cave in to the old Keynesian orthodoxy once tutored by the responsible members of Washington insider-dom. What this view missed, however, was the degree to which the old establishment had exhausted itself fighting the losing battles of the seventies. Once the Reagan entourage came to town, exuding confidence in themselves and cloaking their economic policies in patriotic metaphors, the emasculated political class, tired of feeling helpless in the face of economic equations it could no longer understand, simply threw up its hands and shot craps with the nation's monetary and fiscal policy. Although most insiders did not even pretend to understand it, they were sufficiently riled up by the supply-siders' apocalyptic rhetoric to act upon the ever present American compulsion to *do something.* As monetarist Herbert Stein wrote on the *Journal* op-ed page:

> Economists cannot say that they know with certainty that the Kemp-Roth tax cut would not raise the revenue. They can, or should only say that the available evidence makes the outcome extremely improbable. It may turn out that there is human life on Mars. But I would not invest much in McDonald's franchise on the planet, and I wouldn't bet the nation's economic policy on the assumption that the tax cut will increase the revenue.

Whatever defects Wanniski or Bartley are likely to admit regarding the "riverboat gamble" they helped inspire, they blame on the manner in which it was implemented. Wanniski says he tried to warn Stockman that "interest rates would not come down without recession, unless there was a monetary reform, that it was not a fiscal problem, and deferring the tax cuts would only invite recession and expand the deficits." But Stockman who, according to Wanniski, "never really understood the supply-side framework," was determined to do it his way, with budget cuts, massive military spending increases, and without controlling the money supply. The result was a kind of superheated military Keynesianism, replete with exploding government debt, declining savings, decreased national investment, and a massive redistribution of national income from the poorest Americans to the richest. * In short, the plan accomplished none of what its promoters had promised

---

*During the 1980s, according to Congressional Budget Office data, the richest 1% of U.S. families enjoyed 60% of the nation's after-tax income gain. See Sylvia Nasar, "The 1980's: A Very Good Time to Be Very Rich," *The New York Times,* March 5, 1992, p. 1.

and made our economy's most important problems worse. "The big problem with Dave," Wanniski later insisted, "was his youth."

Stockman's various decoys and dissimulations during the early days of the supply-side adventure at least had the virtue of demonstrating for all to see just how supine the punditocracy can be in the face of a concerted White House propaganda barrage. When then–*Washington Post* editor William Greider published OMB director Stockman's confessional in the November 1981 *Atlantic Monthly* nine months into the Reagan administration, insider Washington reacted as if the President had suddenly been found to be selling arms to the Ayatollah. In language that anticipated the upcoming Savings and Loan scandal—the legislative basis of which the *Journal* editorial page had supported wholeheartedly just six months earlier—Stockman observed that the Reagan administration had "lost control" of its supply-side tax cut policies, leading powerful and influential "hogs" to "feed" on the new Reagan ideology.* The fact that supply-side economics had been nothing more than a "Trojan horse to bring down the top rate" of taxation for America's richest citizens, as Stockman said, should have come as no surprise to those insiders plugged into the political process. All that was required was an ability to read the coded dialogue of administration press leaks. Yet, as Greider noted, "it was as though editors and reporters had no memory of what they themselves had been reporting for months."†

Clearly the economic pundits had failed the American public. They had no inkling whatever that the man most responsible for turning the President's confident economic philosophy into policy viewed the entire episode as a cynical manipulation of the public's gullibility for the purpose of raiding the Treasury and feeding the "hogs." But they had done so by fooling themselves as well. The relentless amnesia of the American political process was never more apparent than in the days that followed the Stockman article's appearance. The President's men concocted a story line in which young Davey was taken to a metaphorical "woodshed" by an angry but forgiving President, who whipped some sense into his errant young adviser,

---

*With regard to the S&L scandal, the *Journal* promised in June 1981 that "complete deregulation would allow [the thrifts] to do all the things that banks can do: make all types of loans and enlarge the scope of their investments." In what may go down as the worst prediction in all economic forecasting history—quite a statement, I know—Bartley and company observed that "the beauty of these solutions is that they're cheap." See "Thrift Sale," *The Wall Street Journal*, June 29, 1981.

†"It's kind of hard to sell 'trickle down,' " Stockman explained, "so the supply-side formula was the only way to get a tax policy that was really 'trickle down. . . .' Supply-side is 'trickle-down' theory." See William Greider, *The Education of David Stockman and Other Americans*, rev. edn. (New York: New American Library, 1986). These quotes appear on pp. 47, 48, and 55.

presumably eliciting a promise never to tell the truth to the American people again. In fact, Reagan never expressed much anger toward Stockman. The "woodshed" meeting was a complete fiction, generated to take the political heat off the moment and submerge the truths laid bare in the Stockman story into the mythical image of Reagan as a strong but merciful patriarch.

The substance of Stockman's story could hardly have been more devastating to the Reagan administration. He was saying that at base, the entire edifice was phony. There was no "there" there. Literally "no one" knew "what was going on with the numbers." The costs of the willful self-deception involved in conferring competence on the Reagan administration would be demonstrated over and over again during the course of the next eight years, but the insider dialogue continued to focus almost exclusively on the alleged personality conflicts. It did not even matter, as in the case of Stockman, that these conflicts existed only in the fevered imagination of the President's image consultants. No story, it appeared, was too trivial, too clichéd, or too far-fetched to excite the passions of the punditocracy, so long as it had good guys, bad guys, and the right ones won out at the end.

Robert Bartley, it should surprise no one, thinks the supply-side experiment turned out just fine. Bartley says he has learned to live with, if not quite love, the deficits, now approaching $350 billion a year. In the first place, he insists, they are a "secondary issue" irrelevant to what takes place in the "real sector." Secondly, they are a matter of spending policy rather than tax policy, and can be closed by "moderate budget restraint." Third, rather than condemn the deficits and the interest payments they demand from the taxpayer, Bartley wants to know what those funds would have gone toward. "It's certainly true that the government can spend money to increase production or on defense which increases production. But, on the other hand, if it's going to spend it on increased transfer payments, I'd rather have them pay it out in interest and let the private economy use it."

What Bartley is in effect saying here, as Wanniski puts it, is that "there are deficits and there are deficits." He would rather see Americans pay a healthy percentage of their taxes to the rich foreigners who hold our debt than have the money available for rebuilding our public infrastructure, cleaning our air and water, providing resources to keep our neighborhoods safe from drugs and crime, improving our national education system, and retraining our workers to compete in the global economy. This is, historically speaking, a respectable philosophical position within the conservative camp. But it is hardly one that the majority of the country can be expected to embrace.

The economist Herbert Stein is credited with being the first to affix the new-fangled name of "supply-side fiscalism" to these policies in 1976, and

George Bush, in a brief moment of ludicity four years later, called them "voodoo economics." The characterizations have a nice ring to them; yet a more accurate depiction might have employed a more old-fashioned term, but one that remained taboo within the punditocracy during the entire Reagan era: "class warfare."

9

"EVEN THE NEW REPUBLIC . . ."

I don't know if any of you have heard of a magazine called *The New Republic*," said then–Treasury Secretary Donald T. Regan to an assembled group of reporters in early 1985, but, as he soon made clear, this hallowed home of historic heartbleeders, this perfidious parlor of pointy-headed pinkos, this effete embankment of Eastern Establishment elitism, had just "endorsed" Ronald Reagan's tax reform plan. *What a victory for common sense.*

Of course Regan, the no-nonsense former Merrill Lynch CEO, did not bother with the rhetorical flourishes attributed above. But the thrust of his comments was clear. It was a thrust that the Reagan administration and its allies found extremely useful during the 1980s whenever they needed to demonstrate just how silly and sectarian their adversaries were being. "My God," opponents of the nuclear freeze, proponents of the MX, boosters of the Contra war, critics of the civil rights movement, etc., could now say, "*even the liberal New Republic* understands this issue well enough to see we're right. What can possibly be the matter with my distinguished opponent?" Michael Kinsley, editor for much of the period, once suggested that the magazine change its name to "Even the liberal New Republic . . ."

The degree of cultural hegemony exercised by *TNR* over right-thinking Washington insiders is difficult to explain outside the purview of its tiny empire. A simple chart detailing the various activities of the magazine's editors extending into all three rings of punditocracy tells a part of the story (see chart on page 178). But it is only a part. The ubiquitous presence of

The New Republic in the Media

FRED BARNES

Senior editor, *The New Republic*
Regular panelist, "The McLaughlin Group"
Frequent substitute host, CNN's "Crossfire"
National editor, *The Washingtonian*
Frequent contributor, *The American Spectator*
Roving editor, *Reader's Digest*
Frequent contributor, *Vogue*

SIDNEY BLUMENTHAL

Senior editor, *The New Republic*
Contributing editor, *Vanity Fair*
Frequent contributor, *GQ*

HENDRIK HERTZBERG

Senior editor and former editor-in-chief, *The New Republic*
Frequent contributor, *Esquire*

MICHAEL KINSLEY

Senior editor, TRB columnist, and former editor-in-chief, *The New Republic*
Co-host, CNN's "Crossfire"
Regular columnist, *The Washington Post* (syndicated)
Regular columnist, *Time*
Frequent co-host, "Firing Line"
Former regular columnist, *The Wall Street Journal*

MORTON KONDRACKE

Senior editor, *The New Republic*
Regular panelist, "The McLaughlin Group"
Former regular panelist, "This Week with David Brinkley"
Host, "American Interests"
Former regular columnist, *The Wall Street Journal*
Former bureau chief, *Newsweek*
Senior editor, *Roll Call*
Former national editor, *The Washingtonian*

CHARLES KRAUTHAMMER

Contributing editor, former senior editor, *The New Republic*
Regular columnist, *The Washington Post* (syndicated)
Regular columnist, *Time*
Regular panelist, "Inside Washington"
Editorial advisory board member, *The National Interest*
Editorial board member, *The American Scholar*

LEON WIESELTIER

Literary editor, *The New Republic*
Former music editor, *The Washingtonian*
Former contributing editor, *Vanity Fair*

its editors throughout the opinion business adds up to considerable collective influence. But the overall effect was even greater than the sum of its parts. Tastemaker *Vanity Fair* instructed its readers on two separate occasions between 1985 and 1988 that no fashion-conscious politico could aspire to hipness without "the smartest, most impudent weekly in the country" and the "most entertaining and intellectually agile magazine in the country." A *New York Times* cultural critic observed that *TNR*'s influence, as the 1990s began, seemed "to be at, or certainly near, a new height." Right-wingers, in particular, could not get enough of this liberal magazine. Norman Podhoretz called it "indispensable." George Will referred to it as "currently the nation's most interesting and most important political journal." Buckley's *National Review* thought it "one of the most interesting magazines in the United States." The White House had twenty copies messengered every Thursday afternoon, minutes after the magazine returned from the printer.

As the above statements testify, *The New Republic* was, during the 1980s, the single most important repository of ideas and political ideology in the entire insider constellation. Excluding the nonpartisan *National Journal*, TNR was the only regularly read Washington-based magazine in which ideas and policy problems could be fleshed out to a degree that remotely reflected their contextual complexity, allowing for possible objections and meeting them with fully reasoned responses. Moreover, in a town where the standards of literary eloquence are embodied by General Accounting Office reports with titles like "Administrative Systems: NASA Should Reassess Its Automated Information Management (AIM) Program and Rescind Its IBM-Compatible Policy" (May 1990), the damn thing was actually fun to read. TNR was well written, perfectly attuned to the rhythms and genuflections of the insider dialogue, and extraordinarily—oftentimes diabolically—clever. Even those offended by its know-it-all tone or rightward political leanings could not help but admire its zippy writing style and engaging humor.

TNR's victory as the heavyweight champion of pundit-powered publications was partially a reflection of the state of its competition. Other magazines published important articles, but their influence rested largely upon the reputations of their authors.* The only weekly periodical with comparable cachet to that of *TNR* was *The Economist* of London. While American journalists read *The Economist* with a degree of reverence that borders on worship, no magazine written and published across the Atlantic could seriously expect to be a decisive influence in the opinion-shaping game in Washington. The insider dialogue responds to stimuli so capricious and

Foreign Affairs and *Foreign Policy*, being specialized quarterly publications, speak to a slightly different audience.

arcane that no one who is not fully immersed in it can expect to master it in a meaningful way for other insiders. *TNR* editor Mickey Kaus once lamented the difficulty of attempting to keep track of the insider dialogue from Los Angeles. "By the time you've heard Pat Caddell is touting Bruce Springsteen for president," Kaus bemoaned, "he has already switched to Dwight Gooden."

To the degree that *TNR* had any competition in the big idea business, it derived not so much from other publications as from television's two "quality" television interview programs, "Nightline" and "The MacNeil/Lehrer Newshour." In terms of pure starmaking ability within the punditocracy, "Nightline" host Ted Koppel fell just percentage points behind God. Since the program surreptitiously hatched itself amidst the media chicanery surrounding the 1979 Iran hostage crisis, Koppel and company managed to forge a truly unique combination of highbrow respect and network financial support. To be interrupted in a meeting by a call from "Nightline" became the ultimate insider status symbol. To be invited on the show was akin to winning the lottery. Best of all was to be asked on to discuss a subject in which one had no particular expertise, which meant that Koppel had anointed you as an all-purpose Wise Man. *New Republic* editors Michael Kinsley, Hendrik Hertzberg, Charles Krauthammer, and Leon Wieseltier have enjoyed this honor repeatedly. But "Nightline" did not set out to shape intellectual fashions so much as it mirrored them. For that reason, it suffered from many of the same defects that plague most objective journalism. As is also the case with "The MacNeil/Lehrer Newshour," most of its invited experts were either public officials or former public officials. In an era dominated by conservative administrations, their minions enjoyed a considerable "Nightline" advantage.* Moreover, since many of the Reagan administration's battles were fought between its incumbent "pragmatists" and "ideologues," the left/right split that television producers customarily sought for their guest spots usually featured a "liberal" supporter of the Reagan administration along with a representative of a position so extreme that not even Ronald Reagan could sign off on it.

The New Republic occasionally divided along these lines as well. Despite all evidence, Morton Kondracke continued to insist that he was not a conservative, and so in the magazine's syndicated radio program, he would

---

*In an examination of the "Nightline" guest list for the period January 1, 1985, to April 30, 1988, the most frequently called upon guests were Henry Kissinger, Alexander Haig, Elliott Abrams, and Jerry Falwell; 89% were men and 92% were white. See William Hoynes and David Croteau, "All the Usual Suspects: MacNeil/Lehrer and 'Nightline' " (New York: FAIR, May 1990).

set himself up as the "liberal" in order to support Reagan foreign policies. As late as August 1991, extreme conservatives like James J. Kilpatrick were still touting Kondracke's "liberal" bona fides in celebration of his endorsement of their views. Were this the sum total effect of the magazine's efforts to undermine liberalism in the 1980s, it could be considered merely a pale, unimportant version of "The McLaughlin Group." But the magazine's assault on liberals and liberalism was far more interesting—and confusing—than that seen anywhere else in the punditocracy.

Somehow, during the 1980s, *The New Republic* managed to carry on its masthead at least a half-dozen of the most interesting and original liberal writers in America, while at the same time providing conservatives with their most potent political/ideological weapons in the punditocracy's war of ideas. TNR argued the Reagan administration's case with far greater sophistication and nuance than did the administration itself. Moreover, by publishing hard-line Reaganite views alongside those of its traditional liberal writers and insisting that both formed part of a single project designed to rejuvenate liberalism, the magazine succeeded in giving the fundamental precepts of Reaganite foreign policy—the military buildup, the proxy wars, the contemptuous unilateralism—what former editor-in-chief Hendrik Hertzberg called an important dose of "intellectual cachet." Proponents of old-fashioned liberal values—nonintervention, multilateralism, social justice, and redistribution of wealth—were left with nowhere to go but *The Nation*, which, for most practical purposes, was considered so politically extreme that most insiders were afraid to pick one up without lead-lined gloves.

The act of retaining a liberal readership while publishing a flagship conservative publication was by definition a delicate one. The magazine's answer to its ideological conundrum was to seek refuge in a psychological term that previously had been taken to indicate a severe psychological disorder. Owner and president Martin Peretz bragged that "some people say we are schizophrenic, yet these are times when even the most thoughtful people are ambivalent."

In addition to "schizophrenia," the magazine's editors had great success in renegotiating the political connotation of the word "unpredictable." This term, for which *Roget's Thesaurus* offers "capricious, careless, immature, irresponsible, undependable and untrustworthy" as imperfect synonyms, became during the reign of *TNR* the certifying adjective: the word that admitted formerly boring liberals into the exclusive club of the politically relevant and culturally chic. To be "predictable"—that is, to remain consistent to some definable set of principles or world view, became, in

TNR's lexicon, akin to cowardice, lily-livered nostalgia, soft-headness, and stilted mental growth. *The Nation* was predictable. Feminists were predictable. Civil rights leaders were predictable. But "the one sure thing," promised Peretz, "about this unpredictable magazine is that we will go on being unpredictable."

The unpredictable/schizophrenia strategy simultaneously won the magazine the new, influential audience it sought without driving away too many of the liberals who formed the backbone of its readership. It was also extremely helpful to the magazine's ability to secure corporate advertising. Freed from what publisher Jeffrey Dearth called the "philosophical albatross" of the "dead-weight of knee-jerk liberalism," *TNR* was able to woo new corporate advertisers to its pages. More to the point, however, was its ability to sway the insider dialogue. Just how, through the personality of its writers and editors, the magazine arrived at its "iconoclastic" definition of modern liberalism was a subject of endless speculation on the insider cocktail circuit in Washington. Everyone read the magazine, liberals angrily and conservatives with ill-concealed glee. Feminists, though put off by its Harvard frat-boy atmosphere—Henry Fairlie once compared it to an ancient Greek gymnasium—nevertheless appreciated its pro-feminist politics. Radicals on both sides of the political divide agreed that the only reason Washington seemed to find the magazine's arguments so fascinating was the fact that its conservatives insisted upon called themselves liberals. As *Nation* columnist Christopher Hitchens complained:

> The preface to this was always to be able to say, "Look, I've been a liberal all my life, it is in my roots, my fingertips and my hair, and it is in that capacity that I say I like the contras, or I like the MX, or what's so wrong with Ivan Boesky?" These are statements which would be perfectly trite on their own—they almost would have some distance to go before reaching trite—but because of the "I'm a liberal" preface, they are invested with a kind of daring and appear brave.

Then–Heritage Foundation editor Dinesh D'Souza concurred:

> Articles triumphantly circulated on the Right would probably be ho-hum items if they appeared in *National Review* or the *American Spectator*. . . .
> Perhaps *TNR's* only new idea is that its old ideas aren't very good. . . .
> But if *TNR* articles give credibility to the right, perhaps the magazine considers this a small price to pay for getting itself taken seriously by conservatives—who happen to be in power.

However unimpressed were critics like these, the benefits of calling oneself liberal while endorsing Reaganite goals were manifestly apparent at the magazine's November 1984 seventieth anniversary party. There among the silk cummerbunds and caviar blinis, editors heard themselves praised by such liberal luminaries as Patrick Buchanan, Jeane Kirkpatrick, Irving Kristol, and Henry Kissinger. Dr. K (to whom, in 1977, the magazine had bid farewell with an editorial entitled "Good Riddance") complained with a straight face that the evening had been "traumatic" for him. "I have been photographed with so many liberals, my semiannual visits to the White House will now be even less frequent."

One of the enduring mysteries about *TNR*'s role in the political and cultural wars of the 1980s was the fact that, while its liberals were considered by far more talented and interesting than its conservatives, it was the latter whose political views defined its stature within the punditocracy. This was even stranger given the fact that for much of the period, its editor-in-chief was the writer widely recognized as the most talented liberal pundit in more than a generation.

To say that former editor-in-chief Michael Kinsley has led a charmed life is to commit oneself to considerable understatement. Compared to Kinsley, Dobie Gillis grew up in downtown Baluchistan. Loving parents, suburban Detroit childhood, Harvard, Rhodes Scholarship, Harvard Law School, five summers working for Ralph Nader, one summer as managing editor of the neoliberal *Washington Monthly*, and finally at the ripe old age of twenty-five (and still in law school) managing editor of *TNR*. With a kind of glamourous nebbishness that frequently lands him on the top of Washington's "most eligible bachelor" lists, Kinsley somehow lived up to all the myths that New Republicans tried to create about themselves. He was ideologically anti-ideological. He had an unerring eye for cant, hypocrisy, and sanctimony. He was hysterically funny and, perhaps most important, politically fearless.

Kinsley turned sacred cows into hamburger without regard to political or ideological affinity. During the eighties he scorched the earth on targets ranging from Jonathan Schell's high-minded nuclear apocalyptism to his own magazine's infatuation with anti-Communist guerrillas, welfare programs for the wealthy, and the unfairness of the Social Security tax. His column on the latter issue inspired Daniel Patrick Moynihan to introduce a bill cutting the tax, thereby throwing the Democratic party into yet another unsolved identity crisis and forcing the entire Congress to calculate the size of the deficit slightly less dishonestly. His satires on the self-important stupidity of such Washington pundits as Hugh Sidey and the cast of

"Agronsky and Company" were funnier and more biting than anything in this book.

But however talented as writer or critic he may be, Kinsley does not inspire. He laughs, he cajoles, he mocks, and he satirizes, but even the most astute reader of his work would have a hard time conjuring up what motivates Kinsley's political zeal. Kinsley credits neoliberal guru and *Washington Monthly* editor Charlie Peters with inspiring his personal philosophy, but after two decades of neoliberal proselytizing, its fundamentals still appear decidedly fuzzy. Kinsley is against overtaxing poor people and subsidizing wealthy ones. He is an ardent free-trader, and believes that capitalism would benefit from a collapse in real estate prices. He seems to admire Ralph Nader, his former employer, whom he sees as "operating on the mental fringe where self-abnegation blurs into self obsession." But Kinsley himself is obsessed by nothing. He dedicates himself simply to delineating the foibles of contemporary Washington life. Kinsleyism might fairly be called technocracy with a sense of humor. However high-minded and personally engaging it may be for upper-middle-class yuppies, this is not the foundation of a resurgent liberalism.

Whenever Kinsley got fed up with taking orders from Peretz, he would resign as the magazine's editor and be replaced by Hendrik Hertzberg.* Kinsley had no competition as the most talented liberal pundit in Washington, but if he had, it would have been Hertzberg. Emanating from a less ambivalently bleeding heart, Hertzberg's politics derived from exactly the emotionally driven sense of commitment that was lacking in Kinsley. A onetime *New Yorker* editor and Carter speechwriter, Hertzberg was a traditional social democrat who wrote with an engaging sense of humor and a wonderful feel for political irony. Here is Hendrik Hertzberg on the 1988 Iowa primary:

> The big Democratic winner, of course, was Richard Gephardt, a man who puts me in mind, unreasonably to be sure, of an earthling whose body has been taken over by space aliens. I keep expecting him to reach under his chin and peel back that immobile, monochromatic, oddly smooth face to reveal the lizard beneath. Perhaps the aliens are from the planet Bryan. How else to explain the fact that Gephardt, who until a few

*The reverse was also true until Hertzberg retired again in September 1991, and Kinsley, ensconced at "Crossfire," *Time*, and the *The New Republic*'s TRB column, was no longer available. This time Peretz chose twenty-eight-year-old Andrew Sullivan, a gay British Catholic Tory who wrote bravely and brilliantly about the gay predicament in the age of AIDS, but professed little concern with the magazine's historic *mishigas*.

months ago was sort of a neoconservative, neoliberal, has suddenly begun talking, in his slow robotic voice, like a devotee of Populism?

Rounding out the liberal stable at the magazine during the 1980s were Sidney Blumenthal and Leon Wieseltier. Blumenthal, who spent much of the decade at *The Washington Post*, nevertheless contributed to *TNR* a powerful ability to mine the underlying cultural elements of American politics. Wieseltier, a brilliant medieval Jewish scholar whom Peretz plucked from the elevated vines of Harvard's Society of Fellows, was an extremely ambivalent liberal, who tended to arrive at conventional liberal political positions via almost Hegelian intellectual complications. *

If the four writers discussed above were given free rein to write and publish *TNR*, supplemented by thoughtful liberal contributing editors such as Michael Walzer, Louis Menand, Ronald Steel, Robert Reich, Bob Kuttner, and Mickey Kaus, *TNR* would most likely have been exactly the challenging liberal publication that American politics so sorely lacked in the 1980s. Such a magazine would have been decidedly less radical than *The Nation*, but better able to integrate moral, political, and social questions into a policy framework. Such a magazine would also have been at the cutting edge of Democratic party politics, helping the more progressive elements of the debate fashion a coherent response to the breakdown of the social contract that for years ensured the primacy of the New Deal coalition. But then, of course, no one would have had occasion to beat down his liberal opponents by insisting that "even *The New Republic*" understood the necessity of whatever Reaganite measure happened to be on the table.

When Martin Peretz took over *The New Republic*, both had reached their respective political and philosophical dead ends. Peretz had attended Brandeis before becoming a left-wing (graduate) student activist at Harvard. The child of a devoted Labor Zionist and right-wing Jabotinskyist, with many millions of dollars at his disposal, he had given up trying to overthrow the system and was now ready to work within it. Peretz and the New Left parted company when black revolutionaries began to condemn Israel as a racist and imperialist outpost. He felt a deep devotion to the Jewish state, explaining to Henry Kissinger during the 1967 Arab-Israeli War that his "dovishness stopped at the delicatessen door."

Peretz and his second wife, the Singer Sewing machine heiress Anne

---

*This was truer later in the decade rather than earlier. Wieseltier supported aid to the Contras and the MX missile, but his cultural revulsion with Reaganism led him further toward the liberal side as the decade wore on.

Labouisse Farnsworth, had funded some of the decade's most ambitious political efforts along with some of its most disastrous ones.* Peretz had invested himself wholeheartedly in the movement, and its collapse left him at loose ends. One freshman at Harvard in 1966, James Fallows, who says he was "straight off the boat" from the Goldwaterite conservatism of his Southern California upbringing, applied to join a seminar Peretz was conducting on the Vietnam War. Fallows recalls feeling Peretz's "withering contempt" for someone who, like this California rube, was not "sufficiently or stylishly anti-American in his view of the war."† By the early seventies, with Peretz's academic career stymied and his politics moving on a rightward arc, however, the couple was looking for new political investments.

The New Republic, meanwhile, had drifted into a kind of courtly irrelevance. Its post-Lippmann zenith had taken place more than a decade earlier when the handsome young President emerged from Air Force One ready to lead the Free World, holding a copy of that week's issue beneath his arm. But the ideological ferment of the 1960s, coupled with the failure of liberalism's wars—on the Vietnamese in Indochina and on poverty in America's cities—had left its most venerable institutions exhausted and confused. *TNR* was no exception.

The Peretzes purchased the magazine from owner-editor Gilbert Harrison in 1974, with the understanding that Harrison would remain editor for three years. That arrangement lasted ten months. One day Harrison entered the stately 19th Street townhouse to find his Queen Anne desk and John Marin paintings in the hallway and Martin Peretz sitting in what had until the day before been Harrison's office. *The New Republic*'s era of "unpredictability" had begun.

In the beginning, there were the words. Upon taking over the magazine, Peretz would frequently subject the holdover staff to profane verbal abuse before firing them, says Philip Terzian, an editor whom Peretz fired. Harrison's staff feared Peretz would turn *TNR* into a liberal version of *Commentary*, with all issues decided on the basis of what was "good for the

---

*According to Gwenda Blair, Peretz married Linda Heller, a Brandeis classmate, the daughter of a wealthy citrus grower, in 1962. The marriage lasted "a year or two" and Peretz moved into Kirkland House, a Harvard residential hall. He married Farnsworth in June 1967 after she separated from her first husband in the mid-1960s. It was at this point, according to Blair, that Peretz became "a husband again, a stepfather, and a very rich man." See Blair, "Citizen Peretz," *Esquire*, July 1985, pp. 89–90.

†"The contempt is more or less the same now," Fallows said twenty-five years later. "It's just pointed in the opposite direction." Historian Barton J. Bernstein, who attended graduate school with Peretz in the early 1960s, adds: "It's funny. Most of the people, pro and anti, who've known Marty over the years see him the same way—as somebody on the make. The dispute most often is on the value of whatever his cause is." Author's interviews with James Fallows and Barton J. Bernstein.

Jews." Peretz went so far in this direction, says Terzian, that he instructed him to pick up material from the Israeli Embassy that he would later run as *TNR* editorials.* "It was a very wild place," recalled Henry Fairlie, who remained close to Peretz until his death in 1990, "run by a sort of Jewish cowboy with an open shirt."

Peretz originally told *The Washington Post* that he planned to "toughen *The New Republic*'s liberalism with more aggressive, sharply argued opinions now being exploited by conservatives." But the most obvious manner in which these positions were sharpened and toughened up was by heaving them overboard. The political retooling of the magazine began immediately but proceeded fitfully during the Ford and Carter eras, and not always according to political principle. This confused readers and writers alike. Speaking of a book review commissioned more than a dozen years earlier, Peretz recalled to the literary critic Alfred Kazin in 1989 that "the worst thing I ever did to you was when I suppressed your [negative] review of Lillian Hellman. She scared me shitless."

While Peretz allowed Kinsley and his cohorts a generally free hand with much of the magazine's domestic agenda, he gradually reshaped its foreign policy to reflect the contours of the emerging Counter-establishment realignment. Michael Ledeen, a shadowy, failed academic accused of plagiarism by his colleagues, and a man with still-murky ties to the Italian Secret Service, began to appear prominently in the magazine.† Kenneth Adelman, Reagan's future anti-arms-control adviser, also saw his right-wing polemics featured frequently. Other invited neocons included Jeane Kirkpatrick, Edward Luttwak, and the ubiquitous Irving Kristol. The only point of contact between the old liberals and the New Rightists was a consistently pro-Israel hard line.

Unlike Norman Podhoretz's monochromatic *Commentary*, Peretz's neoconservative leanings stretched him in many directions simultaneously. First came the most conventional: Peretz hired Morton Kondracke from the *Chicago Sun-Times*, and the reporter quickly converted from liberal to neoconservative in tune with the tenor of the late Carter era. When Kondracke left on his brief *Newsweek* sojourn, he was replaced by the even more conservative Fred Barnes. When Kondracke returned, Barnes re-

---

*Peretz declined to be interviewed for this book.

†This is the same Michael Ledeen who helped broker Oliver North's arms sales to the Ayatollah. It is also the same Michael Ledeen who once offered to put the author's head "through the living room window," if the author asked him another question about why Ledeen had ended his academic career under a cloud of plagiarism charges at Washington University at St. Louis. See Eric Alterman, "Michael Ledeen: His Shadowy World Is None of Your Business," *Regardie's*, April 1987, p. 38.

mained. Both men made their livings by professing faith in the conventional wisdom of the moment. Neither one proved an intellectual match for the magazine's liberals, but each had qualities that endeared him to insiderdom.

The charitable explanation for Morton Kondracke was simply that he was a likable fellow who had fallen in with the wrong crowd. Kondracke worked hard, but suffered from a built-in homing device for conventional insider thinking regardless of the issue. Without trying or perhaps even being aware of it, Kondracke speaks, as Kinsley has noted, with the voice of "official" Washington.* As one TNR editor put it, "Central America is wherever Mort is."

Fred Barnes, a born-again Christian, was less a member of the close-knit Peretz *mishpacha* than Kondracke, but excelled as the kind of inside pooper-scooper who kept TNR on the punditocracy's cutting edge. White House sources knew his to be a sympathetic ear and thus went to great efforts to fill it early and often. They would leak to him on Tuesday to make his TNR deadline and then again on Friday morning for "The McLaughlin Group."

Barnes and Kondracke kept the magazine current, but it was Charles Krauthammer who undertook a five-year mission to shape its liberal philosophy and boldly take it where no liberal had gone before. Almost alone among TNR's neocon stable, Krauthammer brought both arguments and an intelligence that were taken seriously by its liberal half. As Kinsley put it, "Before I know my argument is sound, I like to run it hypothetically through Charles."

Krauthammer had been chief resident of Psychiatric Consultation Services at Massachusetts General Hospital before coming to Washington with one of his professors in 1978. After a stint as Walter Mondale's speechwriter, he joined TNR as a senior editor, later expanding his portfolio to op-ed pages, newsweeklies, and pundit sitcoms. As with most neocons, Krauthammer was never willing to give up his insistence that *he* was the real liberal. Hendrik Hertzberg, whose job it was to argue with him, calls Krauthammer a "left-wing neocon on domestic matters and a hard-right neocon on foreign policy." This is in contrast to Peretz, who, according to Hertzberg, had been a "left-wing neocon" both foreign and domestically, during the eighties. These distinctions are important. For, as Kondracke reveals, while both he and Krauthammer began as "disciples of Peretz at the outset, increasingly Peretz and I became inspired by Krauthammer."

During the Krauthammer ascendancy, TNR editorials took a progressively harder line, and developed a frequent habit of questioning the motives

---

*The quote from which I derive this view reads: "I think we can hear the official view making itself heard through my friend Mort Kondracke in last week's *New Republic*." See Michael Kinsley, "Yes, We Have No Bananas," *The New Republic*, November 24, 1979.

of its opponents. The sentiments underlying these editorials often recalled a different McCarthy than the one whom Peretz had helped bankroll in 1968. Those who did not see things the magazine's way became "second-rate thinkers," "self-indulgent, solipsistic," "Sandinista sympathizers," "fellow-travellers and their ilk." One editorial accused "Democrats, including some in Congress," of "positively identifying with the Sandinistas, their social designs, their political ends and even their hostility to the United States." This tactic infuriated Wieseltier, who explains:

> Charles's great contribution to the debate was to question the motives of his opponents. One of the great neoconservative habits—[Norman] Podhoretz has perfected it—was that since your own view is obviously correct, anyone who disagrees with you must suffer from a human frailty. The explanation cannot be intellectual, it must be psychological. Because if the intellectual differences were granted, that would imply there was something to argue about. But there is nothing to argue about. So it is obvious that there must be something the matter with that person, and so you look to his ambitions, his motives, his wife. Something.

The questioning of liberal motives during the Reagan years was part of a frontal assault by the magazine upon the chastened, post-Vietnam internationalism that characterized the Democratic party's mainstream. At the beginning of the Reagan administration, when its opponents coalesced behind a proposal for a mutual, verifiable freeze on the production and development of nuclear weapons, the magazine attacked both the proposal and its partisans. When the Conference of Catholic Bishops proclaimed nuclear deterrence to be immoral, *TNR* wrote that "there are few greater sins against sanity than the weakening of deterrence. Like the president, the bishops have sinned." "Utopian thinking has always offered lofty rationalization for risk, for tampering with the foundations," explained *TNR*'s editors in yet another editorial that equated the willingness to negotiate a reduction in arms with the Soviets with "utopianism" and "risk," but "this time the risk is too great, the foundations too shaky."*

Opposing the peace movement and arms-control caucuses within the Democratic party, the magazine threw its considerable persuasive powers behind the construction of two new ICBMs, the ten-warheaded MX, and the single-warheaded Midgetman. In 1983, when the Reagan administration

---

*"Nuclear Fantasies," *The New Republic*, April 18, 1983, p. 10. Needless to say, had Mikhail Gorbachev thought this way, we'd still be fighting the "evil empire."

engineered the "Scowcroft Report"—a propaganda document conceived by one of the decade's many bipartisan commissions of conservative Democrats and Republicans, to build support for otherwise unsupportable Reagan administration policies—*TNR* wrote: "The Commission has accomplished nothing less than a revolution in doctrine." What this revolution constituted in political terms, however, was merely the agreement of the administration to build Midgetman missiles in addition to its beloved MX. *TNR* professed to detest the MX, observing at one point that "only if we wish to start a nuclear war—do we need the MX." But it was willing to endorse its development as a means to persuade the Reagan administration to build a fleet of Midgetman missiles as well. The "revolution," however, never arrived. The Reagan administration got its MXes, to be sure, with crucial New Republican Democrats supporting it. But none of the administration's promises with regard to the Scowcroft Commission report were ever fulfilled.

Although it was passionate in support of the continuance of the nuclear arms race, the magazine reserved much of its most vociferous rhetorical support for the administration's proxy wars in Central America. With regard to El Salvador, the magazine's editors managed to convince themselves that by 1986, "the military and police, which rightist thugs once dominated, are slowly but meaningfully becoming more professional and apolitical." El Salvador, wrote the editors, "is a democracy in the process of becoming, and it is therefore a big credit on Ronald Reagan's ledger—and also on the ledger of moderate Democrats who weren't afraid to cross the partisan line." This claim, in fact, stretched the truth to such extreme proportions that not even the U.S.-supported, right-wing president of El Salvador, Alfredo Christiani, pretended to believe it. * According to figures assembled by the human rights office of the Catholic Archdiocese in San Salvador, in the period between 1980 and 1989, government-sponsored or -assisted death squads killed 41,048 citizens. The equivalent figure for the left-wing guerrillas, including kidnappings, was 776. When, in November 1989, these same U.S.-equipped and trained, "professional and apolitical" soldiers chose among their grisly victims six Jesuit priests and their cook and her daughter, and then, following their murders, conspired to cover up their responsibility and protect the guilty parties, the magazine (with the exception of Kondracke) began to backpedal. With between 50,000 and 70,000 lives and nearly $6 billion wasted in the endless Salvadoran civil war, the country made a mockery of the magazine's

---

*Upon signing a peace treaty with the rebels in early 1992, Christiani announced that his country had been fighting a war with "profound social, political, economic and cultural roots." Chief among them, he said, was "the absence of a truly democratic order for the Salvadoran people." Quoted in James Le Moyne, "Out of the Jungle," *The New York Times*, February 9, 1992, p. 29.

1986 insistence that "what has happened there should cheer all who welcome the strengthening of the democratic center in Central America."*

While *TNR* fought hard to win support for the Reagan administration's policies in El Salvador, its heart belonged to the Contras. For *TNR's* neocons, the Nicaragua of the 1980s was not a country but an existential opportunity. In the overblown rhetoric used by Contra supporters during the various battles, one could hear echoes of Seville, Munich, and Saigon. Nicaragua was where good and evil were facing off for what promised to be a final showdown: The "Communist totalitarians" vs. the "Democratic resistance."

It was through the invention of the Reagan Doctrine, with its ire focused on pathetic little Nicaragua, that Krauthammer and *The New Republic* demonstrated decisively how central punditry had become in the formation of the insider consensus that ruled American policy in the 1980s. The idea steamrolled through all three rings of the punditocracy, aided considerably by Krauthammer's unmediated access to each of them. The advantage of having a "doctrine" to defend their lies and dissimulations was considerable to the likes of Elliott Abrams, William Casey, and Oliver North. They could sell it to private contributors, manipulate it in government white papers, and seize on it as a justification for lying to the Congress and the American people, and in the case of the latter two, trading arms for hostages, and diverting money to their friends. Details about this or that massacre or drug-smuggling operation could be swept under the rug on behalf of the exalted moral calling the "doctrine" invoked. Everyone likes to think they are toiling on behalf of some greater idea larger than themselves—larger even than the country for whose interests they labor. Krauthammer's creation not only flattered these people, it inspired them; some so much they were later indicted by a Washington grand jury.

But more than a mere higher calling was involved. Washington public

*"Democrats and Commandantes," *The New Republic*, July 28, 1986, p. 7. The figures come from Charles Lane, "The War That Will Not End," *The New Republic*, October 16, 1989, p. 23. Immediately following the massacre, Kondracke tried to blame the Jesuits' murder on the rebels. Speaking on "The McLaughlin Group," he noted, "You can either say it was the right-wing death squads, and that's what the Communists will say and that's what the left wing in the United States will say, but it could have been the [rebel] FMLN." He made this statement despite the fact that just five days later, he wrote a *TNR* editorial that admitted it had "almost certainly" been the army that was responsible. When asked about this apparent contradiction, Kondracke replied, "I sort of hope, frankly, that the left did it." A November 1991 investigative report authored by House Democrats found what it termed to be "strong circumstantial evidence" that the crime was plotted at the highest levels of the Salvadoran military, including perhaps its defense minister at the time, General Rene Emillio Ponce. Kondracke's explanations come from the author's interview. See also Eric Alterman, "Shooting from the Lip," *The Washington Post Magazine*, March 18, 1990, p. 30, and Clifford Krauss, "Panel Links Chief of Salvador Army to Jesuit Killings," *The New York Times*, November 17, 1991, p. 1.

relations firms—the people who are paid good money to understand these things, however subliminally—knew a milk cow when they saw one. They flew the Reagan Doctrine flag and lobbied administration officials to include their well-paying anti-Communist clients on the list of U.S.-funded Reagan Doctrine "freedom fighters." Rival public relations firms adopted Marxist regimes as their clients in order to fight them. Thus, Reagan's closest friend, Robert Gray, head of the powerhouse Gray and Company, adopted the cause of the Marxist government of Angola, only to give it up when young Reaganites picketed his stately Georgetown offices. Soon, the South African creation in Mozambique—RENAMO—and the non-Communist guerrillas in Cambodia attached themselves to the Reagan Doctrine teat, basking in all the pro-freedom and democracy rhetoric that passionate supporters of the Afghans and Contras were generating. Right-wing adventurer Jack Wheeler revealed something of the value of Krauthammer's service to the cause when he told Sidney Blumenthal, then of the *Post*, that "we had him [Krauthammer] in for an off-the-record lunch with the president. He popularized the term, a rallying point for conservatives. . . . I love that guy Krauthammer for inventing the 'Reagan Doctrine.' "*

While the Reagan Doctrine knew no borders, the object of its most passionate affections was always Managua. When push came to shove on a crucial congressional vote, virtually the entire edifice of the nation's foreign policy seemed to rest on these agrarian democrats. According to one Krauthammer-authored editorial, "the liberation of Angola, Afghanistan, and Cambodia would not have one-tenth the geopolitical importance—and psychological importance for other oppressed democrats—that the replacement of the Sandinista regime with a democratic government in Managua would." The upcoming vote somehow became "one of the most important foreign policy votes of the decade."

Charles Krauthammer's Nicaragua editorials are among the most significant documents of the entire era. They embraced all of the clichés of the Reaganite mind-set, with regard to both the "moral equivalent of our founding fathers" in Nicaragua and the functional equivalents of Neville Chamberlain at home. Krauthammer rested the Contras' Jeffersonian bona

---

*Quoted in *The Washington Post*, June 19, 1986. Krauthammer's specific response to these criticisms—he has responses to all the other criticisms as well—is that all of the cases he chose were "tentative, leaky colonies that did not quite have legitimacy and who engendered authentic, indigenous resistance." He specifically left out RENAMO in Mozambique and felt considerable discomfort with regard to Cambodia. As to Nicaragua, "Yes, much of the leadership was Somocista and America-guided. But by the mid-eighties, Arturo Cruz, who is someone I respect, said it had become an authentic peasant army." Author's interview. (Note: Cruz was on Oliver North's payroll at the time.)

fides upon the allegedly "impeccably democratic" shoulders of its civilian directorate, Arturo Cruz, and former Coca-Cola magnate Adolfo Calero. He did so despite the fact that Robert Owen, the man appointed by both Abrams and Oliver North to act as a go-between for the Contras and the American government, was describing the civilians in a secret memo as "a creation of the USG to garner support from Congress." Those Americans who observed that the Soviets and Cubans were more than ready and willing to match our own military commitment in Nicaragua were smeared as "the council of pure defeatism." To those who noted the fact that Nicaragua's neighbors preferred a peaceful solution, Krauthammer and company insisted that these countries were merely reading the tea leaves of liberal cowardice. Seeing "an isolationist Congress and a rising military power in Managua," they fell into the grip of public appeasement and private duplicity. Secretly, *TNR* assured its readers (apparently on the basis of mass mental telepathy), Nicaraguans were "desperate to see the United States get rid of the Sandinistas for them."

The editorial, noted Contra supporter Wieseltier, was "the worst piece of *agitprop* writing I have read since I got here. It talked about the other side's motives, and it made the case in the administration's words, rather than in our own." Twelve *TNR* contributing editors apparently agreed and banded together to sign a letter of protest that was summarily buried in the magazine's back pages. Kinsley ripped the editorial to pieces in his own column, calling the logic it employed "preposterous," "fatuous," and a "logical contortion." Hendrik Hertzberg did not critique the piece in public, but believes that sentiments such as these finally led him to resign as editor. "The magazine was playing a role," he explained, "where I just couldn't be the front man for it any more."

What Hertzberg had in mind here was not merely the Krauthammer/Peretz powers of persuasion evinced in the magazine's editorials, but also the efforts of a group of formerly liberal political operatives to use it. Saluted in the pages of the magazine as a "handful of young Democratic intellectuals and activists, Robert Leiken, Bernard Aronson, Bruce Cameron and Penn Kemble [who] will have been found . . . when the history of the American debates over Nicaragua is written . . . to have transformed both public discussions and public policy," these apostate liberals worked closely with Abrams and Oliver North to try to sway the swing votes in Congress. Their vehicle of choice was *The New Republic.* As Sidney Blumenthal observes, these "pro-Contra operatives were able to use the pages of *TNR* to develop a public strategy to complement a political strategy that they were working on inside Congress. This gave legitimacy to the whole effort." It also helped Aronson earn Elliott Abrams's old job in the Bush administration. Not a bad day's work for a magazine whose editors lectured poor Salman Rushdie that "it is the place of the writer and the intellectual to be outside, not inside; not to be a part of, but to be not a part of."

Because the endless Contra debate in Congress focused on the votes of fewer than two dozen swing Democrats in the House of Representatives, these interventions would prove absolutely crucial in convincing Congress to approve military aid. Pat Buchanan was calling the Democrats "the party of Communism" at the time, and Norman Podhoretz insisted that "in a conflict where the only choice is between Communists and anti-Communists, anyone who refuses to help the anti-Communists is helping the Communists." The Democrats could not allow themselves to be perceived to be responding to threats quite this vulgar, but they were looking for cover from them nevertheless. The most influential of these swing votes, House Armed Services Committee Chair Les Aspin, and Coalition for a Democratic Majority member Dave McCurdy, were particularly susceptible to the compliments heaped upon them by the editors of TNR, who noted the willingness on the part of these "moderate Democrats who weren't afraid to cross party lines" and who were willing to "lead and to take risks." Aspin even briefly hired Leiken, TNR's pro-Contra policy entrepreneur, as an informal adviser and paid his way to Nicaragua to survey the situation. Together, they prevailed upon the key swing Democrats to back Contra aid and allow the war to continue at crucial moments in the debate. This pattern repeated itself for two years, until Oliver North and Robert McFarlane put an end to it with a Bible and a birthday cake in Tehran.

When the Contra cause crumbled, Krauthammer and company only heated up their rhetoric even further, employing language that turned out to be wholly inaccurate but that should have sent a shudder down the spine of those dedicated to free public debate. Borrowing a page from Podhoretz, Krauthammer compared Contra/Sandinista cease-fire accords to "the similar speedy peace" that "Congress brought Indochina in 1975." Going back even further in the history of stab-in-the-back politics, he also promised that "who lost Central America will become an issue some day and on that question it is worth keeping the record straight and the memory fresh." Democratic Speaker Jim Wright had, in Krauthammer's evocative words, "made Central America safe for Communism."

Aside from the violence it inflicted upon the English language, the most significant damage inflicted by the neoconservative view of Latin America was the inexplicable importance it placed on Nicaragua to the exclusion of the rest of the region. The magazine's friend and confidant, Assistant Secretary of State for Inter-American Affairs (and admitted liar) Elliott Abrams, said he spent almost half his time on this one tortured nation. In the meantime, staggering economic debts in Latin America, coupled with extremely fragile democratic development and environmentally unsustainable investment patterns across the continent, were undermining the long-term viability of the truly strategic nations of the region. In Argentina, by the end of the decade, inflation reached 3,700 percent while the government accumulated an unpayable debt of $65 billion. Brazil, another nation of enormous strategic importance, saw its inflation rate rise to 1,765 percent in 1989, with an accompanying debt of $100 billion. Closer to home, Mexico, a nation of millions of potential economic refugees, saw its debt shoot up to $107 billion in 1987 with a relatively modest inflation rate of 160 percent. The Andean nation of Peru, a supplier of much of the U.S. cocaine market, experienced an inflation rate of 2,275 percent and a 10 percent drop in growth in 1989 alone. Bolivia, another cocaine-producing nation, may have set the all-time world's record with an annual inflation rate of 8,170 percent in 1985. Environmental destruction in these places also approached crisis proportions. In Peru, farmers were even razing sections of the Amazon rain forest to sow coca crops. All of these countries are unarguably more important to the future economic and political security of the United States than either Nicaragua or El Salvador. Yet, owing in part to the punditocracy's Reagan Doctrine–inspired obsession with these two countries— including, particularly, arguments calling this or that Contra vote "one of the most important foreign policy votes of the decade"—not one of them attracted a fraction of the attention necessary to fashion a coherent American response.

It is impossible to write about *TNR* without coming to grips with Peretz and Israel. It is not enough to say that *TNR*'s owner is merely obsessed with Israel; he says so himself.* But more importantly, Peretz is obsessed with Israel's critics, Israel's would-be critics, and people who never heard of Israel, but might one day know someone who might someday become a critic. "Israel, lion of nations, loyal ally and democratic outpost, Israel, gateway of Meccas, is of course, a land of religious reasonance and geopolitical significance," wrote James Wolcott, trying to describe Peretz's mind-set on the subject. He understated the case considerably.

One could, if one were sufficiently conspiratorially minded, draw a political *TNR* map of the world based wholly on the Israel connection. The Sandinistas were bad because they accepted PLO advisers. The United Nations was useless because it invited Yassir Arafat to speak. Jesse Jackson was dangerous because he sang "We Shall Overcome" with West Bank

*"My own passions coincided with those of the founders, the cause of a free Israel among them. My critics say it is an obsession. I confess. It is my obsession. And why shouldn't it be?" Taken from a subscription appeal from Peretz to American Jews, July 1991.

Palestinians and spoke up for their right to statehood. The Salvadoran government was deserving of U.S. military support because it accepted Israeli military trainers and voted with the Israelis in the United Nations. Bill Moyers was a fraud because he once spoke up for the right of Arab-Americans to criticize Israel in the media.*

Of course *TNR*'s flight into the arms of the right was based on political and psychological factors far more complex than just Israel, but the notion retains a subliminal credibility. Since he gave up on revolution, Peretz has devoted himself to fighting for Israel on all fronts, a crusade not uncommon among neocons. Influential intellectuals of both the right and left in Western Europe hold the rather oversimplified and unsophisticated view that the entire rightward drift of American liberalism during the sixties and seventies can be viewed as a result of the change in Israel's geopolitical status from the spirited Socialist David of its early years to the pro-American empire, post-1967 military Goliath. (The Six-Day War was important to the birth of neoconservatism, but so were the New York city teachers' strike and the blatantly anti-Semitic rhetoric of much of black America's most vocal leadership.) Still, there are uncountable ironies involved in *TNR*'s treatment of Israel's critics—not least the fact that, while few people are so frequently reviled in *TNR*'s editorials as those who openly call for the establishment of a Palestinian state living in peace alongside Israel, no fewer than four of the magazine's editors (Kinsley, Hertzberg, Blumenthal, and Wieseltier) all say they would support the establishment of such a demilitarized state. Wieseltier, a onetime member of the Jewish Defense League and every bit as devoted a Zionist as Peretz, says he would give his right arm to see it tomorrow.

TNR's role in the Arab-Israeli debate is at once simple and complicated. Norman Podhoretz has argued that "the role of Jews who write in both the Jewish and general press is to defend Israel." Critical reporting of Israel, Podhoretz insists, "helps Israel's enemies—and they are legion in the U.S.—to say more and more openly that Israel is not a

---

*The Moyers case is of particular interest because it is the one example where *TNR* attacked somebody wealthy enough to buy more than equal response time in the magazine. In defending his unsuccessful attempt to destroy Moyers's reputation as a thorough reporter and an honest man, the writer *TNR* commissioned to do the job, Andrew Ferguson, admitted that he "could not afford the three or four hours it would have taken [him] to get to Mr. Moyers," who had offered him a face-to-face interview, and thus rejected the opportunity to interview the subject of his hatchet job in person. This did not appear to bother the magazine's editors, who ran the article beneath the self-revelatory tag-line, "Bill Moyers, Liberal Fraud." See Andrew Ferguson, "The Power of Myth," *The New Republic*, August 19 and 26, 1991, and the correspondence pages, coupled with Moyers's paid response in the October 7, 1991, issue.

democratic country." Peretz has never advocated anything quite this explicit, but one could argue, not wholly inaccurately, that his primary task as editor and owner of *TNR* has been to praise Israel and subvert those he deems its opponents.

Marty Peretz does not like Arabs. They have, he argues, "a national characterological inability to compromise," and tend toward the "violent," "fratricidal," "unreliable," "primitive," and "crazed." Even worse, however, are Palestinian Arabs. *TNR* editorials often treat the word "Palestinian" as a synonym for "terrorist." In an interview with the Israeli newspaper *Ha'aretz* during the 1982 Israeli invasion of Lebanon, Peretz explained that the Israelis should administer to the PLO "a lasting military defeat that will clarify to the Palestinians living in the West Bank that their struggle for an independent state has suffered a setback of many years. [Then the] Palestinians will be turned into just another crushed nation, like the Kurds or the Afghans. . . . [The problem] is beginning to be boring."* When asked what he objected to most about the magazine he edited, Michael Kinsley responded, "I have a problem with some of the needlessly vicious things about Arabs that we publish."

Another significant responsibility Peretz has undertaken on behalf of Israel's interests has been the ideological policing of the American media. Peretz calls U.S. media coverage of the Middle East "an obsessive wound in my heart." If so, he has managed to offer this pain considerable balm in the editorial pages of his magazine. This wound accounts for what one *TNR* editor calls "Marty's ridiculous obsession with [*New York Times* columnist] Tony Lewis."† It also seems to account for the magazine's shameful vilification of I. F. Stone over a period of decades. During the 1982 Israeli siege of Beirut, when Israel turned off all water and electricity services to Muslim sections of the city, Peretz spotted Stone's name on an appeal for "the victims *including* hundreds of thousands trapped in West Beirut without water, essential services and medical supplies." Peretz singled out Stone, a devoted friend of Israel's peace camp, from the list of signatories and accused him of caring "*only*" for those "trapped in West Beirut," whom he insisted

---

*See Peretz interview with Benny Landau, published in *Ha'aretz*, December 9, 1982. Note Peretz's implied analogy between the moral behavior of the Israeli occupying forces and those of Saddam Hussein and the pre-Gorbachev Soviets. Note also that following the Persian Gulf War, Peretz wrote an article vociferously objecting to any comparison between the Kurds, whom he insisted were entitled to their own state, and the Palestinians, who were not. See Martin Peretz, "Unpromised Lands," *The New Republic*, June 3, 1991, pp. 20–23.

†Author's interview. Lewis responds, "I don't understand what it is about me that so enrages Marty. I don't think it is a difference in policy or theology. I think he is kind of obsessed with me." Author's interview with Anthony Lewis.

were trapped not by the surrounding Israeli Army but by the PLO. "So this is what I. F. Stone has come to," wrote Peretz, "asking his admirers to put up money so that the PLO can continue to fight, not simply against Israel but against the possibility of a peaceful Lebanon." "I do think sometimes we attack people unfairly," admits Wieseltier. *

Peretz's most ambitious media enforcement operation of the eighties came during the Israeli invasion when he wrote a cover story entitled "Lebanon Eyewitness." After being treated to a brief tour of the war zone by Israeli military intelligence, Peretz assured his readers that the news reports they had read and television coverage they had seen were simply false. He would single out for particular opprobrium *The Washington Post* and ABC News. One cannot hope to judge how journalists fudged their stories, or did not report them at all, in order to avoid being selected for treatment like this. "We're the cops" on Israel, explains one *TNR* editor. "Marty really put the fear of the devil into the media after Lebanon." † With more than $4 billion in aid monies riding on perceptions of Israel in Congress each year, the importance of this kind of police work can hardly be overestimated.

But Peretz is only half the story. Leon Wieseltier is correct when he says, "There is no question that on Israel we have had it a million ways. Yes, our rhetorical heat has been out front, but we have published some of the most anti-Israeli policy stuff anywhere." *TNR* has published a cover with a map of the Middle East featuring a Palestinian state on it. Wieseltier, Irving Howe, and Michael Walzer have all written articles extremely critical of the policies of the Israeli government. During the eighties, the magazine called on Begin to resign and made an enemy of Yitzhak Shamir. It has published Robert Kuttner's attack upon the "unholy alliance" between Jewish PACs and Far Right politicians on the cover as well. In a seminal issue published during the height of the Intifada in March 1988, Wieseltier endorsed many

---

*Author's interview with Leon Wieseltier. During the Persian Gulf War, Peretz complained in a column entitled "Blacklisted" that, despite repeated efforts to volunteer his services, he was perhaps "the only writer on the Middle East who had not been invited by PBS or NPR to speak about the Gulf," while other writers with less "definite views" such as Anthony Lewis and Harvard professor Roger Fisher had been extended such invitations. Peretz apparently neglected to ponder the possibility that with the exception of fellow millionaire magazine owner (and Israeli partisan) Mortimer Zuckerman, he was also the "only writer on the Middle East" who owned, published, and edited the forum that so prominently featured his views. See Martin Peretz, "Blacklisted," *The New Republic*, April 15, 1991, p. 42.

†Author's interview. Peretz also trumpets his magazine's reception of an accuracy award from an organization called CAMERA—the Committee for Accuracy in Middle East Reporting. As most journalists covering the area can attest, the word "accuracy" in CAMERA's title is about as relevant as the word *Pravda* ("Truth") was in the Communist Party's official publication. CAMERA is an enforcement organ for supporters of the Israeli right wing, but with tactics far more vulgar and transparent than anything even that has appeared in *TNR*.

of the PLO's demands for a mini-state alongside that of Israel. Even Peretz declared "the policy of occupation and settlement" to be "in ruins." It fell to Krauthammer to defend the hawkish ground that *TNR* had historically occupied, arguing that to cede any territory to the current generation of Palestinian leadership would constitute "surrender" to "rioting."

TNR's dovish pieces on the Middle East, particularly those by Wieseltier, have been tremendously important within the American-Jewish community in legitimizing the kind of dissent from the Israeli party line that Peretz and Krauthammer have made a career of attacking. On the one hand, this is a confusing phenomenon. Why would Peretz—whose attacks on the likes of Stone, Lewis, Edward Said, and others associated with criticism of Israel or support for Palestinian rights are almost unparalleled in their bile and venom content—allow his magazine to be used to publicize these same positions in the mouths of others? Part of the answer lies in the magazine's celebration of political diversity, which in the matter of Israel extends beyond the parameters of its American agenda. Perhaps more significant, however, is the fact that support for a Palestinian state or criticism of Israel's occupation is not the point. The point is who is doing the criticizing. Those whom Peretz determines to be criticizing Israel out of genuine concern for its soul, its safety, and its security are generally left alone. Those whose primary concern appears to be the conditions of Palestinian life are savaged within an inch of their professional reputations.*

One question liberals asked constantly during the eighties was why, if a primary function of *TNR*'s liberal editors-in-chief was to make the magazine's neoconservatism more palatable, did they stick around for the party? The answers, like everything at *TNR*, are complicated. Kinsley says that his decision to edit a magazine whose political thrust he did not support was, in essence, "a Faustian bargain." The bargain amounted to the fact that he could publish whatever he wanted:

> The price was I had to publish things I didn't want. I thought that was a pretty good arrangement. It comes out every week. There is a lot of crap in it, but if I have anything I want said or want to say, I can say it in a national magazine without having to pay the bills. Yes, the war in Nicaragua bothered me as did our endorsement of it, but I was considerably soothed by being able to publish the opposite view, and it seems to me that anybody reading both would think that I was right.

Hertzberg's refusal to adopt Kinsley's strategem (that is, to publish a

---

*For the record, the author would put himself, Stone, and Lewis in the former category. Edward Said's primary sympathies lie, quite properly, I think, with his own people.

liberal magazine within a conservative one) led to frequent "Fuck you, Ricks" and "Fuck you, Martys" shouted in the hallways of the magazine during the early eighties, with Hertzberg telling one reporter that Peretz was "oafish and bullying." "The initial way I dealt with the tension," recalls Hertzberg, "was to resign. . . . I became sufficiently disturbed with the role of TNR and the general thrust of the role that I was playing in the Reagan years that I left. I didn't feel alienated to the point that I wasn't perfectly happy to write for the magazine, but I didn't want to be a front man for it any longer."

In addition to the Contras, Hertzberg was angered by the public role played by TNR in undermining the nuclear freeze movement and supporting the MX. "I wanted our position to be one of critical support rather than critical opposition. Instead, the magazine showed contempt for its [the freeze movement's] arms-control thinking and questioned the backgrounds of many of the movement's leaders." It does not bother Hertzberg that the magazine subjects civil rights or social policy organizers to fine-tooth scrutiny. "What the magazine should be criticized for," he allows, "is for not subjecting power to the same kind of criticism."

Beginning in late 1986, the magazine began to draw itself away from Reagan and Reaganism and concentrate a bit more of its fire on "power." The magazine's October 13, 1986, editorial on "The Reagan Hangover" was among the first frontal attacks on the legacy of Ronald Reagan in the mainstream media, and unlike most, preceded the revelations of the Iran-Contra scandal. But during the 1988 election, TNR's editors, like much of the punditocracy, focused on the wholly ir-relevant question of which Democratic candidate would likely be toughest on the Russians. They attacked Dukakis for his willingness to "parrot the left isolationist line," his "standard issue McGovernite left worldview," and his refusal to endorse the TNR theology on the nuclear freeze, the MX, and most particularly, the Reagan Doctrine. The magazine chose as its favored candidate former Peretz student and Midgetman booster Albert Gore of Tennessee. Gore ran a perfectly conceived neocon campaign, talking tough to the surrendering Gorbachev, and prostrating himself before the Shamir government to curry favor with New York's Jews. Advised extensively by Peretz and Wieseltier, his campaign fizzled in New York, where even the Jews found his hawkishness a bit too kosher for comfort. With its anemic 10 percent of the total Democratic vote, the Gore campaign in the end proved to be a kind of metaphor for just how far The New Republic had drifted from the concerns of the sophisticated Democratic voters for whom the magazine's editors had, for the previous decade, pretended to speak.

CONSEQUENCES:
THE BUSH YEARS

"I miss it, the Cold War. It gave you a reason to get up in the morning."

—HARRY "RABBIT" ANGSTROM, IN JOHN UPDIKE'S
RABBIT AT REST (1990)

THE MAN WITH NO NEW IDEAS

Long after names like Krauthammer, Kondracke, and Kissinger have receded into the dustbin of history, scholars of the American past will scrutinize the records of contemporary public discourse for the answers to an historical enigma: How was it, they will ask, that a nation so blessed with economic advantage, with such abundant natural resources, and with so sophisticated a guiding political class allowed itself to squander its national treasure and destroy the foundations of its prosperity and security in pursuit of enemies that had long ceased to threaten it? By what paradoxical rule of political science, they will wonder, did the United States embark on an orgy of military spending and colossal debt creation just as its enemy was collapsing and its own economy eroding? And why, most curiously of all, they will puzzle, were the architects of this disaster, the men and women whose every pronouncement regarding the character of the nation's challenge had been belied by reality, nevertheless celebrated as heroes and champions of an imaginary American renaissance? Such scholars would do well to begin their investigations with a detailed examination of the Washington punditocracy.

Drawing upon fragments by the Greek poet Archilochus, Isaiah Berlin divided Russian thinkers into foxes, who knew "many things," and hedgehogs, who "know one big thing." Each point of view has its advantages, but the world is probably a safer place with fewer hedgehogs. Being a fox can be uninspiring, but being a hedgehog is often worse. What happens when your One Big Thing turns out to be wrong?

In March 1985, Eduard Shevardnadze, Mikhail Gorbachev's closest friend and adviser, turned to his new boss, the General Secretary of the Communist Party, and blurted out the fact that had eluded virtually the entire Soviet leadership since Stalin's time. "Everything's rotten," observed Shevardnadze, "it has to be changed." Through their willingness to accept this awful truth into their collective political psyche, the two men converted themselves from hedgehogs into foxes. Gorbachev was not exaggerating in the slightest when he explained that things were so bad that "everything pertaining to the economy, culture, democracy, foreign policy—all spheres—had to be reappraised."

The pre-Gorbachev Communist Party had known One Big Thing: Soviet-style communism was the highest order of ideological and economic development known to humanity. This knowledge blinded its members to the facts that were obvious to virtually any tourist who spent more than a week traveling the country: The Soviet experiment, initiated in 1917, was over. It had ended in almost unmitigated failure. Although the Gorbachev "revolution from above" was also a failure in many important respects, it at least created a political space for the even more revolutionary efforts of Boris Yeltsin and the final, incredible implosion of 1991. For all its fits and starts, it was an effort of almost unprecedented existential audacity.

The Reagan-era punditocracy, meanwhile, was comprised of no fewer hedgehogs than the Brezhnev-era Politburo. Its consensus also insisted upon One Big Thing: that America's "long twilight struggle" in the Cold War took precedence over all competing national priorities and goals. By the mid-1970s, however, this view was only slightly less useful in determining the true interests of the United States in a multipolar and economically driven world competition than Stalin's constitution was to the Soviets. Although certainly not "everything" in American economic and political life had become rotten, many things had, and more were in the process of becoming so. The rot permeated the nation's manufacturing industries, its environment, and much of its political and social structure. That we were still in much better shape than the Soviets should have offered precious little comfort, given the fact that our true competition—the Germans and Japanese— were walking away with the most rewarding aspects of the new international economy. But because of the dramatic difference in degree between our own problems and those faced by the Soviets, the United States failed to produce any leadership with the vision or clarity of purpose necessary to pierce its intellectual delusions. Incredibly, not even the public surrender of the enemy proved sufficient to disturb our self-satisfied complacency.

During the final years of Ronald Reagan's presidency, the punditocracy withdrew even more deeply into its insider cocoon. The central problem of

American political life, it insisted, remained the need to educate and fortify the attentive public to resist the implacable expansion of international communism. The United States, as the only Western power with both the will and the means to resist this expansion, would continue to be required to expend vast amounts of blood and treasure in this never-ending conflict. The doctrines that ruled the punditocracy mind-set were in most cases internally consistent. This enabled its members to fit virtually any development anywhere in the world into its basic model without upsetting any core assumptions. That core formed the minimum intellectual requirements for admittance into the club of the politically relevant. Yet despite the rigidity with which they were enforced, many pundit beliefs were unique to insider Washington. The combination of the intensity with which these notions were held, coupled with their frequently tangential relationship to reality, often left European and other observers shaking their heads in astonishment.

The world view through which punditocracy perceptions were filtered was a mixture of the pre-Vietnam centrism coupled with the hard-line revisionism of the Reaganite Counter-establishment. Where the former gave way to the latter was not in its recognition that the United States was engaged in a timeless duel to the death with the Soviet Union—this was already a given—but in the Whittaker Chamberslike pessimism with which it regarded the likely outcome.*

Zbigniew Brzezinski, who as Jimmy Carter's national security adviser approached the dovish edges of respectability, published a guide to U.S.-Soviet relations in 1986, positing as its "central proposition" that "the American-Soviet contest is not some temporary aberration but a historical rivalry that will long endure." The contest was being fought, in Brzezinski's view, for "nothing less than global predominance," and would long ago have been settled by war were it not for the deterrent power of nuclear weapons. "Never has there been a contest," including that between the United States and Nazi Germany, Brzezinski argued, "between two powers so fundamentally different" as this one.†

The reasons to doubt the eventual triumph of good over evil in this contest

---

*Chambers worried that communism (which, more than three decades before Ronald Reagan, he called "the focus of the concentrated evil of our time") was certain to triumph over freedom as "the world outside Communism, the world in crisis, lacks a vision, and a faith." See Whittaker Chambers, *Witness* (New York: Random House, 1952), pp. 3–22.

†Zbigniew Brzezinski, *Game Plan: How to Conduct the U.S.-Soviet Contest* (New York: Atlantic Monthly Books, 1986), pp. 8, 12–15. In the book, Brzezinski argued on behalf of a military strategy designed to maintain what he modestly termed necessary to achieve an "integrated capability" for "surface, sea, and space combat as the central point of departure for the waging of an enduring and consuming political contest for earth control" (p. 259).

lay in what one neoconservative writer called our country's "excess of virtue." Democracies were fickle fighters and unwilling to sacrifice themselves for total victory. Jeane Kirkpatrick argued in her seminal essay, "Dictatorships and Double Standards," that "the history of this century provides no ground for expecting that radical totalitarian regimes will transform themselves." Kirkpatrick's was a perfectly rational reading of history, but it came to be understood during the Reagan years to mean simply that, while democracies were fragile flowers, Communist dictatorships, like diamonds, were forever. Jean-François Revel, a right-wing French intellectual who became to the punditocracy of the 1980s what Regis Debray was to the student movement of the 1960s, saw democracy as "a historical accident, a brief parenthesis that is closing before our eyes." In his influential text, *How Democracies Perish*, Revel complained that while democracies face an "internal enemy whose right to exist is written into the law itself," communism was both "durable and immutable." "Totalitarianism liquidates its internal enemies," wrote Revel, "or smashes opposition as soon as it arises; it uses methods that are simple and infallible because they are undemocratic. But democracy can defend itself from within only very feebly; its internal enemy has an easy time of it because he exploits the right to disagree that is inherent in democracy."

Revel's ideas were much popularized by George Will. Arguing that time was not "on the side of the bourgeois societies of the West," Will insisted that totalitarian regimes, "for all their stupidities have one strength, staying power." After a mere six decades in power in the Soviet Union, the Communists had "achieved the closest approximation to permanency in politics." When, in the early 1980s, Senator Joseph Biden argued on behalf of keeping U.S. sanctions on the Soviet Union so long as its troops remained in Afghanistan, Will guffawed. "Biden, 37," he predicted, "will not live to see the troops withdrawn."

The irreconcilability of Soviet and American systems coupled with the enemy's immutability added up to only one of two possibilities: we had either to fight or switch. Under Jimmy Carter, went the argument, the country had come dangerously close to switching. Under Ronald Reagan, we would be fighting again.

Because nuclear weapons had raised the cost of typical world wars to prohibitive levels, the Third World War was conducted by means of military spending and proxy warfare. Throughout the 1980s, the leading voices of the punditocracy argued on behalf of vast increases in America's weapons budgets, the rapid expansion—into outer space if possible—of its nuclear weapons capabilities, and a series of U.S.-funded-and-supplied proxy wars against Soviet military clients. The justification for these efforts rested on the allegedly urgent need to demonstrate to friend and foe alike that we had every intention of resisting Communist expansion. The punditocracy's Cold War became a war of symbols, to be won not merely with blitzkriegs or flanking maneuvers, but with line items, flow charts, and disinformation.

Aside from the disastrous intervention in Lebanon, a couple of bombing missions in Libya, and a holiday takeover of the nutmeg-producing island of Grenada, the only fighting and dying done on behalf of this strategic vision was done by foreigners. Throughout the period, however, a number of the punditocracy's most distinguished members were itching to go further. The Soviets, said Irving Kristol, were driven by "a self-conscious and fully articulated secular-messianic religion." Kristol recommended a U.S. invasion of Nicaragua in order to teach the mini-messiahs there a lesson. Edward Luttwak, the punditocracy's favorite military strategist, lamented that military pacifists had been successful in making even *tactical* nuclear weapons unfashionable in U.S. military doctrine. "Unless we refute the counsel of impotence," he insisted, "the only possible choices left to us will be appeasement or outright retreat."

The problems with even the most moderate versions of this world view were threefold. First, because it was not shared by the very allies we were hoping to impress, our demonstrations of will and resolve prove counterproductive; not unlike that of a man who tries to win a vegetarian woman's affection by showering her with steaks and pork chops. Second, it proved extremely expensive, in both real terms and in its opportunity cost. Third, it had precious little relationship to the alleged object of its attention—the phenomenon of post-Stalinist Soviet communism. It therefore demanded sacrifices of the American people and the victims of its proxy wars that were wholly unnecessary and doubly self-defeating for being so.

As amazing as it sounds, the most important country in the world to the Reagan-era punditocracy, excluding the Soviet Union itself, was brave little Finland. Throughout the decade, the example of Finland was held up as the ultimate threat to the safety and security of the American people—the geopolitical dagger we saw before us. Finland, argued Charles Krauthammer, "had earned its independence at the cost of its dignity." It lived behind not an Iron Curtain, explained William Safire, but "a kind of beaded curtain . . . subservient to Soviet security and foreign policy domination." The theory of "Finlandization" was an existential version of the domino theory: Communist conquests came not in the form of small subjugated Asian countries but of psychologically dispirited Europeans. Unless the United States showed itself willing to do all the things the neoconservatives were demanding of it, they warned, Western Europeans would lose heart and decide that they, too, had no choice but to purchase their independence at the cost of their dignity. It is this logic that explains George Will's otherwise wholly nonsensical statement that "If Cuba cannot be 'Finlandized' by the United States, then Western Europe eventually will be by the Soviet Union."*

The Finlandization argument was originally trotted out during the Carter presidency by members of the Committee on the Present Danger on behalf of the MX missile and reappeared as late as June 1989 in a Jeane Kirkpatrick column. As with its larger strategic umbrella, it suffered from no end of difficulties when confronted with the realities it alleged to address. For starters, it painted a wholly false picture of Finland. That frozen nation, as William Pfaff and George Kennan have noted, actually served to deter Soviet expansion, so that by the 1980s, Soviet influence over Finnish affairs had declined precipitously. †

The audience at this costly spectacle, the Europeans themselves, found the entire intellectual exercise to be so vain and misguided that it often seemed to call into question both the judgment and the values upon which

---

*George F. Will, November 7, 1983. The official manifestation of the Finlandization argument can be seen in Ronald Reagan's April 27, 1983, insistence, in a speech to a joint session of Congress, that "If we cannot defend ourselves [in Central America], we cannot expect to prevail elsewhere. Our credibility would collapse, our alliances would crumble and the safety of our homeland would be put in jeopardy." This argument was an even greater exaggeration of those put forth by his predecessors in seeking to justify the American war in Indochina. When defending his 1970 invasion of Cambodia, Richard Nixon argued that "If, when the chips are down, the world's most powerful nation, the United States of America, acts like a pitiful, helpless giant, the forces of totalitarianism and anarchy will threaten free institutions throughout the world." Similarly, Lyndon Johnson defended his escalation of the Vietnam conflict by insisting that if the United States did not prevail there, "We'll lose all of Asia and then Europe, and then we'll be a rich little island all by ourselves. That means World War III." For a useful discussion of the legacy of these doctrines in American life, see the afterword in Jonathan Schell, *Observing the Nixon Years* (New York: Pantheon, 1989). The Nixon and Johnson quotes appear on pp. 254–55.

†Finnish security was guaranteed by the Finns themselves, who, through a variety of political, economic, and military measures, successfully raised the cost of Soviet domination to prohibitive levels. See William Pfaff, *Barbarian Sentiments: How the American Century Ends*, p. 88, and George F. Kennan, *The Nuclear Delusion* (New York: Pantheon Books, 1982), pp. 70–72. Moreover, for all the very real danger to Finland from Soviet power, the majority of its people nevertheless managed to achieve an average per capita income higher than that of the United States, and according to a 1991 UN survey, scored higher on an international "freedom" index. According to the statistical supplement to the "OECD [Organization for Economic Cooperation and Development] Observer," June/July 1990 edition, Finnish per capita income stood at $21,266, while that of the United States was pegged at $19,558. The 1991 UN Human Development Report ranked the United States thirteenth among the forty criteria chosen to measure international freedom. Finland ranked fourth behind only Sweden, Denmark, and the Netherlands.

the Atlantic partnership was alleged to be based. To observant European elites, the concept of "Finlandization" lacked both simple cogency and elementary dignity. Its primary purpose, in their eyes, was to provide an all-but-transparent gloss for the Reagan administration's own deadly crusades in Central America. *

The most serious problem with the argument was its catastrophic misreading of the basis of Soviet power. The image of the insatiable Russian Bear, whose power was increasing with every unchallenged conquest, bore little relationship to the exhausted, emaciated economy upon which the Soviet military rested. The punditocracy was by no means solely responsible for this situation. Soviet secrecy had created a kind of black box in the American imagination into which all our fears and neuroses were poured. Certainly some of these were justified, as attested to by the writings of Alexander Solzhenitsyn among others, along with the easily observable miseries of Afghan and East European life. But these fears, coupled with the difficulty in acquiring dependable data from the Soviets themselves, led the government's national security apparatus to invent a capability for the Soviet Union that vastly exceeded its pathetic economic output. As a result, the Pentagon regularly flooded the American media with a steady stream of falsehoods about the Soviet military machine, and the CIA provided enormously inflated estimates of Soviet power throughout the bureaucracy. The 1989 edition of the *Statistical Abstract of the United States,* citing the CIA, reported the per capita GNP of East Germany to be larger than that of West Germany. The CIA's annual *Handbook of Economic Statistics* reported that the growth of the Soviet economy during the years 1981–85 exceeded that of the European community by more than 25 percent. Employing such figures, the White House, State Department, and private defense contractors and consultants operated what former neoconservative Senator Daniel Patrick Moynihan called a "national security state" based on a "vast secrecy system which basically hid from us our own miscalculations."

Building upon the false figures and the infectious atmosphere of government secrecy, the punditocracy vision of an implacable enemy on an immutable march toward our shores caused American politicians to inflict enormous damage upon American long-term interests. While the investment-oriented societies of East Asia and Northern Europe were laying

---

*In the summer of 1986, a top official of Margaret Thatcher's Foreign Office—a representative of the only government that even pretended to support U.S. global counterrevolution—complained to a visitor, "If you Americans want to behave like brutes in Central America, go ahead. But for goodness sakes, leave us out of it!" Author's interview.

the groundwork for their massive industrial expansions of the 1980s and 1990s, the United States engaged in the most expensive military buildup in peacetime history. Coupled with massive increases in luxury consumption inspired by the supply-side tax cuts, this had the effect of accelerating the deindustrialization of the nation at a time when massive public and private debt made ever larger demands on our dwindling productive capacities. The net result was a steady decline not only in the economy's annual productivity gains but more concretely in the living standards of most Americans—a decline that becomes more difficult to reverse with every passing moment.*

Strobe Talbott, a *Time* magazine pundit and well-respected guru on Soviet affairs, published a brave *mea culpa* in early 1990, in which he deplored the fact that "for more than four decades, Western policy has been based on a grotesque exaggeration of what the Soviet Union could do if it wanted, therefore what it might do, therefore what the West must be prepared to do in response . . . where the West thought the Soviet Union was strong, it was in fact weak."

Conversions such as Talbott's and Moynihan's, however admirable, were not sufficient to overcome the punditocracy's ideological preoccupation. For according to the ideology of the 1980s punditocracy, the very idea of Mikhail Gorbachev was impossible. Almost until the very moment the Berlin Wall came crumbling down in November 1989, there was simply no room in the insider mind-set for a weakening base of Soviet power, an end to the Cold War, and the possibility of a cooperative superpower relationship. Regardless of whatever the Soviets may have said or done, the punditocracy knew better.

On the balmy Moscow morning of March 11, 1985, members of the Central Committee of the Communist Party of the Soviet Union gathered inside the Kremlin to choose a new leader. When it was over, the victor was fifty-four-year-old Mikhail Sergeyvich Gorbachev. Two days later, as Chopin's Funeral March drifted through Red Square, mourners marched to the burial of the morally and intellectually barren Brezhnevite, Konstantin Chernenko. With him was buried Moscow's collaboration in the construc-

---

*Real weekly earnings in 1987 per average American family were no higher than they were in 1973, despite a major increase in the number of two-income families. See Bennett Harrison and Barry Bluestone, *The Great U-Turn: Corporate Restructuring and the Polarizing of America* (New York: Basic Books, 1988), pp. 6–7. Excluding the wealthiest 20% of Americans, family incomes began losing ground in 1987 and declined steadily through the end of the decade. See Louis Uchtelle, "Not Getting Ahead? Better Get Used to It," *The New York Times* "Week in Review," December 16, 1990, p. 1. (Data based on U.S. Bureau of Labor Standards.)

tion of the Cold War ideology that had sustained the American leadership class since the end of World War II. As François Mitterrand, Helmut Kohl, Margaret Thatcher, and George Bush stood quietly by, Mikhail Gorbachev threw in the first shovelful of earth.

On the opposite side of the world, in northwest Washington, DC, the punditocracy scrambled to reconstitute itself into its "Something's Up in Russia" mode. For approximately two weeks thereafter, a window opened inside the inner rings of the punditocracy ·into which climbed those Sovietologists and former officials who had made the final cut on the rolodexes of the senior producers and op-ed page editors the last time a General Secretary had died. Fax machines hummed, and satellite hook-ups buzzed with the juice of instant strategic analysis.

In a rare moment of both humility and candor on the day of Gorbachev's appointment, Henry Kissinger admitted to a *Washington Post* reporter that "nobody really knows what the younger generation thinks in the Soviet Union. We don't have any contact with them." America would have been well served by its Sovietology industry if Kissinger and company had just stopped there. Alas, that was not an option. "It will be two to four years before he can consolidate his power," Kissinger continued. Minor-league Kissingers took a similar line. "There will probably be a long period of transition to adjust to the new generation," explained former Secretary of State Alexander Haig. "It will be more like three years or so for the new leader to establish himself in a position of pre-eminence," noted former Secretary of Defense Harold Brown.

Complete ignorance of Gorbachev's views was not considered a serious handicap in the punditocracy. Its ideological assumptions told the chosen pundits all they needed to know. Soviet leaders came in only two categories: just as bad, and even worse. Thus, virtually all the expert reactions solicited in the media during this period fell into one of two persuasions: boredom or alarm.

The bored pundits complained that Gorbachev was simply old-hat. How could he be anything else? The man was a product of assembly-line totalitarian immutability. Carnegie Endowment Sovietologist Dimitri Simes forthrightly stated to reporters that Gorbachev had "no new ideas." "You don't survive the winnowing-out process in the Politburo unless you are cut from the same cloth as your fellow members," explained former CIA man George Carver. "[George] McGoverns and Jimmy Carters do not rise to the top in the Soviet Union." "You don't get into the Politburo by being a liberal," seconded Russian historian Peter Reddaway. "The real question," added *Time*'s Talbott, "was not whether he [Gorbachev] will pursue a course different from that taken by his predecessors, but whether he will pursue it more effectively."

A more alarmist tone was taken by a second faction of Soviet experts. As former Kissinger aide Helmut Sonnenfeldt explained, the Soviets had "an advantage now that they have a living, breathing leader who can deal with European leaders." Sonnenfeldt was alluding to the fact that the first five years of Reagan's presidency had been conducted opposite three sick, aged Soviet leaders who could barely muster the strength to stand up between them. Gorbachev's ability to walk up and down the Kremlin steps without assistance, coupled with what these experts perceived to be the American public's desire to love their adversary, could, if not thwarted in time, lead to catastrophe. *

The problem, according to Arnold Horelick of the Rand Corporation, was that "everyone is waiting for someone to appear on the Soviet side in whom you can invest some illusions." Punditocracy Sovietologists put the kibosh on that one almost before you could say "Henry Wallace." Georgetown University's Angela Stent warned that it was "very dangerous to think that Gorbachev will be any more 'liberal or flexible' on foreign relations" than his predecessors. Zbigniew Brzezinski promised that the United States could expect "a much more skillful, energetic—but in many respects, more dangerous sort of leader." Adam Ulam, head of Harvard's Russian Research Center, predicted that "Gorbachev may be even more rigorous with intellectuals, writers and dissidents than in the past." His colleague, Marshall Goldman, added the view that in his acceptance speech, Gorbachev had called for "an intensification of social production . . . and the economy" which, according to Goldman, was "usually a catch phrase meaning 'more discipline.' "†

These statements all have a number of characteristics in common. Most obviously they were incorrect. But they were incorrect in important ways. Almost all seem to preclude the possibility of alternative interpretations. Moreover, all share the assumption that any optimism with regard to the de-escalation of Cold War tensions is both foolish and dangerous, and deserves no place in the discussions of serious men and women. Aside from the special case of the émigré Dimitri Simes, those Sovietologists who had spent extended periods of time in the USSR during the previous decade, or who had significant

---

*Midge Decter explains, "Americans always love Soviet leaders—not Chernenko, but we didn't really get the chance. But beginning with Khrushchev—Khrushchev was a terrific guy. We really loved that guy." See the Committee for the Free World, *Does The West Still Exist?* (New York: The Orwell Press, 1990), p.19.

†Goldman added, "If he masters the system—rather than its mastering him—this may augur bold moves in domestic and foreign policy. Don't bet on it." See Marshall I. Goldman, "Will Gorbachev Be Brezhnev II?" *The New York Times*, op-ed page, March 12, 1985.

contacts at numerous levels of Soviet society and understood the broad middle-class stirrings for change, were generally excluded from adding their strokes to the incipient Gorbachev portrait. The more dovish inhabitants of ex-officialdom were not only not consulted, but were held up as objects of ridicule. George Carver had only to mention the names "McGovern" and "Carter" to discredit any views that diverged from the punditocracy hard line.

To the degree that American attitudes were capable of influencing the behavior of the Soviet leadership, these views may have been self-fulfilling. As was true of the Soviet belligerence quoted and magnified in the American media, hawkish quotes from one side feed and empower hawks on the other. This symbiosis was demonstrated time and again, by comments like those of the retired dovish Soviet Army colonel who explained to a British journalist in 1984 that "We need an economic reform. We need to expand human rights in our country and to further develop Soviet democracy. And we can only make headway in tackling our problems under conditions of prolonged detente. We need detente, lots and lots of detente."

They didn't get much of it from Ronald Reagan or the Reagan-era punditocracy. But in Mikhail Gorbachev, the Soviets had happened upon something truly new in the history of great power politics. Throughout the next four years, the most influential members of the punditocracy virtually tied themselves to the mast of Stalin-era Manichaeism, dismissing what were once colossally unthinkable Soviet concessions as mere propaganda moves designed to confuse Western audiences or to thwart our sense of purpose. When the charade proved no longer maintainable, the world had changed forever: geopolitics had entered an entirely new era, and the United States, the primary architect of the previous one, had been dragged along kicking and screaming.

The period between Gorbachev's initial rise to power and the final American agreement to accept the Soviet forfeit of the Cold War was one of endless confusion within the punditocracy. It was as if a slow-motion earthquake was shattering its ideological foundation brick by brick. With each falling fragment of the edifice, pundit after pundit scrambled to deny either the reality or the significance of the bricks, insisting the whole while that the lumps they appeared to be taking were all part of some larger pattern—a pattern that, despite all evidence, they had predicted all along.

Addicted to a wholly superficial level of analysis, the pundits sealed themselves off from the wide-ranging ideological debate that had commenced in Moscow. This dialogue, which encompassed not only military strategy but also the entire economic and social structure of the Soviet Union, contained within it the seeds of an astonishingly broad social and intellectual revolution inside much of the Soviet leadership class.* Had U.S. experts better understood the implications of this discussion, it might have been possible in certain limited instances to try to influence Moscow to move in more pacific and cooperative directions. The inability of the punditocracy even to consider the possibility of internal change within the Soviet civil and military mind helped lead to a series of belligerent statements and actions that impeded the progress of those Soviet leaders and intellectuals who were arguing for a whole new focus for Soviet strategy. Once the strategic shift was finally accomplished, the punditocracy's inability to perceive it crippled Washington's ability to help shape it and pursue our own interests accordingly.

Skeptical observers can be forgiven for failing to embrace the changes represented by Mikhail Gorbachev purely on the basis of a new rhetorical style. Soviet leaders had long demonstrated an embarrassing affinity for a kind of surreal flower-power rhetoric that could not have been more inconsistent with their government's own behavior. But if Gorbachev also rewrote the Soviet style book in his speeches, it was his actions that provided the more serious evidence that something profound was under way in the Soviet Union. And it was the significance of these actions, rather than the new rhetorical style, to which the punditocracy willfully blinded itself.

The punditocracy reaction to Gorbachev during his first four years in power can be roughly divided into three segments: First came the "It's All a Trick" period. When this was no longer sustainable, the "He's Just Resting" or *Peredyshka* interregnum took over. When this justification collapsed, the pontificators returned with a new theorem: Gorbachev was a fine fellow, yes, but unfortunately he was about to be overthrown. Proving that he was always a man just slightly ahead of his time, Charles Krauthammer came close to rolling all of these genuflections into three consecutive sentences in November 1987, when he observed that "We don't know if Gorbachev is sincere. If he is, we don't know whether he will succeed in winning over his bureaucracy. If he does, we don't know if he will last." Under any and all of these conditions, however, the proscribed American response remained the

*This analysis relies heavily upon that put forth by Michael McGwire in *Perestroika and Soviet National Security* (Washington, DC: The Brookings Institution, 1991), pp. 115–258. It is not inconsistent with those appearing in: Stephen M. Meyer, "The Sources and Prospects of Gorbachev's New Political Thinking on Security," *International Security*, Fall 1988, pp. 124–63; Robert Legvold, "War, Weapons and Foreign Policy," in Seweryn Bialer and Michael Mandelbaum, eds., *Gorbachev's Russia and American Foreign Policy* (Boulder, CO: Westview Press, 1987), pp. 97–133; Jack Snyder, "The Gorbachev Revolution: A Waning of Soviet Expansionism," *International Security*, Winter 1987/88, pp. 93–127; Matthew Evangelista, "The New Soviet Approach to Security," *World Policy Journal*, Fall 1986, pp. 561–89; and Raymond Garthoff, "New Thinking in Soviet Military Doctrine," *The Washington Quarterly*, Fall 1988, pp. 131–58.

same: Stand Tall, Remain Firm, Keep Your Powder Dry, Avoid "Euphoria," and most importantly, *Do Nothing.*

The new era of U.S.-Soviet relations can be dated approximately to April 17, 1985, when Gorbachev proposed his first nuclear-testing moratorium. Three months later, in July, he announced a unilateral testing moratorium, promising to extend it indefinitely should the United States follow suit. Two months after that, he proposed a chemical weapons "free zone" in Central Europe, offering to destroy Soviet stocks in exchange for a reciprocal gesture by the NATO powers.

All of these measures were viewed in Washington as simple propaganda measures, no different than the cynical and insincere crowing that Gorbachev's predecessors regularly undertook on behalf of the "peace-loving peoples of the world." That Gorbachev might have had something new in mind did not really occur to anyone within the punditocracy until April 1986. Then, in response to Chernobyl, Gorbachev requested assistance from the West German and Swedish governments. On May 14, he proposed a four-point program to strengthen Soviet cooperation with the International Atomic Energy Agency (IAEA), thereby reversing a decades-old policy of total secrecy in all nuclear-related matters. Soviet experts found this behavior intriguing, and were even more surprised when, three months later, Gorbachev released a remarkably candid and self-critical report on the accident.

In mid-December, Gorbachev pulled a final Christmas rabbit out of his fur cap when he phoned Andrei Sakharov in Gorki and told the Soviet Union's leading dissident to return to Moscow and "go back to your patriotic work." Many hundreds of thousands of Americans had campaigned for Sakharov's freedom and were initially overjoyed by the news. This was a foolishly naive reaction, according to punditocracy prognosticators. George Will, who little more than a year earlier had attacked Gorbachev for heading a regime that "tortures its most distinguished citizen, Andrei Sakharov," entitled his column on the subject "Sakharov's Release: It's Just Business as Usual." Dimitri Simes, writing in *Foreign Affairs*, insisted that Gorbachev's decision "changed little," and was probably undertaken only to avoid being "blamed for Sakharov's de facto murder."

The coming winter proved a brutal one for punditocracy ideology. It began in late January 1987 when, in a plenum of the Party Central Committee, Gorbachev introduced *perestroika*, charging the party with stagnation and systemic failures, and calling for the introduction of secret balloting, a choice of candidates in party elections, as well as experiments in giving Soviet citizens a choice in general elections. Three weeks later, he announced the pardoning of 140 political prisoners, the largest number since

1956, with promises of more to follow. On February 28, Gorbachev ended the stalemate in the U.S.-USSR intermediate nuclear force (INF) negotiations by simply caving in to all American demands. Lest anyone get the idea that serious change was taking place, Henry Kissinger, invited by *Newsweek* to explain these bewildering developments, harkened back to the much-overinterpreted Kirkpatrick doctrine. "The Soviet Union is a totalitarian state today and it will be a totalitarian state even after the reforms are completed," Kissinger reassured his readers. "They seek efficiency, productivity—not democracy. They need a respite in the international field to accomplish these objectives: they have not been converted to Western pacifist notions."

Still Gorbachev's response to the Soviet crisis continued unabated. In May 1987 he announced that the Soviet Union would no longer jam Voice of America broadcasts. In June, at another Central Committee plenum, he called for the partial dismantling of centralized economic control and irrational pricing methods. Five days later, on June 30, Gorbachev announced an appeals process for Soviet citizens unjustly treated by party officials. That summer he began withdrawing Soviet troops from Afghanistan. Upon returning from his summer vacation, in September, he invited three American congressmen and two journalists to inspect the disputed radar station at Krasnoyarsk, which American officials had long maintained was a violation of the 1972 ABM Treaty. Next, in November, after proposing a mutual U.S.-USSR 50 percent cut in nuclear weapons, Gorbachev took the opportunity of the seventieth anniversary of the Bolshevik Revolution to denounce Stalin's Terror and to rehabilitate his more liberal adversary, Nikolai Bukharin.

Within the scholarly Sovietological community, excitement over Gorbachev's ultimate direction, piqued initially by Chernobyl, was reaching a fevered pitch. "History is on the move again in Soviet Russia," announced the distinguished emeritus professor of politics at Princeton, Robert C. Tucker:

> The signs are abundant, among them the proclaimed need for public openness or "glasnost," steps toward structural economic reform, the legalizing of limited forms of small scale individual and cooperative enterprise, a lively ferment in the arts, a drive against the mass scourge of alcohol abuse, the freeing of some prominent dissidents, the release of Andrei Sakharov to return to Moscow from Gorki exile, and moves on the international chessboard. . . . The fundamental fact about the Soviet Union today is that a struggle is taking place over reform of the established political culture—the customary ways of thinking and acting handed down from the past.

Tucker had the reputation of being a conservative Sovietologist. His article, which appeared in the spring of 1987, had been preceded by any number of pieces by less cautious Soviet experts proclaiming the onset of a new era in Soviet political culture.* By September, Robert Legvold, director of the most prestigious center of Soviet study in the country, Columbia's W. Averell Harriman Institute for the Advanced Study of the Soviet Union, explained that he did not think "there is anyone in academic circles who doubts that Gorbachev is committed to far-reaching changes within the Soviet Union, including a re-examination of foreign policy ideas."

In the American public, too, Gorbachev struck a remarkably responsive chord. Popularity polls indicated that Americans admired him even more than their own leaders. Japanese economic domination replaced Soviet military power as the most feared threat to the country's well-being. When Gorbachev came to Washington at the end of the year and stepped outside his limousine on Connecticut Avenue, the nearby pedestrians started screaming, jumping up and down, and reaching over to try to touch the great man's garment.

Yet academic and popular enthusiasm for Gorbachev only seemed to inspire the punditocracy to new heights in its attempts to deny the reality of substantive change. William Safire promised his readers in November that no matter what Gorbachev said about Stalin himself, the General Secretary would "break few Stalinist icons." Safire saw *glasnost* and *perestroika* as a means to achieve not "peaceful competition but to get a second wind—to carry out their now unspoken mission to dominate the world." Should real trouble break out in Eastern Europe, Safire promised, Gorbachev could be counted upon to "crack down as Mr. Stalin would have, fraternally, rolling in the tanks and shooting the dissenters."† His colleague, A. M. Rosenthal, attributed Gorbachev's behavior to a "brilliant strategy" designed "to attain full moral equality with the United States without essentially changing the system upon which the Soviet dictatorship and his own power rests." The intention, Rosenthal insisted, was to "erode our values and vision and compassion."

The Springsteenlike reception accorded Gorbachev during the Decem-

---

*A special citation is due here to the series of prophetic articles on the emerging changes in the Soviet Union and their implications for U.S. strategy published by Soviet experts Archie Brown, Matthew Evangelista, Robert C. Tucker, and Michael McGwire that appeared in *World Policy Journal* during the period of late 1986 through 1987 under the guidance of its editor, Sherle R. Schwenninger.

†Quoted in Walter Shapiro, "Prolific Purveyor of Punditry," *Time*, February 12, 1990, p. 62. Safire also noted on March 27, 1989, that "when the Poles or the Hungarians rebel, Russian tanks will likely roll, corking genies and pushing back toothpaste with a vengeance."

ber 1987 summit seemed to drive the punditocracy to desperation. Charles Krauthammer chalked it up to the fact that the city had somehow "lost its head." Americans were "getting dizzy on Gorbachev." George Will relied on a similar explanation: Americans were simply "drunk on detente."

Because Gorbachev seemed to be caving in to American demands on all bilateral issues related to human rights and arms control, post–Cold War Cold Warriors had to reach out to find other important areas of conflict to make their case that the conflict still remained essentially unchanged. The obvious target here became Nicaragua. As the punditocracy mind-set insisted that Third World revolution was by definition a function of Soviet meddling, the fact that the Sandinistas did not roll over and play dead as a favor to Gorbachev was seized upon as a telling example of the General Secretary's true deviousness. Instead of being cast as a mere symbol of the larger ideological conflict between the United States and the USSR, proxy warfare in Nicaragua—and, to a lesser extent, Angola, El Salvador, and Afghanistan—became the essence of the conflict itself.

The Nicaragua fetish during this period produced a wonderfully emblematic moment in the history of punditocracy strategic analysis. In early November 1987, Edward Luttwak spied a photo on page one of The New York Times posing Nicaragua's Daniel Ortega beside Erich Honecker of East Germany and Poland's Wojciech Jaruzelski at the opening of the 19th Party Congress in Moscow. The photo, wrote Luttwak in The Washington Post, proved that the Sandinistas had been admitted to the "very exclusive club of governments the Soviet Union regards as permanent, organic allies," and thus "settled conclusively" the argument over "the nature of the Sandinista regime and its intent in regard to the peace plan." One of the many problems with Luttwak's analysis was that the photo did not exist, and neither, so far as anyone else knew, did the club. The Times had simply published two photos adjacently with only a tiny border between them. *

If the punditocracy's stubbornness with regard to Mikhail Gorbachev's 1987 initiatives appeared to have an element of tragedy, its continuation in the face of Mr. Gorbachev's 1988 performance demonstrated a distinct touch of farce. In early February, Gorbachev announced that the Soviets would withdraw unilaterally from Afghanistan. Ten days later, in Yugoslavia, he signed a joint statement in which he blamed the USSR for the two nations' historic conflict, renounced the "pretension of imposing concepts of social development on anyone," and rejected the use of force or "interference in the affairs of other states." In May, Ronald Reagan was invited to lecture Soviet students

---

*Philip Geyelin was the first person to point this out. See The Washington Post, November 29, 1987.

on human rights at Moscow State University. In June, the Russian Orthodox Church celebrated its one thousandth anniversary with the full support and cooperation of the Soviet government. At the end of the month, at the first All-Union Communist Party Conference since 1941, Gorbachev outlined his plan for a transition to democracy, which included a plan for local elections and a democratically elected bicameral legislature. Three weeks later, he offered to dismantle the disputed radar station at Krasnoyarsk.

This pattern continued throughout early December, when Gorbachev, demonstrating a true showman's flair for the single dramatic gesture, piled up all of his proscribed doctrinal changes in Soviet behavior and dumped them on an unsuspecting world at the United Nations in New York. For good measure he threw in a unilateral 20 percent cut in Soviet military forces. His speech out-McGoverned George McGovern with its internationalist rhetoric and electrified both the media and the American people.

But even now, Gorbachev had still not managed to impress the influential Cold Warriors within the punditocracy. Following the UN speech, *The Washington Post* op-ed page seemed to mirror the various stages of Gorbachev denial. George Will fell back on the now dated "he's trying to get us to drop our guard" standby, arguing that "Gorbachev may, without reversing Soviet economic decline, achieve a relative enhancement of Soviet military power."* (Will would hold fast to this line right up through the time that Gorbachev agreed to dissolve the Soviet Union four years later.)† Charles Krauthammer went with the current fashion of the waiting-period argument. He observed that Soviet leaders "always talk this way when they are looking for a period of *peredyshka* [breathing space]." Sovietologist Dimitri Simes saw a need to get out in front of his nonspecialist colleagues, and used the page to argue that Gorbachev was "a beleaguered imperial leader in desperate need of foreign successes to compensate for domestic setbacks." He was therefore making "a virtue out of necessity" in order to "use Soviet limitations to enhance Moscow's global influence." No matter what the prognosis, the administered cure never seemed to change. At all costs, insisted Dr. Kissinger eight days later, the thing to do was to avoid

*George F. Will, December 9, 1988. This was similar to the Safire line of the day. He noted that the speech was a combination of "audacity and mendacity," while arguing that if Gorbachev were really sincere, he would show it by "tearing down the Berlin Wall." See William Safire, December 9, 1988.

†"Gorbachev placed only an instrumental value on freedom," Will wrote of the man then being held in captivity in the Crimea. In a column entitled "So Much for a Master Tinkerer," Will complained that the man he would call a "retrograde force" favored "only small, conditioned doses of freedom, only because and to the extent that they would serve economic efficiency and hence Soviet power." See George F. Will, August 22, 1991, and August 24, 1991.

"wishful thinking" and, of course, "euphoria." In the end, counseled Kissinger, "peaceful coexistence must be based not on public relations spectacles but on a reciprocal respect for the other side's vital interests."

European leaders found the American response puzzling. A *Manchester Guardian* reporter in Bonn observed, "The German Question is suddenly quite simple: what on earth is the matter with the Americans?"* Unencumbered by the simple moral certainties of the early Reagan era, the Europeans were sufficiently agile, intellectually and diplomatically, to negotiate an entirely new foundation for their relations with the East. The Germans, in particular, achieved once unthinkable strategic gains from *perestroika* and new thinking because they were quick to recognize the opportunity and seize it with both fists. They not only united their homeland, but maneuvered themselves into a relationship that left them poised to exploit the Eastern transformations for long-term growth and environmental security.

It is instructive to examine the case of German Foreign Minister Hans-Dietrich Genscher, as an example of just how insistent were the punditocracy nay-sayers in denigrating the possibility of peaceful cooperation between East and West. Genscher saw in Gorbachev the opportunity to make peace and end the division of Europe as early as August 1986. He announced a few months later that if such a chance existed, "It would be a mistake of historical dimension for the West to let this chance slip just because it cannot escape from a way of thinking. Let us not sit back idly and wait for Mr. Gorbachev to deliver," he advised. "Let us rather try to influence, expedite, and shape developments from our end."

Such talk was heresy at the time in Washington, and Genscher soon became a despised figure in the punditocracy, his name converted into an epithet of unadulterated perfidy. *Newsweek* devoted a cover story to the threat of "Genscherization" of European foreign policy. Evans and Novak quite predictably beat this drum on the *Post* op-ed page, but the usually staid James Hoagland also joined in, calling Genscher "a master contortionist," willing "to mix domestic politics and East-West policies when it helps his favorite cause— himself." William Safire, however, took his place as leader of this particular pack. He warned of "the Genscherite appeasement bloc," led by "Germany's devious foreign minister," a man who saw "a Fourth Reich rising from NATO's ashes to dominate Europe's economy." Employing a textbook "When did you stop beating your wife?" construction, Safire inquired whether

---

*See W. L. Webb, "West Germans Baffled by American Attitudes," *The Manchester Guardian Weekly*, May 28, 1989, p. 10. Webb quotes one SDP politician observing that "the Russian enemy image has been the basis of their ideological identity, the one sure thing in an insecure world of daunting debt and declining economic power. Where the Germans offend is in not letting them preserve this image of an enemy."

"the export-loving foreign minister, Mr. Genscher, approve[s] of the way West German missile experts are providing Third World nations with the technical means to build delivery systems for gas bombs." It is a demonstration of just how thoroughly Cold War myopia dominated the punditocracy mind-set that its most influential member, William Safire, could accuse an allied foreign minister of being "export-loving" and make it sound evil.

Protected by the distance of the Atlantic Ocean and his status as the most popular politician in Germany, Genscher survived the punditocracy attack. In a front-page story dated July 20, 1990, *The New York Times* reported that while "the man of the hour of German Unity may be Chancellor Helmut Kohl . . . the man who first saw it coming was certainly Foreign Minister Hans Dietrich Genscher." He went on, with Kohl, to achieve not only German unity but, as the *Times* reported, "a comprehensive package of arms reductions, an all-European security structure building on the mechanisms set up in 1975 by the Helsinki Conference on Security and Cooperation in Europe, large-scale Western financial help for the Soviet Union to modernize its economy and a gradual end to the divisions of the continent." Needless to say, none of this would have been possible if Genscher had a punditocracy to worry about.

As a direct consequence of its inability to adjust to the prerogatives of the new world era, meanwhile, the United States was rapidly losing influence in Europe while excusing itself from the new political and economic arrangements negotiated under the shadow of Gorbachev's initiatives. The new European Bank for Reconstruction and Development was set up under the leadership of the Bundesbank and chaired by Jacques Attali, an adviser to François Mitterrand who considers America to be "Japan's grainery." *Washington Post* foreign editor David Ignatius noted shortly after the Berlin Wall fell that, while America's economic competitors had representatives in Warsaw, Budapest, Prague, and Moscow, "making contacts, making loans, making business," the United States had generally restricted itself to reactions amounting to "Whoopee! We won the Cold War. . . ."* The apparent paralysis of the nation's leadership in addressing the country's mounting fiscal crises—from the budget deficit to the trade deficit to the S&L scandal to the increasing weakness of the American banking system—all contributed to the impression in Europe that, as one reporter put it, the United States was becoming "the sick man of the new world economic order."

---

*Of 940 joint ventures in the Soviet Union reported as of October 1, 1989, U.S. companies had participated in only 97, compared with 595 for Japan and Western Europe. PlanEcon, a Washington-based consulting firm for Eastern-Europe related business, noted that 75% of its clients were European or Japanese. See David Ignatius, "While Washington Slept," *The Washington Post*, Outlook section, November 19, 1989, p. 2.

*   *   *

If Mikhail Gorbachev had taught the nation's leading political pundits anything at all, it should have been the value of a little humility. In the years following his 1985 ascension to power, all one would have needed to do to embarrass most pundits was to read aloud their previous predictions. Unfortunately, Gorbachev had no more success in reforming the deeply ingrained practices of the punditocracy than he had had with Soviet agriculture.

A few pundits were sufficiently honest to own up to the fact that their ideological compasses had veered off-kilter. Shortly before the Berlin Wall came down, Meg Greenfield admitted that "What we are confronting is the destruction of many of our premises and expectations. . . . Our pat arguments don't work anymore. We can no longer put our minds on automatic." Most, however, simply continued to dig themselves further and further into their early-Reagan-era ditches. In February 1989, Zbigniew Brzezinski told the editors of *The Washington Times* that further upheaval in Poland could discredit Gorbachev's efforts at political liberalization to the point that it would spark a Soviet military takeover *in Moscow*. A George Will column dated November 9, 1989, the very day of the fall of the Berlin Wall, contained these immortal words: "Liberalization is a ploy . . . the Wall will remain."

When a lost driver asks a pedestrian for directions, only to find out later the destination in question was actually hundreds of miles from the place the pedestrian said it would be, the driver usually knows better than to go back for more advice. Fortunately for the employment status of the punditocracy, a similar standard does not appear to operate with regard to the American news media and matters of war and peace. The pundits who had blithely predicted that Gorbachev would never do everything he had just done continued to pontificate as if their dismal records had no implications for their newest pronouncements. Yet so long as their analysis erred on the side of "caution," of "prudence," of doing nothing and above all, of avoiding "euphoria," the pundits risked little.

To those who argue that it matters little what pundits say, since it is the politicians who ultimately must make the decisions, the 1988 American presidential election provides a useful demonstration of the strictures that the punditocracy can impose upon political debate irrespective of either public opinion or political reality. Though he had not yet made his UN address or allowed the collapse of his Eastern European empire, Gorbachev had, by the fall of 1988, gone quite a distance in addressing the major concerns of the United States regarding Soviet intentions. The American people, moreover, were consistently telling pollsters that they no longer worried about the Soviet military. Yet, as Sidney Blumenthal demonstrated in *Pledging Allegiance*, the presidential election was conducted as if none of this were happening.

The campaign was characterized by the bizarre spectacle of each serious contender's seeking to prove his political manhood by demonstrating just how "tough" and "strong" he could be in the face of the surrendering Soviet leader. The less cooperation a particular candidate received in this regard from his punditocracy audience, the more he felt it necessary to take the responsibility upon himself. In a speech before the New Hampshire Knights of Columbus, the Democratic victor, Michael Dukakis, used variants of the word "strength" thirty-eight times in twenty-five minutes. The result was a pathetic spectacle that disintegrated into an argument over whether any of his opponents was sufficiently "tough" and "strong" enough, in Dukakis's words, "to use force to defend our territory," as if a potential military attack upon the United States was somehow the most pressing danger facing the next American president.

Early in the race a few candidates had attempted to move their dialogue off the shopworn penny of Korea-era machismo, but they were quickly slapped back into line. Albert Gore, for instance, had begun his campaign by speaking of the dangers posed by the greenhouse gases and the need for a high-tech infrastructure to support American technological research and development. Gore was laughed off the podium by George Will for addressing himself to issues that "were not even peripheral." Sufficiently chastened, Gore quickly embraced the hairy-chested neoconservative rhetoric crafted for him by his advisers, two of whom doubled as editors of *The New Republic*. This succeeded in convincing Will to endorse Gore as the only Democratic candidate who was "not a foreign-policy naif." Meanwhile, the public dialogue on America's problems inspired by the race began absurdly and degenerated from there.*

An interesting dichotomy developed during this period between reporters and op-ed writers, which served to demonstrate just how powerfully the punditocracy's Reagan-era obsessions impeded its ability to judge the candidates. While news pages were filled with incredible report after incredible report about the Soviet Union, the pundits kept insisting that such things were simply not possible. This tension was clearly illustrated during the election by the reporting and editorial staffs at *The Wall Street Journal*. Extrapolating from the changes inspired by Gorbachev and the emergence of

---

*When Dukakis observed that if a Central American nation wished to have friendly relations with the Soviet Union, this did not constitute an a priori justification of a U.S. military invasion, Gore insisted that this meant "it would be perfectly all right with him for the Soviets to create a client state in the Western Hemisphere." This, in turn, inspired Dukakis to return fire as if preparing for a fifth-grade playground fight at recess: "I don't think he is the toughest," declared Dukakis. "I don't think he's the toughest at all . . . I don't yield to Gore in toughness in any way, shape or manner." See Toner, "Dukakis Talking Tough, Marches into Dixie," *The New York Times*, February 17, 1988, p. A19.

the economic power of Japan, among other developments, two journalists reported quite undramatically in August 1988 that the postwar era was over. On the newspaper's front page, they noted:

> the containment of Communism and its chief proponent, the Soviet Union . . . tailored to the two-power world of 40 years ago, doesn't fit an era in which the Soviet Union is struggling to restructure its ossified economy, Communism is in decline as an ideology and the American people worry more about economic competition with Japan or terrorist attacks against the U.S. than superpower confrontation.

Yet a month after the story appeared, the *Journal*'s editorial page savaged Michael Dukakis for allowing even a hint of such a commonsense approach to cloud his vision. "A bipartisan postwar consensus has sustained a policy of 'containment' against Soviet and Communist expansion," argued Mr. Bartley and company. "Mr. Dukakis supports containment in Europe, but he won't support Freedom Fighters in the Third World." These sixteen words constitute a masterpiece of punditocracy subterfuge as they contain three simultaneous intellectual sleights of hand together with an attack on their subject for failing to address the phony issues posited in the first place. By insisting upon the continued relevance of the "bipartisan consensus" on containment, the editors ignore the consequences of the Soviet military's commitment to New Thinking and the Reasonable Sufficiency doctrine.* (The editors' hero, Margaret Thatcher, declared the Cold War over in November.) The *Journal* editors moreover equated support for Third World guerrillas with this same outdated policy of "containment" in Europe, which, when it was still relevant, had been significantly weakened by exactly these adventures. Finally, they insisted upon calling those revolutionaries "freedom fighters" though their ranks were largely populated by persons whose ideas and motivations can be said to have little or nothing to do with the idea. Jonas Savimbi's "freedom fighters" in Angola were murderous Maoists, while the *Mujahedeen* in Afghanistan were largely Islamic fundamentalists with a heavy concentration of heroin smugglers. The brigades of

---

*"Reasonable sufficiency" consisted, according to Robert Legvold, of "pared-down nuclear arsenals capable only of launching a secure second strike; conventional forces capable of defending, not conducting major offensive operations, and interventionary forces capable of deterring an aggressor in regional crises but insufficient to prop up a regime incapable of defending itself." These ideas were footnoted to articles published in the Soviet press between June and September 1987. See Robert Legvold, "War, Weapons and Foreign Policy," in Seweryn Bialer and Michael Mandelbaum, eds., *Gorbachev's Russia and American Foreign Policy* (Boulder, CO: Westview Press, 1987), p. 113.

the Nicaraguan Contras were filled with similarly unsavory types, as evidenced by what one reputable human rights organization called their "routine attacks on civilian populations," including "the kidnapping, torture and murder [of] health workers, teachers and other government employees."

Because he had neither the courage nor the vision to defend his own conception of the changes under way in the Soviet Union or the proper role of the United States in a changed world, Michael Dukakis constantly found himself the helpless victim of the punditocracy's 1946 world view. If he spoke of his intention to move away from Reagan-era confrontation, these sentiments were attributed to his softness; views that were "standard-issue McGovernite Left," in the words of The New Republic, "pure McGovernism," as William F. Buckley called them, or even vintage Henry Wallace, as the Journal editors intimated.

But if, in contrast, Dukakis folded completely and endorsed the punditocracy viewpoint that Ronald Reagan's toughness had won whatever meager concessions Mr. Gorbachev had offered, he was attacked for having opposed most of these policies in the first place. After noting that Gorbachev would never reject terrorism or permit freedom of religion or free emigration as Dukakis would "challenge" him to do, Charles Krauthammer maintained that "Reagan's successes, which Dukakis is quick to applaud, happened not because he challenged the Russians to be nice but because he forced them to give in." In what must qualify as one of the least flattering presidential endorsements in American history, Krauthammer and his New Republic colleagues noted that their candidate, as President,

> would have endorsed the nuclear freeze, thereby denying us the INF treaty that saw the removal of Soviet missiles in Europe. He would have cut off the contras early on, leaving us today with a consolidated and expansionist Marxist regime in Nicaragua. Whether a Dukakis foreign policy would have produced the Soviet pullout from Afghanistan, the impending settlement in Angola, and other successes of the Reaganite hard-line is dubious at the least.

The obvious loser in this process was not Dukakis but the American political process. William Safire says he thinks his political influence is at a peak during election season. This is because the candidates must campaign for many months before they face an electorate. Voters are not invited into the process until the shape of the debate has already been determined. The pre-campaign campaign is about two things: money and recognition. The former often follows the latter. While handlers, pollsters, moneymen, and volunteer workers all have a role to play, the pundits are the only constant determinant of how much and what kind of attention each candidate can be expected to receive.

Thus it was wholly irrelevant to the 1988 campaign that vast majorities of the American people had ceased to view the Soviet military as an important threat to their well-being. Nor did it turn out to matter much that economic power and influence had come to play a far more important role on the world stage in determining a nation's well-being than the size of its military, and that more than two thirds of Americans surveyed at the time felt that way.* To William Safire, George Will, Charles Krauthammer, Henry Kissinger, most of the panelists on "The McLaughlin Group," and the neoconservative editors of *The New Republic*, the rise of Mikhail Gorbachev did not fundamentally affect the power calculation that lay at the root of all great power politics. The American purpose, as it were, remained resistance to Soviet Communist domination. Those candidates who refused to place this contest at the very center of their political agendas—and who refused, therefore, to subordinate all other national problems to its achievement—were to be dismissed as foolish, naive, and "McGovernite." Their funding and hence recognition levels diminished accordingly. † Thus a candidate who sought to engage Gorbachev in ending the Cold War or merely one who sought to subordinate what remained of the East-West competition to what appeared to be more pressing domestic and international needs was simply not to be taken seriously. The environment, our education system, our economic infrastructure, the health of our cities, our ability to compete on par with Germans and Japanese—these were issues that, when push came to shove, were "not even peripheral" when compared with the long twilight struggle of the never-ending Cold War.

*Both of these statements are evident in "Defining American Strength: Results of a Survey of American Voters Conducted by The World Policy Institute, October 15 through October 20, 1987" (Washington, DC: Mellman and Lazarus Research, 1987). See also Stanley Greenberg, "Looking Toward '88: The Politics of American Identity," *World Policy Journal*, Fall 1987. These numbers, moreover, remained firm throughout the year. According to a later poll, taken in May 1989 and therefore more than six months before the fall of the Berlin Wall, a full 4% of Americans surveyed considered "Soviet aggression in the world" to pose "the greatest danger to America today," while just 2% thought it represented "the most important problem facing America today." The latter number was one tenth of those who chose "education" and one seventh of those who chose "rising costs for young families." Recognizing this, a full 73% of those surveyed wanted the government to recognize that "the greatest threat to American security is the economic challenge posed by Japan, and we should shift military spending to favor domestic investment." See "Defining American Priorities: Results of a Survey of American Voters Conducted for The World Policy Institute by Greenberg-Lake, The Analysis Group, May 18 through May 23, 1989."

†Jesse Jackson is obviously his own special case here.

When Michael Dukakis debated George Bush for the presidency of the United States, both spoke as if Mikhail Gorbachev did not exist. American Sovietologists regarded Gorbachev as the most remarkable development in the past two centuries of Russian history. The American people considered him among the most impressive men on the planet. But because neither group had the means to puncture the closed circle of self-reinforcing punditocracy ideology, neither group's views proved relevant to the electoral discussion. The Cold War therefore lived on in the American political imagination long after it had ended in the geographical space it was said to occupy, crippling our political dialogue and warping our national priorities.

In 1988, the American people elected a man who attributed the rise of Mikhail Gorbachev solely to "our strength . . . steadiness . . . our resolve," but who nevertheless compared negotiating arms-control treaties with the man to ignoring the lessons of Auschwitz. His running mate told reporters that he considered *perestroika* to be "nothing more than refined Stalinism" and Gorbachev to be "no different than Brezhnev or anybody else." The brazen foolishness of these statements was made possible by three years of punditocracy denial, distortion, and distrust. As a result, the United States entered the decade of the 1990s with an intellectually crippled political leadership, incapable even of acknowledging, much less addressing, the fundamental challenges we faced as a nation.

11

WINNING ISN'T EVERYTHING . . .

The final, undeniable implosion of the Eastern bloc in late 1989 presented innumerable problems for punditocracy. There was the "winning" of the Cold War to be celebrated, certainly; seminars to be given, conferences to be attended, and memoirs to be invented. But beyond that, all was mist.

The grand contest was over. "History" had come to an end. "The American idea" had triumphed. Still, the punditocracy seemed discomfited. There were no ticker-tape parades in Times Square, no drunken soldiers reveling until all hours of the night receiving kisses from women they never met, no joy across the land. "All over the world everything is going our way," noted *The New York Times* "Week in Review" editors. "So Why Then Doesn't It Feel Better?"

It was not as if there were no post–Cold War agenda out there waiting to be addressed. The eighties, as that conservative social critic, the late Harry Angstrom, reminds us, were a time of "everything falling apart, airplanes, bridges, eight years under Reagan of nobody minding the store, making money out of nothing, running up debt, trusting in God." But none of the dormant issues of the 1970s and 1980s proved terribly galvanizing to the punditocracy. The deindustrialization of the American economy—its disintegrating transportation infrastructure, global warming, ozonosphere depletion, soil erosion, increasing infant mortality rates, declining SAT scores, growing illiteracy, and racial tension in cities across the country—these were problems with complex, multifaceted roots that could not be solved without massive amounts of long-term investment, and in many cases, tedious international cooperation. They had none of the romance of maintaining one's vigilance for a Long Twilight Struggle. They did not, in the words of the "End of History" ideologist Francis Fukuyama, inspire "the struggle for recognition, the willingness to risk one's life for a purely abstract goal, worldwide ideological struggle that called forth daring, courage, imagination and idealism." In fact, noted Fukuyama, they could be summed up in a single word: "boredom." Our future, Washington pundits seemed to fear, was behind us.

The Cold War's end, to punditocracy commentators, came as an unalloyed American triumph. William Safire, almost alone among influential pundits, continued to argue even after the Wall came down that the battle would be over "only when the Soviet Union demonstrates its willingness to end the practice of imperialism." But even Safire's editor at the time, Leslie Gelb, noted that he had long since lost that battle.

"History," noted George Will, was "marching to the cadences of an American President." "What has happened is a clear victory for the traditional principles on which American and Western democracies are based," observed Jeane Kirkpatrick. "As our one great adversary implodes," argued Charles Krauthammer, we are "alone on the world stage." In perhaps the most enthusiastic example of the genre, neoconservative pundit Ben Wattenberg practically watusied across the pages of *The National Interest* with his proclamation that:

> America is and will be Number One. . . . Today only American democratic culture has legs. Only Americans have the sense of mission— and gall—to engage in global cultural advocacy. We are the only mythic nation . . . we have the highest standard of living . . . we have the best filmmakers . . . America is the number one tourist destination. . . .*

*Ben J. Wattenberg, "Neo-Manifest Destinarianism," *The National Interest*, Fall 1990, pp. 51–54. The purest demonstration of these sentiments can actually be found in the writing of the proudly incorrigible P. J. O'Rourke. Writing in the January 11, 1990, edition of *Rolling Stone*, O'Rourke announced: "We won and let's not anybody forget it. We the peoples, the free and equal citizens of democracies, we the living exemplars of the Rights of Man, tore a new asshole in International Communism. Their wall is breached. Their gut string is busted. The rot of their dead body politic fills the nostrils of the earth with glorious stink. We cleaned the clock of Marxism. We mopped the floor with them. We ran the Reds through the wringer and hung them out to dry. The privileges of liberty and the sanctity of the individual went out and kicked some butt. . . . They have had the soldiers, the submarines, and the fine-sounding ideology to sucker in the eggheads and the nitwit Third Worlders, but we had all the fun. Now they're lunch and we're number one on the planet."

Beneath the triumphalism, however, lay a number of uncertainties about the future plans for this mythic nation of ours. A few Old Rightists, led by Pat Buchanan, reverted to pre–Cold War isolationism. Ironically, it was the neoconservatives who indirectly inspired the growth of this isolationism with their insistence upon profligate weapons spending and indiscriminate military intervention during the Reagan era; yet it was also they who denounced it most vociferously. Liberals spoke woozily of a "peace dividend" to be derived from funds no longer necessary to fight Communists. Conservatives focused on the dangers presented from new external threats ranging from drug-smuggling Latin American generals to terrorist-minded cross-dressing Arab dictators. Both problems fell under the general rubric of "instability," and required roughly the same level of military investment and worldwide intervention that the Cold War had. That the United States also had urgent internal problems with which to deal was granted in a kind of abstract manner by most participants in the insider debate. But however dire each of these problems may have seemed in isolation, none was considered remotely as serious as the various military perils that continued to preoccupy the punditocracy.

That the United States had seriously weakened itself and its ability to compete in the postwar world did not much enter into discussions of the post–Cold War era. Denouncing the notion of America's economic decline had been a brief punditocracy obsession just a year before the 1989 revolutions. But by the time the Cold War's remaining ideological flotsam had been sufficiently cleared away to air the issue again, in spite of its allegedly defeatist imputations, it had already been disposed of and replaced by the psychologically far more endearing notion of an America-inspired "end of history."

The decline of so many of the qualities that had given the United States its special advantages in the world was not exactly a secret during the 1970s and early 1980s. The theme made its academic debut when Cornell professor Richard Rosecrance published a book entitled *America as an Ordinary Country* in 1976. Analysts and academics James Chace, Mancur Olson, David Calleo, Walter Russell Mead, and Rosecrance himself all published major works throughout the eighties delineating the collapsing economic position of the United States and warning of the consequences of continued denial on the part of our leaders. But it was still "morning" in the punditocracy, and all opposing arguments sank from public debate without a trace.

It was not until Yale Professor Paul Kennedy published his massive tome *The Rise and Fall of the Great Powers* that "late afternoon" or even "evening" managed to insinuate themselves into the punditocracy's metaphorical clocks. Published in late 1987, Kennedy's book shot up both *The Washington Post* and *New York Times* bestseller lists early in 1988, and remained in both places for most of the year.

Though based on years of research and flooded beneath an ocean of footnotes, Kennedy's thesis was a simple restatement of Walter Lippmann's commonsense observation that to be economically and politically solvent, a nation must bring "into balance . . . the nation's commitments and the nation's power." The power of Kennedy's version lay in the five hundred years of history he had summoned to prove it. Beginning with Ming China, the soft-spoken North Country Englishman demonstrated that the decline of the United States was not only unarguable, it was the fulfillment of an historical pattern that had been repeating itself for centuries.

The same pattern of "imperial overstretch" had felled the Spanish/ Austrian Habsburg Empire of the sixteenth and early seventeenth century, the French Empire that followed, and the British Empire that inherited the post-Napoleonic order. The game of empire was by definition an expensive one. Whenever a nation extended its armies and military commitments across the globe, it inevitably invested great sums to protect its position. These investments had the effect of eating away at its own fundamental sources of productivity until the nation was finally forced to retrench. Unfortunately, noted Kennedy, great powers in relative decline had a habit of responding to that decline by spending even more on "security," thereby "diverting potential resources from 'investment' and compound[ing] their long term dilemmas." Retrenchment could be planned for, or it could be thrust upon us, but the message of every one of Kennedy's nearly seven hundred pages of historical facts and figures was that it could not be prevented merely by asserting our "will," "credibility," and "resolve."

The book, and its implications for the upcoming election, became the dominant topic of punditocracy conversation in early 1988. Exactly why Kennedy's tome managed to penetrate the ideological wall constructed by punditocracy Cold Warriors is an interesting, though not fully answerable question.* It is hard to imagine that many of the pundits who attacked the book had read it. Some may not even have bothered to read the sections on contemporary Russia and Japan. Understandably, perhaps, the punditocracy argument over Kennedy's book focused exclusively on the .03 percent of it that dealt with the present-day United States.

Ideologically, Kennedy and the "declinists" provided a refuge for those pundits seeking to tiptoe out of the Reagan camp in order to catch the next

---

*Front-page raves in both *The New York Times* and *The Washington Post* book review sections provided necessary but not sufficient conditions.

ideological wave. *The New Republic* editors had already positioned themselves for such a move a year earlier with their discovery of the "Reagan hangover" the country was about to experience. With the era winding down and the magazine knowing, as George Will put it, "in its DNA structure" that it would be compelled to endorse a Democratic candidate within the year, its editors saw in Kennedy's thesis an appropriately muscular alternative to the Reaganism it had been promoting for the previous seven. The (Kondracke-authored) lead editorial provided an important tastemaking boost, as did Kondracke's prediction on "The McLaughlin Group" that it would become the "book of the year." David Broder, another crucial barometer of punditocracy precipitation, devoted a New Hampshire-based column to Kennedy. He, too, wondered if "balancing" might not mean "taking a broader measure of national strength than the number of warheads, divisions or ships we can deploy. . . ."

Kennedy also benefited from the ire of his enemies. Neoconservatives considered Kennedy's demonstration of America's vulnerabilities to be a kind of grand metaphysical insult, akin to Nietzsche's rhetorical assassination of God. Norman Podhoretz took up the cudgel against the dangerous moral equivalence he detected in Kennedy's comparison of the American empire to those that had come before it. "To Kennedy," he lamented in *The Washington Post*, "America represents nothing special in history, nothing of any permanent or universal validity or value."* Joining Podhoretz across a religious but hardly political divide was the neoconservative Catholic theologian Michael Novak. The latter feared that Kennedy's declinist arguments have "unforgivably damaged our national morale."

Recognizing that they had no chance to engage Kennedy on his home turf of scholarly research, right-wing pundits generally contented themselves with the suggestion that whatever the data might imply, it was irrelevant to the United States' predicament, owing to our special grace. Jeane Kirkpatrick, positing no evidence, insisted that there was no connection between defense expenditures, economic growth, and national decline. Like Podhoretz, she saw America's problem as merely a "loss of national will." George Will attempted to discredit the thesis by viewing it through the prism of small, strategically insignificant, and (as yet) uninvaded Latin American nations. "Imperial overstretch," he chuckled. "The Sandinistas and Noriega

---

*Norman Podhoretz, "The Decline of America: A Best Selling Theme," *The Washington Post*, February 26, 1988. Kennedy replied that "of course the United States is special. So is France. So is India. So is Norway. All countries are, in their various ways, special. All are, as Ranke would put it, 'immediate to God.' But when their inhabitants start boasting about being 'special,' it is time to be disturbed, because it usually indicates a profound contempt for other peoples who are not so special."

rejoice that America's real problem is understretch, the atrophy of underused muscle."

By far the most energetic and creative attempt to shift the ground beneath the bleakness of Kennedy's mountain of statistical decline was that of Harvard Professor Joseph Nye, who blanketed the punditocracy's third ring with articles in the *Times*, the *Post*, *Foreign Policy*, *The Atlantic Monthly*, and finally in his own book, *Bound to Lead*. Nye granted much of the substance of Kennedy's thesis, but insisted that his instruments of measurement were obsolete. Nye preferred to rest his case against decline on what he called "soft" power assets such as the spread of American popular culture, the use of English as the lingua franca worldwide, and the fact that no other "number one" was emerging on the horizon. A key adviser to the patriotically anti-declinist presidential campaign of Michael Dukakis, Nye insisted that "withdrawing from international commitments might reduce American influence overseas without necessarily strengthening the domestic economy."

The debate over Kennedy's thesis, however uplifting for those waiting in vain for the introduction of even a thimbleful of unpleasant reality into the punditocracy debate, proved nevertheless to be a major disappointment. The Bush presidential campaign picked it up, kicked it around, and turned it into yet another manifestation of Democrat-induced "doom and gloom." As with most Bush attacks, the Dukakis campaign ignored its substance and hoped it would go away.

While Kennedy was initially accepted into the debate in large measure because of the undeniable moderation of his presentation, he may, in the end, have been undermined by the very same quality. For before the full extent of American decline could be thoroughly demonstrated to a skeptical public, the revolutions of 1989 appeared, only to be followed by the drama of the Persian Gulf crisis. In both instances, conservatives could once again make the case that America was "winning." Czech and Chinese student leaders were quoting Jefferson. The Soviet Union was imploding. Berliners were dancing on the Wall, and the United Nations was happily endorsing our willingness to send our soldiers to die in the desert to expel Saddam Hussein from Kuwait. At the surface level of political analysis, where pundicratic debate takes place, the nation's emotional clock had been set back, once again, to morning in America.

In late 1989, as the declinist thesis was being carefully swept under the rug, Washington latched onto yet another "big idea," this one far more consistent with a nation enjoying an orgy of self-congratulation. "The End of History," as then–State Department official Francis Fukuyama called his theory, was not posited as a response to Kennedy, but was used as one nevertheless. The article in which Fukuyama presented his case was promoted in George Will's column and funded and disseminated with the help of the Far Right Olin Foundation and its neoconservative journal, *The National Interest*, published by Irving Kristol. Though dressed up in some extremely intimidating Hegelian garb, the Fukuyama thesis, as the historian William McNeill would later explain, "simply reformulate[d] a long-standing vision of the United States as embodying an earthly perfection toward which all other peoples have been expected to aspire." As Fukuyama put it, to the delight of his neoconservative patrons, "What we may be witnessing is the end point of mankind's ideological evolution and the universalization of Western liberal democracy as the final form of human government."

Fukuyama's strange notions of daring, idealism, imagination, and courage, coupled with the astonishing cultural arrogance of his use of the word "history," occupied the punditocracy long enough to free it from the albatross of Paul Kennedy.* But once the Hegelian philosophical gloss was wiped away, Fukuyama was simply saying what everyone had known all along: market economies were more efficient than centrally planned economies. Freedom was better than unfreedom. No one of political significance or intellectual substance in the United States had argued otherwise for nearly thirty years. The argument, rather, has been between differing versions of capitalism: social democratic, as in Northern Europe; laissez-faire, as in Reaganite America and Thatcherite England; or corporatist/interventionary, as in Japan and South Korea. Judging by the recent productive performance of the economies in question, it is hardly clear that the American model is most inspiring of these three. In any case, the pretense of the debate over whose system was more efficient, ours or the Communists', had become by the 1970s largely a means of avoiding a confrontation with our own failures.

Late in 1990, George Will, sounding extremely Fukuyamian, argued that

An argument that has convulsed the politics of this century and enlivened intellectual life for longer than that, is now over. On one side were those who argued that justice required society to be run from above, from the center, by the commands of a cadre claiming privileged insight into the inexorable, inevitable unfolding dynamic of history. On the other side—the American side—it is fair to call it—were those who argued that justice demands wide dispersal of decision making, broad scope for the private pursuit of happiness as individuals envision it, a pursuit protected

---

*Fukuyama writes, "For our purposes, it matters very little what strange thoughts occur to people in Albania or Burkina Faso, for we are interested in what one could in some sense call the common ideological heritage of mankind." "The End of History?" *The National Interest*, Summer 1989, p. 9.

and facilitated by government deriving its powers from the consent of the governed.

Like Fukuyama, Will was picking on the strawest of men. Both writers make frequent reference to Berkeley and Cambridge—in jest, one assumes—as the last remaining outposts of academic Marxism. But Marxism/Leninism, as both men surely must know, has had absolutely no standing whatever in American progressive thought since the collapse of the New Left in the early seventies.* As one *Financial Times* columnist pointed out, by Fukuyama's (and Will's) yardstick, "History must have ended a very long time ago in America: indeed, perhaps it never even started there."

The pathetic level of discussion over "declinism" and "endism" illustrated nothing so much as the decline of American public culture and the end of any hopes for a measured, rational discussion of its increasing political and economic insolvency. Paul Kennedy assembled a vast array of facts and figures during his years of researching *The Rise and Fall of the Great Powers*. But perhaps his most astute observation came when he told a *New York Times* interviewer that "anybody advocating American perestroika is going to have a hell of a fight on his hands."

That the idea of America's economic decline remains controversial even today, when so much incontrovertible evidence has arisen in support of it, is a tribute to the clout of the punditocracy's ideological fixation. It is also a measure of the power of One Big Thing in a hedgehog-driven political culture.

That the United States has undergone a relative decline from the artificial heights it occupied in the immediate postwar period is granted by all sides in the debate. Indeed, our economic policies were designed to cause exactly that process to reduce our manufacturing surpluses in order to bring Europe and Asia to the level where they could compete effectively under an American-policed system of free trade. If these war-torn competitors needed to adopt temporarily unfair trading practices to protect their infant industries against the behemoth American multinationals, so be it; in the end, this would strengthen our allies for the really important contest: the one against communism.

The process worked beyond our wildest dreams. Protected by a series of both formal and informal mechanisms, the European and East Asian nations

---

*Even within the New Left, self-described Marxist/Leninists were nevertheless quite critical of the ossified Stalinist structure of the Soviet Union, which was considered as much an enemy of popular liberation as the United States.

which formed the basis of our worldwide anti-Communist alliance rebuilt their economies to the point where their capacities for innovation and low-cost production exceeded those of American firms. Between 1975 and 1989, the American share of the global product fell 6 percent while Japan's rose 15 percent. Our share of global equities diminished by half during the eighties, while the value of Japanese stock assets increased five hundred-fold. Crucial industries such as consumer electronics and machine-tool production have all but disappeared from our shores. Computers, semiconductors, and automobiles may be next.

Wall Street Journal editor Robert Bartley, still battling declinist remnants in March 1992, argues that "for all the accomplishments of the industrious Japanese, America still dominates scientific innovation." It is a measure of punditocracy desperation that so savvy a player as Bartley is forced to revert to such unsupportable (and unsupported) assertions. Japan has already surpassed the United States as the world's top patron of industrial research and development, and its corporations top the world competition for the creation of newly patented products and ideas.

The single most important determinant of the health of a nation's economy is its ability to improve its productivity rate. The reason the United States was able to catch up to, and later surpass, Britain's standard of living during the nineteenth century was its tiny but consistent advantage in productivity performance. In the past twenty years, however, U.S. productivity increases have been declining steadily. The past two decades constitute the worst performance by this country during the entire century.

Added to declining productivity levels in the early 1980s was the assumption, by the U.S. economy, of huge amounts of new debt. This debt explosion was a direct outgrowth of the punditocracy-inspired doctrines of massive military spending coupled with equally massive supply-side tax cuts for the wealthy. At the crossroads of these two perfectly contradictory policies, in conjunction with declining productivity rates, was the conversion of the American economy from the world's wealthiest to its most indebted. America's borrowing binge has also contributed to the relative lack of investment funds that would have been available to finance improvements in our miserable productivity numbers. Since 1980, federal borrowing has absorbed almost 75 percent of all net savings done by American families and businesses combined. New investment in plants and equipment—the building blocks of productivity increases and long-term prosperity—is now lower in the United States than at any time since World War II. In a nutshell, explains *BusinessWeek*, "America simply isn't competitive with other nations."

The eighties *were* kind to millionaires. Their numbers increased from 180,000 in 1972 to over 1.3 million by 1988. The average total compensation for an American CEO in 1989 exceeded $2 million a year. Meanwhile, living standards for the vast majority of Americans either stood still or began to decline. Accounting for inflation, average hourly wages for American workers fell by almost 10 percent during the 1980s, having been flat since 1973. Their benefits fell even more. Even *Commentary* magazine has been forced to admit that during the past two decades, American wage earners have seen their salaries regress to the point where by 1990, both "non-farm" workers and corporate executives were earning on average no more than they had in 1965, allowing for inflation. What's more, the U.S. Census Bureau admitted in early 1992 that the number of Americans who could call themselves middle class was now shrinking. The news gets even worse when one considers the fact that to the Census Bureau, a family of four living on an annual income of only $18,576 qualifies as "middle class."

To make matters even worse, the problems created by this type of decline are self-reinforcing. America already has the worst primary education system in the Western world. We have the highest drop-out and illiteracy rates among Western industrialized nations and our students consistently perform near the bottom on international examinations. An uneducated work force virtually ensures even greater declines in productivity, and hence, the same vicious cycle.

The same depressing pattern is discernible in America's collapsing economic infrastructure. During the past decade, the federal government has allowed the country's infrastructure to decline to a state of near collapse. This not only invites avoidable catastrophes, such as falling bridges and disintegrating tunnels, but also ensures excessive costs and delays in the production of American goods. Yet once again, we find ourselves victims of a vicious cycle; without increases in productivity, we will have insufficient revenue to fix our infrastructure. Without a better infrastructure, it will be nearly impossible to increase productivity.

Inseparable from America's economic decline are a series of world developments that were either ignored or improperly understood while they were occurring owing to our national obsession with the Soviets. The rise of the world's most powerful economic power, Japan, and its systematic, government-supported attack on many of America's most important industries, provides a perfect example. This extended assault went all but ignored in Washington while it was taking place. Afraid to alienate geopolitical allies in the grand competition with the Soviet Union, the United States allowed itself to become the patsy of its trade competitors, offering one trade concession after another in order to keep peace for our military alliances. Nowhere were the sacred vows of the free-trade regime defended more vociferously than within the punditocracy.

Ironically, the United States went to its greatest lengths to subjugate its long-term economic health to its metaphysical military battle just as the rest of the world seemed to recognize the increasing primacy of economic influence over military force. Intoxicated by the romance of the Reagan Doctrine, the United States intervened throughout the 1980s in Central America, the Middle East, Southern Africa, and Southeast Asia. None of these places showed any signs of achieving greater stability or addressing their long-term problems as a result. Meanwhile, Japan spent the decade deploying its newfound economic influence, carving out its sphere of influence in Asia, and working out a modus vivendi with its regional rival, China. Germany and the European Community followed a similar path, proving once again that surplus capital is never lonely. In the end, by concentrating upon a Cold War geopolitical strategy rather than a post–Cold War geoeconomic one, the United States lost influence in one strategic nation after another, while doing nothing for the internal victims of our erstwhile allies.

If the American economy were the only element of our national culture in decline, then the problems ignored and exacerbated by punditocracy Cold War obsessions might be less worrisome. But the economy constitutes only one aspect of a negative spiral toward national insolvency and domestic insecurity. Even more daunting in many ways are the threats we face in preserving our natural environment.

Environmental danger suffers in the public imagination from its lack of romance and its general slow-burning demeanor. This may sound strange, given the romance the issue has generated among Hollywood's political aristocracy. But however well meaning, the celestial-induced feel-goodism of Earth Day and its well-tanned ambassadors does not begin to address the elaborate series of interlocking phenomena that must be ameliorated if we are to avoid unprecedented natural upheavals.

The environmental threats we face are, without exception, painfully gradual ones. They do not inspire pop culture nightmares as a surprise Soviet missile attack or an Arab hijacker might. The only credible villain in the story is a worldwide economic system that places less value on the destruction of an entire ecosystem than it does on a barrel of oil. Moreover, our understanding of the relationships between these complex phenomena is extremely hazy. It is as if we are feeling our way through a room filled with ever-expanding pockets of invisible, odorless poison gases. We know they are there, and we know they are bad for us. We can't be sure just what the effects of this unknown gas will be; we can only be certain they won't be pleasant.

The costs of decades of short-sighted energy and industrial policies are now only dimly apparent. We see them throughout the economy—in rising health-care costs associated with increased cancer rates, in the reduced productivity of our farmland, in the enormous expense of nuclear waste and toxic-site cleanup, and in the intangible costs to our society of dying forests, ruined lakes, and the loss of biodiversity. We see them most poignantly among our dead soldiers in the Persian Gulf.

The intellectual void we face with regard to the environment is more worrisome than most of our other problems because it is impossible to address without unprecedented international cooperation—yet another sensible notion that fell into disrepute under the influence of the Reagan punditocracy. Ozone rays and greenhouse gases recognize no borders.

To make matters worse, many Third World populations are struggling to survive—and are thus not terribly interested in assuring a better quality of life for future generations. Many have enormous debts to pay to Western banks. This leads some of the world's poorest nations to pursue some of the world's most awful environmental practices. The net result can be seen in the growing rate of tropical deforestation, particularly in, but not limited to, Amazonia.

The severe environmental problems of Third World countries affect our own health and security not only through environmental processes like global warming but also through increased political and economic instability. In many developing countries, the combination of expanding populations, soil erosion, tropical deforestation, and other resource constraints is destroying fragile ecosystems and stunting economic growth, thereby intensifying internal conflict. This in turn adds to political tensions, reduces productivity, and decreases our potential markets. Fewer markets means a worse economy, less money for environmental protection, increased political tension, and a continued decline in the overall quality of American life.

The unhappy effects of our own economic decline and social disintegration are already apparent in most of the nation's urban centers, though Cold War hedgehogs in the punditocracy are particularly adept at averting their eyes. George Will makes much political hay out of the notion that "the Soviet Union is the first industrialized society to achieve" a decline in the life expectancy rates of its citizens "during peacetime and in the 1970s was the only nation of any sort with such a decline, except Cambodia." Actually, the United States has achieved a similarly awful state of affairs for its black males, whose life expectancy rates began declining in the mid-1980s. To be born black or Hispanic in the United States is, in all probability, to be in the equivalent of a poor, dangerous, and dirty Third World nation. Black wealth per capita is approximately one tenth that of white wealth, with Hispanics only slightly better off. For a black male born in the past twenty-five years, the chances are better that he will end up in jail than in college, in this, the world's most incarcerated society.

The nation's economic decline and social decay have made American cities all but unlivable places for much of the middle class. Drugs, crime, the AIDS virus, inadequate housing stock, unmet infrastructural needs, increasing illiteracy, and declining employment opportunities have combined to turn major sections of New York, Washington, DC, Chicago, Detroit, and Los Angeles into the functional equivalents of downtown Beirut. In the United States, 9,536 people were murdered in 1989. In Britain, the number was seven. Moreover, home ownership, college education, and health insurance—the very foundations of middle-class American life—are also under siege. Given rising costs and falling family incomes, the American Dream is now out of reach for most Americans.

The final relevant aspect of American decline lies in the area that we regularly trumpet as our most important contribution to civilization: our political system. Even so sophisticated an observer as the New Republic literary editor, Leon Wieseltier, feels no compunction in simply asserting that "the United States has provided for its citizens a system of government that is morally, socially, and culturally superior to any other system in the world." Once upon a time that statement was undoubtedly true. Today, however, the idea that the United States can claim itself to be a model democracy, with incumbent reelection rates exceeding 95 percent, with fewer than half its citizens on average bothering to vote, and with a Congress that is rife with officially sanctioned corruption in the form of PAC contributions, is curious, to say the least. When one factors in the content upon which our political contests are decided, the claim sounds even more bizarre.

As Christopher Lasch has argued, perhaps the worst effect of the Cold War has been "to undermine confidence in government, to weaken our public culture and to destroy the delicate fabric of trust on which civic life depends." True, the United States may retain the world's most impressive Constitution. But all too frequently in the Cold War era, it has given way under the strain of the government's demands for secrecy and unfettered freedom of action. As a result, a number of the Constitution's most important provisions have been effectively revoked. The Fourth Amendment right "of the people to be secure in their persons, houses and effects, against unreasonable searches and seizures" has collapsed beneath a presidential directive that allows the government to search American citizens' homes and place wiretaps on their telephones so long as the U.S. Attorney General deems the individual to be working as an "agent of a foreign power."* No proof is necessary. The secrecy under which the United States budgets its intelligence functions is also in violation of the Constitution. The latter specifically enunciates the principle that "no money shall be drawn from the Treasury but in Consequence of Appropriations made by Law." Yet the CIA is currently authorized to transfer and receive funds from other agencies in secret with only the approval of the Office of Management and Budget, an office answerable only to the President. Since the onset of the Cold War, moreover, the United States government has seen fit to overturn constitutional and lawful protections regarding freedom of travel, the free flow of information, the prior restraint of free speech, privacy of individuals, and even protection for the environment.† The forfeit of Congress' warmaking powers, evident in every single postwar use of American military force save that of the Persian Gulf, is yet another casualty of our Cold War fixation.

The punditocracy cannot be fairly said to have simply ignored these developments during the past half-decade. Rather, it has simply treated them as isolated phenomena, worthy of only temporary attention and occasionally, minor adjustments.

The threat of ecological catastrophe earned its fifteen minutes of fame during the scalding-hot summer of 1988. It garnered *Time*'s coveted "Planet of the Year" award and some extremely ambitious rhetoric about the need to face up, once and for all, to the destructive byproducts of our present course. *The New York Times* editorial board wondered aloud how we would find the courage and foresight to prevent the impending catastrophe. Its liberal columnists, Tom Wicker and Anthony Lewis, devoted enormous amounts of column space to the need for sweeping change domestically and massive cooperation internationally. In 1990 *The Washington Post* hired its first-ever environmental columnist, Jessica Tuchman Matthews. The vice-president of the World Resources Institute, Matthews can claim authorship of one of the most ambitious pleas for environmental sanity ever to grace a mainstream punditocracy publication. Arguing in the Spring 1989 issue of *Foreign Affairs* that "the 1990s will demand a redefinition of what constitutes security," Matthews noted that while "in the seventies, the concept was

*The language is that of the Fourth Amendment to the United States Constitution. The law currently in force is Ronald Reagan's Executive Order 12333 Section 2.4(b), which authorizes "unconsented physical searches" by the FBI.

†In 1981, the Supreme Court unanimously held that information that is properly classified is exempt from the National Environmental Policy Act of 1969. For information on this and other erosions of civil liberties related to the Cold War, see the American Civil Liberties Union, "Ending the Cold War at Home: A Public Policy Report" (Washington, DC: ACLU, 1991).

expanded to include international economics . . . global developments now suggest the need for another, broadening definition of national security to include resource, environmental and demographic issues." The concurrent issue of *Foreign Policy* proved even more ambitious and far-sighted than its competitor. Leading with two important articles entitled "Climate Chaos," and "Environment and Security," the magazine eschewed the traditional geopolitical definition of national security and instead addressed itself to the emerging national and international trends—environmental and otherwise— that threatened America's future. Among these were mildly prophetic contributions from editor Charles William Maynes on remaking American foreign policy, MIT professor Charles H. Ferguson on the alarming decline in the nation's high-technology industries, and private economist David Hale on the enormous costs to the American economy of Reagan-era indulgences. Still, for all the apparent movement away from the traditional concerns of Cold War issues, the essential priorities that had dictated the course of American decline in all of these areas generally escaped notice. The casual connections between Cold War military spending and the inadequacy of financial resources to address the various pathologies that continue to plague us went unremarked. Our pressing need to recast the entire investment strategy went unraised. And because the problems were still viewed as isolated rather than interconnected phenomena, they remained buried beneath the daily avalanche of stories and issues dictated by the obsolete, postwar mind-set. As the imperatives of the emerging post–Cold War agenda failed to capture the punditocracy's imagination, the old reflexes soon reasserted themselves as if almost nothing at all had changed. The Soviet Union had forfeited its Eastern European empire, but Gorbachev's ill treatment of its non-Russian republics suddenly became the primary issue in determining, yet once again, whether or not he was "for real." When the discomfort levels of summers of 1989 and 1990 did not match that of 1988, the issues of global warming and ozone destruction, too, fell off the punditocracy agenda. Two years later, in the spring of 1992, Fred Barnes felt free to make the bizarre claim on "The McLaughlin Group," that "the whole global warming issue is a hoax." His alleged evidence? A pseudo-scientific report issued by a tiny Counter-establishment think tank originally set up to do battle on behalf of Star Wars.

Particularly with regard to the economy, the Bush-era public dialogue has had a quality of otherworldliness to it. In an early 1991 *New York Times* book review of Alfred L. Malabre's *Beyond Our Means*, Christopher Lehmann-Haupt criticized the author for presenting "the litany—the annual budget deficits, the huge national debt, the negative balance to trade, the mounting private debt, the dependence on foreign investment, the Savings and Loan crisis, the downturn in the business cycle"—and then complained that "for all their reality, they've become boring to read about." At the risk of offending the world's most influential book reviewer, that's just the problem. Our opinion makers likewise grew bored with discussions of what Mr. Lehmann-Haupt calls "the litany," but right up to the 1992 election, came no closer to a strategy of national priorities that might seriously address it.

A healthy portion of the blame could be ascribed to the fact that pundits and politicians are simply incapable of focusing on more than one, extremely narrowly defined issue at a time. During the course of the first three years of the Bush presidency, attention lurched back and forth between the ever-exploding Savings and Loan crisis, the mushrooming federal deficit, and the allegedly salutary effects of lowering the tax rate on capital gains. It stayed with none of them long enough to allow discussion of the fundamental political and strategic doctrines that underlay their development.

The most successful attempt to puncture the punditocracy's smug complacency during this period came from a conservative Republican political analyst, Kevin Phillips, who published *The Politics of Rich and Poor* in the spring of 1990. The book documented the enrichment of the wealthiest strata of American society at the expense of its poor and middle classes, and single-handedly catapulted the issue of tax unfairness into the epicenter of punditocracy argument. The Democratic party, both nationally and in Congress, seized upon Phillips's argument as the centerpiece of its 1990 campaign and budget strategy. One Vermont Republican was even seen on national television denouncing a sheepish-looking George Bush, who, having flown into town to make a campaign appearance on the man's behalf, was treated to a Phillips-inspired lecture upon the need for rich people to pay higher taxes.

Phillips's success owed much to an interesting reversal of the 1980s "even *The New Republic* . . ." principle. His analysis, though forcefully argued and competently organized, was old-hat. The fact that Donald, Ivan, and Leona were throwing lots of parties with their newly undertaxed incomes as the rest of us took home smaller and smaller pieces of the pie was well known to those who cared to look. The Economic Policy Institute tried to call attention to this trend as early as October 1986. In early 1988, the economists Barry Bluestone and Bennett Harrison published a book-length economic treatise demonstrating that "for every affluent 'yuppie' in an expensive big-city condominium . . . there are many more people whose wages have been falling and whose families are finding it more and more difficult to make ends meet." Nobody cared. Pundits accused those liberals who raised the issue of "practicing the politics of class warfare." The only thing worse than to lose a class war during the 1980s was to be accused of being willing to fight one.

Not until Phillips, who, as the creator of Richard Nixon's racially divisive "Southern strategy" in 1968, possessed unimpeachable conservative credentials, started knocking around the issue did it succeed in capturing the punditocracy's imagination. Were the Republicans really "the party of the rich," asked op-ed writers and talk-show hosts. Was the "little guy" finally striking back? Was a populist tax revolt in the offing? What did a populist look like, anyway, and what if one wanted to marry your daughter?

Lost amid the hoopla was the larger context of Phillips's critique. As he explained in the book's introduction, the reason these disturbing events had proceeded unchallenged for more than a decade owed a great deal to what he called "the critical weakness of American politics and governance . . . a frightening inability to define and debate America's problems." American politics, he announced, was "brain dead."

While Phillips allowed that pundits such as himself were not "providing great insights," he defined the problem primarily in terms of America's political parties: both the Democrats and Republicans were "out of sync with the times," prisoners of what he called the "irrelevant consensus phenomenon." American politics, said Phillips, was addicted to "outdated ideologies . . . about to be retired by history." Along with virtually everyone else outside Washington, Phillips was disgusted with the pathetically meager content of American politics. Historic battles were being fought in the streets of Prague, Beijing, Moscow, and Berlin. Even in South Africa, previously considered among the world's most reactionary nations, F. W. DeKlerk and Nelson Mandela were engaged in a minuet of diplomacy and power politics that impressed the most visionary observers. Yet in the United States, the political process was deadlocked in a debate over flag-burning and capital gains taxes. Public opinion surveys consistently demonstrated considerable unease among the populace about the path the nation was taking. Even Republican pollsters were finding majorities of Americans feeling that the country was "seriously off track." BusinessWeek discovered that 64 percent of Americans expected the economy to be dominated by foreign companies. Those who paid close attention to public affairs were well aware of the symptoms of the problem: "the litany," as Christopher Lehmann-Haupt called it, had been repeated by so many reputable figures one wondered if somewhere someone had invented word-processing software that simply plugged it in next to the escape key.

But the forces of American decline nevertheless continued to accelerate. The would-be public policy doctors focused on the strictly surface-level symptoms while the disease continued to eat at the body. So long as the country's intellectual leadership defined the problem exclusively in terms of its individual components, the logjam remained impenetrable. Congress, dominated by lobbyists and PACs, could not muster a majority in favor of substantive change absent an intellectual revolution. But this revolution lay stillborn—"brain dead," in Phillips's evocative phrase—the victim of a guiding class of punditocracy gatekeepers who continued to insist on fealty to the priorities of a bygone era.

America's problems in the early 1990s were still by and large soluble. The forces of our national decline were proceeding apace, but still had not kicked in full force. The nation retained the resources, economic and intellectual, to revitalize our economy, rebuild our cities and educational institutions, and begin the process of international negotiation to blunt the catastrophic effects of environmental neglect. In Louisiana, the country was given a preview of the future politics of decline in the race-baiting, "blame the poor" election campaign of former Nazi sympathizer and Ku Klux Klan Grand Wizard David Duke.* Yet even this barely roused the punditocracy. The central hurdle preventing an intelligent reassessment of America's long-term needs and strategic interests remained the inability of its leadership class, guided by the punditocracy, to come to terms with the reality of American decline in an economically more competitive and environmentally more fragile world than that it had previously known. The Cold War and its accompanying mental straitjacket paralyzed the American strategic mind and apparently destroyed what was once a national genius for innovation.

George Will, by fortunate coincidence, provided an archetype of the punditocracy's insistence upon fretting only about the symptoms of decline while ignoring the disease itself. Will wrote powerfully of the failures of the American system to provide for its neediest. "Nineteen nations have better infant mortality rates than the United States," he noted.

> The infant death rate in Japan is less than half the U.S. rate. . . . The infant death rate in the nation's capital and in Detroit and Baltimore is humiliatingly close to a Third World rate. It is higher than in Jamaica and Costa Rica. The rate among black American babies is worse than among Hungarian and Polish babies. Nothing that happens in Bangladesh should be as interesting to Americans as the fact that a boy born in Harlem today has a lower life expectancy than a boy born in Bangladesh.

Will took the opportunity of the President's 1991 State of the Union address to blithely remind his readers that the same nation that had manufactured those Patriot and Tomahawk missiles that exploded so

---

*Michael Kinsley made this point quite eloquently in "David Duke and American Decline," *Time*, November 25, 1991, p. 110.

beautifully over Baghdad had lost virtually its entire presence in the consumer electronics industry. It was also a nation, he noted, that had more and more difficulty producing "successful schools" and "children from functional families, walking to school down streets free from gunfire."

In some senses, Mr. Will's belated awakening was laudable. But it also proved irrelevant. Ironically, but hardly uniquely, no one in America was more influential than George Will in ensuring that the United States continued to invest itself in the kind of military hardware and geopolitical adventurism that all but ensured that those shaming statistics would continue to grow worse. Will's addiction to the expensive and debilitating drug of Cold War machismo affected his judgment capabilities with embarrassing results during the short-lived Soviet putsch of August 1991. The coup, which collapsed almost before it began, led Will to consign the "timid," "tinkering," and "temporizing" Mikhail Gorbachev and his liberalization efforts to the dustbin of history, along with any notion that Americans might entertain about reduced military spending. "The essential U.S. policy is still: Keep our powder dry and have lots of powder. The peace dividend will be a little late again," he cautioned. * As with his comments about the permanence of the Berlin Wall, dated the day of its destruction, Will's unlucky timing—together with Charles Krauthammer's equally military-minded response to the coup—spoke volumes about the punditocracy's inability to cast off its Manichean world view in the face of even cataclysmic change in the conditions that inspired it. †

George Smiley, the now retired legend of John LeCarré's London circus, evidences considerable pain over the fact that, as he puts it, "It was their emperor, not ours, who had the nerve to mount the rostrum and declare that he had no clothes." But in a way, this was no accident of history. Moscow's Cold War myopia had led to so dreadful a state of internal affairs in the Soviet Union that it eventually led to a second Russian Revolution. In the United States, however, the punditocracy's reaction to the sight of our enemy's admission of nakedness was to continue to insist upon the durability and warmth of our own now shabby and threadbare, fifty-year-old frock.

---

*Note that Will, together with Charles Krauthammer, was among the most vociferous supporters of the post–Cold War effort to build the $70 billion B-1 bomber fleet as well.

†Weeks *after* the coup failed, Krauthammer called recommendations to cut defense spending "the height of irresponsibility," adding, "Is it not time to get serious about strategic defense?" Charles Krauthammer, September 6, 1991.

12

OPERATION PUNDIT STORM

I

Few events in recent American history demonstrate the destructive power of the punditocracy with greater clarity than America's decision to go to war with Iraq in January of 1991. Casting about for a replacement of its One Big Thing in the aftermath of the Cold War, the punditocracy found itself at sea in a world without clear enemies to condemn or a credible international crusade to exhort. Dogged by increasing evidence of protracted decline and diminished international influence, the insider political dialogue manifested a kind of inchoate desperation—not altogether unlike that communicated by George Bush's syntax. "If only we knew who the bad guys were," the pundits seemed to be saying, "we'd know who we were again."

How it happened that the extrication of the Iraqi Army from the kingdom of Kuwait came to be *the* most important priority of the American people in the winter of 1991 can only be understood in this context. George Bush's success in leading the American public into war might never have been possible without the energetic cooperation of the punditocracy who, for a brief shining moment, found a new Big Thing to demonstrate its self-worth. The punditocracy's role explains not only the delusion of omnipotence that seized the nation in the aftermath of the hundred hours' fighting, but also the presumably serious insistence on the part of almost everyone who appeared in the media at the time that the defeat of a nation with a gross domestic product the size of Kentucky's somehow represented America's "defining moment."

During the six months that George Bush, Dick Cheney, Colin Powell, and Norman Schwarzkopf laid the groundwork for their successful assault on Saddam Hussein's army, a tiny cadre of mostly neoconservative pundits performed a similarly delicate operation on elite Washington opinion. Although it was undoubtedly President Bush's actions on behalf of Operation Desert Storm that spoke loudest during this period, the punditocracy's battle plan proved, in many respects, no less effective. The pundits concentrated their fire on a few superficially simple issues in this Arabian drama and treated them in a highly inflammatory fashion, thereby simultaneously constricting and distorting the war's public discourse. In the debate that led to Congress's decision to declare war, as well as during the fighting itself, the punditocracy shaped the political dialogue in a manner that substituted the Iraqi bogeyman for their fallen Stalinist icon and celebrated American military prowess with a degree of reverence that bordered on worship. Then, in the war's aftermath, they proceeded to ignore many of its considerable costs, as well as nearly all the fundamental questions it should have raised about America's future.

In the languid months that preceded the Iraqi invasion of Kuwait, Washington was having a difficult time convincing itself that it still mattered. David Broder helped get the year off to a depressing start by telling the city's powermongers—in a front-page article, no less—that they didn't matter any more. "Nation's Capital in Eclipse," explained Broder's headline, "As Pride and Power Slip Away."

In the White House, tempers were flaring over the reemergence of the dreaded "wimp issue" just in time for midterm elections. The exploding budget deficit forced the President to publicly repudiate his "no new taxes" pledge, infuriating conservatives who began, once again, to search for a potential challenger. One of their favorites, Patrick Buchanan, could be seen every day on television accusing the President of "refusing to stand up and lead our side in the great fight," and looking "like a wimp on the tax issue." Meanwhile, as Bush watched his approval ratings sink to new depths, his son Neil got himself embroiled in the ever-burgeoning S&L debacle. Neil Bush took to defending himself with abusive phone calls to reporters in the middle of the night and by treating live television cameras to the kind of language unheard from presidential family members since the heyday of Billy Carter. *

Life was no prettier in the punditocracy. Robbed of its Big Thing, its ideological flailings had the character of Churchill's pudding: they lacked

*Neil Bush charged that the accusations leveled against him were "absolute bullshit." His taped performance was shown on "The McLaughlin Group," July 14, 1990.

theme. Of course the pundits hated environmentalists, taxers and spenders, terrorists, and particularly, drug-smuggling dictators, but clearly passions were waning. One well-known Cold Warrior speculated about trying a second career as a novelist or a jazz critic. The beat went on, but the thrill was gone.

Tax rises, oil spills, flag-burners, Jesse Helms, and Piss Christ: every issue seemed more depressing than the last. Just days before the Iraqi invasion, "The McLaughlin Group" spent a good portion of the show discussing what should be done about Roseanne Barr's mangling of "The Star-Spangled Banner" at a baseball game. Morton Kondracke insisted that Americans boycott her sponsors because Ms. Barr was "unpatriotic," and "down on the country."

As if sent directly from Central Casting, Saddam Hussein rode in on his black horse, and rescued Washington from all this and the gratitude was almost palpable. Ben Wattenberg headlined his column: "Thanks Saddam, We Needed That." "In a way," observed the editors of *The New Republic*, "Saddam Hussein did the world a favor . . ." Suddenly Washington was in the grip of what *New York Times* bigfoot R. W. Apple, Jr., called "the heavy speculation, the avid gossip, the gung-ho, here's where it's happening spirit that marks the city when it grapples with great events." "Hey, whaddya know," quipped Michael Kinsley, "we're not declining after all." America was "back," yet again.

Hussein, among others, had a right to be surprised by all this. Right up until the day he invaded Kuwait, the very same Mr. Hussein had been considered a valued commercial customer and regional balancing force by at least three American presidents. Before, during, and after his invasion of Iran, Hussein had enjoyed private weekly screenings of U.S. satellite intelligence data. When the war with Iran ended and he turned his poison-gas pellets on his own Kurdish population, Hussein continued to receive sophisticated American technology and taxpayer-subsidized loans for his grain and technology purchases. President Bush himself had approved these loans earlier in the year. Assistant Secretary of State John Kelly, meanwhile, had testified before Congress in support of more loans to Hussein just *three days* before the invasion. Bush's State Department had allegedly gone so far as to frustrate official criminal inquiries into Hussein's U.S. loan network, in order to ensure that his cash-for-weapons pipeline continued unobstructed.

Though it could not compete with Hussein's regime in the cruelty and aggression departments, Kuwait, meanwhile, was not exactly the ideal place to mount a principled American defense of freedom and democracy. The ruling al-Sabah family ran a theocratic dictatorship in which Jews and Christians enjoyed virtually no rights. Its leader, the emir, made a regular practice of "marrying" young virgins on Thursday nights, the eve of the Islamic Sabbath, and "divorcing" them the next day. In the United Nations, the Kuwaiti regime attacked the United States with greater frequency and often stronger rhetorical violence than did the Soviet Union. And when one of our ships, the U.S.S. *Stark*, was torpedoed by Iraq while protecting *Kuwaiti* shipping in 1987, the Kuwaitis refused permission to allow America's dying sailors the right to use their hospital facilities.

President Bush's motivations in deciding to opt for war are not fully knowable. A late-afternoon meeting with Margaret Thatcher on August 2 was apparently quite influential, as were the parallels in the President's own mind drawn between Hussein and Hitler.* Foreign policy crises, moreover, were not exactly unwelcome in the Bush White House, for the President's approval ratings took a nose dive whenever he was forced to deal with domestic matters. His chief of staff, John Sununu, reportedly called the prospect of a short, successful war "pure gold" for the President.† The evidence is sketchy, but one can also postulate an important contribution by the punditocracy. James Fallows, for instance, discerns a powerful combination of Bush's own political and psychological weaknesses with hairy-chested pundit rhetoric to transform the President from wimp to war hero. "Following Bush's conversion," observes Fallows,

> instantly, all the pundits who had been grumbling about Bush wimping out on "no new taxes" and insisting that he had no backbone were now talking about how he had been transformed into the man of greatness standing up to Iraq. Bush's turnaround seemed to me to be a virtually— almost structurally—pundit-driven activity, and it confirmed his two worst tendencies: not wanting to get involved in domestic politics and thinking that this was the transcendent issue of all time.

Whether Bush himself was swayed by punditocracy intimations regarding his political manhood, the issue's transcendence is explicable only in terms of the particular ideological framework constructed for the invasion by Bush and his neoconservative allies in the punditocracy. The ability of both of these parties to manipulate the public dialogue—the pundits by word and Bush by deed—ensured that the truly essential questions about the war and U.S. national interest would never be asked. Instead, the

---

*"Remember, George," was President Bush's recollection of the soon-to-be-deposed prime minister's warning, "this is no time to go wobbly." George Bush quoted in Martin Walker, "Victory and Delusion," *Foreign Policy* 83, Summer 1991, p. 167.

†As indeed, it was. John Sununu quoted in Elizabeth Drew, "Letter from Washington," *The New Yorker*, February 4, 1991, p. 83.

debate was driven by the President's willingness to ratchet up the size and scope of the American commitment unilaterally and the pundits' ability to reinforce the pro-war agenda at crucial moments in the debate. This latter contribution turned out to be crucial during the belated congressional debate in early January 1991, when a deeply divided Congress accepted the punditocracy's definition of the stakes of the conflict and acceded—reluctantly—to the President's war plans.

In the immediate aftermath of the Iraqi invasion of Kuwait, America's media discovered two facts about the U.S. political debate it apparently found surprising. First, the Reaganite coalition of Old Right conservatives and New Right neoconservatives was in the process of imploding; and second, the debate's center of gravity could now be found in the punditocracy.

In the latter case, editors and news reporters who had historically prided themselves on ignoring their own editorial pages suddenly found themselves interviewing columnists and talk-show regulars with the respect and attention they would normally reserve for congressmen and cabinet secretaries. When they asked one another why they were doing this, the answers came back, "Congress is out of town," or, "The Democrats are afraid to undercut the President." Both were true, but neither fully explained why the reporters had no choice but to rely on the punditocracy. The true reason was that there was no other debate to report; the punditocracy was it. Not only was the only coherent opposition to George Bush's initial decision to deploy 200,000 troops to the desert pundit-centered, but with the exception of Stephen Solarz and a few others, so, too, were the only coherent explanations as to why war was necessary. Not coincidentally, Solarz's most complete and cogent presentation of the pre-war argument appeared in *The New Republic*.

The displacement in the public debate of Congress and the old-line political establishment by the punditocracy had been evident for more than a decade. Its widespread recognition in August 1990 became necessary only because the stakes were suddenly so high. On an issue as large and symbolically potent as taking the country to war—a war that had been unimaginable until just days before its planning began—most of the nation's hypercautious, poll-driven politicians were helpless to form independent judgments without first hearing the parameters of the debate communicated to them by the pundits. As Patrick Buchanan explained beneath a *New York Times* headline reading, "The Battle of the Columnists: Telling Leaders How to Think":

> The war between the interventionists and the neo-isolationists has moved
> to the weekend talk shows and the op-ed pages. It is not only among

journalists, like Buchanan and Safire, but between Brzezinski and Kissinger, and it moves onto shows like "The Capital Gang," "Crossfire," "The MacNeil/Lehrer News Hour," David Brinkley's Sunday show and "Nightline." This is where the debate is played out. It is an unrecognized sea change in American politics.

Jude Wanniski, now a consultant and media critic, concurred:

> In order to narrow down the options for where the country should be moving it is important that the intellectual cadre be engaged in discussion to do that. Politicians no longer have time, so it is the business of the professional opinion leaders—the pundits.

Similarly, the Old Right/neocon coalition had been crumbling for quite a while as the glue of anti-communism grew increasingly less cohesive. With the Soviets down for the count, the neoconservatives were eager to press for the establishment of a global *Pax Americana*—the "universal dominion" of the United States, in Charles Krauthammer's phrase, whereby America and its Western allies would undertake the liberalization of foreign nations across the globe by political, military, and economic means. Much of the Old Right, however, had reverted to its pre-World War II "America First" roots. Led by Buchanan, they were not interested in spreading democracy, but only in defending their vision of it at home. Buchanan accused the neoconservatives of practicing what he called "democratism," a form of "idolatry" that substituted "a false god for the real, a love of process for a love of country."

Between the neocons and isolationists lay a host of post-Reaganite positions that embraced neither one. The fervently anti-Soviet Zbigniew Brzezinski reconsidered his support for U.S. policy based on "earth control," and retreated into a more modest vision of global security via an American/ European/Japanese trilateral compact. Edward Luttwak, the strategic genius behind so many punditocracy war plans of the 1980s, had, by August 1990, come around to the view, originally enunciated by Sherle R. Schwenninger four years earlier, that traditional geopolitical conflicts such as that between Iraq and Iran no longer had much relevance to the overall security and prosperity of the United States. In the "main struggle of the main arena of international life," Luttwak explained, a nation's power and influence were determined not by its geopolitical assets but by its geoeconomic ones. "Disposable capital is increasingly displacing firepower, civilian product development is displacing military innovation, and market penetration is displacing the possession of foreign garrisons and bases" as the coins of the strategic realm.

Clearly, ideological fault lines had shifted. While Ronald Reagan could count on a popular punditocracy front to support him in every foreign endeavor involving the U.S. military, the contingent working the field for George Bush was considerably smaller. Fortunately for the President's war plans, Washington's post–Cold War intellectual transformation remained for practical purposes largely rhetorical. Although the Soviet threat was gone, the minds shaped by the Cold War remained programmed for permanent crisis. Even while some of the most influential members of the punditocracy were evolving into neo-isolationists and geoeconomists, the Cold War consensus they helped to create came back to haunt them. The idea of conservatives opposing a war thus produced a kind of cognitive dissonance in insider Washington that, however interesting, enjoyed little influence in the system itself. As "the unchallenged superpower . . . the center of world power" and "the apex of the Industrial West," in Charles Krauthammer's evocative phrasing, we simply *had* to do something. And given a mind-set shaped by the Cold War, that something had to be military. Daniel Patrick Moynihan dissected this phenomenon on the Senate floor:

> What we find is a kind of time warp in which we are acting in an old mode in response to a new situation. . . . It is in that mode of which we are in a bipolar, permanent crisis with the enemy. It used to be totalitarian, Leninist Communism. Without a moment's pause almost, we shifted the enemy to this person at the head of this insignificant, flawed country whose boundaries were drawn in 1925 in a tent by an English colonial official, an artifact of the Treaty of Sèvres.

What is easy to forget in light of the obliteration of the Iraqi Army is just how shocking was the idea of war in the first place. Indeed, when Washington first received word of the Iraqi campaign, few insiders seemed to be aware that any "defining moments" might be in the offing. On "The McLaughlin Group," Fred Barnes predicted that "it would be crazy to think that we're going to send troops over there and defend Kuwait." He was joined by fellow inside dopester Robert Novak, who promised, "We're not going to send troops in there. C'mon, there's no chance of that." These observations were consistent with the early readings of the President as well. Following an early-morning meeting of the National Security Council, President Bush told the press that intervention was "not being considered," and, "we're not contemplating such action."

Outside of the Gulf itself, world reaction was hardly thunderous. In Germany and Japan, both of whom lack the internal oil resources enjoyed by the United States, the invasion was a ho-hum affair. As Japanese Consul General Msamichi Hanabusa explained, "Who will control oil . . . is not a very serious issue for Japan. It is of course better that oil is in friendly hands. But experience tells us that whoever controls oil will be disposed to sell it . . . oil is a fungible commodity." If awoken at all by news of the invasion, our economic competitors simply turned over and went back to sleep.

Virtually alone in Washington, William Safire and the neo-conservative pundits called for immediate war. The groundwork for Operation Pundit Storm actually began three months earlier, shortly after Hussein threatened to "incinerate half of Israel" with a gas attack should he be attacked first. This alerted the powerfully pro-Israel neocons to the fact that they had an enemy in the Middle East to whom they had been paying insufficient attention. William Safire, much to the amusement of less principled commentators, had been raising hell about Hussein's gassing of the Kurds in 1988 and the United States' generally shameful history with respect to their unhappy struggle for autonomy.* Safire, together with Jim Hoagland, also conducted a lonely campaign during the first two years of the Bush administration to expose Hussein's manipulation of U.S. banking and agricultural credits to feed his military appetite and intimidate his neighbors. Once the threat to Israel was made explicit, however, they were joined in this campaign by A. M. Rosenthal, Mortimer Zuckerman, Charles Krauthammer, and others. The latter holds the honor of first

---

*Of all the egregious actions for which Safire has forgiven his friends Richard Nixon and Henry Kissinger during the past two decades, none should have been more difficult than the moral callousness with which they manipulated the doomed rebellion of Iraq's Kurds almost twenty years before George Bush did so. At a May 30, 1972, meeting in Tehran with the Shah of Iran, Nixon and Kissinger agreed to institute a $16 million CIA covert aid program to aid the rebellion in order, in the Shah's words, to "help the Kurds make life difficult for our Iraqi neighbor and enemy." In fact, neither the Shah, nor Kissinger, who acceded to the request, had any interest in seeing the Kurds succeed. According to a bipartisan congressional investigation commission, "the President, Dr. Kissinger and the foreign head of state [the Shah] hoped that our clients [the Kurds] would not prevail. They preferred instead that the insurgents simply continue a level of hostilities sufficient to sap the resources of our ally's neighboring country [Iraq]. The policy was not imparted to our clients, who were encouraged to continue fighting." U.S. aid to the Kurdish rebellion was, in Kissinger's words, "merely an instrument to dissuade Iraq from international adventurism." When, in 1975, both the Shah and the CIA cut them off, the rebels were summarily slaughtered. Kissinger's explanation: "Secret service operations are not missionary work." See Karl E. Meyer, "Kurds Are Not Pawns," *The New York Times*, March 6, 1991, p. A17; Christopher Hitchens, "Why We Are Stuck in the Sand," *Harper's*, January 1991, p. 71; and Hersh, *The Price of Power: Kissinger in the Nixon White House*, p. 542n.

affixing the adjective "truly Hitlerian" to Hussein, almost a week before the invasion.*

Once news of the invasion came through, so, too, did the neocon calls for Saddam's head. *The New Republic* editors recommended an immediate "massive bombing campaign" launched "at the slightest provocation" to destroy Hussein's military machine. "The United States must act," they insisted, "the sooner the better." Krauthammer predicted that if Saddam were not stopped by force, the United States would face "a nightmare not just of indiscriminate aggression, but of indiscriminate aggression with missiles, poison gas and soon nuclear weapons." He chastised the President for being unwilling to stop this "thug on the loose" because Bush was "not eager to get bogged down in a land war in a God-forsaken patch of desert," and anyway, had been "shamelessly propitiating [Hussein] since it helped him win the Iran-Iraq war in 1988." Safire took aim at the President's "past appeasement of Saddam Hussein" as well. He titled his first column "Now or Later?" Fewer than three weeks into the crisis he insisted, "The question is no longer 'Will there be a war' between the world and Iraq but 'What is the best strategy to win the war already begun?' "†

A. M. Rosenthal, positively aflame with war fever, generously granted that "not every Iraqi is an evil dreamer of death," but nevertheless saw U.S. hostages in Iraq—soon to be released unharmed—as "tethered . . . sacrificial goats," at the mercy of "the one, true Muslim conqueror, crying destruction to the Jews, and death to all Arabs who question his vision, course and glory." Like Safire, he insisted that we were already "at war with Iraq." Perhaps the most ambitious of the hawks were Robert Bartley's crew at *The Wall Street Journal*, who recommended that American forces simply "take Baghdad and install a MacArthur regency." The pro-war punditocracy's first team was rounded out by columnists Ben Wattenberg, Richard Perle, David Gergen, and Mortimer Zuckerman of *U.S. News*; Fred Barnes and Morton Kondracke in *The New Republic* and on "The McLaughlin Group"; the eloquent Johns Hopkins professor Fouad Ajami in both *The New Republic* and *U.S. News*; and James Hoagland in *The Washington Post*.

Two warriors who were a little slow off the mark were Jeane Kirkpatrick

---

*"What makes him truly Hitlerian is his way of dealing with neighboring states." Charles Krauthammer, July 27, 1990.

†William Safire, August 7, 1990, December 27, 1990, and August 20, 1990. The columnist recommended that we "(1) suppress Iraqi air defense; (2) take out war production at the 26 key targets; (3) launch a three-front land-war at the Turkish, Syrian, and Kuwaiti borders, coincident with an internal uprising to establish an independent Kurdistan, and (4) increase the blockade and air attacks to simulate riots and a coup. If we cannot win we should disband our armed forces and rely on Star Wars." William Safire, August 22, 1990.

and Henry Kissinger. Initially, Kirkpatrick said she saw "no distinctive U.S. interest" in the Gulf and she cautioned against precipitous action there. Over time, however, she joined Stephen Solarz's pro-war organization and proclaimed in early November that "obviously it is time to begin the defense of Kuwait." Kissinger, as always, proved the most slippery. Three days into the conflict, he predicted that "Iraq [would] have to withdraw" if an "effective" economic blockade were instituted for "several months," recommending that "before we station troops in Saudi Arabia," the United States should "try these other measures." Yet just two weeks later, following what he called Bush's "courageous," "skillful," and "flawless" performance in wholly rejecting his advice, Kissinger reversed himself and became one of the most forceful pro-war pundits in the country. "The United States cannot afford to be diddled," he insisted, "and it simply cannot afford to lose."

Kissinger's judgment as a pundit may, in this instance, have been clouded—at least initially—by Kissinger's judgment as the proprietor of a multi-million-dollar conglomerate. A little more than a year before the invasion, Kissinger Associates senior economist Alan Stoga participated in a Baghdad meeting between Saddam Hussein and an advisory group called the U.S./Iraq Business Forum. The meeting's agenda focused on ways Hussein could obtain Western loans at favorable rates. Marshall Wiley, a participant, told CBS's "60 Minutes" that Stoga's "association with Kissinger" was "probably the primary reason" he had been invited, and that he participated in advising Hussein on the restructuring of his debt.

When reporter Joe Conason wrote the story up in *The New Republic* in October 1990, Kissinger reacted furiously, denying any and all allegations of impropriety. Martin Peretz later wrote to "60 Minutes" to disown the article, insisting that it had not been given proper "scrutiny" and admitting that he "regret[ted] retailing it." Peretz's lawyer then called the show and asked that the original letter not be aired—a request that was denied.

Meanwhile, before illustrating at length Kissinger's ability to orchestrate powerful interference with his own coverage in the media, "60 Minutes" went on to outline yet another potential connection between Kissinger Associates and Hussein's financial machinations. According to the program, the Atlanta branch of the Italian Banca Nazionale del Lavaro (BNL) participated in illegal loans to Hussein for the purposes of feeding his military machine. Deputy Secretary of State Lawrence Eagleburger, a former top-level employee of Kissinger's consulting firm, supported allowing even larger loans to Hussein, although, according to "60 Minutes," "it is unmistakably clear from Eagleburger's memo that he was aware that BNL was already under investigation because its previous loans had been used for military supplies."

The investigation resulted in a 347-count indictment of a number of former BNL employees. BNL was a client of Kissinger Associates throughout this period, although this was concealed from the public until the House Banking Committee started investigating the illegal loans. Committee Chair Henry Gonzalez (D-Tex.) explains that "Many Kissinger Associates clients were doing business with Iraqis as a direct result of the unreported four billion in BNL loans to Iraq."

Kissinger told *The Financial Times* (London) that he had resigned from the BNL Advisory Committee just days before the indictments were handed down. This is false, according to "60 Minutes." Kissinger resigned in August 1991, long after the invasion had taken place. He also explained that he "didn't have an idea of what BNL was doing in Iraq." But Kenneth Timmerman, author of *The Death Lobby: How the West Armed Iraq*, finds this implausible in the extreme. "With his contacts in the intelligence community, his contacts in the companies that were actually doing the bidding," and with his former employees, Brent Scowcroft and Eagleburger, holding the top job at the National Security Council and the number-two spot at the State Department respectively, Timmerman observes, "you couldn't be better plugged in than that."

Whatever its motivations, the punditocracy drumbeat seemed to echo that of the Hearst newspapers' "Remember the *Maine*" campaign that preceded the Spanish-American War, albeit in far more sophisticated form. * Its most potent weapon in this crusade was the same impatience with complexity and nuance that had helped make the growth of its power and influence possible in the first place. Those who questioned the wisdom of threatening war over Kuwait were consistently written off as "pro-isolationism," "pro-appeasement," or, in the case of Patrick Buchanan, pro-anti-Semitism.† Those who did so with the added disadvantage of

---

*In this regard, George Bush's performance during the conflict was eerily reminiscent of William McKinley's during the war with Spain. McKinley gave Admiral Dewey instructions to destroy the Spanish Fleet at Manila, sent American troops there to fight, and only then presented his plans to Congress as a fait accompli. For a surprisingly salient discussion of that war and its implications, see Richard Hofstadter, "Cuba, the Philippines and Manifest Destiny," in Hofstadter, ed., *The Paranoid Style in American Politics and Other Essays* (New York: Alfred A. Knopf, 1965), pp. 164–87.

†Abe Rosenthal's accusation that alleged Jew-hater Patrick Buchanan was guilty of "blood libel" and worse for his contention that those, like Rosenthal, who wanted war were more concerned with Israel than with the United States, has already received far more analysis and argument than it deserves—including that provided by the author. Even if Buchanan does have a problem with Jews—a question upon which I remain divided—the salient point here is the ugly shadow Rosenthal's hysterical imputations cast over the entire debate. This shadow further constricted discussion and confused the relevant issues at hand. For further discussion, see Eric Alterman, "Semites and Anti-Semites: The Pat and Abe Show," *The Nation*, November 5, 1991.

professional expertise were contemptuously branded "Arabists" and "fellow travellers" by "McLaughlin Group" panelist Morton Kondracke.*

Guided by the twin influences of these pundits and the President's unilateral measures, the public debate proceeded on an uneven and often uneasy course to war. Bush's own role was paradoxical. On the one hand, by declaring that the invasion "would not stand," deploying 200,000 troops in Saudi Arabia, doubling that number four months later, and positioning those forces for an offensive war, Bush restricted the terms of the debate in such a fashion that a decision for peace would have necessitated a humiliating public retreat.† He secured countless votes in Congress and percentage points in approval for the war option in U.S. opinion polls simply by successfully equating a diplomatically brokered solution with an ignominious defeat for the United States. But however valuable the President's willingness to stretch his constitutional prerogatives may have been, he never proved able to articulate a consistent rationale as to why this war was necessary. He could not seem to make up his mind about his reasoning and therefore frequently confused people by switching from economic to moral to political rationales from moment to moment. Bush attempted to demonize Hussein as "worse than Hitler," but he sounded small and petty doing so.‡ As Charles Krauthammer complained in late November, "Bush has been so clumsy in advancing his case as to have nearly discredited it." Fortunately for the President, however, the pundits were more than willing to take over.

Throughout the fall, much of the subsequent public discussion inspired by the President took place on a rhetorical level so silly that many pro-war pundits could not bring themselves to support it. Bush's alleged devotion to

---

* This took place on "The McLaughlin Group," January 19, 1991. It should be noted that in the same discussion, Kondracke praised Martin Indyk, as the "smartest person on this." Indyk heads up the Institute for Near East Policy, an outgrowth of the American-Israel Public Affairs Committee (AIPAC). Kondracke did not mention that Indyk's institute sponsored his trip to the Middle East and offered former AIPAC staffer Seth Carus to co-author an article with him in The New Republic. The article largely endorsed the agenda of the institute and the AIPAC lobby.

†Despite the approval ratings, Bush did not enjoy a public mandate for a course toward war. A New York Times/CBS Poll published August 10 indicated that 68% of Americans questioned felt that the United States should not go on the offensive to liberate Kuwait. An August 12 poll found that 40% thought that Bush was "too quick to send troops." This figure held a week later. Cited in Bennet, "How They Missed That Story," The Washington Monthly, December 1990, p. 13.

‡Sir Michael Howard, considered by many to be the English-speaking world's most distinguished living military historian, and a supporter of Bush's war policy nevertheless, called the comparison "demeaning to the president and misleading to the American people." See Michael Howard, "The Burdens of Victory," U.S. News & World Report, May 13, 1991, p. 48.

the idea of a "new world order" was explicitly disavowed by pro-war pundits from Krauthammer to Kristol to Kissinger. Such talk was directed strictly at what Washington calls "the hustings," and taken seriously by almost no one, save perhaps A. M. Rosenthal and the soon-to-pay-for-it Kurds.* Going to war "for good against evil," to "combat aggression," or to defend "national sovereignty" also did not enter into the punditocracy's reasoning in any serious fashion. †

A cousin of the "new world order" argument that was taken seriously, however, was the insistence by many liberal pundits that the President was dedicated to the 1940s ideal of entrusting the United Nations to secure the peace in an otherwise anarchic world. This belief was encouraged, no doubt, by the Bush administration's newly minted enthusiasm for the approval of the Security Council for its actions, coupled with its success in convincing thirty-three nations to provide either token fighting forces, materiel, or medical teams to the war effort. These were no small achievements. But when Richard Cohen wrote that "maybe the most important consequence of the Gulf crisis has been the revival of the United Nations," he demonstrated nothing so much as how easy it had become to snow desperate liberals. It had been a point of pride within the Reagan administration for the entire decade

*At one point during the crisis, Rosenthal published a column entitled "New World Order" which consisted entirely of previously published news reports side-by-side with streams of Rosenthal's ungrammatical consciousness. One such entry read: "Jew kills Arab, Arab kills Jew, big news, Arab kills Arab, who gives a damn? Hypocrisy column? Everybody inured to hypocrisy. Try just clippings, documents." See A. M. Rosenthal, October 24, 1990. It is interesting to note that whether for reasons of national character, political culture, or simple expediency, there has been remarkably little change in the character of U.S. wartime propaganda during the twentieth century. In their history of the Creel Committee, Woodrow Wilson's propaganda team in World War I, James R. Mock and Cedric Larson note the committee's objective to convince the people of the world:

1. That America could never be beaten . . .
2. That America was a land of freedom and democracy; and therefore that it could be trusted.
3. That, thanks to President Wilson's vision of a *new world order* and his power of achieving it, victory for the Allied arms would usher in a new era of peace and hope [italics added].

See James R. Mock and Cedric Larson, *Words That Won the War: The Story of the Committee on Public Information 1917–1919* (Princeton: Princeton University Press, 1939), p. 247, cited in David M. Kennedy, *Over Here: The First World War in American Society* (New York: Oxford University Press, 1980), p. 353.

†No one in the punditocracy has suggested the United States go to war to end Turkey's military occupation of Cyprus, China's brutal domination of Tibet, or Indonesia's eradication of East Timor. The United States, moreover, is not exactly strategically well placed among great powers to launch a credible campaign on behalf of wars in defense of another nation's national sovereignty, given recent unilateral U.S. military actions in Libya, Grenada, Nicaragua, and Panama.

of the 1980s to mock the self-righteous moralizing of that pathetically ineffective debating society on Manhattan's East River.* If, after more than a decade of contempt, George Bush had truly gotten religion regarding the United Nations' potential, he could have secured a resolution under Article 43 of the body's Charter, creating a true UN force with a UN military staff. Such a path would have helped spread international costs and contributions evenly among the world community and could have saved James Baker the humiliating spectacle of traveling the globe, tin cup in one hand, billy club in the other. But it would also have restricted the President's freedom of action in exactly the fashion envisioned by the UN founders. As such, it was never seriously considered.

The "war for oil" argument, though stronger than the "new world order" counterpart, was never sufficiently powerful to stand on its own. It is hardly prudent to fight a war to ensure one's oil supply, as the Japanese consul general pointed out, when one can simply pay for it. The key weapon in the warriors' political arsenal therefore was the fear inspired by the idea of a nuclear-armed Saddam Hussein. William Safire introduced this argument—by coincidence the only justification, according to a CBS/New York Times poll, acceptable to a majority of Americans to support an offensive war—just five days into the crisis. Initially, Safire predicted that the Iraqis would have a nuclear bomb ready to deliver to the United States by 1994. ("The first city he will take out is New York.") A few months into the crisis, in the midst of four consecutive

---

*The devotion shown to the United Nations by both the Bush administration and the punditocracy was particularly difficult to square with extremely recent American history. The United States was condemned by the World Court in June 1986 for its "unlawful use of force" in mining Nicaragua's harbors, supporting the Contras, and conducting illegal economic warfare there. The United States vetoed the November 1986 Security Council resolution, passed 11–1 with 3 abstentions, calling on the United States to observe international law in the case of Nicaragua and then lost a 94–3 vote in the General Assembly calling on it to comply with the World Court's decision. In 1987, during the INF summit, the General Assembly voted 154–1 to oppose the buildup of weapons in outer space. It voted 135–1 against the development of new weapons of mass destruction. The United States provided the lone dissent in both votes. In the same session, the General Assembly passed a resolution condemning "Terrorism Wherever and by Whomever Committed." The vote was 153–2 this time, with Israel and the United States in opposition. The two nations objected because the resolution's text contained the words that nothing in it "would prejudice the right of peoples, particularly those under colonial or racist regimes, or under foreign occupation or other forms of domination, to struggle for self-determination, freedom and independence, or to seek and receive support for that end." In January 1990, during the first year of the Bush administration, the Security Council voted 13–1 (with Britain abstaining) to condemn the sacking by U.S. troops of the residence of the Nicaraguan ambassador in Panama. See Alexander Cockburn, "The Sinners Cast Stones at Iraq," Los Angeles Times, August 12, 1990, Opinion section, p. 7.

columns on the subject, the *Times* man moved the deadline up a year, to 1993. Along with his compatriots in the pro-war punditocracy, Safire argued that we were no longer talking simply about oil, peace, order, or democracy: We were "dealing with our own survival."

Unfortunately, neither Safire nor anyone else in the West had any dependable information about the Iraqi nuclear program. The data managed to evade Western experts throughout the war, coming to light only when an Iraqi defector provided blueprints in its aftermath. At the time of the Safire columns, even Colin Powell saw the threat as years away.* Yet even if Safire's predictions had been based on fact rather than conjecture, his insistence upon immediate war begged all kinds of questions about both the self-enforcing aspects of nuclear deterrence, and the less drastic means at America's disposal for reducing or eliminating Hussein's nuclear threat. In any event, in the course of the war, the United States still failed to eliminate most of Iraq's nuclear infrastructure. Had Hussein really been interested in nuclear blackmail—and his decision to invade Kuwait *before* his plans achieved operational capability belies this hypothesis—the war would likely have given him his excuse to use it. †

Iraq's invasion of Kuwait did present a complicated problem for the United States. We are dependent on cheap oil from a region that has always been an unfriendly neighborhood, characterized by violent autocracies and unstable political relationships. As Zbigniew Brzezinski noted, "There [was] no easy solution to the crisis." But the Reagan administration and its punditocracy cheerleaders had inoculated the insider dialogue to the idea that there was *any* problem facing the United States that did not have an easy solution—particularly if the latter included an opportunity to flex American military power. In the case of Iraq's invasion of Kuwait, the punditocracy treated the inherent complexity of the problem as something that would go away just as soon as the United States proved it meant business.

*In December 1990, General Colin Powell said that Iraq was still some distance from joining the ranks of the nuclear powers. A comprehensive survey published in the March 1991 issue of the *Bulletin of Atomic Scientists* also concluded that "Iraq was many years away from developing usable nuclear weapons." At the time this book went to press, the most recent report on the subject, written by a top-level UN delegation in early April, concluded that it would have taken Iraq "at least" two to three years to build a bomb, owing to what one inspector called "several important bottlenecks" and a "fundamentally flawed" design plan. See Charles William Maynes, "Dateline Washington: A Necessary War?" *Foreign Policy*, Spring 1991, and Paul Lewis, "Iraq's A-Bomb Capability Overrated, UN Now Says," *The New York Times*, May 20, 1992.

†Moreover, the pro-war position in this instance implies that an Iraqi invasion of Kuwait was worth the risk of a nuclear attack on the United States—quite an assumption, I would say.

* * *

Throughout the autumn of 1990, the President and the punditocracy worked in tandem to create a heightened sense of crisis over the Iraqi occupation of Kuwait and thus an increased sense of inevitability about the war should Hussein refuse to capitulate. Liberals, in particular (along with those pundits unfairly perceived as liberals), were tremendously eager to be seen as supportive of the President during this period. David Broder found it "almost impossible to imagine a more serious, calm, cautious, rational and prudent set of people than those this president has assembled" in his tiny coterie of advisers. Richard Cohen expressed awe over the President's "masterful assembling" of the crisis. Haynes Johnson congratulated Bush for his "skill and sureness of purpose." And Anthony Lewis applauded the President's "wisdom . . . professionalism and care for long-term interests" of the nation. This strategy of rallying round the Commander-in-Chief, backfired, however, when it became clear that he had no intention of using his newly discovered "mastery," "skill," and "wisdom," etc., for anything but offensive war.

As Charlie Peters complained on the *Times* op-ed page, there was nothing inevitable about any of this. "The conditions that created the pressure to go to war were the results of choices made by George Bush." Yet Bush succeeded in constructing his own cage so skillfully that he now seemed to be "its victim rather than its architect." Peters argued bravely and frantically on the morning of January 16 that the nation did not "have to accept the trap he has created. We can tell him not to go to war." But of course we could not have. Bush may not have had much support for his commitment to war when he first made it.* But once the President committed himself, he committed not just the reputation of one, politically savvy individual who happened to occupy the Oval Office at the time; he committed—with the help of the punditocracy—the power and prestige of the United States of America.

Had it been up to George Bush and a healthy proportion of the punditocracy, the decision to go to war would have been left entirely to them. Richard Cheney noted in early December that, in the opinion of the administration, George Bush had all the authority he needed to go to war

---

*According to an ABC/*Washington Post* poll taken on January 9, 1991, only 39% of Americans questioned thought that the United States should go to war "immediately" after the January 15 UN deadline passed; 35% thought the crisis could be solved by additional negotiations, and a full 66% believed that the United States "should agree to an Arab-Israeli conference if Iraq agreed to withdraw from Kuwait." The poll results were reprinted in the *Congressional Record* of January 12, 1991, as part of a statement by Senator Robert Byrd of West Virginia.

with or without congressional approval. Charles Krauthammer gratefully observed around the same time that Congress had been completely "irrelevant" to the decision-making process regarding the war. Fred Barnes argued that "Congress has no business getting involved. They would stew and whine and yap and they couldn't even pass a budget." Morton Kondracke seconded Barnes's analysis, adding, "Congress is chicken."

By the time Congress finally did get around to exercising its constitutional prerogative to determine whether to commit the nation to war, it had almost ceased to matter. The punditocracy had succeeded in defining the debate so narrowly and perversely that the anti-war position would be considered the functional equivalent of national humiliation, retreat, denial, and general cowardice in the face of evil.

Twenty-four of the nation's twenty-five largest newspapers endorsed George Bush's strategy to risk war on behalf of Kuwait.* David Broder considered this near unanimity of opinion a mark of maturity, noting approvingly that "almost none" of the President's domestic critics "disputes his decision to intervene. Nor does any Democrat challenge Bush's view that America's vital interests are at stake." Leslie H. Gelb, who inaugurated his foreign affairs column in *The New York Times* at exactly this propitious historical moment, caught the appropriate wave perfectly. As a "liberal," he conceded all the major points of contention to the President. Bush was "right on the fundamental issue. If war is not justifiable here, then where?" The only "realistic alternative" was sanctions. But the advocates of continued sanctions could not "convincingly show that Iraq will crack before the alliance crumbles." Just why Bush was "right" on the fundamental issue, Gelb did not bother to explain. Nor was it necessary for him to demonstrate why it was so important for Iraq to "crack" before the alliance crumbled. Colin Powell reportedly believed that U.S. objectives could be accomplished over time without a war, and Norman Schwarzkopf argued that "if the alternative to dying is sitting out in the sun for another summer, that's not a bad alternative." This view was seconded by the vast majority of living ex-Secretaries of Defense and Chairmen of the Joint Chiefs of Staff. But given the President's rhetorical commitments and the pundits' consistent ideological bombardment, by early January 1991 sitting and waiting had become no alternative at all. "Politically," George Bush allegedly explained to his top military officer, "I don't think there is time." Pro-war pundits have a right to a certain pride of accomplishment in the President's statement. For

---

*The exception was Denver's *Rocky Mountain News*. See Vincent Carroll, "The Scarcity of Anti-War Editorial Voices," *Washington Journalism Review*, January/February 1991, p. 14.

when the crisis began and no one save the pundits wanted war, "politically" the President had had all the time in the world.

Here was the field upon which the congressional debate was finally conducted during the second weekend of 1991. Instead of addressing the difficult considerations about the American national interest the crisis posed, Congress simply asked itself the question Safire had posed more than six months earlier: War "Now or Later?" Senate Armed Services Committee Chairman Sam Nunn had single-handedly slowed the pro-war juggernaut with his late November committee hearings, but his argument for continued sanctions was nowhere near strong enough to stand up to the patriotic crescendo orchestrated by Bush and the pundits. With the honorable exception of Pat Moynihan, most senators were largely mute over just what it was about the tiny, anti-democratic, anti-Semitic, and anti-American kingdom of Kuwait that justified an American-led war on its behalf.* Senator Nunn, the axis around which all Democratic defense debates revolve, disposed of that problem when he explained, "the question is not whether military action is justified. It is." Senate Majority Leader George Mitchell concurred. As he introduced the Democratic position when the debate began, he reassured the nation that "this is not a debate about whether force should ever be used. No one proposes to rule out the use of force."

David Broder saw fit to laud Congress for dealing with the question of war "in a manner befitting the gravity of the subject," with a debate that was "civil and somber, always serious and often eloquent." Again, this was less a reflection of the subject of Broder's commentary than of the deterioration of his own standards. In fact, no debate worthy of the name even took place. Members read their remarks to largely empty chambers, with little substantive intercourse, exchange of ideas, or engagement of their colleagues' positions. The Republican war supporter, Arlen Specter, complained that "there have not been very many senators on the floor and there has not been the kind of exchange which I think a matter of this gravity deserves." Another senator commented that he did not see "a single senator trying to persuade another senator" during the entire three-day period.†

The body's "debate," moreover, revealed a distinctly Orwellian cast. The war's margin of victory was provided by lawmakers who claimed to prefer continued sanctions. Specter, for instance, said he would have "preferred to

---

*As a reward for his courage, Moynihan was greeted immediately following the war with a full-page advertisement in *The New York Times*, paid for by the New York Conservative Party, accusing him of "opposing" the "values of proud Americans" and being a "spokesman for appeasement." March 6, 1991.

†For a useful discussion of the Senate debate, see James Bennet, "The Senate's Lame Doves," *The Washington Monthly*, March 1991.

give sanctions more time to work and would not have set the January 15 deadline," but voted for war because, he said, it offered "a unique opportunity to promote world peace." Republican Minority Leader Robert Dole insisted that his vote for war should be considered a vote "to strengthen [the President's] hand for peace, not war but for peace." Frank Murkowski of Alaska argued that "for those who believed in allowing the sanctions to take effect, the only responsible action to take now is to grant the president his request for a realistic threat of force." Senators J. Bennett Johnston, Jr., Albert Gore, and James Jeffords also indicated that they would have preferred continued sanctions, but voted for war because the President had already committed the nation so far toward war. Senator John Kerry of Massachusetts estimated during the course of the debate that "75 percent or more of those who will vote for the use of force do not want it to be used, and a significant number will vote for it only because they want to prevent the president from being reversed." Kerry may have been right; he may have been exaggerating to strengthen his own argument. But such distinctions were quickly left to the historians once the final vote was tallied up and the bombs began to fall.

II

As the U.S. Air Force lit up the dark Arabian sky with its eerily beautiful arsenal on the morning of January 17, 1991, George Bush went before the American people to explain why "the world could wait no longer," and the confusion level within the American political dialogue achieved a kind of perverse epiphany. False information, incomplete field reports, and raw Pentagon propaganda were transmitted across the American airwaves unfiltered by editors, producers, or any of the traditional gatekeepers of independent journalism. Retired colonels, admirals, and Pentagon consultants paraded through the punditocracy's third ring as the networks' impartial experts and pronounced every aspect of the effort to be an unqualified success—and a morally exemplary one at that. On the op-ed pages and weekend talk shows, the punditocracy discovered in victory not merely the vindication of Bush's war strategy but a reaffirmation of every dogma its members had ever wanted to believe: America's decline was a myth; military power remained the only important determination of national strength and international influence; and we lived in what would always be, as Ben Wattenberg put it, "the most powerful nation in the world."

The victory in Iraq inspired what seemed to be a metaphysical trend in punditocracy analysis. Even before Hussein's tattered troops made it home from Kuwait, commentary was beginning to exhibit an almost supernatural hue. Fred Barnes called George Bush's performance "flawless, daring, bold and fantastic," indicative of what he termed to be "the greatest presidential leadership ever." On the same show Morton Kondracke praised the President's "vision, guts, and grace," terming the U.S. ground war "an act of mercy." Evans and Novak professed to detect a "fearsome, transcendent America emerging from Bush's flawless conquest of Saddam Hussein," coupled with "something . . . intangible and mystical in the new relationship that now appears to bind the president and his country." Pat Buchanan, too, saw George Bush as "the most effective war president of our lifetime"; a man who "doth bestride our narrow world like a colossus." Even allowing for the fully understandable sense of relief inspired by the war's surprising end, one could not help but be amazed, once again, by the precarious intellectual foundation upon which America's new political theology was being forged.

Punditocracy discussions of the Gulf War never came to terms with the single most important determinant of their content: the Pentagon censors. Having been shamed and embarrassed by critical reporting of Vietnam, Pentagon public affairs officers had spent the better part of twenty years thinking up ways to control the flow of news from any prospective battlefield.* Following trial runs in Grenada and Panama, they were ready with a smorgasbord of strategies that combined to present an almost perfect version of a Steven Spielberglike movie called *War in the Gulf*. They were so good at their jobs, in fact, that they did so while the media paid their transmission costs.

The Pentagon's information control system had a haphazard quality to it, but this did not adversely affect its effectiveness. Sometimes news reports

---

*The problem was not, as so many pundits insisted, that the military blamed the media for "losing the war." That opinion may be held by individual officers and servicemen, but in truth, the war's legacy to the U.S. military is considerably more complex than punditocracy commentary would admit. For instance, the official United States Army history concluded that "most of the public affairs problems that confronted the United States in South Vietnam stemmed from the contradictions implicit in Lyndon Johnson's strategy for the war. . . .

"Believing that the press had in most cases supported official policies in earlier American wars, especially in World War II, many members of the military expected similar support in Vietnam. When the contradictions engendered by President Johnson's strategy of limited war led instead to a more critical attitude, the military tended increasingly to blame the press for the credibility problems they experienced, accusing television news in particular of turning the American public against the war. . . .

"It is undeniable, however, that the press reports were still often more accurate than the public statements of the administration in portraying the situation in Vietnam." See William M. Hammond, *The United States Army in Vietnam: The Military and the Media* (Washington, DC: U.S. Army Center of Military History, 1988), pp. 387–88.

were censored.* Sometimes reporters were lied to.† Sometimes they were even arrested.‡ But such extremes were rarely necessary. By creating a pool system whereby only a tiny number of favored reporters were allowed to observe and interview only pre-selected soldiers in the presence of an all-powerful public affairs officer, there was little chance that anything terribly unpleasant about the war would turn up in a correspondent's report.‖ If by some miraculous chance a critical observation did make its way into a pool report, then the officer in charge could send it home via military press headquarters in Dhahran for "security review." There the military would enjoy yet another opportunity to alter, delay, and otherwise emasculate whatever did not please it. If all that was not enough, the Dhahran office might send it to an air base in Omaha or Nevada for more "review." Given the "degree of surveillance and control the military exercised over the correspondents' reports," *Times* Gulf reporter Malcolm Browne compared his role and that of his colleagues to "the PK," referring to the *Propaganda Kompanic*, the Nazi propaganda corps. For the duration of his experience as a pool reporter, Browne lamented, he was little more than an "unpaid employee of the Department of Defense."

Aside from its troubling First Amendment implications, the system's upshot from the point of view of public debate was that the entire game was fixed. Punditocracy discussion of the war was largely a product of tainted information provided by a supremely interested party. The only major outlier in the system of Pentagon information control was Peter Arnett's reporting

---

*Malcolm Browne describes an almost comical example of the kind of censorship that was ongoing during the conflict. In a pool report he co-authored, public affairs officers changed his adjective describing pilots from "giddy" to "proud." The words "fighter-bomber" in the story were also changed simply to "fighter," in Browne's estimation so as not to jeopardize funding for the B-2 Stealth bomber by making it seem redundant. Following these changes, the story was sent to officials at the Tonopah Test Range in Nevada, where the entire piece was deemed a breach of security. It was cleared twenty-four hours later, however, long since dated and already irrelevant. Malcolm W. Browne, "The Military vs. the Press," *The New York Times Magazine*, March 3, 1991, p. 45.

†When asked about the military's deliberate deception of the media, Pentagon spokesman Pete Williams did not deny the allegation, but responded, "We were not trying to deceive the press. We were trying to fool Saddam Hussein." See Jim MacNeil, "The Big Ten Gulf Myths," *In These Times*, April 3–9, 1991, p. 12.

‡*The Washington Post* reported on February 11 that *New York Times* correspondent Chris Hedges was detained a day earlier by U.S. military authorities after interviewing shopkeepers in Saudi Arabia. Hedges was held for two hours and then sent back to his hotel without his press credentials.

‖The pool from which the pool was chosen was itself pre-selected by the Saudis who, advised by their Washington public relations staff, frequently denied visas to reporters likely to be too tough on the kingdom.

from Iraq. But owing to extensive Iraqi censorship, this could hardly be considered much more reliable. Thus, our high-tech weaponry performed flawlessly because the people paid to requisition it said it did. Loss of Iraqi life on the ground was minuscule for similar reasons. What's more, explained such credible and disinterested television pundits as the recently cashiered Air Force Chief of Staff and NBC News consultant General Michael Dugan, the United States would never deliberately harm civilians in wartime. The happy circle was completed by civilian analysts such as right-wing Republican congressional aide and former Pentagon employee Anthony Cordesman, who appeared fifty-six times to reassure the skeptics in ABC's viewing audience not to worry, "The Pentagon is giving it to you absolutely straight."*

Whatever their individual motivations, were many of the "experts" who appeared on television at this time giving testimony in a court of law, they would be looking at multiple perjury charges. Even the most celebrated American weapons—particularly the "smart bombs" and Patriot missiles— did not work remotely as advertised.† Iraqi battle deaths were enormous, though just how high we will never know.‡ And a major part of the reason Dugan was available for day work at all was his untimely revelation as Chief of Staff that in the event of war, the Air Force planned to target such noncombatants as Saddam Hussein's family and mistress. What's more, the massive rout of the Iraqi forces that Americans found so wonderfully

---

*In most cases, Cordesman was identified not by his employment history, but simply as a professor at Georgetown University, where in fact he is only adjunct. He is quoted in Verne Gay, "Instant Stardom for War Experts," Newsday, January 23, 1991, p. 59.

†The Patriot anti-missile system was, in the words of one MIT analyst and former Pentagon adviser, an "almost total failure," causing "greater ground damage" than would have been experienced had they never been fired. According to Professor Theodore A. Postol of MIT, who reviewed technological data provided by the Israeli military, "during the period of Patriot defense there were 15 percent fewer Scud attacks relative to the period when there was no defense, yet the number of apartments reported damaged almost tripled and the number of injuries from attacks increased by almost 50 percent." A second equally egregious example were the reports of "80%" accuracy of U.S. bombing missions over Iraq that appeared in virtually every news outlet in the early days of the war. In fact, according to a postwar briefing by Air Force General Merrill A. McPeak, of the 88,500 tons of bombs dropped on Iraq and Kuwait, approximately 70% missed their targets. See Patrick E. Tyler, "Did Patriot Missiles Work? Not So Well, Scientists Say," The New York Times, April 17, 1991, p. 1; William J. Broad, "Critic of Patriot Missile Says It Was 'Almost Total Failure' in War," The New York Times, January 9, 1991, p. A8; and Barton Gellman, "U.S. Bombs Missed 70% of Time," The Manchester Guardian Weekly, March 24, 1991, p. 18.

‡Even today, no one knows how many Iraqis were killed in the war. Ted Koppel reported on "Nightline," January 9, 1992, that despite an official initial estimate by the Pentagon's Defense Intelligence Agency of "approximately 100,000" Iraqi deaths in Kuwait, it is possible that the number may have been as low as 10,000.

surprising may not have been such a shock to those with accurate inside information. Before the war began, the Pentagon leaked vastly inflated estimates of its likely cost, including exaggerated assessments of the number of Iraqi troops dug into Kuwait, the kinds of weapons available to them, and the number of American combat deaths the two together were likely to cause.* The Iraqis' crumbling under the weight of American airpower and running for cover during the ground assault were wholly attributed to the brilliance of our strategic doctrine and the awesome powers of America's (Japanese) technology. A better explanation, though one rarely heard at the time, would have been that the Iraqis were never as strong as everyone had been led to believe.

Almost as alarming from the point of view of a sensible, measured debate was the incredible rush to judgment by the pundits, as if the long-term consequences of the conflict could be determined on the morning the fighting began. Within twenty-four hours of the beginning of the initial bombing campaign, the punditocracy concluded that the war had been a brilliant, unmitigated success. Literally hours into the fighting, A. M. Rosenthal started tallying up its political winners and losers. All of the winners, by coincidence, had been on Rosenthal's side of the argument in the first place. George Will, who had opposed the war as ill-considered, was nevertheless swept away by the "technological prowess and moral purpose" of a nation that had become "the symbol of Western political values and of cultural modernity." It was Will's hope that the explosions would provide "the thin edge of a large wedge sufficient to pry parts of Arabia into participation in the modernity" capable of producing such wonders. Richard Cohen got so caught up in the euphoria of the moment that he seriously entertained the notion that Hussein's defeat would introduce "a wholly different Middle East."

Punditocracy commentary throughout the conflict jumped from one false report to another, occasionally pausing long enough to inflate misleading data into a full-fledged doctrine. The wholly misleading progress reports

*The Pentagon ordered 16,000 body bags and told reporters to expect between 20,000 and 30,000 casualties. Moreover, it estimated Iraqi strength in Kuwait at 540,000 front-line troops. This turned out to be roughly three times the number of ill-equipped, second-rank soldiers who were really there. The vast majority of Hussein's elite Republican Guard remained in Iraq, where they were needed for Kurdish and Shi'ite population control following the war. See "Hunger and the Butcher's Bill," *The Economist*, September 8, 1990, p. 45, and Committee on Armed Services, U.S. House of Representatives, "Defense for a New Era: Lessons of the Persian Gulf War" (Washington, D.C.: U.S. Government Printing Office, 1992), pp. 29–33. Note: Whether these estimates were purposefully inflated is not known at present, but in any case, intentionality is peripheral to the issue at hand.

for the Patriot missile kills, for instance, became absolute proof of the efficacy of SDI—an argument that would not have made sense even if the Patriots had worked as trumpeted. George Will nevertheless insisted that "there's more to SDI than the Patriot, as you will learn to your pleasure sooner or later." Fred Barnes asserted the same day that the Patriot battles had proved that "We need SDI." "When President Bush goes before Congress for his State of the Union address," added Patrick Buchanan, "he ought to insist on the restoration of full funding for SDI. And entertain no counterargument. The debate is over." *The Wall Street Journal* editors concurred, arguing that "The epic debates over ABM and SDI, after all, were over whether to give American civilians the kind of protection Israeli civilians have just received." Now, even according to the information provided by Israeli military and U.S. Defense Department officials, the Patriots hit fewer than 20 percent of the incoming Scuds launched at the Jewish state. If the United States were to counter a full-fledged nuclear attack equally effectively, Will, Barnes, Buchanan, and the editors of *The Wall Street Journal* would all be incinerated.

Mikhail Gorbachev's desperate attempts just before the ground war began to broker a diplomatic solution that would achieve virtually all the goals it eventually earned at immeasurably less cost met with a similarly unhappy fate within the punditocracy. Conventional wisdom—with only Anthony Lewis dissenting—assumed that Gorbachev had no real interest in peace, but was only looking to resume his arms pipeline to Hussein while simultaneously spoiling America's triumph and heating up what Charles Krauthammer called "Cold War II" as an added bonus. A dispute arose, however, as to whether Gorbachev had intended to do this all along, and had therefore submitted to the entire war effort as a grand set-up, or had merely reverted to "evil empire" form. Evans and Novak straddled their respective horses, detecting a "reversion to old-style diplomacy" coupled with the insistence that Gorbachev was "playing a double game all along." A. M. Rosenthal went whole-hog with the latter view as well, arguing that Gorbachev was trying to "retain his old pal, Saddam Hussein," because "the Moscow-Baghdad alliance was never dissolved." William Safire did not take a position on the theological dispute, though he did employ an almost textbook-perfect "war is peace" construction, accusing Gorbachev's "perfid-[ious]" peace efforts of potentially costing "thousands of American and allied lives." Morton Kondracke, the alleged reporter among the group, went so far as to insist that Gorbachev already was "rearming Hussein," though of course he neglected to posit any evidence. It was, to say the least, hardly the punditocracy's finest hour.

*　　*　　*

The U.S.-led ground assault lasted just one hundred hours, but the brevity of the conflict only seemed to intensify the transcendence discovered in the victory in the punditocracy's postwar analysis. We not only "kicked" the Vietnam syndrome; we were the envy of the world. A new era of *Pax Americana* was in the offing, based on "a single pole of world power" with "the United States at the apex," argued Charles Krauthammer. Pat Buchanan, hardly a stern critic of the excesses of American jingoism, nevertheless recoiled from the "hubris, the sense of omnipotence," he detected in post-Gulf Washington; the "feeling that as Mr. Bush exults in the world today, what we say goes."

Needless to say, this state of affairs owed more to the distortion of fact engendered by the punditocracy's willful self-delusion than to any development that had taken place in the Gulf region. What the punditocracy was trumpeting as a wondrous victory in the Gulf rapidly turned into a quagmire of unending frustration. The war was not without significant accomplishments. *The Economist* numbered these as the need "to stand up to the Iraqi dictator, both to prevent him from extending his tyranny to countries beyond Iraq and Kuwait, to deny him the wealth of oil that would have fueled that extension and to deter other aggressors who might have taken inspiration had they seen him get away with such a rich grab." The magazine's editors had insisted all along that these gains could not have been achieved without war, but that hypothetical can never truly be answered. Let us grant it for the sake of argument. A true accounting would weigh these accomplishments against the enormous physical destruction and human dislocation the war produced. But because of the punditocracy's intoxicated embrace of the conflict as the ultimate demonstration of American power and beneficence, such an accounting became impossible.

Had the pundits been willing to examine the results of the war from the perspective of a strict, nonideological cost-benefit analysis, the claims of any kind of meaningful "victory" would have become less overwhelming with each passing day. True, fewer than three hundred Americans died overall in the war, a much smaller number than anyone publicly anticipated. But one does not judge the wisdom of a given war on the basis of how many casualties each side experienced. Millions died in World War II in a thoroughly worthy military conflict. Conversely, the U.S. Army suffered far fewer battle deaths than its enemy in Vietnam but it lost the war nevertheless. The proper question regarding battle deaths is not how few died relative to one's enemy, but whether the war turned out to be a strategically prudent and morally sound use of military force.

Take for instance the case of oil. Although not the primary justification for the war, the need to assure a secure supply of petroleum nevertheless transformed Kuwait from a nasty little autocracy into a "vital interest" of the United States. Unless we were willing to go to war, *The New Republic* editors argued at the outset of the crisis, a "large scale American military presence in the Persian Gulf" would be necessary "to protect the oil. . . ."

In fact, the war significantly decreased the amount of oil available for U.S. import for at least the next five years by destroying or inspiring the destruction of much of Kuwait's production potential and even more of Iraq's. Saudi Arabia and the rest of OPEC moved quickly to take advantage of this state of affairs on March 12, by announcing that member production would be further curtailed. By the spring of 1991, the price of a barrel of oil reached nearly $21—almost exactly the level Saddam Hussein had been demanding of OPEC just before the invasion. In January 1992, the Saudis made another cut in production of 100,000 barrels a day.

Moreover, despite our apparently unquenchable thirst for oil, we suffer from an even more demanding dependence on credit. Our net indebtedness to foreigners is expected to reach a trillion dollars by the time George Bush leaves office. Far more important to the overall health of the American economy than who controls a minor portion of our oil imports will be the interest price we pay on that trillion-dollar debt. Although wholly unnoticed by any major pundits, the war ensured that borrowing that money will be more expensive in the future. For rather than paying for postwar reconstruction by liquidating assets, both the Saudis and the Kuwaitis elected to borrow the necessary tens of billions. A 1991 Morgan Stanley study predicted that partially as a result of Saudi and Kuwaiti borrowing, worldwide demand for capital will likely exceed the world's supply by more than $200 billion a year within a few years. This will significantly increase its cost, and may ultimately strangle any hopes for a major economic recovery in the United States.

From a strategic standpoint, the punditocracy saw the war as an almost unmitigated success. Even the faultlessly moderate Jim Hoagland, winner of the 1991 Pulitzer Prize for commentary, observed that "the United States has not been so dominant on the world stage since the brief period after World War II." David Broder saw the war as a victory for "peace and the rule of law" as well.

So it seemed in the thick of battle. But from the distance of just a few weeks' perspective, the gleam of war's strategic brilliance grew decidedly dimmer. The allies did succeed in briefly weakening Saddam Hussein, but they did not by any stretch of the imagination cripple him. CIA Director Robert Gates told a Senate committee in early 1992 that Hussein's military forces remained "a great challenge" to the United States, armed with "a cadre of scientists and engineers . . . able to reconstitute any dormant program rapidly." Following the ground war, Hussein retained at least 700 tanks, 1,400 armored personnel carriers, 340 artillery pieces, and 20 divisions, including Republican Guard divisions, who remained wholly untouched by the fighting and who could hardly be said to be at "peace" with the Kurds and Shi'ites. Most of the Iraqi Air Force sat out the war as well. Within a year of the triumph, hawkish columnists James Hoagland, A. M. Rosenthal, and William Safire were calling for yet another war against Hussein, this one to accomplish all the things the last one had failed to do.

In the region, the war's benefits were no less murky. Turkey, a nation whose strategic importance dwarfs that of Kuwait, panicked under the threat of a massive Kurdish exodus from Iraq—a threat that became even more dangerous when Hussein decided to start arming Turkey's Kurds in revenge. Iran, meanwhile, emerged as the dominant power in the region, as Iraq's role as a buffer against the export of Islamic extremism passed into history. Its revolutionary regime began purchasing massive amounts of discarded Soviet weaponry and pursuing its own nuclear research program following the war. The war also complicated the Middle East peace process, conferences notwithstanding. While it did weaken the forces of Arab rejectionism—in part the result of the Palestinians' foolish and self-defeating support for Hussein's murderous invasion—it nevertheless hardened them in Israel. The Shamir government used the war to invite an avowedly racist party into its coalition, to jail a moderate Palestinian philosophy professor for three months without charge, and to break ground on a massive series of new Jewish settlements in the occupied West Bank, confiscating many thousands of acres of Palestinian farmland in the process.

However costly the victory may have been, argued Charles Krauthammer in mid-April, "the primary gains of the war—the liberation of Kuwait and the destruction of Iraq's potential for aggression—remain." But Krauthammer's latter claim is simply untrue. The war did not destroy Hussein's potential for aggression; it merely caused him to confine it, quite briefly, to those unlucky enough to live within his borders.* As for the much-publicized "liberation" of Kuwait, this is a curious choice of words to describe a nation that does not enjoy freedom of speech, freedom of assembly, freedom to vote, or freedom of much of anything else; where

---

*In addition to the unhappy fate that befell the Kurds and Shi'ites, Hussein also began arming Kurdish fighters on Turkey's southern border, turning them from a "rag-tag terrorist band," according to one Western diplomat, to a "viable guerrilla army." See Chris Hedges, "Iraqis Are Arming the Rebel Kurds in Turkey's South," *The New York Times*, October 20, 1991, p. 1.

outspoken advocates of democracy are shot in the streets; where the penalty for wearing a politically incorrect T-shirt is fifteen years in jail; and where Charles Krauthammer would be denied entry because he is a Jew.

More than half of Kuwait's citizens did not bother to show up for their liberation. By early May, nearly a third of those who had stayed in the country during the occupation also departed, leaving perhaps only 100,000–150,000 actual Kuwaiti nationals in their own homeland. To the degree that these few remaining patriots did consider themselves free of their Iraqi oppressors, they were liberated to live under what are perhaps the most oppressive environmental conditions in human history. The war created an unprecedented ecological catastrophe which, while it may not be as toxic as was once feared, nevertheless poisoned the air, land, and sea of the entire Gulf region and threatened the health of millions.* Kuwait may have been freed from Iraqi plundering, but from a public health standpoint, saving the country all but destroyed it.

To the degree that the remaining Kuwaitis felt any sense of well-being, their good fortune was purchased at an extraordinary expensive price in innocent human misery. The most immediate victims of Kuwaiti freedom were the tens of thousands of soldiers and civilians who died during the war and its buildup. The number of Iraqi casualties remains murky, but perhaps as many as two thousand Iraqi conscripts, according to Pentagon calculations, were simply buried alive.†

A second set of victims were those Palestinian, Iraqi, and Jordanian nationals who had the misfortune to find themselves alive and unprotected in liberated Kuwait. According to human rights organizations present at the time, these innocents were the victims of widespread kidnapping, rape, torture, and occasionally murder—treatment that sounds quite similar to the horror stories told by Kuwaitis of the Iraqi occupation. Additional victims

---

*Accurate assessments of the degree of environmental damage to the region were stymied by the inability of the United States, Kuwait, or any international agency to conduct a systematic study. See John H. Cushman, "Environmental Claims for Damage Go Begging for Data," *The New York Times*, November 12, 1991, p. B7.

†See Eric Schmitt, "U.S. Army Buried Iraqi Soldiers Alive in Gulf War," *The New York Times*, September 15, 1991, p. 8, and Patrick J. Sloyan, "U.S. Defends Burying Alive Iraqi Troops," reprinted from *Newsday* in the *San Francisco Chronicle*, April 11, 1992, p. A10. The Pentagon later explained that a "gap" in the laws of warfare made it legally permissible to bury its enemy alive. According to the Pentagon report, "Many Iraqis surrendered during this phase of the attack and were taken prisoner. The division then assaulted the trenches containing other Iraqi soldiers. Once astride the trench lines, the division turned the plow blades of its tanks and combat earth movers along the Iraqi defense line.

"In the process, many more Iraqi soldiers surrendered; others died in the course of the attack. . . ."

would have to include the roughly 18 million Iraqi civilians who saw their country bombed into conditions a UN commission termed "near-apocalyptic" immediately following the war. To liberate tiny, anti-democratic, anti-Semitic, and anti-American Kuwait, allied bombing turned the city of Baghdad into a hellish cauldron. Over time, moreover, sanitation systems failed, infectious disease thrived, food became scarce, and child mortality figures apparently tripled, vastly increasing the number of deaths the war would eventually cause. The only crime these children committed, let us recall, was to be born inside a country governed by Saddam Hussein.

Then there were the betrayals. George Bush repeatedly called upon the Iraqi people to "take matters into their own hands" and force Hussein to "step aside." The "Voice of Free Iraq" radio station, broadcasting from Saudi Arabia under what is universally assumed to be CIA sponsorship, encouraged the rebels to form a unified military command and "to swoop in on the regime of the Saddam Hussein gang and destroy it." But when the Shi'ia Muslims of southern Iraq heeded this call, the U.S. Army was ordered to stand by silently just a mile away from the killing grounds as Hussein's murderous minions slaughtered them by the tens of thousands. In the north, the Kurdish rebellion against the man Bush called "worse than Hitler" was met with official U.S. indifference as the President took a fishing vacation simultaneous to one of the worst man-made humanitarian disasters in modern history. Nearly 2 million Kurdish refugees were created almost overnight following the President's decision to allow Hussein's forces to employ rotary attack planes in their merciless slaughter of the men, women, and children who had paid heed to Bush's call for an uprising *after* the President had publicly promised that the choppers would not fly. The predictable result here was yet another massacre numbering in the tens of thousands, as well as the heart-wrenching sight of pregnant women, babies, and small children freezing and starving to death in the mountains.

The President explained himself by professing an unwillingness to "intervene militarily" in what he called "Iraq's internal affairs." As he uttered these words, the U.S. military occupied between 15 and 20 percent of Iraqi territory. By the time Bush reversed himself and joined Britain and France in helping to construct refugee camps for the wretched survivors, the President succeeded in earning the United States the worst of both possible outcomes: our military stood by in the face of genocide and it still risked involvement in a long-term, long-distance quagmire. A year after the war ended, more than 800,000 Kurds remained homeless in northern Iraq. Meanwhile, in order to accomplish what the Kurds had intended in the first place with their uprising—the overthrow of Hussein—Bush reverted back to economic sanctions, thereby further punishing the innocent victims of

Hussein's megalomania. The sanctions, which Bush and the punditocracy had insisted would never dislodge Hussein from Kuwait, were now alleged to be the mechanism through which we would dislodge him *from Iraq.*

The punditocracy did not spare George Bush any of its capacity for moral outrage over his willingness to sit back and allow this terror to take place. William Safire compared it to the Bay of Pigs. Haynes Johnson chose the Hungarian uprising of 1956. Charles Krauthammer preferred the metaphor of Tiananmen Square. A. M. Rosenthal borrowed the parallel of the Red Army at the Vistula, going so far in another column as to promote the Kurds to the status of honorary Jews. But for all of the punditocracy anguish voiced during this period, it remained beyond the parameters of the dialogue to question the wisdom of having started the war that had helped set all of these simultaneous catastrophes in motion in the first place. Apart from the extremes of the "Buchanan/McGovern axis" (Pat Buchanan, Anthony Lewis, Tom Wicker, and Mary McGrory), almost no one in the punditocracy asked whether, after all was said and done, the war had been a mistake. *

It was certainly too bad about the Kurds though. Jim Hoagland complained that the Kurds and Shi'ites had "embarrassed" George Bush and "tarnished the glory of the victory of Operation Desert Storm," with George Bush "accomplishing less than he did in Panama. . . ."† Charles Krauthammer admitted only to "enormous disappointment," following "seven months of brilliant, indeed heroic presidential leadership." The punditocracy argument seemed to rest on a distinction by which Bush had conducted the war

---

*The punditocracy view of the war throughout the conflict, it is worth noting, was largely at odds with that voiced in the public opinion polls. Majorities of the American people were initially opposed to the President's decision to launch the war immediately after the UN deadline came up; they supported the organization of a prewar peace conference to deal explicitly with the Palestinian issue. Ten days before the ground war was launched, they expressed themselves against the idea by a nine to one margin; within a few weeks of the war's end, they had already decided that the war could not in good conscience be called a "victory." For the early war and Palestinian peace conference poll figures, see the January 9, 1991, *Washington Post*/ABC poll printed in the *Congressional Record* of January 12, 1991, by Senator Robert Byrd of West Virginia. For the poll figure on the ground war, see the CBS/*New York Times* poll and Charles Krauthammer, March 1, 1991. For the figure on Americans believing the war was not a "victory," see Morton Kondracke, "Gun Shy," *The New Republic*, May 20, 1991, p. 19.

†Jim Hoagland, April 22, 1991. Regarding Bush's magistral accomplishment in Panama, we learn according even to the U.S. State Department that Panama remains "a major transshipment point for cocaine destined for the U.S. and Europe." A General Accounting Office report, moreover, cited a U.S. Drug Enforcement Administration agent who "believes that trafficking may have doubled" since the American invasion of December 1989. See David Johnston, "The Noriega Verdict," *The New York Times*, April 11, 1992, p. 1.

beautifully, only to choke somewhere near the finish line. "Brilliant, heroic, flawless, fantastic, daring, bold, masterful" George Bush had launched the war. But the wimp had retaken possession of the President's body before the final mopping up could be completed. The post-Iraq political spectrum lay somewhere between Morton Kondracke, who argued in *The New Republic* that "although the Democrats were wrong to oppose America's war against Saddam Hussein, they have every right to second-guess the administration's handling of the postwar endgame," and Charles Krauthammer, who denied prewar critics the right to postwar criticism. "Erstwhile antiwar critics," he argued, were "quite prepared to consign Kuwait to the fate they now bemoan in Kurdistan," and would thus do better to hold their tongues.

None of the war's punditocracy promoters appeared willing to recognize that the unhappy fate of the Kurds, the Shi'ites, and even the innocent tortured nationals of pro-Saddam nations inside Kuwait was visited upon them directly as a result of the American decision to launch a war for Kuwait. The chaos and suffering caused by the war were thus treated in the American political dialogue as if they had come about wholly independently of the war that had sown them. "The peace," observed George Will with deadly seriousness, "is not nearly as much fun as the war was."

Even more dangerous than the war itself to long-term American interests, however, may be its political legacy. The war's end saw the pro-war pundits' influence reach its pinnacle inside Washington, just as the assumptions underlying their analyses grew ever more remote from the realities they were alleging to interpret.

Initially, the war seemed to imperil the future of the two-party system. Richard Cohen gloated over the Democrat's "isolationist chickens coming home to roost." David Broder insisted that the war "showed the nation once again that Democrats cannot define the destiny of America." *The Wall Street Journal* editors wondered how "so many elected members of a political party could end up on the opposite side from the American people? Especially after so many of them endured a failed tryout of this act with the invasion of Grenada." A. M. Rosenthal's barely coherent fulminations contained this warning: "A party that is not strong enough to fight evil abroad cannot be trusted to fight evil at home." There was simply no way that "Americans would put their affairs into the hands of a candidate who not only opposed military action against Saddam Hussein but is too murky-minded or arrogant to drop the heavy baggage of that mistake and goes staggering on under it, crying, 'What mistake? What baggage?'"

Leaving aside the fact that the more serious consequences of the war were not and could not yet possibly be apparent just one week after the initial cease-fire had been announced, these analyses were also flatly contradicted by public opinion polls at the time.* But because they accurately reflected punditocracy conventional wisdom, the Democrats by and large accepted their punishment quietly, and tried to keep their heads down. At the Democratic Leadership Council (DLC) meeting in early May, the "centrist" delegates dropped plans to make prewar support for Bush an explicit litmus test for a presidential race, but passed a resolution saluting their political adversary for his "well conceived and superbly executed strategy" in the war anyway. As the organization's favorite son, Arkansas Governor Bill Clinton, put the finishing touches on his pro-war presidential candidacy, such previously vocal opponents as Senators John Kerry and Barbara Mikulski offered up *mea culpa* mass mailings celebrating the war and intimating that they, too, had been on board, sort of, right from the start.

In the longer term, the punditocracy employed the war to shape the overall direction of American strategic policy. Enough of doom-sayers, conservationists, butter-before-guns types, and liberals who whined about bad schools and unmanageable debts. Everything was just fine. The war had proven us to be, in Ben Wattenberg's words, "the most influential nation in history." In the sands of Kuwait, the punditocracy decided it had finally found incontrovertible proof that those nagging declinists had everything wrong. Charles Krauthammer argued that the defeat of Iraq demonstrated that the very idea of American decline was "nonsense." He deployed as his sole piece of supporting evidence a comparison between the relative difficulty the United States had faced in defeating North Korea in 1950 with that of defeating Iraq forty years later. The war had proven, added Michael Novak, "the end of the decline . . . the decline of the declinists . . . the daughter of disaster for the declinists."

These arguments were so transparently specious that the mere fact that such respected and influential political intellectuals felt no compunction in offering them is itself evidence of the alarming decline of the standards of Washington debate. As a basis for a sensible, prudent comparison of America's relative power in 1950 and 1990, Krauthammer's analogy is intellectually indefensible and wholly unworthy of so thoughtful a writer and

---

*A poll taken by the *Los Angeles Times* at the height of the war euphoria in early March found that only a tiny plurality (21% to 19%) of those questioned thought that a vote against war had been an exercise of "good judgment." Asked how the war had affected their impression of the Democrats, 11% said they were less favorably inclined toward the Democrats, 3% said they were more favorably inclined toward the Democrats, and 85% said their view of the Democrats had not changed. E. J. Dionne, "Democrats Remain Split Over Policy," *The Washington Post*, March 17, 1991, p. A6.

thinker.* As for Novak's claim, widely endorsed throughout the punditocracy, it, too, asks much merely to be taken seriously. None of the supposedly humiliated declinists upon whose graves he is so eager to dance ever remotely implied that as a result of its inability to fashion a decent education system, a healthy economy, or a stable urban society, the United States would therefore be incapable of winning a war against so pathetically mismatched an opponent as Iraq. The argument, rather, insisted that America's obsession with military force at the expense of its economic, social, and environmental health had undermined its productive capabilities and ensured the long-term degradation of its living standards. And that argument stands.

History is replete with examples of empires mounting impressive military campaigns on the cusp of their impending economic collapse. Spain sent a massive army to Germany in 1634 to fight in the Thirty Years' War, Paul Kennedy reminds us, but the kingdom was bankrupt within a decade. Britain demonstrated a daunting "force projection" capability when it transported 300,000 troops from all over the world into the Transvaal in 1899–1900. Yet it too had already begun its decline and started to come apart fourteen years later.

Punditocracy celebrations of the "unity of purpose" Americans allegedly achieved during the Gulf War were similarly woolly-minded. In his *National Review* column, ominously entitled "Rebirth of a Nation," Reagan/Bush appointee and newly minted neocon pundit William J.

---

*The Korean War, he noted, "lasted three years, cost 54,000 American lives and ended in a draw," while the Iraqi War lasted six weeks, cost 196 American lives, and ended in a rout. "If the Roman empire had declined at this rate," he quipped, "you'd be reading this column in Latin."

Cute, but for starters, Krauthammer might have acknowledged that the Korean War was fought not only against Koreans but against the massive army of Mao's China as well. He might also note that a significant proportion of the 54,000 Americans who died in Korea died not from battle wounds but from sickness and disease—something only Iraqis died from in the Gulf. Third, Krauthammer would do well to deal with the fact that the United States could not and did not initiate a worldwide embargo against Korea before going to war, thereby depriving its military of key spare parts and maintenance equipment. Fourth, Korea had not just exhausted itself in an endless war against its neighbor, as had Iraq against Iran. Fifth, the North Koreans had the Soviets in their corner, offering a degree of support and materiel which is still unclear, while the Soviets were allied with us against Iraq. Sixth, the United States ended military action in the Gulf after it liberated Kuwait. Had the Army stopped after liberating South Korea, the war would have ended within four months. General MacArthur captured Pyongyang, the North Korean capital, on October 19, 1950, a little over three months after U.S. and allied troops initially landed. For something approaching the whole story, see Bruce Cumings, *The Origins of the Korean War: Liberation and the Emergence of Separate Regimes, 1945–1947* (Princeton, NJ: Princeton University Press, 1981), and *The Origins of the Korean War*, Vol. II: *The Roaring of the Cataract, 1947–1950* (Princeton, NJ: Princeton University Press, 1991).

Bennett posited that the war's success would henceforth become "one of the defining events in the American psyche." The foundations for this much-expressed hope were sketchy, but appeared to rest primarily on the fact that Americans watched even greater than usual amounts of television during the war and told pollsters of their near-unanimous approval of Bush's conduct of the conflict. Yet even were this more than punditocracy wishful thinking, it is doubtful that it would have any significant implications for addressing the sources of America's predicament. Michael Howard observes that Britain achieved its greatest moment of "national unity" under Winston Churchill in 1944–45 following its victory in World War II, yet this period also coincided with that of Britain's most pronounced national economic decline.

From the standpoint of the problems that truly threaten the nation's future prosperity and security, the Persian Gulf War was little more than a wasteful diversion from the difficult tasks at hand. While the nation remained focused on Scud attacks and Patriot kills, the remaining productive forces within the economy continued on their steadily deteriorating path. According to Commerce Department figures, real GNP in the United States dropped at an annual rate of 2.1 percent during the buildup, making it the largest single downturn since the 1981–82 recession. This slide worsened during the months of the war and its aftermath. The number of Americans applying for unemployment insurance also reached an eight-year high, as official U.S. statistics, it was later revealed, vastly undercounted the rise in the number of jobless. This undercount was the result, according to a Reuters' report, of "many small companies that went bankrupt and the job losses when some workers were called to serve in the Persian Gulf War," and appeared to have had a "big impact," according to private analysts, on the U.S. economic downturn that began in July 1990. Banks went bust at record, post-depression rates, and business failures jumped over 20 percent. The big-three auto companies lost a total of $2.4 billion in the quarter that George Bush went to war and $4.5 billion during the entire crisis. General Motors, it would later be revealed, was on its way to posting the largest annual loss in U.S. corporate history. The United States, moreover, for the first time in twenty-seven years, dropped out of the world's top five machine-tool manufacturers. Overall, roughly a million jobs disappeared from the American economy in the six months it took George Bush to mass his fighting force on the Kuwaiti border alone.

Inside our cities, the number of people gunned down during the hundred hours of Desert Storm equaled our battle casualties in the Persian Gulf. More than one in eight American children were found by one study to be going hungry. The number of families requiring aid for dependent children hit an all-time public record. As the war wound down, the state of Maryland announced that 9,300 women and children would be cut off from receiving free milk, cheeses, eggs, juice, and peanut butter each month because of decreased funding in the federal government's nutrition program. Similar cuts had been announced in Virginia a week earlier.

With regard to the battle to address the nation's many environmental threats, punditocracy armchair generals were, as usual, AWOL. The Environmental Protection Agency discovered shortly after the war's end that the depletion of the ozone level over the United States was proceeding twice as fast as had earlier been expected. This implied, according to government calculations, that over the next 50 years, 12 million Americans would develop skin cancer and more than 200,000 would die as a result.

The balance of American foreign policy in the non-Gulf world suffered from malign neglect during this period as well. The punditocracy barely paid attention while the most important political development of the postwar era—the political experiment under way in Mikhail Gorbachev's Soviet Union—became unglued as the Soviet Union slipped into what appeared to be unending chaos. Yet U.S. public debate treated these dramatic developments almost exclusively in terms of their implications for Bush's Gulf War script. As the fate of *perestroika* hung in the balance throughout the fall and winter of the war months and conservative coup plotters in Moscow gathered strength, attacking Gorbachev and Eduard Shevardnadze for behaving as American handmaidens in the Gulf, the punditocracy could hardly be roused to notice, excluding a few ritual denunciations of Gorbachev's peacemaking perfidy. The British journalist Martin Walker noted during the height of the ground war that the failure of Gorbachev's reformist agenda was at least in some measure the cost of Washington's "obsession with the essentially regional problem of Saddam Hussein." Had the August coup turned out differently, the reformist impulse in the Soviet Union might have been the final victim of the punditocracy's fatal preoccupation in the Gulf.

In most of these cases, the punditocracy's sins were those of omission rather than commission. Only A. M. Rosenthal went so far as to criticize those few journalists who did continue to discuss America's more serious problems. The unfortunate "sob-sisters of journalism, politics and academia," cried Rosenthal, were still offering "sophomoric lectures" about "how the war would still leave us with all the domestic problems bedeviling the country: drugs, crime, race, AIDS, S&Ls, homelessness, recession, teen-age pregnancy, graffiti, garbage, loud radios and paper cracklers at the movies," when they should, like him, have been devoting their columns to dewey-eyed tributes to the manliness and grace of their president.

Perhaps the most dangerous idea to emerge from the detritus of Baghdad's destruction was the notion that the Gulf War provided a worthwhile model for a future international security system. Despite the obvious costs involved, the idea of the United States serving as the gendarme of the Western world, putting our massive military might at the service of Western interests, swelled punditocracy breasts with pride. Anthony Cordesman, who won William Safire's award for the most impressive television pundit of the war, greeted New York Times readers on the morning after the cease-fire with a paean to "America's new combat culture," based, at least in Cordesman's hope, on what would be a further redistribution of money and resources to military means. Charles Krauthammer sketched out the contours of this culture's foreign policy in his plea for a new Pax Americana based on unilateral U.S. military intervention on a worldwide basis. "Our best hope," argued Krauthammer, "is in American strength and will, unashamedly laying down the rules of world order and being prepared to enforce them," the ultimate goal being the use of American "dominance to achieve American ends throughout the world." As always, Krauthammer's candor and eloquence were instructive. His use of the word "dominance" does not refer to economic dominance, political dominance, or even the kind of intellectual or cultural dominance to which Americans once aspired. It refers explicitly and exclusively to military power. As Robert Bartley, his neocon comrade, later admitted, "on the Right, the notion of decline faded as Ronald Reagan filled the military spare-parts bins, frankly labeled the Soviet Union an 'evil empire,' invaded Grenada, bombed Libya and revived the option of missile defense." Now that "an American-led attack [had] decimated" Iraq, "the world's new military balance was clear." America, Bartley insisted, "has not declined, it has prevailed." It was military power and military power alone though which the United States retained its status as the world's premier nation.

This superiority, though Krauthammer and his punditocracy colleagues refuse to acknowledge it, has been purchased at a devastating cost to the economic and ecological health of the nation. In a complete reversal of the conditions of the immediate postwar world, the work forces of our Western allies are now better skilled, better educated, safer in their homes, and more secure in their jobs than their counterparts in the United States. At the lowest end of the scale, the citizens of neither Western Europe nor Japan were subjected to the subproletarian conditions which vexed so much of America's all but hopeless poor. Health, employment, and retirement in Western Europe are insured at a level, as William Pfaff argues, that "many Americans still find scarcely credible." In Japan, Edward Luttwak bemoaned the tens of thousands of young Americans "living as illegal immigrants," supplemented by so many American prostitutes that "their services no longer command a premium—though there is still a fair demand for blondes." Traveling in Berlin while the United States was preparing to fight Iraq and ogling what appeared to be the enormous expense—in dollar terms—of everyday items, the Hungarian-born American historian John Lukacs was moved to wonder, "Has it ever happened, in this century, that an American traveling abroad found that he was poorer there than were the natives of his own class? Perhaps less elegant, less sophisticated, less worldly. But poorer?"

When the rest of the world looks at the condition in which America currently finds itself, there is barely a hint of the gratitude or envy so frequently trumpeted by the punditocracy. Instead, we find a mixture of bemusement and pity among our friends, and contempt among our adversaries, for a nation whose productive capacities have been almost willfully crippled. In the "fearsome, transcendent" America whose "dominance" is so apparent to the punditocracy, our competitors see what Edward Luttwak has aptly described as a "no-skill, no-money, have-gun-will-travel society whose geo-economic failure now seems quite predictable." As the United States was seeking to extend its influence throughout the Gulf by bombing Iraq into the Stone Age, Japanese businessmen were buying up one of our last great movie studios for more money than they were originally willing to pledge to the Gulf effort. In Germany, politicians were biding their time, unconcerned about who ran which Middle Eastern kingdom while so much of their own country required massive educational, environmental, and capital investment. "Let them call us draft dodgers," wrote Marion Grafin Donhoff in Die Zeit, "What do we care?"

If the United States is ever to regain the economic dynamism of Germany and Japan, much less reverse the dangerous diminution in the quality of life of the majority of its citizens in the social, environmental, and competitive realms, it will first need to undergo a near-complete intellectual revolution as to the ordering of its national priorities. As Luttwak explained before a shocked Senate Armed Services Committee:

> The great questions to be resolved in the main arena of international life
> have not been changed at all by Iraq's invasion of Kuwait: who will
> develop and market the next generation of computers, civilian aircraft,
> advanced materials and other high added-value products. For that it is not
> expeditionary armies that are needed but abundant, patient capital, not
> impressive warships but educational investment in a highly skilled labor
> force.

The example of Luttwak's experiences is instructive. No one in the punditocracy underwent a more startling intellectual transformation in the wake of the end of the Cold War. Once prized by the Reagan punditocracy as the most creative mind in its consensus of belligerence, Luttwak became during the prelude to the war the most eloquent American voice of the new—geoeconomic—world order. He also became, in the wake of the war, perhaps the single most ridiculed figure in punditocracy discourse, as numerous publications—including *Commentary*, the *Post* Style section, *The New Republic*, and *The Washington Times*—singled him out for the alleged lunacy of his analysis. Now, this brilliant and quirky Transylvanian did not simply reverse himself on the great issues of the day and go over to the liberal side. He continued to mock welfare queens, attack environmentalists, and denounce the dangers of liberal "communitarianism" with the same fervor he once reserved for KGB saboteurs. But as the KGB's minions were treading home from Eastern Europe and no remotely comparable threats to American security seemed to be materializing on the horizon, Luttwak was sufficiently confident in his intellectual abilities to see the new world anew. The punditocracy, however, as if engaged in an unspoken conspiracy of intellectual obsolescence and political intolerance, took the opportunity of Luttwak's volte-face to cast him as the villain in what appeared to be an archetypal cautionary tale. The lesson for any major intellectual figure who enjoyed the largesse of punditocracy respect and admiration could hardly be clearer. Travel beyond the bounds of what we define to be acceptable political discourse and prepare, politically speaking, to die.

The point here is not that anyone—indeed, even his friends and family—need worry about Edward Luttwak. His career as a respected voice in the debate quickly recovered as he reintegrated his analysis into the delineated boundaries of punditocracy discourse. Lost, however, are the ideas, the challenges, the intellectual interplay that such a voice would have offered. And it is precisely such voices that a guiding elite requires if it is to avoid falling into comfortable, though largely nostalgic, categories of thought in seeking to determine the nation's future.

"Every other nation on earth would like to be in our position," insisted Charles Krauthammer who, in the wake of the war, had come closest to fulfilling Lippmann's mantle as the most influential intellectual voice in elite political culture. "Why not enjoy it?" Both the statement and the question that follow are an invitation to complacency. If we are the envy of the world, then why worry about our computer industry, our banking industry, our auto industry, our third-rate educational system, our health-care crisis, our manufacturing base, our unsafe cities, our drug epidemic, our collapsing infrastructure, and our degraded environment? In this fashion, America's "victory" in the Gulf, as interpreted by the punditocracy, will all but ensure the acceleration of America's decline as a secure and prosperous nation. The unlimited opportunities opened up by the collapse of the Cold War will go unexploited. Although the enemy had self-destructed and his stand-in had proven to be a fraud, the system was predicated upon eternal enemies, and the system worked—sort of. In March 1992, the Pentagon leaked a draft "Defense Policy Guidance" report calling for the investment of yet another $1.2 trillion over the next five years to ensure, virtually unilaterally, that the United States be able to defeat not existing adversaries, but "potential competitors," lest they "aspire to a larger regional or global role."* Bartley, Will, Krauthammer and company had a right to be proud. The Pentagon document represented, as the *Times* noted, "the only effort so far to put together a coherent blueprint for the post–Cold War era" more than a year after the Gulf War had ended. Fewer than thirty days later, the Senate passed a budget resolution calling for $291 billion in military spending for fiscal year 1993. Despite all the earth-shattering transformations the planet had undergone during the previous decade, there would be no new thinking in Washington so long as the punditocracy reigned.

---

*Despite the best efforts of Krauthammer, Bartley, and others to publicly congratulate the Pentagon for the perspicacity of its analysis, the document's rhetoric revealed more about the administration's true mind-set than it had intended. In the document's final version, its unilateralist language was toned down, though its strategic priorities—along with the planned weapons spending that underlay them—remained essentially unchanged. See Patrick E. Tyler, "Pentagon Drops Goal of Blocking New Superpowers," *The New York Times*, May 24, 1992, p. A1.

CONCLUSION

The punditocracy's attempt to schedule George Bush's postwar coronation proved a bit premature. The Gulf War did cast a shadow over the electoral campaign, but it was hardly the one presaged by the triumphalism of early 1991. By the time of the New Hampshire primaries a year later, Saddam Hussein remained firmly ensconced in power, his military intact and his nuclear weapons program the subject of continued nervous speculation. Neither Kuwait nor Saudi Arabia proved ready to tolerate democratic dissent, nor recognize the legitimacy of Israel. At home, the U.S. economy continued on its tailspin and the Bush administration reverted to chaotic form. The President scheduled a hasty trip to Japan in the hopes of portraying himself as the unchallenged leader of the world's only superpower. Instead, he ended up cutting a ribbon on a toy store and throwing up on the prime minister's shoes. He returned home empty-handed to a media suddenly picturing him as a rudderless politician, increasingly out of touch with the fear and anger of everyday Americans, and vulnerable to political challenges from both his right and left.

The punditocracy, meanwhile, was proving itself no less fickle than the public. While most pundits continued to celebrate the munificence of the American military power, they too soured on the commander-in-chief. The pundits were angry at Bush for letting Saddam get away, abandoning the Kurds, and failing to force our erstwhile allies in the region to reform themselves politically. But most of all, the pundits were furious at the President for what they perceived to be his strong-arm tactics regarding Israel.

In attempting to force Israel to freeze settlement activity on the West Bank, the President, many pundits believed, displayed a dangerous inability to appreciate Israel's security concerns and political sensitivities, particularly given the dual strain it was undergoing from massive Soviet Jewish immigration coupled with its participation in U.S.-sponsored peace talks. In addition, he appeared to them to be flirting with political anti-Semitism. During the height of the settlement controversy, Bush insisted—quite ridiculously—that he was nothing more than "one lonely little guy" standing up to "something like a thousand [pro-Shamir] lobbyists on the Hill working the other side of the question." These words sent a chill down the spine of Israel's partisans throughout the insider universe.

The issue came to a head when Jewish pundit/politician Ed Koch revealed that Secretary of State James A. Baker had allegedly said, "Fuck the Jews; they didn't vote for us, anyway," at a cabinet meeting. Baker's assessment may have been factually correct, and in fact, even many American Jews supported the administration's willingness to ask Israel to choose between continued expansion of the occupation and the possibility of peace with its neighbors. But—incredibly—this consummate political smoothie failed to include the power of the punditocracy in his calculations. Its influence far exceeds the voting power of any American ethnic minority, Jews included. Reports of the comment, which the Secretary of State denied, provided something of a final nail in the administration's political coffin in neoconservative circles, inspiring new fears and stoking smoldering embers. William Safire, to no one's surprise, set the pace. First he beat up on the President and "his hatchetman at State" for deliberately "humiliating Israel" by trying to force its people to "sit up and beg" for housing-loan guarantees. Second, and far more impressive, were Safire's unsparing efforts to promote the administration's coddling of Saddam Hussein into a full-blown Watergate-type scandal, replete with a "criminal conspiracy" including the "fraudulent use of public funds, its sustained deception of Congress and its obstruction of justice." Safire returned to this subject over and over again, as only Safire can do, going so far in one eight-day period as to title two columns "Crimes of Iraqgate."* By the end of 1991, the millennialist rhetoric of February and March seemed a distant memory and the punditocracy was in the market for a new President.

*See William Safire, March 2, 1992, May 18, 1992, and May 25, 1992. For a rather less agile defense of the Shamir government's behavior, see A. M. Rosenthal, May 29, 1991, where he claims—straight-faced—that the problem with the Israeli Prime Minister is that "Mr. Shamir's particular personality manages to obscure his own commitment toward autonomy for Palestinians."

Under normal circumstances, the pundits would have been delighted to embrace one of their own as a hard-line Republican alternative to George Bush. But Patrick J. Buchanan—the anti-Desert Storm, possibly anti-Semitic, pro-Fascist, pro-Palestinian, McCarthyite, tribalist, protectionist, isolationist—was no normal circumstance. With the exception of a tiny minority of pundits who had worked closely with Buchanan and insisted that the anti-Semitism charge was unfair, the punditocracy recoiled in horror from the man Charles Krauthammer called "a woolly mammoth, frozen in Siberian ice as a perfectly preserved specimen of 1930's isolationism and nativism."

Of course the debate over Buchanan's psychological motivations once again had the effect of obscuring any possibility of examining the problems faced by the nation.* The tenor of political discussion was nicely illustrated on the December morning that Buchanan appeared on ABC's "This Week with David Brinkley" just days before he announced his candidacy. The program was something of an historic first, as three television pundits spent an hour asking a fourth about what he would do as President. Sam Donaldson chose as the basis of his attack the confused accusations of yet another pundit, A. M. Rosenthal. Unfortunately, Donaldson misread Rosenthal's column and therefore mischaracterized what were Rosenthal's "almost criminal distortions" of Buchanan's views in the first place. Through this comedy of errors, Buchanan got himself released from the burden of having to explain some of his most offensive comments, and could respond, quite legitimately, "that's false . . . that's false . . . where did you get these quotes . . . where did you get these quotes?" etc. Following even more misrepresentations of his views by Donaldson, Buchanan decided he would rather discuss Slovenia.

On the Democratic side, punditocracy politics were slightly less confusing but certainly no less complicated. The punditocracy's unanimously anointed candidate was Arkansas Governor Bill Clinton. As Evans and Novak reported, when Clinton came to Washington in September 1991, "as a newly minted candidate but by no means the front-runner," he described himself to an insider breakfast gathering as "the party's only candidate who solidly supported the [Persian Gulf] war." The effect of this performance, they reported, could "not be minimized," as it allowed Clinton to present himself as "the one candidate able to confront George Bush on what then seemed a transcendent issue." In fact, Clinton's support for the pro-war position was

---

*Though the choice between the perceived anti-Israel bias of Bush and Baker, and the assumed anti-Semitism and naked pro-Palestinian bias of Buchanan, did have the virtue of illuminating just how foolish Jewish neoconservatives like Irving Kristol and Norman Podhoretz had been in insisting, throughout the 1980s, that "Jewish interests" in America lay with a switch from the Democrats to the Republicans.

quite a bit more equivocal than he let on.* Moreover, as indicated earlier, the American people no longer cared about the war by the time of the election. No matter. The punditocracy cared passionately, and it would be choosing its candidate long before any voters had anything to say about the matter.

Clinton was the only conceivable choice for the punditocracy, given the character of its Reagan-era obsessions. In addition to his Desert Storm bona fides, he was also willing to credit Ronald Reagan's weapons spending with ending the Cold War, and even wanted to build nuclear submarines that the Bush administration insisted it wanted to scrap.† With regard to Israel, Clinton stood foursquare behind the Shamir government's demand for loan guarantees without making any concessions over a freeze on new settlements. Just before the New York primary, Clinton went before a group of Jewish leaders to accuse the Bush administration of eroding "the taboo against overt anti-Semitism" through its use of "strident rhetoric, public and private, against Israel." On social matters, Clinton adopted a number of neoconservative positions regarding the family and the importance of personal responsibility for those on welfare. He proved particularly agile at, and genuinely committed to, defusing America's explosive racial problems. Moreover, as virtually every reporter who covered the campaign was willing—privately—to testify, Clinton was simply a hell of a guy: charming, funny, able to laugh at himself, and a brilliant back-room politician to boot. If some Dr. Frankenstein of the political process had crafted all of the punditocracy's wishes and dreams onto a handsome cadaver and plugged him in, he could hardly have manufactured a politician more appealing than Bill Clinton.

The punditocracy swoon for Clinton was so powerful and so pervasive that it soon became a story in its own right. The *Times*'s Washington bureau

*Evans and Novak reported that they could not find any Clinton statements on the record in support of ending sanctions and beginning a war before the vote actually took place. The closest the Clinton campaign could come to substantiating its claim, they said, was the governor's statement made two days after the vote, reading: "I guess I would have voted with the majority if it was a close vote, but I agree with the arguments the minority made." An AP report also quoted him as saying the opposite—that he would have voted with the minority—but the Clinton campaign called this story "incorrect." See Rowland Evans and Robert Novak, March 4, 1992. Note: All the quotes in the text refer to the columnists', not the candidate's, quotes.

†For the defense of the Reagan buildup, Clinton insisted at an October 1991 *Washington Post* editorial board meeting that Reagan deserved credit for "the idea that he wanted to stand up to them," praising Reagan's "rhetoric in defense of freedom" and his role in "advancing the idea that Communism could be rolled back." The punditocracy also appreciated statements like that of Clinton deputy campaign manager and spokesperson George Stephanopoulos, who called the Seawolf nuclear submarine program "an important part of our defense posture." See E. J. Dionne, "Clinton Credits Reagan for Fall of Communism," *The Washington Post*, October 17, 1991, p. A4. Stephanopoulos quoted in *San Francisco Chronicle*, March 2, 1992.

chief, Howell Raines, noted what he called the "extraordinary burst of journalistic fawning" detected among punditocracy personages, and singled out the editors of *The New Republic*, who had tried and failed to play the same role for Albert Gore four years earlier. The editors, including owner Martin Peretz, were even seen "spinning" the room of journalists on behalf of Clinton following a Democratic debate. Given the vagaries of the American electoral process, this kind of help can be quite important. Hardly anyone in true-life America watches the debates themselves, but impressions of competence and eloquence do filter through news reports. Spin, therefore, is everything.

The effect of this support on the shape and character of the 1992 race was manifest and manifold, and the Clinton campaign was quick to deploy it to maximum advantage. The punditocracy's ability to shape an election campaign is of a different character than its influence over insider policy issues, owing to the variety of intermediaries it must work through to influence the tens of millions of people who choose a party's nominee. To shape the debate of the candidates, the punditocracy needs to work through these intermediaries—be they the moneymen, the campaign reporters, or the television producers—in order to try to shape the larger discussion upon which the media feels compelled to report every four years.

The Clinton campaigners understood this process perfectly and did their best to employ their punditocracy advantage to create a ripple effect throughout the entire media and create the impression that their candidate was the man to beat. Clinton's foreign policy speeches, for instance, explained deputy campaign manager and spokesperson George Stephanopoulos, were crafted specifically with the punditocracy in mind. "They write the columns, the experts and the diplomats read the columns, the reporters interview the experts, the producers read the reporters and the next thing you know, Clinton's made the evening news, looking like a president." The tactic was first deployed in December 1991, when Clinton made his first major foreign policy address at Georgetown University. The campaign made what Stephanopoulos calls "a deliberate decision to leak the speech to [the *Times*'s] Leslie Gelb to jump start the process. And it worked." Indeed, Gelb wrote an influential column in the *Times* just before Clinton's first major foreign policy address, praising the governor's ability to "appreciate the value of military power." As *Post* media reporter Howard Kurtz noted, "Favorable notices such as the Gelb column percolate through the political community, reinforcing the elusive notion of 'momentum.' " Soon, Evans and Novak, Jim Hoagland, and Jack Germond began to treat Clinton's front-runner status as an accomplished fact. Morton Kondracke went so far as to insist that the party was in a state of panic over the possibility that Clinton might stumble, given the fact that "below Clinton, there's nothing there." As always, no evidence was posited. When William Safire called upon "front-runner" Clinton as his chosen vehicle with which to bash Bush for being insufficiently sympathetic to Israeli sensitivities just nine days into the new year, and *The New Republic* followed shortly thereafter with an incredibly laudatory Sidney Blumenthal cover story on the man, the contest was declared all but over. * This wholly manufactured political "momentum" helped Clinton outpace his rivals in the fundraising contest, and thereby buy himself sufficient television time and campaign staff in New Hampshire and elsewhere actually to earn himself the front-runner position in the real election. This, in an election process, is the meaning of pundit power.

Had Clinton remained altogether faithful to his wife, fought in Vietnam, or even won the New Hampshire primary, the punditocracy primary might have ended the Democratic contest then and there. But of course, duty called again and again in the winter of 1992. In *L'Affaire* Flowers, the question of marital fidelity needed to be delegitimated and the character of the attacker destroyed. This process was well under way even before the story broke. In a preemptive attack, noted Raines, *The New Republic*, "aware of festering rumors, tried to inoculate him [Clinton] against disclosures with an editorial arguing that personal questions from back home were out of bounds." Al Hunt called it "a shabby accusation" that "distorted and contaminated not only the political system but the judgment of some in the news media." "Pornographers," cried Thomas Oliphant of "Inside Washington," and the *Boston Globe*, were trying to "hijack democracy." Charles Krauthammer congratulated the highbrow media for underplaying the story as a newfound sign of its newfound responsibility, while A. M. Rosenthal lauded his own paper for playing the story "exactly right," in his humble opinion. Almost no one, including the few feminist columnists in the business, thought the adultery issue worthy of consideration. Nor did any wonder whether Clinton's nondenial denial raised any other important questions about his fitness for the job.† As for Ms. Flowers, never in presidential history has anyone's decision to change her hair color been the subject of so much high-minded editorializing. Sidney Blumenthal, for instance, called Flowers "the woman in red, trimmed in black to match the roots of her frosted hair." She suffered, it appeared, not only from the

---

*Clinton, who attacked the Bush administration's concerted opposition to Israeli settlement policy, was, according to Safire, admirably "on top of the issue." See William Safire, January 9, 1991. Blumenthal's cover story, "The Anointed," appeared in early January, though the magazine is dated February 3, 1992.

†This is not to imply that the author disagrees with this judgment; I do not. But I do find the unanimity of this bit of conventional wisdom striking, particularly since I share it.

inconvenience of her story but also the perceived content of her tabloid character: Ms. Flowers, it appeared, was *not* the kind of woman who subscribed to *The New Republic*.

The Flowers affair had a number of interesting and unremarked undercurrents. The media, obsessed by celebrity, could not resist succumbing to the story, even as it hated itself in the morning for doing so. Ted Koppel, scooping even *The Star* on "Nightline" the night before the story broke, snuck it through journalistic customs, as *Newsweek*'s Jonathan Alter pointed out, by pretending it was really a story about media ethics. In a confusing moment of post-modern political warfare, Clinton partisan Mandy Grunwald attacked Koppel on the air for defining those ethics—and defining them into the gutter—as he pretended to explore them.

The punditocracy, moreover, had an additional incentive for venting its wrath on the media for tawdry sensationalism over the Flowers affair. George Will had seen allegations of his marital problems splashed across the media and John McLaughlin had been the subject of any number of stories alleging sexual harassment of his female employees, as well as his recent *War of the Roses*–style divorce. High-profile members of the punditocracy, in other words, had become "celebrities" in the same sense that "Bill and Hillary" had, and were therefore just as vulnerable. A final irony in the episode lay in the fact that the punditocracy's arbitrary test of Clinton's "electability" rested on his ability to convince Democratic primary voters that questions of adultery were irrelevant to his candidacy. As these same pundits have been complaining for two decades now, however, Democratic primary voters constitute a puny minority of the voting public, and their numbers this year were even smaller than usual. A paltry 7 percent of eligible voters in New York bothered to show up for its primary.* Extreme liberals make up a far greater percentage of this tiny electorate than they do in the general election. The fact that primary voters may not care about Bill Clinton's sex life was therefore hardly proof positive that the issue would not destroy him in November 1992.

A similar dynamic seemed at work in the election season's second scandal—that of twenty-three-year-old Billy Clinton's letter to his Arkansas draft board. Once again, the punditocracy had no one but itself to thank for the alleged salience of the issue. More than any other institution in American society, it had been insisting upon the paramount importance of the Vietnam War as the primary determinant in America's pre-Reagan fall from grace. But this time, Clinton had two more factors working in his favor:

*Voters in New York turned out at the lowest rate since the present system was adopted in 1980. See Sam Roberts, "Voter Turnout Is Ominous Sign for Candidates," *The New York Times*, April 9, 1992, p. A11.

First, he repudiated the substance of his youthful views, and no longer believed in the right of selective conscientious objection. Meg Greenfield and the *Post's* editors called this position "not a view a president can easily hold."

Second, Clinton enjoyed an unspoken feeling of generational solidarity on the part of the people writing about him. This was clearest in the case of fellow Rhodes Scholar, friend, and former anti-Vietnam activist Strobe Talbott, whose influential columns in *Time* magazine and comments on "Inside Washington" were intended to exonerate Clinton of all charges. So were the ad hoc contributions of another friend and former Rhodes, nuclear strategist Michael Mandelbaum, who blanketed the *Times* op-ed page, "The MacNeil-Lehrer Newshour," and *The New Republic* with spirited defenses of his former classmate's character. But the appeal of Clinton's explanations was no less powerful with those pundits without such Clintonesque personal histories. Virtually everyone within the punditocracy who had been of draft age during Vietnam had also skipped the war—in graduate school or elsewhere—and was therefore vulnerable to the same charges. As with the infidelity issue, they had a fundamental interest in seeing that one's "youthful exuberance" not interfere with one's middle-aged political relevance.

In addition to blunting the power of the main scandals, the punditocracy worked to win Clinton the Democratic nomination in other important ways. One of the stranger ones—though it seemed to work perfectly—was the attempt to declare Clinton winner of the New Hampshire primary despite his apparent second-place finish to Paul Tsongas. For instance, "Nightline" pundit Jeff Greenfield announced in late February—when Clinton had still not won a single contest—that "We've had four primaries and four winners, five if you count Bill Clinton in New Hampshire." Just why one would count a second-place finish in New Hampshire as "winning," Greenfield did not feel compelled to explain. When, on the night of his victory there, Paul Tsongas exclaimed, "Thank you New Hampshire, you've done it. You've proven the pundits wrong," it soon became clear that he was taking this voting business altogether too seriously.

As if all this were not enough, the punditocracy, led by *The New Republic* once again, also devoted a great deal of energy to destroying Clinton's opponents. The strangest of these attacks was Morton Kondracke's attempt to pummel Paul Tsongas. Reading the piece gave one the feeling of living in a time warp, as if Kondracke had written it four years earlier with Michael Dukakis in mind, but had penciled in Tsongas's name just before deadline. In March of 1992, when the Soviet Union no longer existed, when Nicaragua, Grenada, and El Salvador no longer mattered, and when the truly massive problems that faced the country were finally becoming evident for all to see, Kondracke complained of the former Massachusetts senator that he "argued against the invasion of Grenada," he opposed the Contras as "terrorists . . . he urged a negotiated settlement between Communist FMLN guerrillas and the government of El Salvador in 1983 even though the FMLN was still bent on a takeover at the time."*

Pundit sit-com panelists seemed virtually unanimous in their choice of Clinton, and so were the regulars on the *Times* and *Post* op-ed pages. In fact, when quizzed, Clinton aide Stephanopoulos was incapable of naming a single member of the punditocracy whose leanings did not seem to favor the Clinton camp. Still, there were subtle and not-so-subtle ways to manifest this. Always one for flooring the gas pedal just as his car is approaching the edge of a cliff, the *Times*'s Rosenthal wondered aloud whether New Yorkers could escape their present incarnation as a "giant bowl of malevolent jelly quivering with eagerness to swallow [Clinton] whole," and, instead, "show themselves smart enough, mature and sophisticated enough," to be worthy of the candidate.

Undoubtedly the most valuable pundit (MVP) in the entire Clinton constellation, however, was *The New Republic*'s campaign correspondent, Sidney Blumenthal. Freed from the pretense of objectivity in his reporting, Blumenthal aimed his considerable intellectual firepower on Clinton's opponents like a SWAT team sharpshooter, picking them off one by one with a ferocious tenacity and razor-sharp wit. The first contestant to suffer Blumenthal's wrath was Senator Tom Harkin (D-Iowa), whose candidacy the author likened to "a primal scream." Next came the hit on Robert Kerrey (D-Neb.), who, after reading Blumenthal's unflattering cover story depicting him as a confused character in an absurd existentialist political narrative, mentioned a desire to "loosen one of [Blumenthal's] teeth" and unburden him of his "preppy little smile." Then came Ms. Flowers and her tacky brunette roots. Following these patriot missives, Blumenthal turned his sights onto Clinton hater Mario Cuomo ("The Coward"), and remaining opponents Paul Tsongas and Jerry Brown.

In the Tsongas case, the Blumenthal attack set the tone for a number of anti-Tsongas stories that soon filled the media, helping to destroy the aura of uncommon political virtue that had been the candidate's primary selling point. In the case of Jerry Brown, Blumenthal used the *Times* op-ed page the weekend of the New York primary to compare him to punditocracy Beelzebub, Oliver Stone, for allegedly promoting "conspiratorialism about the evil of the political system and the government," relying on "the appeal

*Morton Kondracke, "Punch Puller," *The New Republic*, March 16, 1992, pp. 11–14. Were I Morton Kondracke, I would say as little about El Salvador as possible. See chapter 9 for details.

of the irrational presented as super-rational." That there were real evils in the American political system that Brown—however flawed as a messenger he may have been—was simply exposing, was apparently ruled out as a subject of legitimate debate not only by Blumenthal but by the entire lovestruck punditocracy. Following Clinton's victory in New York, Blumenthal set his sights on those congressmen and senators who worried that Clinton's nomination might spell disaster in November. Their ranks, he insisted, were largely composed of the "get-a-diaper crowd," filled with representatives "playing the role of Chicken Little," augmented by the "continuing self-defeating behavior" of "losers." This compared to the "unslick . . . empathetic . . . intelligent . . . technically precise . . . earnest . . . activist-scholar" these politicians had the temerity to oppose. Blumenthal's pro-Clinton tear earned him an affectionate tweaking in *Doonesbury*, along with the deserved reputation as America's sharpest deconstructor of election parapolitics. It also proved influential.

Just how important was the punditocracy anointment of Bill Clinton as its choice for the nomination is difficult to overstate. In the first place, winning the punditocracy primary allowed Clinton to raise piles of early money and buy himself into the front-runner's position in New Hampshire and elsewhere. Second, it is simply inconceivable that any candidate could have expected to survive both the Flowers episode and the draft controversy.

It is hardly a coincidence, therefore, that an insurgent candidate like billionaire businessman Ross Perot should emerge in a punditocracy-driven election process. The American people—as we have noted—have long considered themselves to be irrelevant to the nation's political discourse. Here, for the first time in modern political history, an independent candidate not only was offering to "send Washington a message" but was willing to pick up the tab for the call. Perot's refusal to play the election game by its traditional rules—his "Larry King Live"/"Today" show campaign tactics—proved to be a brilliant means of exploiting Americans' sense of betrayal over what they considered to be the hijacking of their democracy by the pundits, the elite media, and the money men. The more the punditocracy attacked Perot, the more his popularity seemed to soar. Meanwhile, suitably "responsible" punditocracy-approved politicians found themselves laden with the albatross of being considered "insiders" and hence "part of the problem."

Aside from giving those few people who managed to get through to Perot and Clinton on the network phone-in shows a sense of participation in the process, however, it is difficult to imagine just how these changes will address the problems of America's irrelevant public discourse. As virtually all of the candidates' frequent 1992 appearances on various call-in and show-and-tell election programs demonstrated, it is no less difficult for a popular politician to manipulate a discussion fed by anonymous callers who lack access to complete information and are given no opportunity to ask follow-up questions than it was for Ronald Reagan to win the affection of "The McLaughlin Group." Though President Clinton's admirable abilities as a political articulator provide a welcome change from the Reagan/Bush era, the fact remains that as long as American politics remains in thrall to show business values, the best we can hope for from our national discourse is that it keeps us entertained.

Clearly, the problems that plague our political discourse are far more serious than we have previously been willing to admit. They are embedded in our political culture and will remain so, absent a concerted effort to address them. Moreover, as the nation's economic and environmental decline grows more pronounced and our international influence continues to wane, these difficulties are likely to be exacerbated. Externally, this implies future alleged Hitlers; internally, more David Dukes and Patrick Buchanans. These quixotic pursuits will only further divert attention from the urgent tasks of national economic reconstruction and ecological protection, thereby inspiring more of the same in an apparently endless vicious cycle. At the end of this road lies an America unable to cope with the challenges of securing its own prosperity and security in the coming century, as its intellectual leadership remains mired in what George Will terms the "tawdry ferocity" of American public discourse.

There is considerable irony in all this. The American body politic is sick and getting sicker as our democratic muscles atrophy from disuse. The very pundits who bemoan the degraded state of American political debate are themselves in part responsible for its dilapidated condition.* For except in the most extreme cases it is the punditocracy, not the general public, to whom our politicians have become answerable.

As we have seen, excluding questions of major wars or minor taxes, the public has precious little interest or influence in Washington's insider

*A perfect example of this phenomenon can be found in Robert Bartley's anti-declinist manifesto of March 1992. In it, the *Journal* editor quotes a former French foreign minister arguing that "It's hard to take seriously that a nation has deep problems if they can be fixed with a 50-cent-a-gallon gasoline tax." Were any American politician foolhardy enough to propose such a measure, however, he would be immediately denounced and relentlessly ridiculed by none other than Robert L. Bartley and his anti-tax crew at *The Wall Street Journal*. See Bartley, "Is America on the Way Down?" *Commentary*, March 1992, p. 25.

debate. Few Americans bother any more to inform themselves about political matters, and those who do are generally stymied in trying to make their influence felt. Congress does face the electorate every few years, but incumbent reelections—at least until 1992—have become a foregone conclusion for all but a statistically insignificant minority. In between these generally bewildering and frequently demeaning contests, Congress and the President are graded every day not by the public but by the punditocracy. For all the attention paid to the extensive polling undertaken by both the Bush and Reagan White Houses, it is pundits, not the public, who administer the daily rewards and sanctions of the political system and who determine the width and breadth of public debate. That they do so on the basis of values and ambitions that have precious little relevance either to the country's primary failings or to the expressed desires of the American people is perhaps the central sclerotic artery in our political and intellectual paralysis.

The problem does not lie with the American people. A decade of public opinion polling suggests a general public that is in profound ways more sophisticated than its ideological interlocutors. The public recognized opportunities to move beyond the strictures of Cold War thinking long before such ideas were taken seriously within the punditocracy. It was also much quicker to recognize the urgency of economic, social, and environmental threats to its well-being. Though it supported the Reagan military buildup in its earliest years, the American people lost interest in the Soviet threat beginning in the mid-1980s. By 1986, only 20 percent of those questioned considered the Soviet Union to be "a very serious threat" to the United States, and by early 1988 a full two thirds rejected the notion that "the military threat from the Soviet Union is constantly growing and presents a real, immediate danger to the United States." These same surveys, conducted by both Democratic and Republican pollsters, found a three to one majority insisting that economic strength was more important than military strength in determining a nation's influence, and a five to one majority favoring increases in domestic spending over that for the military. Respondents deemed threats to the global environment to be more serious than Soviet military threats as well by a margin of three to two.

The American public has also consistently evinced much greater concern with the decline of the nation's productive capacities than its insider counterparts. Worried more about the quality of their own lives than any global chess match, Americans are far more likely to locate the sources of the nation's power and greatness at home than abroad. They believe, by wide margins, that to build the world's "strongest education system" is more important to the nation's well-being than to accumulate its "strongest military force."* In an extensive fall 1990 survey of the foreign policy beliefs of the American public compared with those of its appointed "opinion leaders," the Gallup organization found that fully 28 percent of the American people considered "crime" and "poverty" to be among the nation's "two or three biggest problems." The two categories did not even place among opinion leaders. Analogously, nearly one in five leaders responded that "Iraq" belonged in the "biggest problem" category, while the respondents questioned in the larger public survey did not even mention it.

The American public is also considerably less enamored of the use of military force than are its opinion leaders. Ronald Reagan used every trick in his Great Communicator's book, backed up by all those in the punditocracy's as well, but neither one could convince more than a third of the American people that the prevention or overthrow of Marxist revolution in Central America justified the sacrifice of a single American life. The Persian Gulf War polls require a deeper reading but demonstrate a similar trend. In a November 1990 Gallup Poll taken after three months of Bush administration and punditocracy scare tactics, only 42 percent of the public supported the use of troops "if Iraq refused to withdraw from Kuwait," while 55 percent of the leaders did. Immediately following the cakewalk military victory, a majority of Americans were still opposed to the proposition that the United States should take "the lead military role where there are problems in the world requiring a military response." Now, the punditocracy constituted by far the most belligerent faction of the American political establishment in favor of the war. Moreover, it proved almost mystically infatuated with the conflict's regenerative powers for the nation, irrespective of the protracted decline the nation has experienced in the economic and environmental quality of its life. One can therefore safely conclude that the punditocracy, as it is presently constituted, presents a significant barrier between the American people and the enactment of the kind of progressive domestic revitalization program they desire.†

Given both the punditocracy's intellectual shallowness and political precariousness, one is tempted to argue that simply by bypassing the pundit world view and appealing directly to the American people, a credible

---

*This was true as early as mid-1987, where nine of ten voters supported the education proposition, while a bare majority, 51%, signed on to the military power notion. The poll is cited in Stanley B. Greenberg, "The Politics of American Identity," *World Policy Journal*, Fall 1987, p. 698.

†Contrary to hallowed punditocracy dogma, a full 66% of the public concur with the statement that our economic problems have "caused this country to decline as a world power." See Reilly, *American Public Opinion and U.S. Foreign Policy*, p. 27.

progressive presidential candidate could conceivably transform American politics as thoroughly as Franklin Roosevelt did in the election of 1932.* Such a campaign would undoubtedly increase the meager excitement quotient of our presidential campaigns. It might even win; but the chances of this are slim. They are even worse for the wholesale transformation of the political dialogue necessary to give such a program a chance to work. For the punditocracy is only one aspect—both a symptom and a cause—of a much larger and more daunting problem: a problem that keeps us from even recognizing the extent of our contemporary crisis, much less beginning the national political dialogue necessary to address it.

While the pundits are perhaps the most important determinants of the size and scope of the American political dialogue, they cannot in good conscience be credited with full responsibility for the decrepit state of our democratic institutions. Were the punditocracy problem to be solved by, say, a meticulously placed earthquake or a one-way shuttle launch, this would ameliorate but not end the problem of the mutually reinforcing nonsense that rules the American political dialogue. Large corporations would continue to exercise a preponderance of political power by virtue of the system's dependence upon their financial largesse. Television production values would retain their dictatorship over the kinds of information Americans receive through the de facto censorship of the nine-second sound bite. Right-wing biases within media corporate ownership would continue to dominate discussion. Americans would continue to insist upon being ceaselessly entertained and comforted by our politicians, rather than instructed or inspired by them. Tax phobias and racial animosities, both exacerbated by the Reagan and Bush presidencies, would also stymie sensible discourse. Alienated perhaps irretrievably from the political realm, half the nation's citizenry might still not bother to show up on election day. And by and large, the American political process would continue to operate on the basis of its own bizarre internal logic rather than any recognizable representation of the reality beyond most of our narrowly conceived day-to-day lives.

The problem, at bottom, is that even if someone like Ross Perot seriously wished to address the cancers that are eating away at the country's future, he (or she) would have difficulty not only being heard but also in making himself understood. For we have lost the language we need to discuss the reconstruction of our political culture.

The young Walter Lippmann grappled with the forerunners of this

---

*The word "credible" here is explicitly added to exclude Jerry Brown from the category of qualified applicants.

problem more than seven decades ago and all but threw up his hands in despair. To Lippmann, the "crisis of Western Democracy" was really "a crisis in journalism." The difficulty derived from the imperfections of journalistic communication coupled with the inability of most people to pay sufficient attention to politics. Together, these forces created a false political consciousness that Lippmann termed a "pseudo-environment." In its pre-television, pre-punditocracy incarnation, this pseudo-environment consisted not simply of imperfect representations of truth but merely "reports, rumors and guesses" about it. Thus the entire reference for political thought and action had become, in Lippmann's view, "what somebody asserts, not what actually is." People under the influence of this pseudo-environment, Lippmann warned, "lost their grip upon the relevant facts of their environment" and thus became the "inevitable victims of agitation and propaganda." Lippmann had no viable solutions for this problem after he gave up his ill-conceived House of Lords idea, and ended up merely offering up his own analytical abilities as a kind of thrice-weekly democratic defense.

Today Lippmann's pseudo-environment is further complicated by the onset of what the historian Daniel Boorstin termed "the pseudo-event." The latter, whose existence Boorstin proclaimed in 1961, represented an entirely new development in the increasing corruption of political culture. A pseudo-event is not spontaneous, he noted,

> but comes about because someone has planned, planted or incited it. . . .
> It is planted primarily (not always exclusively) for the immediate purpose
> of being reported or reproduced. . . . Its relation to the underlying reality
> of the situation is ambiguous. Its interest arises largely from this very
> ambiguity. Concerning a pseudo-event the question, "What does it
> mean?" has a new dimension.

Boorstin's dissection of pseduo-event-driven political culture built upon Lippmann's already troubling analysis. For not only was the media confusing and distorting the "pictures in our heads," but its spillage was corrupting "the world outside" as well. Public perceptions of American politics were no longer based merely upon an imperfect and therefore artificial comprehension of reality. Instead, media culture had created its own parallel artificial reality alongside that which had previously constituted "the news." This pseudo-reality was far more comforting for its audience, and offered a more clearly discernible story line. Because it was thoroughly man-made, it could be scheduled in advance for the convenience of a television audience or a particular politician's personal ambition. That gave pseudo-events a distinct advantage over "real life," which tended to take place beyond the purview of television cameras and often at inopportune viewing times.

As with cheap money in an inflated economy, pseudo-events drove out much of what was once true life from our politics. Interviews and ceremonies came to replace—or at the very least determine—the actual issues they were alleging to address. Meaningless budget accords, arms-control treaties, and trade agreements—to say nothing of visits to flag factories and attacks on imaginary television characters' out-of-wedlock pregnancies—were negotiated for no other reason except to give the (televised) appearances of politicians *doing something*. More often than not, the actual problems themselves were ignored. Viewed in this context, George Bush's decision to drive Iraq from Kuwait was the product of a pseudo-environment comprised largely by pseudo-events. True, the Iraqi invasion was definitely a "real life" event, but why did George Bush feel compelled to respond with the American war? What did the President mean when he said, "The world could wait no longer," the night he launched his invasion? Clearly, most of the world could have waited forever, since most of the world could not have cared less who runs Kuwait. The American people would have been happy to wait a bit longer as well, as majorities told pollsters that they opposed a decision to launch a war immediately after the UN deadline expired. Congress certainly would have been happy with a bit more patience, since those senators who provided the winning margin for the war resolution insisted that they were voting, as Republican Minority Leader Robert Dole explained, "for peace, not war but for peace." Bush's chief military advisers, Colin Powell and Norman Schwarzkopf, also had no problem with, say, another year of sitting in the desert sun. So the only people who could truly "wait no longer" were George Bush and the pro-war punditocracy. Together these two forces operated through the media, creating pseudo-event after pseudo-event, to precipitate an air of inevitability for a war considered unthinkable just seven months earlier. What took place on a rather grand scale in the case of the Gulf War provides a model for almost all of what constitutes the American political agenda on a daily basis.

It was probably unavoidable, given these developments, that our political language would succumb to a similarly destructive virus. The "pseudo-language" of American politics, circa 1992, is the byproduct of the particular pseudo-environment of the Cold War, filtered through pseudo-events manufactured by a nexus of insider politicians, pundits, and news/entertainment producers. It is simultaneously a combination of conservative political double-speak overlaid with frivolous Hollywood hoopla, as if the fears implied by George Orwell and Aldous Huxley had materialized in tandem. And the manipulation of this false language has become so crucial to the successful exploitation of the American political system that few of us even recognize it has replaced what once were real politics.*

Our political pseudo-language represents an unhappy marriage between what Boorstin had considered contradictory phenomena: pseudo-events and propaganda. According to Boorstin, "a pseudo-event is an ambiguous truth" that thrives on "our honest desire to be informed." "Propaganda," however, "is an appealing falsehood" that "feeds on our willingness to be inflamed." While propaganda substitutes opinion for facts, pseudo-events are synthetic facts that move people indirectly by providing the "factual" basis on which they are supposed to make up their minds. Propaganda moves them directly by explicitly making judgments for them.

American political pseudo-language accomplishes all of these tasks simultaneously. It substitutes pseudo-event for reality, and judgment for fact, to the point where the honest desire of the citizen to become informed is transformed into a process whereby his passions are inflamed and his reason impaired. The language itself has become so soaked with the assumptions of the American political pseudo-environment that it becomes almost useless for the purpose of addressing contemporary reality.† The consequences of this are far more serious than we have so far been able to admit. For instead of furthering political communication, public discussion within the punditocracy and larger political arena actually thwarts it—surrounding our political conversations with a kind of impenetrable pseudo-linguistic force field. This explains the otherwise bizarre finding by three University of Massachusetts academics who, while polling 250 people selected at random from the Denver phone book during the Gulf War, discovered that the more television news and commentary the respondent claimed to have watched

---

*The historian Gordon Wood identifies a moment during the Constitutional debates of 1787 when the Federalist side decided to "appropriate and exploit the language that more rightfully belonged to their opponents" as the "beginning of a hiatus in American politics and ideology and motives that was never again closed." In doing so, Wood argues, they created a "distinctly American political theory but only at the cost of eventually impoverishing later American political thought." The argument is brilliantly conceived, but the evocation of a lost Eden of honest and appropriate political rhetoric ultimately fails to convince. See Gordon S. Wood, *The Creation of the American Republic, 1776–1787* (New York: W.W. Norton, 1969), pp. 562–64.

†"We are in an odd situation," observes William Pfaff. "At one level of intelligence or consciousness, Americans . . . know their political language is false and their ideas are sentimental." But "it is the only language we have—drained of content though it may be." See Pfaff, *Barbarian Sentiments: How the American Century Ends*, pp. 10–11.

about the conflict, the less he or she was likely to understand about its causes and consequences.

Our political pseudo-language is not only strained and sentimental; it is also deceptive and manipulative. The problem is not merely that we destroy villages in order to save them. At least that level of linguistic contortion still retains the capacity to offend. But much of our political terminology has slipped into Orwellian contradiction without causing any commotion at all. Consider the terms "freedom," "leadership," "democracy," "strength," "credibility," "security." All can be said to represent fundamental virtues to which Americans profess allegiance and which American politicians promise to uphold. Yet in the context of the contemporary American politics, all have become buzzwords for nothing more than the willingness to go to war, to threaten war, and to fund, subsidize, and prepare for war. We defend tyranny in the name of freedom. We behave obsequiously in the name of leadership. We subvert elections in the name of democracy. We allow ourselves to be crudely manipulated in the name of strength. We lie in the name of credibility. And we poison our beautiful country in the name of national security.

Political language, Orwell reminds us, has always been the purview of scoundrels.* But in the context of the Washington punditocracy, we have a situation akin to a convent run by sex criminals. The same people charged with upholding the value of our political language, of defending its honor and protecting its content, are responsible for its manipulation on behalf of powers seeking to exploit its weaknesses. In doing so, they have helped to render our language meaningless and our politics hopeless. And because the terms of our national debate are by necessity formulated according to these perverse linguistic standards and their definitions are in large measure the purview of the punditocracy, our political process has become in many ways simply immune to the influence of elections or public opinion. The game is already won or lost by the time the punditocracy has named the players and determined the playing field. How could any American presidential candidate—Perot included—ever rise above these linguistic perversions and "talk sense" to the American people when the words needed to express the values to which he would appeal imply their definitional opposites? How could Americans hear him?

The reconstruction of a coherent political language is therefore a

*It is, he wrote, "designed to make lies sound truthful and murder respectable, and to give an appearance of solidity to pure wind." See George Orwell, "Politics and the English Language," reprinted in The Orwell Reader (New York: Harcourt Brace Jovanovich, 1956), p. 366.

necessary condition for the revival of a vibrant American political culture. For, in the absence of either one, our political process will continue to be driven by elements that are essentially theatrical. These may consist of foreign wars, or they may consist of proposed education reform, but the drill will remain essentially unchanged either way. Politicians and their handlers will go to great expense to stage-manage their presentations of various issues. The pundits, playing a role not dissimilar to that played by a Broadway theater critic, will inform both the players and the audience the next morning whether the performance can be judged a success. By then, whatever it was that seemed so important will be forgotten, and the players will reconstitute themselves to repeat the same exercise on behalf of yet another impending catastrophe. In the meantime, the original problem will fester, the conditions that forced it briefly into the limelight will deteriorate, and the American people will become further convinced that their government has no useful role to play in improving the conditions of their daily lives. Upon reaching this conclusion they will be congratulated by the punditocracy for their newfound "maturity," and the nation will sink deeper into decline and despair.

I can offer no solution to this complex web of political contradictions, but I do have one modest proposal. The punditocracy may be unredeemable, but it can be made obsolete.

The punditocracy's power and influence derive primarily from the prestige accorded its members within insider Washington. This prestige originates, as George Will explained to Henry Fairlie over a decade ago, from the op-ed pages. Because of the riches, fame, and insider indulgence accorded to these pundits, their frequently ignorant opinions have come to exercise far greater authority over Washington's intellectual universe than the knowledge or expertise that, under normal circumstances, would be expected to inform them. What is necessary to begin to reconstitute a sensible debate about the challenges we face is to destroy the prestige of the instant opinion in Washington and to replace it with a renewed respect for legitimate investigation and scholarship. The best way to do this, I think, is to reformulate some of our ideas about contemporary journalism. The 1992 solution—election by television call-in program—is a response to our predicament, but, as I argued earlier, it is hardly an answer.

The roots of the modern punditocracy, as we have seen, can be found in the early-twentieth-century split between "objective" and "opinion" journalism. Objective journalism was Adolph Ochs's answer to the financial opportunities he gleaned in the commercial and demographic explosions of early-twentieth-century New York. The profession of political punditry came about as a means to fill the vacuum left by the demise of opinionated journalism. For Walter Lippmann, it was the only workable solution he could find to the tangled web of illusion generated by the creation of the American political pseudo-environment. Both developments have helped to make American journalism more reliable and professional, and have done a great deal to improve the status of journalists. But their relationship to the quality and vitality of American political culture is more ambiguous.

The belief in "objectivity," explains the sociologist Michael Schudson, implies that "a person's statements about the world can be trusted if they are submitted to established rules deemed legitimate by a professional community. Facts here are not aspects of the world, but consensually validated statements about it." But as Schudson points out, this is an extremely anachronistic notion for a profession that, unlike medicine or law, requires no special training, licensing, esoteric techniques, or language. What is defined as "objective" in journalism is determined in large measure by market forces. It is hardly the same thing as such humanly achievable goals as "fairness" or "balance," but it has come to be interpreted as such. Instead, objective journalism promotes a thoroughly depersonalized version of events based on what Schudson calls "the ideology of the distrust of the self." Since the "self" in this case is the composite of the journalist's experiences, knowledge, prejudices, and understanding of the contextual environment of a given event, it is difficult to argue that by attempting to rid himself of either relevant context or commonsense judgments, a journalist has somehow served the informational interests of his reader. Unconscious biases remain, of course, but they become shrouded in the guise of objectivity and invested with a kind of farcical authority.

Objectivity, moreover, is an ideology that, in its most pristine form, has no clear preference for fact over fiction. As David Halberstam has observed, "if objectivity in no way conformed to reality, then so much the worse for reality." It is notoriously easy to manipulate by unscrupulous sources who place a higher value on their own personal advancement than on the value of the public knowledge. Because politicians tend to fall into this category, and objectivity is nothing if not deferential to "official" sources, its rules are regularly drafted into service on behalf of the most shameless kinds of demagoguery, lies, and outright thievery. Against the concerted efforts of a high public official to mislead the public, the rules of objectivity render the journalist virtually helpless. Joe McCarthy understood this better than anyone. As Russell Baker complained in his memoirs: "Objective journalism forbade a reporter to go beyond what the great man said. No matter how dull, stupid, unfair, vicious, or mendacious they might be, the utterances of the great were reported deadpan, with nary a hint that the speaker might be a bore, a dunce, a brute, or a habitual liar."

The cult of objectivity is therefore something of a hoax. It is an unachievable intellectual state for our subjective species even when it is not thoroughly compromised by network pressures, advertising revenues, political influence, and individual ambition. Its pretense nevertheless narrows the spectrum of allowable interpretations and restricts the possibilities of thoughtful contextual analyses in journalistic reportage. The net result is the intellectual impoverishment of our political dialogue.

Lippmann's profession, too, has had a devastating impact on the quality of our political debate. Despite his own brilliant example, the job of the prestigious political pundit has developed into the ultimate triumph of power without responsibility; of opinion over knowledge. The artificial journalistic separation between "fact" and "opinion" deprives our public dialogue of even the most rudimentary conclusions of those professional journalists who spend the most time and effort seeking to understand the problems as it simultaneously elevates those who lack even basic competency in the areas they pretend to illuminate. Were this phony split to be undone, journalists would be free to explain their stories as they truly see them, providing enough contextual information for their readers to make more sensibly informed choices. The debate would immediately extend itself into previously taboo areas, and the need for wholly uninformed opinion of the kind provided by so many pundits would decline accordingly. Were today's pundits to retain anything remotely analogous to their current privileged position in the public dialogue, they would be forced to do so on the basis of either legitimate journalistic legwork or superior academic scholarship. William Safire and Michael Kinsley would have nothing much to worry about. Most pundits, however, would have to revert to becoming "real" journalists again, forced to test their desk-hardened opinions against a messy reality. Some might even consider returning to the academy for additional study. There, they could write the occasional op-ed between classes and perhaps inspire their colleagues to return to a level of discourse comprehensible to their fellow, reasonably well-educated citizens, thereby improving the quality of the public dialogue from both ends at once.

Why, moreover, should only multimedia conglomerates be invested with the power to determine the content of our public dialogue? Back in the twenties, Lippmann proposed the creation of a daily paper by labor and "militant liberalism." Conflicting special interests, including those that make up the Democratic and Republican parties, should also be encouraged to participate in this endeavor—not only to inspire increased voter interest but also to try to recreate some of the lost communal bonds within American life. One can imagine any number of short-sighted objections to this scheme, but there is really no inherent reason why this kind of journalism should be impracticable in the United States. Europe is filled with politically interested newspapers, and many practice a higher-quality journalism than do their objective American counterparts. The conservative *Economist* in London observes none of the rules of objective journalism, yet by providing its readership with a thorough context for its reporting and respecting their intelligence sufficiently to indulge its many biases, it manages to provide the sharpest and most engaging reporting in the English-speaking world.* In our own political culture, public television journalist Bill Moyers manages the almost superhuman feat of delving into intricate social and intellectual questions while managing to avoid virtually all of the theatricality and reductiveness that characterizes the rest of television's public discourse. In a small but significant fashion—if only for demonstrative purposes—Moyers's success shows that the medium does have the capacity to stimulate debate without paying heed to the twin shibboleths of objectivity and infotainment.

By destroying the prestige of pure opinion unsupported by factual investigation, a more honest journalism could deal a mighty blow to the power of pseudo-language, pseudo-events, and pseudo-environments in American politics. None of these are completely eradicable. The dilemmas diagnosed by Lippmann predated the birth of the pundit business and they would undoubtedly outlast its demise. The inanity of television culture, as well as the cozy and corrupt political relationships that help sustain the punditocracy, may still thwart the emergence of a more sensible national debate. But once we withdraw the prestige associated with the utterance of wholly ignorant pronouncements in the media, the burden of proof in a political argument would come to rest on a writer's ability to marshal his facts into a coherent context. In such a situation, a writer who wished to use the word "liberation" regarding modern-day Kuwait would be forced to provide some justification for this claim. The assertion that the United States prevented Saddam Hussein's continued "aggression" would be expected to take into account his treatment of the Kurds. And proclamations of the type that claim the United States to be "the most powerful nation in the world" or "the most influential country in history," or even that "every other nation would like to be in our position," would require support from something other than a pundit's patriotic fervor. While television talk shows may continue to program theatrical shenanigans pretending to be reasoned debate, they would come to be appreciated strictly for their entertainment

---

*I say this as someone who shares few of *The Economist*'s biases.

value rather than their pretense of intellectual illumination. Were John McLaughlin universally recognized as a brother and comrade of Morton Downey, Jr., rather than a pretender to the throne of Walter Lippmann, his antics would quickly lose their influence over the flow of our politics.

A second justification for the elimination of the pretense of objectivity is the currently lamentable state of journalistic prose. As Halberstam notes, the rules of objectivity force journalists to write in a "bland, uncritical way" which requires them "to appear to be much dumber and more innocent" than they really are. This is not a trivial issue. Many of the country's most prestigious newspapers are also its most boring, resembling what A. J. Liebling once called "Adolph Ochs' colorless, odorless, and especially tasteless [New York] Times." Newspapers are losing readers in America in large measure because young people do not recognize their relevance to their lives. This is not only unfortunate for their stockholders, but it has an insidious effect on the quality of our political culture and the nature of the country's "culture of communication."

When Lippmann's Public Opinion first appeared in 1922, it became the subject of considerable controversy. The most important response to the book was a lengthy review published by John Dewey in the May 3, 1922, issue of The New Republic, later expanded into a series of lectures and finally published as The Public and Its Problems. Dewey rejected Lippmann's delineation of the basis of public opinion and the role of journalism in society. As James Carey recently explained in Communication as Culture, Dewey took issue with what he called Lippmann's "spectator theory of knowledge." Dewey insisted that public opinion was formed not from allegedly accurate representations of the environment but from the discussion that takes place in community life. Dewey saw the role of the press not as the imperfect representer of reality but as a stimulator of a culture of community conversation. As Carey puts it, "The purpose of news is not to represent and inform but to signal, to tell a story and activate inquiry. Inquiry, in turn, is not something other than conversation and discussion but a more systematic version of it."

Drawing on Carey's work, Christopher Lasch argues that the cult of "responsible" journalism, "professing rigorous standards of objectivity," for which he blames Lippmann's argument, is, in fact, responsible for the decline of public debate in American political culture. If Lippmann's notion of journalism as the scientific demonstration of an objective or "picturable" reality had not triumphed over Dewey's vision of journalism as the cultural agent of community conversation, the United States might still enjoy some of the significant attributes of the vibrant political culture it had in the earlier part of the century. Lasch dates the beginning of the decline of U.S. voter participation, from over 80 percent in 1900, to the adoption by American journalism of Lippmann's standards of objectivity. Having embraced Lippmann's idea, he insists, the press no longer serves to cultivate what Dewey termed "certain vital habits" in the community—the habits which are central to the pursuit of real democracy: "the ability to follow an argument, grasp the point of view of another, expand the boundaries of understanding, debate the alternative purposes that might be pursued."

By attempting to produce an almost scientific representation of political behavior, the cult of journalistic objectivity has plundered the guts out of American politics. Stripped of comprehensible intellectual and emotional context for the news, Americans lose their personal engagement with politics. Requiring some sort of connection to a larger community, they grasp instead for the vicarious emotional fulfillment of the worship of celebrity. The resulting abdication from politics, coupled with the increasing identification with the culture of celebrity, represents, as much as any single development, the foundation of the punditocracy's opportunity to hijack our national political dialogue and direct it toward goals and ambitions that have precious little relevance to most Americans' lives. Were contemporary journalists able once again to recapture the hearts and minds of their readership, the reconstruction of our community conversation might follow.

It is possible to imagine, in such a scenario, the rejuvenation of the American political process as political concerns reenter the emotional and intellectual lives of ordinary Americans. The return of a journalism of engagement would not by itself cure American politics of its many ailments. It certainly will not by itself reverse the nation's long-term economic and environmental decline. It will not even redress the imbalance between conservative and progressive forces that currently dominates our political debate. But by undermining the prestige of ignorant opinion, by reducing the element of pure theatrics from our politics, and by expanding the parameters of permissible political thought, a new American journalism could help to break down the barriers that currently frustrate our ability to address the tasks that lie before us. We cannot begin to solve our problems unless we first learn how to talk about them.

NOTES

PREFACE

xiii "A preface": Joseph Alsop and Turner Catledge, *The 168 Days* (Garden City, NY: Doubleday, Doran & Co., 1938), p. v.

INTRODUCTION

7 Whether the American people: For a useful discussion of the influence of newspaper editorials on the political views of average citizens, see Robert M. Entman, *Democracy Without Citizens: Media and the Decay of American Politics* (New York: Oxford University Press, 1989), pp. 151–53.

8 "No other American": The quote appears in a December 9, 1991, fund-raising appeal Buchanan sent to the author.

9 When Dan Quayle launched: These events are detailed in Bob Woodward and David S. Broder, "The Man Who Could Be President," *The Washington Post National Weekly Edition*, January 13–19, 1992, p. 8.

9 "Auschwitz in the Sand": William Safire, January 16, 1989.

9 "worth two divisions": Johnson is quoted in David Halberstam, *The Powers That Be* (New York: Alfred A. Knopf, 1980), p. 529. *The Jerusalem Post* is cited in Robert I. Friedman, "Selling Israel to America," *Mother Jones*, February/March 1987, p. 25.

10 those same columnists: See, for instance, Charles Krauthammer, April 5, 1991.

10 planting articles: Buchanan explained this technique to Fred Barnes. Author's interview with Fred Barnes.

11 "he who captures": Walter Lippmann, *Public Opinion* (New York: Macmillan, 1922), p. 151.

11 "If politicians": Quoted in Randall Rothenberg, "The Battle of the Columnists:

Telling Leaders How to Think," *The New York Times Week in Review*, September 23, 1990, p. 4.

11 James Fallows . . . recalls: Author's interview with James Fallows.

11 As "freedom fighters": See Charles Krauthammer, "The Reagan Doctrine," *Time*, April 1, 1985, reprinted in Charles Krauthammer, *Cutting Edges: Making Sense of the Eighties* (New York: Random House, 1985), p. 185.

12 "a mass conversion": See George Ball, "The War for Star Wars," *The New York Review of Books*, April 11, 1985, pp. 39–40. Garry Wills argues persuasively that Reagan's idea for SDI derives from his role in the 1940 Brass Bancroft movie *Murder in the Air*, in which the fearless secret agent played by Reagan protected America's wonder weapon, "an inertia projector" that would render enemy airplanes impotent and obsolete by destroying their electrical systems. See Wills, *Reagan's America: Innocents at Home* (New York: Doubleday, 1987), p. 361.

12 The fact that 98 percent: See "The Strategic Defense Initiative: An Opinion Survey of Scientists," Cornell Institute for Social and Economic Research, October 30, 1986. The most telling support for SDI came from Far Right pundit Jeffrey Hart, who noted in *National Review*, "I support SDI even if it doesn't work—at least it would keep money out of the hands of the poor." Quoted in Bob Mack, "The Boys Who Would Be Buckley," *SPY*, June 1989.

12 the program turned out: See Aldric Saucier, "Lost in Space," *The New York Times*, March 9, 1992, p. A15.

15 Independent intellectuals: See Russell Jacoby, *The Last Intellectuals: American Culture in the Age of Academe* (New York: Basic Books, 1987).

17 "When I understood": Author's interview with David Halberstam.

18 "The most important": Author's interview with Leon Wieseltier.

18 "Ignorance is correctable": Neil Postman, *Amusing Ourselves to Death: Public Discourse in the Age of Show Business* (New York: Penguin Books, 1985), p. 108.

1. THE ROAD TO LIPPMANNDOM

21 Its metamorphosis: See William Carey Morey, "Reminiscences of 'The Pundit Club,' " in *The Rochester Historical Society, Publication Fund Series*, Vol. II, Edward R. Foreman, ed. (Rochester, NY: Rochester Historical Society, 1923), pp. 107–11.

21 Having founded: See William Safire, "Pundit Bashing," *The New York Times Magazine*, May 27, 1990, p. 10. Luce also used it for Thornton Wilder.

22 an irreconcilable conflict: The essential text on this question remains Bernard Baylin, *The Ideological Origins of the American Revolution* (Cambridge: Harvard University Press, 1967). For corroborative and competing interpretations, see also chapter 1 of Gordon S. Wood, *The Creation of the American Republic, 1776–1787* (New York: W. W. Norton, 1969), Pauline Maier, *From Resistance to Revolution* (New York: Vintage, 1972), Jack N. Rakove, *The Beginnings of National Politics* (Baltimore: Johns Hopkins University Press,

1979), Eric Foner, *Tom Paine and Revolutionary America* (New York: Oxford University Press, 1976), and Alfred F. Young, ed., *The American Revolution: Explorations in the History of American Radicalism* (DeKalb, IL: Northern Illinois University Press, 1976).

23 Building on the success: See Claude G. Bowers, *Jefferson and Hamilton* (Boston: Houghton Mifflin, 1925), p. 31, and Mitchell Stephens, *A History of News* (New York: Penguin Books, 1988), p. 260.

23 Philip Freneau: Henry Adams described Freneau as "sharing some of the delicacy if not the grandeur of genius." See his *History of the United States, During the Administrations of Thomas Jefferson* (New York: Library of America edition, 1986), p. 87. For Jefferson's recruitment tactics, see Thomas Jefferson, *Writings* (New York: Library of America edition, 1984), pp. 997–1000.

25 "a page treating": Allen Nevins, *American Political Opinions, 1895–1922*, (Port Washington, NY: Kinnikat Press, 1928), p. 112.

26 "We do not mean": Quoted in Willard G. Bleyer, *Main Currents in American Journalism* (Boston: Houghton Mifflin, 1927), p. 240.

26 "to give the news": *The New-York Times*, August 19, 1896.

27 "the fullness": Quoted in Nevins, *American Political Opinions, 1895–1922*, p. 452.

27 the paper that had been losing: See Meyer Berger, *The Story of the New York Times, 1851–1951* (New York: Simon & Schuster, 1952; reprinted: Arno Press, 1970), p. 109. See also Elmer Davis, *History of The New York Times* (New York: The New York Times, 1921), and Gay Talese, *The Kingdom and the Power* (New York: Bantam, 1966).

27 Circulation skyrocketed: *The New York Times*, September 18, 1911, and September 18, 1926, cited in Michael Schudson, *Discovering the News: A Social History of American Newspapers* (New York: Basic Books, 1978), p. 114.

28 "well-heeled readers": Christopher Lasch, "Journalism, Publicity and the Lost Art of Argument," *Gannett Center Journal*, Spring 1990, p. 9.

28 As Godkin's successor: See Oswald Garrison Villard, *Some Newspapers and Newspaper-Men* (New York: Alfred A. Knopf, 1933), p. 8, and Walter Lippmann and Charles Merz, "A Test of the News," *The New Republic*, August 4, 1920.

29 "News comes": Walter Lippmann, *Liberty and the News* (New York: Harcourt, Brace and Howe, 1920), pp. 38–41.

29 "The mass of": Walter Lippmann, *Public Opinion* (New York: Macmillan, 1922), p. 75.

30 "He does not know": Walter Lippmann, *The Phantom Public* (New York: Macmillan, 1924), pp. 13–14.

30 "We must assume": Lippmann (from *The Phantom Public*), in *The Essential Lippmann*, Clinton Rossiter and James Lare, eds. (Cambridge: Harvard University Press, 1982), p. 114.

30 "inevitable victims": Lippmann, *Liberty and the News*, p. 54.

30 At first, in the 1919: Ibid., pp. 79, 101.

30 Even if undertaken: Lippmann, *Public Opinion*, p. 362.

30 In Lippmann's plan: See particularly chapters 25 and 26 of *Public Opinion*.

31 "In this": Walter Lippmann, "The Job of the Washington Correspondent," address to the National Press Club, September 23, 1959, reprinted in *The Atlantic Monthly*, January 1960. The "manufacture the consent" phrase appears in *Liberty and the News*, p. 4.

31 one of the richest: See Ronald Steel, *Walter Lippmann and the American Century* (Boston: Atlantic; Little, Brown, 1979).

32 "a small group . . . identifiable": Quoted in Talese, *The Kingdom and the Power*, pp. 229–30.

33 *TNR's* editors: For the story of the founding of *The New Republic*, see David Seidman's *The New Republic: A Voice of Modern Liberalism* (New York: Praeger, 1985), David W. Levy, *Herbert Croly of The New Republic* (Princeton, NJ: Princeton University Press, 1985), John Patrick Diggins, "The New Republic and Its Times" in *The New Republic*, December 10, 1984, and Steel, *Walter Lippmann and the American Century*, p. 76.

33 the journalist George Polk: See Edmund Keeley, *The Salonika Bay Murder* (Princeton, NJ: Princeton University Press, 1989). See also Kati Marton's *The Polk Conspiracy* (New York: Farrar, Straus, Giroux, 1990) and Ronald Steel, "A Polk Conspiracy?" *The New York Review of Books*, September 26, 1991, for a lively discussion of Lippmann's role in the affair.

33 a 1933 speech: The Hitler assertions are quoted by George F. Will in *Newsweek*, September 11, 1989, p. 68. The second appears in the CBS transcripts of his interviews published as *Conversations with Walter Lippmann* (Boston: Little, Brown, 1965), p. 202.

33 As his friend James Reston: Author's interview with James Reston.

34 Henry Luce's prospectus: Quoted in Halberstam, *The Powers That Be*, p. 49.

35 not until the thirties: See John Kobler, *Luce: His Time, Life and Fortune* (Garden City, NY: Doubleday and Co., 1968), and W. A. Swanberg, *Luce and His Empire* (New York: Charles Scribner's Sons, 1972).

35 Who can believe: Quoted in Steel, *Walter Lippmann and the American Century*, pp. 276–77.

35 "bleeding for the poor": Author's interview.

36 a prophetic resolution: ASNE, "Problems of Journalism," 1938, pp. 157–62, cited in Schudson, *Discovering the News: A Social History of American Newspapers*, p. 214.

37 "if we see": Quoted in Walter LaFeber, *The American Age* (New York: W. W. Norton, 1989), p. 378.

37 "The American people": Quoted in Richard J. Barnet, *The Rocket's Red Glare* (New York: Simon & Schuster, 1990), p. 237.

2. LIPPMANNDOM

39 Lippmann had submitted: See *Life*, November 17, 1947, and March 29, 1943, quoted in Steel, *Walter Lippmann and the American Century*, pp. 410, 447.

39 "afraid of Russia." "They've": Quoted in Richard J. Barnet, "National Security in the Age of Anxiety," unpublished manuscript (1989), p. 17.

40 "considerable political advantage": Quoted in LaFeber, *The American Age*, p. 461.

40 "The atmosphere in": Quoted in Walter Isaacson and Evan Thomas, *The Wise Men* (New York: Simon & Schuster, 1986), p. 440.

42 Lippmann's protégé: See Isaacson and Thomas, *The Wise Men*, p. 409.

43 Together they wrote: See Steel, *Walter Lippmann and the American Century*, pp. 418–19.

43 "What changed his mind": Author's interview.

45 Pegler's ironically titled: See Charles Fisher, *The Columnists* (New York: Howell and Soskin, 1944), p. 166.

45 "the Washington which": Stewart Alsop, *The Center: People and Power in Political Washington* (New York: Harper & Row, 1968), p. ix.

45 In July 1947: See X, "The Sources of Soviet Conduct," in *The Foreign Affairs Reader*, ed. Hamilton Fish Armstrong (New York: Harper and Brothers, 1947), and Walter Lippmann, *The Cold War* (New York: Harper & Row, 1947, 1972). Lippmann did not, as is commonly believed, coin the term "Cold War." His editor at the *World*, Herbert Bayard Swope, used it first in a speech he drafted for Bernard Baruch in 1946. Baruch thought it too strong and did not utter the phrase for another year, by which time Lippmann began publicizing it. In a letter to Lippmann, Swope said he first came up with the phrase in late 1939 or early 1940 to refer to "the opposite of a so-called hot war." See William Safire, *Safire's Political Dictionary* (New York: Ballantine Books, 1978), pp. 127–29.

46 "policy of firm containment": "The Sources of Soviet Conduct," in *The Foreign Affairs Reader*, p. 482.

46 "to the status of": George Kennan, *Memoirs, 1925–1950* (Boston: Atlantic Monthly Press, 1967), p. 356.

46 Lippmann's brilliant critique: For a powerfully compelling argument demonstrating the essential veracity of Lippmann's unhappy prophecy, see Melvin Leffler's massive history of the Truman administration's national security strategy, *A Preponderance of Power: National Security, the Truman Administration and the Cold War* (Stanford, CA: Stanford University Press, 1992). For specific confirmation of Lippmann's predictions regarding the governments of Turkey, Saudi Arabia, Jordan, Iran, and China, see pp. 289–98 and 353–54.

46 "My strongest impression": See Walter Lippmann, November 4, 1947, reprinted in Lippmann, *The Cold War*.

47 Lippmann insisted that: See Steel, *Walter Lippmann and the American Century*, p. 487.

48 "the most powerful voice": Quoted in Merle Miller, "Washington, the World and Joe Alsop," *Harper's*, June 1968, p. 49.

48 "Fat, soft . . ." Joseph W. Alsop with Adam Platt, *"I've Seen the Best of It,"* (New York: W. W. Norton, 1992), p. 71.

48 "a clerk": Quoted in Miller, "Washington, the World and Joe Alsop," p. 49.

48 "whenever I go": Quoted in *The New York Times*, August 29, 1989, p. 86.

49 "was tactless enough": Alsop, *The Center*, p. 7. Alsop added the intriguing detail that "Kennan was seen dancing at a party a few days later over the U.S. decision to commit troops there."

49 "While we sleep": Quoted in Miller, "Washington, the World and Joe Alsop," p. 50.

50 "There is a difference": Quoted in ibid.

50 "Joe was the kind": Author's interview with Tom Braden.

51 "There, that should": Quoted in Karl E. Meyer, *Pundits, Poets and Wits* (New York: Oxford University Press, 1990), p. xiii.

51 "assassins, robbers": Cited in Alsop with Platt, *"I've Seen the Best of It,"* p. 398.

52 "A defeat at ": Cited in Alsop with Platt, *"I've Seen the Best of It,"* p. 472.

52 "had gone collectively": Joseph Alsop, March 16, 1968.

52 Should the United States: Joseph Alsop, March 16, 1968.

52 "you'll be like": Quoted in David Halberstam, *The Powers That Be,* p. 449.

52 "wrong in almost": Ibid., pp. 449 and 530.

53 "could no longer": Alsop with Platt, *"I've Seen the Best of It,"* p. 467.

53 "He would stalk": Tom Wicker's Foreword to Arthur Krock, *In the Nation: 1932–1966* (New York: McGraw-Hill, 1966), p. xiv.

53 "There was an old-fashioned": Russell Baker, *The Good Times* (New York: William Morrow, 1989), p. 258.

55 "This is a country": Quoted in Barney Collier, *Hope and Fear in Washington: The Early Seventies* (New York: Dial Press, 1975), pp. 124–25.

55 "We cannot win": Reston and reviewer Clifton Fadiman quoted in Talese, *The Kingdom and the Power,* pp. 11–12. Reston thinks this is fair—Author's interview.

56 "He used my legs": Author's interview.

56 "wonderful quick": Author's interview with David Halberstam.

56 "There is one": Author's interview with Tom Braden.

56 "There has not been": Alexander Cockburn, "Pundit to Pasture: James Reston," *The Nation,* August 15, 1987, p. 114.

56 Yes . . . : For "Life, tyranny," see James Reston, June 20, 1960. For the "underdeveloped world," see James Reston, November 1, 1961. For "one wonders," see James Reston, December 24, 1961. For "a patient, well-informed people," see James Reston's Gideon D. Seymour Memorial Lecture, University of Minnesota, February 22, 1955.

57 His first move: See Joseph Kraft, *Profiles in Power* (New York: New American Library, 1966), p. 81.

57 "If you spend": Quoted in Stephen Chapman, "Reston on His Laurels," *The New Republic,* April 19, 1980, p. 24.

57 "compulsory plagiarism": James Reston, *Deadline* (New York: Random House, 1991), p. 378.

57 "sometimes plants": Quoted in Elias Vlanton, "The View from Inside," *The Nation,* March 16, 1992, p. 352.

3. POST-LIPPMANNDOM:
THE REST AND THE RIGHTEST

60 "Could you tell": *Conversations with Walter Lippmann,* p. 3.

60 "Television . . . prostitute of": Walter Lippmann, September 27, 1959, reprinted in *The Essential Lippmann,* Rossiter and Lare, eds., p. 412.

61 "They're political bombings": *Conversations with Walter Lippmann,* p. 203.

61 "He must be able": Ibid., pp. 15–17.

62 "A program in which": Quoted in Godfrey Hodgson, *America in Our Time* (New York: Random House, 1976), p. 138.

63 Within four years: See Halberstam, *The Powers That Be*, p. 143.

64 "there is one thing": Irving Kristol, "Civil Liberties, 1952—A Study in Confusion," *Commentary*, March 1953, p. 229. Shirer's version of his dismissal can be found in William L. Shirer, *20th Century Journey: A Native's Return 1945–1988* (Boston: Little, Brown, 1990).

65 Howard K. Smith, the conservative: The details of these historic events can be found in Barbara Matusow, *The Evening Stars* (New York: Ballantine Books, 1983), pp. 179–83.

65 "access to information" and "the main business": These thoughts are expressed by ABC News executive Av Westin in *Newswatch* (New York: Simon & Schuster, 1983), pp. 156–57.

66 "sticking little needles": Author's interview with Jack Germond.

67 television humming: The figures can be found in Richard Schickel's brilliant treatise, *Intimate Strangers: The Culture of Celebrity* (Garden City, NY: Doubleday, 1985), p. 287.

68 a more than two-to-one: Joshua Meyrowitz, *No Sense of Place: The Impact of Electronic Media on Social Behavior* (New York: Oxford University Press, 1985), p. 106.

68 "Television has come": Schickel, *Intimate Strangers*, p. 263.

68 There were 10,000: The figures are given in Phillip Knightly, *The First Casualty* (New York: Harcourt Brace Jovanovich, 1975), p. 412.

69 "necessary illusion": See Reinhold Niebuhr, *Man and Immoral Society* (New York: Scribner's, 1952), pp. 221–23.

70 "was based on": See Meyer, *Pundits, Poets and Wits*, p. xii.

70 "was no longer": Walter Lippmann, *Newsweek*, October 9, 1967.

71 "The country has": James Reston, January 6, 1968.

71 "The nation is": James Reston, April 6, 1968.

72 "most of us": Quoted in Hodgson, *America in Our Time*, p. 375.

72 "the most terrible": Author's interview with Anthony Lewis. The earlier quote is from Anthony Lewis, December 28, 1972.

72 "I realized": Author's interview.

72 "infectious choler": See Mary McGrory, March 3, 1968, and November 9, 1969.

73 "Senators used to tell": Author's interview with Mary McGrory.

73 "And the tragedy": James Reston, May 24, 1973.

73 "If you consider": Quoted in William Safire, *Before the Fall: An Inside View of the Pre-Watergate White House* (Garden City, NY: Doubleday, 1975), p. 360. The entire text of the memo, dated June 10, 1972, appears in Bruce Oudes, ed., *From the President: Richard Nixon's Secret Files* (New York: Harper & Row, 1989), pp. 474–76.

74 "giving the American": The Nixon/Agnew attack on punditry drew on proud Republican history. Dwight Eisenhower never got a bigger ovation in his life than he did at the 1952 Republican Convention when he scornfully derided

"the sensation-seeking columnists and commentators." Agnew is quoted in Jules Witcover, *White Knight: The Rise of Spiro Agnew* (New York: Random House, 1972), p. 47. Eisenhower is quoted in Alsop, *The Center: People and Power in Political Washington*, p. 206.

74 "was not a Conservative": Quoted in William Safire, *Safire's Washington* (New York: Times Books, 1980), p. 7. Halberstam says he was correct to criticize the appointment of Safire, which looked then (and still does) like *Times* publisher Punch Sulzberger's attempt to make "a separate peace" with the Nixon administration. On the other hand, Halberstam considers Safire today to be a first-rate pundit and a tireless reporter. Author's interview with David Halberstam.

74 "reestablish the confidentiality": William Safire, July 19, 1973.

75 as Geyelin recalls: Author's interview with Philip Geyelin.

76 "godfatherly moral attention": Author's interview with William F. Buckley, Jr.

76 As children: See David Remnick, "Buckley: The Lion in Autumn," *The Washington Post*, Style section, December 5, 1985, p. 1.

77 "conservatism was considered": Author's interview with William F. Buckley, Jr.

78 "scientists, teachers": Irving Kristol, *Two Cheers for Capitalism* (New York: Basic Books, 1978), p. 27.

78 "to explain to": Quoted in William Pfaff, *Barbarian Sentiments: How the American Century Ends* (New York: Farrar, Straus, Giroux, 1989), p. 9.

78 "intellectuals to go out": Quoted in Sidney Blumenthal, *The Rise of the Counter-Establishment: From Conservative Ideology to Political Power* (New York: Times Books, 1986), p. 154.

79 "something that looks": Robert L. Bartley, "Business and the New Class," in B. Bruce-Briggs, ed., *The New Class?* (New Brunswick, NJ: Transaction Books, 1979), p. 288. For an extremely learned and trenchant discussion of the New Class war, see Barbara Ehrenreich, *Fear of Falling* (New York: Pantheon Books, 1988). See also Benjamin DeMott's excellent *The Imperial Middle* (New York: William Morrow, 1990).

81 "Abby Hoffman": The Evans and Novak column is quoted in Eric Alterman, "Mr. Nice Guy," *The Washingtonian*, November 1989, p. 278. The Nixon memo, from the President to John Mitchell dated June 6, 1972, appears in Oudes, ed., *From the President: Richard Nixon's Secret Files*, p. 462.

81 "put politics in command": Author's interview with Alexander Cockburn.

82 Author's interviews with Rowland Evans, Robert Novak, and Helmut Sonnenfeldt.

83 "The real lesson": William Safire, January 11, 1979.

83 "Western democracies are": George F. Will, May 1, 1980, and May 21, 1978.

4. THE TRIUMPH OF GEORGE WILL

90 Amid the violent chaos: See John Judis, *William F. Buckley: Patron Saint of the Conservatives* (New York: Simon & Schuster, 1988), p. 290.

90 The incident drew: Said missives, including a partial transcript of the broadcast, can be found reprinted in their entirety in *Esquire's* history of the sixties. See

William F. Buckley, Jr., "On Experiencing Gore Vidal," and Gore Vidal, "A Distasteful Encounter with William F. Buckley, Jr." in Harold Hayes, ed., *Smiling Through the Apocalypse* (New York: McCall Publishing Company, 1969), pp. 911–65.

90 Kenner admonished: See Judis, *William F. Buckley: Patron Saint of the Conservatives*, pp. 290–95, for all the details.

91 "a snotty-nosed": Quoted in Eleanor Randolph, "George Will, the Oracle at Strict Remove," *The Washington Post*, Style section, September 26, 1986, p. 1.

91 "He came along": Quoted in Jane Meyer, "Tory Columnist: Pundit George Will Is a Media Superstar with Plenty of Clout. He has Notable Friends Too, Which Raises Questions on the Right; A Cold Shoulder from Bush," *The Wall Street Journal*, May 7, 1986, p. 1.

91–92 "perhaps the most powerful": The quote, which was taken from the generally unfriendly front-page *Wall Street Journal* story cited above, appears on the back cover of the paperback edition of George F. Will, *The Morning After: American Successes and Excesses, 1981–1986* (New York: Collier Books, 1986).

92 "demeaning": Author's interview with Philip Geyelin.

92 "like some head of state": Quoted in Randolph, "George Will, the Oracle at Strict Remove," p. 1.

92 "the infantilism": See George F. Will, *The New Season* (New York: Simon & Schuster, 1988), p. 20.

96–97 "the undisputed leader": See Charles Krauthammer's review of *The Pursuit of Virtue and Other Tory Notions* in *The New Republic*, June 16, 1982, p. 26.

97 "widely recognized": George Will, November 10, 1985.

98 "He said that": Quoted in James Fallows, "Washington's New Celebrities," *The New York Review of Books*, June 12, 1986.

98 "just back from": Nancy Reagan, *My Turn* (New York: Random House, 1989), p. 292.

98 "be conservative": Author's interview with Joe Cosby.

99 "main feeling": Author's interview with Michael Kinsley.

99 "It is a half-hour": Quoted in Thomas B. Rosenstiel, "Reporters on TV: Is Stardom Weakening the Press?" *Los Angeles Times*, April 26, 1989, p. 1.

99 "Anyone who goes": Quoted in William Henry III, "George Will Among the Polysyllables," *Esquire*, January 1987, p. 92.

100 "When Ronald Reagan": Quoted in Thomas B. Rosenstiel, "Columnist Knows Power of Persona: George Will: Wit, Charm Help Push Conservatism," *Los Angeles Times*, May 29, 1986. p. 1.

100 But the First Lady: See Nancy Reagan, *My Turn*.

100 "The unsurpassed master": Quoted in Meyer, "Tory Columnist: Pundit George Will . . .," *The Wall Street Journal*, May 7, 1986, p. 1.

100 "particularly annoyed": Lou Cannon, *President Reagan: The Role of a Lifetime* (New York: Simon & Schuster, 1991), pp. 132–33.

100 Phil Geyelin . . . recalls: Author's interview.

101 "journalists are spurning": George F. Will, *Newsweek*, September 11, 1989.

Actually, William Safire, at least, knew enough to spurn this choice when it was opened to him.

101 Will and Royko: Cited in Lloyd Tataryn, *The Pundits* (Toronto: Deneau, 1985), p. 80.

101 "I would have": Author's interview with Ben Bradlee.

101 "I don't": Quoted in Meyer, "Tory Columnist: Pundit George Will . . . ," *The Wall Street Journal*, May 7, 1986, p. 1.

102 Will's face: Author's interview with Robert Kaiser.

102 praised his comrade: Author's interview with Charles Krauthammer, and "Washington Diarist," *The New Republic*, April 22, 1985.

102 "Capitalism undermines": George F. Will, August 24, 1980.

102 "to treat laissez-faire": George F. Will, *The Pursuit of Virtue and Other Tory Notions* (New York: Touchstone, 1982), p. 15.

102 "a toothless": Quoted in Dinesh D'Souza, "Op-ed Artists," *Policy Review*, Winter 1985, p. 50.

102 "The United States": George F. Will, *Statecraft as Soulcraft* (New York: Simon & Schuster, 1983), p. 24.

103 He would quiz: The Jesse Jackson interview took place on "This Week with David Brinkley" during the 1988 campaign and is cited in George F. Will, January 28, 1988. The Sartre column appeared February 26, 1976. The Gorbachev quote appeared in Rosenstiel, "Columnist Knows Power . . . ," *Los Angeles Times*, May 29, 1986, p. 1. The first "Richard Coeur de Lion" quote appeared in Will's column on December 20, 1979; the second on December 13, 1987.

104 "the most quoted": George F. Will, July 10, 1983. Eight years later, Will's heirs on "Inside Washington" were still seeking to emulate his magnificent accomplishment. On May 14, 1990, viewers saw a bow-tied, bespectacled pundit complaining of a shortage of "candor and cash" on behalf of the Democrats, in contemptuous tones virtually identical to those of Will's historic pronouncement.

105 "Gadzooks!": George F. Will, September 1, 1980, *Newsweek*, February 2, 1981, and July 10, 1983.

105 "et tu": George F. Will, February 8, 1981, May 20, 1976, February 16, 1987, and March 25, 1990.

105 "one of the most judicious": George F. Will, April 26, 1990, and June 7, 1982.

105 "the Butch Cassidy": George F. Will, October 27, 1980, and *Newsweek*, February 2, 1981.

105 "has been in convincing": Quoted in a 1988 letter published in *The Washington Post* by Robert Borsage (exact date unknown).

106 "during our watch": Quoted in Andrew Kopkind, "Whose Kissinger Now?" *Zeta* magazine, November 1989.

106 "terrorism serve": George F. Will, November 10, 1983.

106 "flows not": "This Week with David Brinkley," June 10, 1985.

106 "it is easiest": George F. Will, September 19, 1983.

107 "born on the farm": Will's Labor Day, 1991, column is quoted in Andy Logan, "Around City Hall," *The New Yorker*, September 23, 1991, p. 103.

107 "Should society": Quoted in Sidney Blumenthal, *The Long National Daydream* (New York: Harper & Row, 1988), p. 34.

108 The columnist insisted: See Henry, "George Will Among the Polysyllables," p. 90.

109 "Thanks, but": Quoted in Victor Gold, "Look Who's Not Coming to Lunch," *The Washingtonian*, April 1990, p. 65.

5. "O.K., LET'S GET OUT"

110 "Sometimes he would": Author's interview.

111 *Rolling Stone* national affairs editor . . . recalls: Author's interview with William Greider.

111 When the Group: "The McLaughlin Group," April 29, 1990.

112 Crocker . . . was forced: Author's interview with Tom Miller.

113 "Don't miss it": The quotes, appearing under the scowling, frightfully serious-minded faces of the four white male regulars, appeared in *The New Republic* on March 21, 1988, p. 4, and September 7, 1987, p. 4.

116 "flesh has an inclination": Quoted in Rudy Maxa, "The Mouth That Roars," *The Washingtonian*, April 1987, p. 127.

116 McLaughlin volunteered: Author's interview with Larry Speakes.

116 McLaughlin called: See Eric Alterman, "Pundit Power," *The Washington Post Magazine*, March 18, 1990, p. 16.

117 McLaughlin lived: Author's interview with Father William O'Halloran.

117 His friend: Author's interview with one such Jesuit grumbler.

117 "the notorious Father": Rowland Evans and Robert Novak, September 30, 1974.

118 Stockman told stories: See Michael Kinsley, review of David Stockman, *The Triumph of Politics* in *The New York Times Book Review*, May 11, 1986. Novak later replied, "Memoir time is payback time. But Mr. Stockman surprised me and I underestimated him. His book suggests no trace of bad blood between us and contains little if any overt criticism of me. Rather I emerge as his willing tool, described variously as his 'dartboard' or 'bulletin board.' Each of four references to me show me slavishly typing his every wish into the Evans and Novak column. . . . In truth, I got that story from a memo from Treasury. Mr. Stockman writes that Mr. Lewis blamed him for our column's treatment of him, and that he 'agreed not to have breakfast' with me 'for a while.' My calendar reflects no such discontinuation of breakfasts."

119 Among the most historically: See Rowland Evans and Robert Novak, May 21, 1986. For a discussion of the columnists' role in protecting North, see Jeffrey L. Pasley, "Inside Dopes: Washington Journalists and Colonel Oliver L. North," *The New Republic*, February 23, 1987, p. 14.

119 An unsuspecting reader: See Michael Massing, "The Prince and the Preppy," *The New Republic*, January 20, 1986, p. 20.

120 During the Iran-Contra scandal: The quotes that follow appear in a profile of Buchanan by Lionel Barber, in the *Financial Times* (London), February 2,

1987, p. 10. The "gay men" quotes appear in Patrick J. Buchanan, *Right from the Beginning* (Boston: Little, Brown, 1988), pp. 339–40.

120 "Let the bloodbath": Buchanan, *Right from the Beginning*, p. 3.

121 "McCarthy was cheered": Ibid., p. 93.

121 Buchanan comes from: Ibid., pp. 72 and 15.

121 "Our political and social": Ibid., p. 337.

122 "from the tradition": Author's interview.

122 "people to the right": Author's interview.

125 Did Kondracke mean: Author's interview with Morton Kondracke.

126 In the latter capacity: See Morton Kondracke, "New Kids on the Block," *The Washingtonian*, December 1989, p. 195.

126 "Mort is conducting": Author's interview with Neal Freeman.

126 Why did Richard Nixon: The quotes that follow are all drawn directly from the Kondracke-Nixon conversation entitled "Richard Nixon Reflects: An American Interests Special," PBS, May 4, 1990.

127 When asked: "The McLaughlin Group," January 12, 1991.

128 "slit his throat": Cited in Edwin Diamond, "Circus of the Stars," *New York*, February 3, 1986. See also David Remnick, "Take One Lapsed Priest with White House Connection, Add a Rumpled Liberal. Throw in a Slick, Neopundit on the Make. Top with Atilla the Hun," *Esquire*, May 1986.

128 "are just going": "The McLaughlin Group," June 18, 1989.

128 "a grade": "The McLaughlin Group," June 29, 1989.

128–29 "the more we know": Ibid.

129 McLaughlin became suddenly: See Alterman, "Pundit Power." p. 33.

129 His assistant: Author's interview with Kara Swisher.

6. ALL THE VIEWS FIT TO PRINT

130 Complaining of: William Safire, March 2, 1987.

132 "afford greater opportunity": *The New York Times*, editorial page, September 21, 1970.

132 "it had not clarified": James Reston, November 5, 1980.

133 "bipartisan foreign policy": James Reston, November 9, 1980.

133 "Worthwhile Canadian": Flora Lewis, April 10, 1986.

134 "I think after": Author's interview with Tom Wicker.

134 "He is not": Author's interview with Michael Kinsley.

134–135 "It's absolutely hilarious": Author's interview with Anthony Lewis.

135 "All of the people": Ibid.

135 "The silent majority": William Safire, November 6, 1980.

135 Safire graded: William Safire, January 22, 1981.

136 "There was lots": Quoted in *The Washington Post*, Style section, August 24, 1987.

137 "When I walked": William Safire, *Safire's Washington*, pp. 7–8.

137 "Bill had not learned": Author's interviews with Harrison Salisbury and William Safire. See also Diana West, "Star Safire," *M inc*, November 1990, p. 30.

139 "brought moral pressure": See William Safire, January 12, 1989.

140 In another variation: See Peter Teeley, "How to Get an Answer from the Vice-President," *The New York Times*, September 9, 1984, p. 24.

141 "There is no doubt": Quoted in *The Washington Post*, Style section, August 24, 1987, p. 1.

141 When asked: Author's interview.

141 He also confesses: Ibid.

142 "Most opinion columnists": See Richard Cohen, "The Syndicated Columnist," *Gannett Center Journal*, Spring 1989, p. 13.

142 Is it any wonder: Bradlee is quoted in Elizabeth Peer with Nancy Stadtman, "Fastest Gun in Op-ed Land," *Newsweek*, April 23, 1979, and in the author's interview.

142 a "libertarian conservative": Author's interview.

142 "The publisher chooses": Author's interview with Leslie H. Gelb.

143 "Even Barbara Walters": A. M. Rosenthal, June 9, 1989.

144 "the saint": A. M. Rosenthal, October 27, 1989.

145 a character in: See Franz Lidz, *Unstrung Heroes* (New York: Random House, 1991).

145 "Rosenthal is": Author's interview with Lars-Erik Nelson.

146 But the overall effect: Author's interview with Leslie H. Gelb.

7. GLASS HOUSES AND REVOLVING DOORS

147 "too gelatinous": Quoted in Chalmers M. Roberts, *In the Shadow of Power* (Washington, DC: Seven Locks Press, 1989), p. 490.

147 he picked Meg Greenfield: Author's interview with Donald Graham.

148 "at the right-ish": Meg Greenfield, *Newsweek*, October 25, 1988.

148 "true audacity": Meg Greenfield, *Newsweek*, November 13, 1989.

148 Donald Graham makes: Author's interview.

151 "The repetitiveness": Henry Fairlie, "How Journalists Get Rich," *The Washingtonian*, August 1983, p. 88.

152 "But wait!": Richard Cohen, "What, Me Worry About Ethics?" *The Washington Post*, Outlook section, August 26, 1989, p. 1.

153 During the 1972 campaign: See Timothy Crouse, *The Boys on the Bus* (New York: Ballantine Books, 1972), p. 96.

153 Broder considers: See David Broder, *Beyond the Front Page* (New York: Simon & Schuster, 1987), p. 332. The Cohen quote appears in Richard Cohen, "The Syndicated Columnist," *Gannett Center Journal*, Spring 1989, p. 14.

153 "the frenzy of": David Broder, October 31, 1967.

154 "The White House propaganda": David Broder, "How Press Secrecy Backfired on Reagan," *The Washington Post*, Outlook section, March 22, 1987, p. 1.

154-155 "The White House has": David Broder, March 22, 1987.

155 Broder wondered why: David Broder, April 5, 1989. Broder later conceded that "there were things that came out of the North trial that improved the historical record—although nothing happened because of it." Author's interview.

156 Bush succeeded: Quoted in Garry Trudeau, "Still a Wimp," *The Washington Post*, November 4, 1988, p. A25.

157 "I am not": Author's interview.

157 "a new hybrid": David S. Broder, "Beware the 'Insider' Syndrome," *The Washington Post*, Outlook section, December 4, 1988, p. 2. For his trouble, Broder was called "a sermonizing, sanctimonious prig, the Malvolio of the print-heads" by Pat Buchanan. "To say that [Nixon speechwriters] Ray Price and Bill Safire's combined decade in Nixon's NFL means they must defer to Broder is like saying that Frank Gifford of Southern Cal and the football Giants ought to give up his seat in the press booth to some pimply-faced kid who covered the Rose Bowl for the daily *Trojan*." Patrick Buchanan, January 6, 1989. Broder replied, "Buchanan has changed hats so often he's forgotten, if he ever knew, the difference between political propaganda and journalism. jIn 1980, while ostensibly a journalist, Buchanan joined George F. Will in rehearsing for his campaign debate—a breach of professional ethics so gross even he might be expected to grasp it." David Broder, January 11, 1989.

157 After all: See Phil McCombs, "David Broder, Roasted and Toasted," *The Washington Post*, Style section, November 30, 1988, p. 2.

158 Concerned about: See Jeane Kirkpatrick, February 19, 1990, and May 14, 1990.

158 In attempting to offer: The column appeared April 23, 1990. Donald F. Graff's letter appeared April 28, 1990.

159 In March 1986: Quoted in Blumenthal, *The Long National Daydream*, pp. 198–99.

159 In another column: See Jeane Kirkpatrick, February 27, 1989, and "Rightists Reject Duarte's Peace Bid," *The New York Times*, February 28, 1989.

159 "no government": Henry Kissinger, June 6, 1989, and August 1, 1989.

160 *The Wall Street Journal* revealed: Quoted from an editor's note distributed by the *Los Angeles Times* to subscribers to Henry Kissinger's column.

160 "never seen the kind": Al Hunt on "60 Minutes," CBS, March 29, 1992.

161 "No one can": Quoted in Walter Pincus, "Kissinger Says He Had No Role in China Mission," *The Washington Post*, December 14, 1989, p. A52. Kissinger's quotes were given on "The MacNeil/Lehrer Newshour" and replayed on "60 Minutes" March 29, 1992.

161 Just five months . . .: "60 Minutes," CBS, March 29, 1992.

161 When asked: Author's interview with Ben Bradlee.

161 Geyelin accuses: Author's interview with Philip Geyelin.

8. "WE ARE THE WILD MEN"

162 Wanniski recalls: Author's interview with Jude Wanniski.

163 "had an absolutely": Wayne Parsons, *The Power of the Financial Press* (New Brunswick, NJ: Rutgers University Press, 1989), p. 149.

163 Few events: For an extremely provocative discussion of aspects of this story, see John Kenneth Galbraith, *The Culture of Contentment* (Boston: Houghton Mifflin, 1992), chapters 7 and 8.

164 Nationally, fewer than: Survey cited in J. M. Rosenberg, *Inside the Wall Street Journal* (New York: Macmillan, 1982), p. 204.

164 is amazed, he says: Author's interview with Robert Bartley.

164 "We are the wild men": Quoted in Alexander Cockburn and James Ridgeway, "The World of Appearance," in Thomas Ferguson and Joel Rogers, eds., *The Hidden Election* (New York: Pantheon, 1981), p. 77.

165 "according to one": Quoted in Rosenberg, *Inside the Wall Street Journal*, p. 206.

165 "Executives and": Ben Bagdikian, quoted in the *Washington Journalism Review*, cited in Rosenberg, *Inside the Wall Street Journal*, pp. 207–8.

165 "the front page has": Author's interview with Robert Bartley.

165 "Mutual Assured Destruction": Ibid.

165 "softness on social issues": Author's interview with Jude Wanniski.

166 "This is not": *Newsweek*, June 22, 1970.

166 "the age of": John Kenneth Galbraith, *A History of Economics* (London: Hamish Hamilton, 1987), p. 166.

167 "I know hardly": *Newsweek*, July 27, 1970.

167 "We have heard": *Newsweek*, August 17, 1970.

167 "It is possible": William F. Buckley, Jr., August 19, 1971.

168 The story of how: See particularly Parsons, *The Power of the Financial Press*, and Sidney Blumenthal, *The Rise of the Counter-Establishment*, upon whose work I have relied for this chapter. For the most exciting though least dependable version, see Rowland Evans and Robert Novak, *The Reagan Revolution* (New York: E. P. Dutton, 1981).

169 "capture some": Quoted in Blumenthal, *The Rise of the Counter-Establishment*, p. 180.

169 "a young assistant": Author's interview with Robert Bartley.

170 "I wish I were": Quoted in Edward Scharff, *Worldly Power* (New York: Beaufort Books, 1986), p. 246.

170 "It was horrible": *The Wall Street Journal*, October 8, 1981.

170 "power of the outrageous": Author's interview with Robert Bartley.

171 "It was our story": Quoted in Blumenthal, *The Rise of the Counter-Establishment*, p. 182.

171 Wanniski stopped into: Author's interview with Jude Wanniski.

172 "thoroughly hosed": David Stockman, *The Triumph of Politics* (New York: Harper & Row, 1986), p. 10.

173 "don't make any sense": Lester Thurow, "Watching the Candidates with the Porcupine and Trying Not to Laugh," *The Washington Journalism Review*, July/August 1980, p. 46.

173 "Economists cannot": *The Wall Street Journal*, April 4, 1980.

173 Wanniski says: Author's interview.

174 "The big problem": Ibid.

175 In the first place: The comments that follow are drawn from the author's interview and Bartley's Introduction to the third edition of Wanniski's *The Way the World Works* (Morristown, NJ: Polynomics, 1990). Bartley expands upon this explanation in Robert Bartley, *The Seven Fat Years and How to Do It Again* (New York: Free Press, 1992).

175 "there are deficits": Author's interview.

9. "EVEN *THE NEW REPUBLIC* . . ."

177 Michael Kinsley . . . once suggested: Michael Kinsley, "No Dogs or Journalists," *The New Republic*, June 3, 1985.

179 Tastemaker *Vanity Fair:* See Stephen Schiff, "Patriarch Chic," *Vanity Fair*, April 1985, p. 43, and James Walcott, "Partisans Reviewed," *Vanity Fair*, November 1988, p. 32.

179 seemed "to be at": See Richard Bernstein, *"The New Republic* Tries to Stay Young at 75," *The New York Times*, October 26, 1990, p. C1.

179 Right-wingers, in particular: The Podhoretz quote can be found in Dinesh D'Souza, "Marty Come Lately: *The New-Republic* Discovers Old Truths," *Policy Review*, Summer 1985. See also George F. Will, November 10, 1987, and *National Review*, December 28, 1984, p. 16.

180 "By the time": Mickey Kaus, Los Angeles diarist, *The New Republic*, August 1986.

181 As late as August 1991: James J. Kilpatrick's column appeared in the summer of 1991. Fred Barnes makes mention of the same point in his October 24, 1991, *TNR* diarist.

181 an important dose: See Hendrik Hertzberg, "Journals of Opinion: A Historical Sketch," in *Gannett Center Journal*, Spring 1989, p. 75.

181 "some people say": Quoted in Dinesh D'Souza, "Marty Come Lately: *The New Republic* Discovers Old Truths."

182 "the one sure thing": Quoted in ibid.

182 the "philosophical albatross": Quoted in Janet Meyers, "*New Republic* Ad Pitch Leaning to the Right," *Advertising Age*, February 10, 1986, p. 32.

182 Fairlie once compared: Fairlie continued, "Marty doesn't take women seriously for positions of responsibility. He's really most comfortable with a room full of Harvard males." Quoted in Gwenda Blair, "Citizen Peretz," *Esquire*, July 1985, p. 91.

182 "The preface to this": Author's interview.

182 "Articles triumphantly": Quoted in Dinesh D'Souza, "Marty Come Lately: *The New Republic* Discovers Old Truths."

183 "I have been": Quoted in Elizabeth Kastor, "Hailing *The New Republic*: Left, Right and Points Between at the Magazine's 70th," *The Washington Post*, Style section, November 28, 1984, p. 1.

184 "operating on": Michael Kinsley, "Saint Ralph," *The New Republic*, December 9, 1985.

184 "The big Democratic": Hendrik Hertzberg, "First Returns," *The New Republic*, February 29, 1988.

185 his "dovishness": Quoted in Gwenda Blair, "Citizen Peretz," p. 92. Together with Michael Walzer, Peretz co-authored an article in the July 1967 *Ramparts*, entitled "Israel Is Not Vietnam."

187 "It was a very wild place": Quoted in Blair, "Citizen Peretz," p. 91.

187 "the worst thing": Author's interview with Alfred Kazin.

188 "Central America": Author's interview.

188 Hendrik Hertzberg, whose job: The Hertzberg quotes derive from the author's interview. The Kondracke quote appears in Morton Kondracke, Charles Krauthammer, and James Fallows, "Washington's New Celebrities: An Exchange," *The New York Review of Books*, September 26, 1986, p. 73.

189 "second-rate thinkers": Quoted in Jonathan Kaufman, *Broken Alliance* (New York: Charles Scribner's Sons, 1988), p. 230. The phrase "Sandinista sympathizer" appeared in Fred Barnes, "The Sandinista Lobby," *The New Republic*, January 20, 1986.

189 One editorial accused: See "Democrats and Commandantes," *The New Republic*, July 28, 1986, pp. 7–10.

189 "Charles's great contribution": Author's interview with Leon Wieseltier.

189 "there are few greater": "In Defense of Deterrence," *The New Republic*, December 20, 1982, p. 9.

190 "The Commission has": "The Scowcroft Revolution," *The New Republic*, May 9, 1983, p. 7.

190 "only if we": "In Defense of Deterrence," p. 7.

190 El Salvador, wrote the editors: See "Democrats and Commandantes," *The New Republic*, July 28, 1986, p. 7.

190 According to figures: Cited in Charles William Maynes, "Dateline Washington: A Necessary War?" *Foreign Policy*, Spring 1991, p. 162.

192 "the liberation": "The Case for the Contras," *The New Republic*, March 24, 1986, p. 7.

193 in a secret memo: The memo in question was reprinted in *Harper's* in October 1987. Note: I do not dispute the fact that Cruz, at least, was a Democrat. He was, however, as Owen indicates, a stooge for the efforts of North, Abrams, and the likes of Somocista commandante Enrique Bermudez. As for the influence of Calero, I quote Owen, who noted that he was surrounded by "liars and greed and power-motivated" people for whom the war was just "a business."

193 "desperate to see": "The Case for the Contras," *The New Republic*, March 24, 1986.

193 "the worst piece": Author's interview.

193 "preposterous": Michael Kinsley, "Manila, Managua," *The New Republic*, March 24, 1986, p. 6.

193 "The magazine was": Author's interview with Hendrik Hertzberg.

193 these "pro-Contra": Author's interview with Sidney Blumenthal.

193 Saluted in the pages: See "Democrats and Commandantes," *The New Republic* July 28, 1986, pp. 7–8.

194 "it is the place": Quoted in "Midnight's Confession," *The New Republic*, January 21, 1991, p. 9.

194 Pat Buchanan was: Quoted in Michael Kinsley, "Taking Responsibility," *The New Republic*, March 19, 1990, p. 6.

194 "moderate Democrats": "Democrats and Commandantes," *The New Republic*, July 28, 1986, p. 7.

194 he also promised: The "who lost Central America" phrase appeared in

Krauthammer's *Washington Post* column, upon the occasion of the first cease-fire/peace accord signed by the Sandinistas and the Contras. My copy is undated. See also Charles Krauthammer, February 10, 1989.

194 The magazine's friend: Author's interview with Elliott Abrams.

194–95 staggering economic debts: See "How Latin America's Economies Look After a Decade's Decline," *The New York Times*, "Week in Review," February 11, 1990, p. 3. See also *International Monetary Fund Annual Report* (Washington, DC: IMF, 1989), Appendix II.

195 In Peru: See James Brooke, "Peruvian Farmers Razing Rain Forest to Sow Drug Crops," *The New York Times*, August 13, 1989, p. 1.

195 "Israel, lion of nations": James Walcott, "Partisans Reviewed," *Vanity Fair*, November 1988, p. 28.

196 no fewer than four: Author's interviews.

196 "helps Israel's enemies": Quoted in Robert I. Friedman, "Selling Israel to America," *Mother Jones*, February/March 1987, p. 21.

197 "a national characterological": Quoted in Gwenda Blair, "Citizen Peretz," p. 93.

197 "I have a problem": Author's interview with Michael Kinsley.

197 "an obsessive wound": Martin Peretz, "Wounds," *The New Republic*. My copy is undated.

198 "So this is": Martin Peretz, "Usual Suspects," *The New Republic*, July 12, 1982.

198 "There is no": Author's interview.

198 During the eighties: See Martin Peretz, "Occupational Hazards," Leon Wieseltier, "Summoned by Stones," and Charles Krauthammer, "No Exit," in *The New Republic*, March 14, 1988, pp. 14–31.

199 "The price was": Author's interview.

199 Hertzberg's refusal: Quoted in Gwenda Blair, "Citizen Peretz," p. 91.

200 "The initial way": Author's interview with Hendrik Hertzberg.

200 "I wanted": Ibid.

10. THE MAN WITH NO NEW IDEAS

203 Drawing upon: See Isaiah Berlin, "The Hedgehog and the Fox" (1951) in Henry Hardy, ed., *Russian Thinkers* (New York: Penguin Books, 1977).

204 "Everything's rotten": Quoted in Serge Schmemann, "Shevardnadze Returns as Soviet Foreign Minister," *The New York Times*, November 20, 1991, p. A7. See also Eduard Shevardnadze, *The Future Belongs to Freedom* (New York: Free Press, 1991), pp. 41–83.

204 "everything pertaining": Mikhail Gorbachev, *Perestroika: New Thinking for Our Country and the World* (New York: Harper & Row, 1987).

206 "the history of": See Jeane J. Kirkpatrick, "Dictatorships and Double Standards," in Kirkpatrick, ed., *Dictatorships and Double Standards: Rationalism and Realism in Politics* (New York: Simon & Schuster, 1982), p. 51.

206 "a historical accident": See Jean-François Revel, "How Democracies Perish," *Commentary*, June 1984.

206 "on the side of": George F. Will, April 17, 1975.

206 "achieved the closest": Will, *The Pursuit of Virtue and Other Tory Notions*, p. 17.

206 "Biden, 37": Quoted in Hendrik Hertzberg, "Casualties of War," *The New Republic*, March 6, 1989, p. 4.

207 "a self-conscious": Irving Kristol, "Foreign Policy in an Age of Ideology," *The National Interest*, Fall 1985, p. 9.

207 Kristol recommended: Quoted in *The Washington Times*, October 2, 1987, p. 10.

207 "Unless we refute": Edward N. Luttwak, "On the Meaning of Victory" (1982), in Walter Laqueur and Brad Roberts, eds., *America in the World, 1962–1987* (New York: St. Martin's Press, 1987), p. 157.

207 Finland . . . "had earned": Author's interview with Charles Krauthammer.

207 "a kind of beaded": William Safire, March 6, 1989.

208 and reappeared: See Jeane Kirkpatrick, June 7, 1989.

209 The 1989 edition: Cited in Daniel Patrick Moynihan, "The Peace Dividend," *The New York Review of Books*, June 28, 1990, p. 3. See also Franklyn D. Holzman, "How the CIA Concocts Soviet Defense Numbers," *The New York Times*, October 25, 1989, editorial page, and Leonard Silk, "Did CIA Distort Soviet Outlays?" *The New York Times*, November 18, 1989, Business section, p. 2. For evidence that the practice may have continued through the 1990 budget cycle, see R. Jeffrey Smith, "Aspin: U.S. Suppressing Data on Cuts," *The Washington Post*, November 17, 1989, p. A10.

209 "national security state": Daniel Patrick Moynihan, "How America Blew It," *Newsweek*, December 10, 1990, p. 14. In 1989, according to the Information Security Oversight Office, located in the General Services Administration, the U.S. government classified 6,796,501 new secrets.

210 "for more than four": Talbott's comments were initially made in the author's interview and appeared shortly thereafter in "Rethinking the Red Menace," *Time*, January 1, 1990, p. 66.

211 "nobody really knows": All quoted in Don Oberdorfer, "U.S. Experts Expect Little Immediate Change in Soviet Policies," *The Washington Post*, March 12, 1985, p. A21.

211 "no new ideas": Quoted in Charlotte Saikowski, "U.S. Analysts Look at Gorbachev and See Shifts in Style, But Not in Substance," *The Christian Science Monitor*, March 12, 1985, p. 1.

211 "You don't survive": Quoted in Norman Kempster, "Gorbachev May Press Drive to Split U.S., Allies," *Los Angeles Times*, March 12, 1985, p. 1.

211 "You don't get into": Quoted in R. W. Apple, Jr., "In West, No Rapid Changes Are Seen," *The New York Times*, March 12, 1985, p. A17.

211 "The real question": See Strobe Talbott, "Both Continuity and Vigor," *Time*, March 25, 1990, p. 23.

212 had "an advantage": Quoted in Kempster, "Gorbachev May Press Drive to Split U.S., Allies," p. 1.

212 "everyone is waiting": Quoted in ibid.

212 "very dangerous": Quoted in ibid.

212 "a much more skillful": Quoted in Oberdorfer, "U.S. Experts Expect Little Immediate Change in Soviet Policies," p. A21. (This quote was considered so insightful either by Brzezinski or the reporters who quoted him that it also appeared in Kempster, "Gorbachev May Press Drive to Split U.S., Allies," p. 1.)

212 "Gorbachev may be": Quoted in Matt Clark, "The Politics of Art," *Newsweek*, March 25, 1985, p. 45.

213 "We need an economic": Quoted in Stephen F. Cohen, "The Failure of the Hard Line" (originally published in *The Nation* on December 15, 1984), *Sovieticus: American Perceptions and Soviet Realities* (New York: W. W. Norton, 1986), p. 151.

214 "We don't know": Charles Krauthammer, "When to Call Off the Cold War," *The New Republic*, November 16, 1987, p. 18.

215 "go back to": Quoted in David Remnick, "The Struggle for Light," *The New York Review of Books*, August 16, 1990, p. 3.

215 George Will, who: The first quote appeared in Will's column on September 26, 1985. The Simes quote and the second Will quote can be found in Michael Massing, "Gorbaphobes in the U.S. Media," *The Nation*, December 26, 1988, p. 713.

216 "The Soviet Union": Henry A. Kissinger, "Kissinger: How to Deal with Gorbachev," *Newsweek*, March 2, 1987, pp. 39–47.

216 "History is on": Robert C. Tucker, "Gorbachev and the Fight for Soviet Reform," *World Policy Journal*, Spring 1987, p. 179.

217 "there is anyone": Quoted in Russell Watson, "A Mellower Moscow," *Newsweek*, September 21, 1987, p. 43.

217 "break few Stalinist": William Safire, November 4, 1987.

217 "peaceful competition": William Safire, December 9, 1987.

217 His colleague . . . : A. M. Rosenthal, December 7, 1987.

218 "lost its head": See Charles Krauthammer, "The Week Washington Lost Its Head," *The New Republic*, January 4 and 11, 1988, and Charles Krauthammer, December 3, 1987.

218 "drunk on detente": George F. Will, December 13, 1987.

219 "always talk": Charles Krauthammer, December 9, 1988.

219 "a beleaguered": Dimitri Simes, "Yes, But," *The Washington Post*, December 9, 1988.

220 "peaceful coexistence": Henry Kissinger, December 20, 1988.

220 It is instructive: See Craig R. Whitney, "Kohl Gets the German Spotlight But Genscher Had the Vision," *The New York Times*, July 20, 1990, p. 1.

220 *Newsweek* devoted . . . : The "appeasement bloc" quote appears in William Safire, July 22, 1990. The "devious" and "Fourth Reich" comments appear in William Safire, May 15, 1989. The *Newsweek* and "export-loving" quotes, along with the beating-your-wife simile, are borrowed from Diana Johnstone, "Washington's Latest Target: Bonn's Hans-Dietrich Genscher," *In These Times*, January 11–17, 1989, p. 9. See also James Hoagland, August 18, 1988.

221 "a comprehensive package": See Whitney, "Kohl Gets the German Spotlight But Genscher Had the Vision," p. 1.

221 The new European Bank: See Jacques Attali, "Lines on the Horizon: A New World Order in the Making," *New Perspectives Quarterly*, Spring 1990, pp. 6–8.

221 The apparent paralysis: See Glenn Frankel, "Europe Views U.S. Crisis as Sign of Economic Ills: Analysts Cite Shift in World's Fiscal Order," *The Washington Post*, October 7, 1990, p. A32, and Hobart Rowan, "Dollar's Fall Causes U.S. to Lose Status as a Safe Investment Haven," *The Washington Post*, October 13, 1990, p. A1.

222 "What we are": Meg Greenfield, *Newsweek*, October 2, 1989.

222 In February 1989: See Martin Sieff, "Brzezinski Sees Soviet System Eaten from Within," *The Washington Times*, February 7, 1989, and George F. Will, November 9, 1989.

223 In a speech before: Robin Toner, "Dukakis Talking Tough, Marches into Dixie," *The New York Times*, February 17, 1988, p. A19.

223 "were not even peripheral": Quoted in Blumenthal, *Pledging Allegiance: The Last Campaign of the Cold War*, p. 218.

223 "not a foreign-policy": George F. Will, February 25, 1988.

224 "the containment of Communism": Walter S. Mossberg and John Walcott, "Strategic Shift: U.S. Redefines Policy on Security to Place Less Stress on Soviets," *The Wall Street Journal*, August 11, 1988, p. 1.

224 "A bipartisan postwar": *The Wall Street Journal*, editorial page, September 13, 1988.

225 what one reputable: See Cynthia Brown, ed., *With Friends Like These: The Americas Watch Report on Human Rights and U.S. Policy in Latin America* (New York: Pantheon Books, 1985), p. 175. For a detailed account of the Contras' sustained pattern of murder and torture of innocent civilians conducted with the full knowledge and tacit cooperation of the CIA and National Security Council, see Sam Dillon, *Commandos: The CIA and Nicaragua's Contra Rebels* (New York: Holt, 1991). See also Fred Bridgland, "Angola's Secret Bloodbath," *The Washington Post*, Outlook section, March 29, 1992. p. 1.

225 views that were: *The New Republic* comment appeared in "Dukakis for President," November 7, 1988, pp. 7–9. Buckley made his comment on a special "Firing Line" debate just before the 1988 election. The *Journal* comment appeared on September 13, 1988.

225 "Reagan's successes": Charles Krauthammer, September 23, 1988.

225 "would have endorsed": *The New Republic*, "Dukakis for President," November 7, 1988, pp. 7–9.

225 William Safire says: Author's interview.

227 "our strength . . . steadiness": Bush speech to the National Press Club on January 5, 1988.

227 "nothing more than": See David Broder, "Thoughts from Quayle on the Campaign Trail," *The Washington Post*, September 6, 1988.

11. WINNING ISN'T EVERYTHING . . .

228 "All over the world": Quoted in Charles Krauthammer, March 9, 1990.

228 "everything falling apart": John Updike, *Rabbit at Rest* (New York: Alfred A. Knopf, 1990), p. 8.

229 "the struggle for recognition": Francis Fukuyama, "The End of History?" *The National Interest*, Summer 1989, p. 18.

229 William Safire, almost alone: William Safire, December 4, 1989, and author's interview with Leslie H. Gelb.

229 "History" was "marching": George F. Will, November 20, 1989.

229 "What has happened": Jeane Kirkpatrick, July 23, 1990.

229 "As our one great": Charles Krauthammer, March 9, 1990.

230 Analysts and academics: See James Chace, *Solvency: The Price of Survival* (New York: Random House, 1981); Mancur Olson, *The Rise and Decline of Nations* (New Haven: Yale University Press, 1982); David Calleo, *Beyond American Hegemony* (New York: Basic Books, 1987); Walter Russell Mead, *Mortal Splendor: The American Empire in Transition* (Boston: Houghton Mifflin, 1987); and Richard Rosecrance, *The Rise of the Trading State* (New York: Basic Books, 1986). See also Richard Rosecrance, *America as an Ordinary Country* (Ithaca, NY: Cornell University Press, 1976).

231 Kennedy's thesis was: See Paul Kennedy, *The Rise and Fall of the Great Powers* (New York: Random House, 1987), p. 534, and Walter Lippmann, *U.S. Foreign Policy: Shield of the Republic* (Boston: Atlantic; Little, Brown, 1943), pp. 7–8.

231 Unfortunately, noted Kennedy: See Kennedy, *The Rise and Fall of the Great Powers*, p. xxiii.

232 The . . . lead editorial: See "Evening in America," *The New Republic*, February 1, 1988, pp. 7–9.

232 He, too, wondered: See David Broder, January 17, 1988.

232 have "unforgivably damaged": Michael Novak, "What Became of the Ugly American?" *Forbes*, April 30, 1990, p. 120.

232 Jeane Kirkpatrick, positing: The "national will" quote belongs to Podhoretz. Both he and Kirkpatrick are quoted in Peter Schmeisser, "Is America in Decline?" *The New York Times Magazine*, April 17, 1988, p. 67.

232–233 "Imperial overstretch": George F. Will, *Newsweek*, January 2, 1989.

233 Nye granted: See Joseph Nye, *Bound to Lead: The Changing Nature of American Power* (New York: Basic Books, 1990). By the time his book was published, Nye had been joined in this endeavor by Henry R. Nau, *The Myth of America's Decline: Leading the World Economy into the 1990s* (New York: Oxford University Press, 1990), and (perhaps ironically) Richard Rosecrance, *America's Economic Resurgence* (New York: Harper & Row, 1990). Kennedy reviewed these three books together with John Chancellor's less ambitious version of same, *Peril and Promise: A Commentary on America* (New York: Harper & Row, 1990), in Paul Kennedy, "Fin-de-Siècle America," *The New York Review of Books*, June 28, 1990, pp. 31–40.

233 "withdrawing from": Nye, *Bound to Lead: The Changing Nature of American Power*, p. 4.

234 "simply reformulate[d]": William H. McNeill, "History Over, the World Goes On," *The New York Times Book Review*, January 26, 1992, pp. 14–15.

234 "What we may be": Fukuyama, "The End of History?" p. 4.

234 "An argument that has": George F. Will, *Suddenly: The American Idea at Home and Abroad* (New York: Free Press, 1990), p. xiii.

235 "History must have": Ian Davidson, "News of the End of History Fails to Reach Europe," *The Financial Times*, September 19, 1989, p. 2.

235 "anybody advocating": Quoted in Schmeisser, "Is America in Decline?" p. 96.

236 Our share of global: See Attali, "Lines on the Horizon: A New World Order in the Making," *New Perspectives Quarterly*, Spring 1990, pp. 6–8.

236 Crucial industries: The United States lost 14% in its OECD export manufacturing share from 1980 through 1987. From 1984 to 1987 alone, the U.S. market share in silicon wafers went from 85% to 22%; its portion of the semiconductors market fell from 54% to 41%. In computers, it declined from 78% to 41%. The past decade has also seen a $20 billion swing in the American electronics trade balance. Our share of the machine-tool industry dropped from 25% to 5% in the last thirty years. *The Economist* has posited that, without major changes, Detroit is unlikely to survive, a view seconded in early 1992 by Clyde Prestowitz of Washington's Economic Strategy Institute. See Lester Thurow, Fred Branfman, and George Lodge, "Fiddling While U.S. Industry Burns, A Rebuild America White Paper" (Washington, DC: Rebuild America, 1990). For the machine-tools figure, see Attali, "Lines on the Horizon: A New World Order in the Making," p. 6.

236 "for all the accomplishments": See Robert L. Bartley, "Is America on the Way Down?" *Commentary*, March 1992, p. 22.

236 Japan has already: See William J. Broad, "Japan Seen Passing U.S. in Research by Industry," *The New York Times*, February 25, 1992, p. B5, and John Eckhouse, "U.S. Firms Get Fewer Patrons," *San Francisco Chronicle*, February 15, 1992, p. B1. The four top recipients of patents in 1990, for instance, were Hitachi, Toshiba, Canon, and Mitsubishi.

236 In the past twenty: The rate of U.S. productivity increases averaged 0.4% between 1973 and 1988. See Paul Krugman, *The Age of Diminished Expectations* (Cambridge: MIT Press, 1990), p. 11.

236 Added to declining: The United States' net investment position (the amount of assets we owned in other countries compared with what they owned in ours) peaked in 1981 at just over $140 billion. By 1989, we were already $650 billion in the red, with the numbers still climbing. By 1988, interest payments on the $3 trillion government debt amounted to nearly 20% of the entire federal budget and consumed all of the tax payments collected west of the Mississippi. See Krugman, *The Age of Diminished Expectations*, p. 40, and Daniel Patrick Moynihan, "The Peace Dividend," p. 3. Japan, by contrast, takes in the equivalent of 4% of its GNP in interest payments and investment earnings. Coupled with its relatively meager military budget, this gives Japanese corporations an investment advantage of 11% of GNP compared with their capital-starved U.S.

competitors. See Sherle R. Schwenninger and Jerry W. Sanders, "U.S. Policy Toward the Alliance," in Archibald L. Gillies, Jeff Faux, Jerry W. Sanders, Sherle R. Schwenninger, and Paul F. Walker, eds., *Post Reagan America* (New York: The World Policy Institute, 1987), pp. 57–58.

236 Since 1980, federal borrowing: See Benjamin Friedman, "Reagan Lives!" *The New York Review of Books*, December 20, 1990, p. 29.

236 "America simply isn't": Karen Pennar, "Can You Compete? A Special Report," *BusinessWeek*, December 17, 1990, p. 63.

237 The eighties *were:* According to the United States Census Bureau, the income of the richest fifth of the country grew 14% after inflation from 1984 to 1988, from $98,411 to $111,770, while the average income of all Americans dropped to $35,752 from $37,012 during the same period. According to the Bureau, the fall is statistically insignificant. See Robert Pear, "Rich Got Richer in 80s; Others Held Even," *The New York Times*, January 11, 1991, p. 1.

237 Their numbers increased: Cited in Kevin Phillips, *The Politics of Rich and Poor: Wealth and the American Electorate in the Reagan Aftermath* (New York: Random House, 1990), p. 10.

237 The average total compensation: Cited in John A. Byrne, "Is the Boss Getting Paid Too Much?" *BusinessWeek*, May 1, 1989, p. 46.

237 Even *Commentary:* See Edward N. Luttwak, "Is America on the Way Down?" *Commentary*, March 1992, p. 21.

237 Americans who could call: The number of Americans who fell into this category decreased by more than 11% between 1969 and 1989. See "U.S. Says Middle Class Shrinking," *The New York Times*, February 22, 1992, p. 4.

237 We have the highest: Forty percent of European high school students can solve math problems that are beyond the ability of 90% of their American counterparts. Japanese high school graduates can solve calculus problems that not even most American college graduates can manage. See Laura D'Andrea Tyson, "Failing Our Youth: America's K-12 Education," *New Perspectives Quarterly*, Fall 1990, p. 28. See also "America's Choice, High Skills or Low Wages," The Report of the Commission on the Skills of the American Workforce, June 1990.

237 The same depressing: "In 1952, infrastructure spending absorbed 6.9% of the non-military budget. During the seventies this figure fell to 1.5%. In the eighties, it fell again to 1.2%." Cited in Robert Heilbronner, "Seize the Day," *The New York Review of Books*, February 15, 1990, p. 30. The U.S. General Accounting Office estimates that $315 billion of new investment will be needed simply to maintain America's infrastructure at 1983 conditions through 2000. See General Accounting Office, "Transportation Issues" (Washington, DC: U.S. Government Printing Office, November 1988), p. 21.

238 In the end . . . : The primacy of the "geoeconomic era" over that of the passing, geopolitical one was first enunciated, so far as I am aware, in Sherle R. Schwenninger and Jerry W. Sanders, "The Democrats and a New Grand Strategy: Foreign Policy for the Post Reagan Era," *World Policy Journal*, Summer 1986.

239 dying forests: Twenty percent of all plant and animal species will be extinct in

the next twenty years. See "Promethean Legacy," *New Perspectives Quarterly*, Spring 1989, p. 25.

239 The net result: Since midcentury, the world has lost nearly 20% of the topsoil from its cropland, a fifth of its tropical rainforests. The rainforest destruction is now occurring at a rate of between 1 and 2% a year in some places. Lester Brown, et al, *State of the World 1990* (Washington, DC: Worldwatch, 1990), p. 3.

239 In many developing: There are now 10 million environmental refugees worldwide. See "Promethean Legacy," p. 25.

239 "the Soviet Union is": George F. Will, January 19, 1987.

239 Actually, the United States: The National Center for Health Statistics figures are cited in Philip J. Hilts, "Life Expectancy for Blacks in U.S. Shows Sharp Drop," *The New York Times*, November 29, 1990, p. 1, and Malcolm Gladwell, "Life Expectancy of Black Males Falls to 64.9," *The Washington Post*, April 9, 1991, p. 5. The 1988 numbers demonstrated the continuation of a four-year trend, based on U.S. Department of Health and Human Services figures. The 1988 figure was the lowest since 1981 and was a full eight years and one month lower than the average life expectancy for white males in the United States.

240 Black wealth: According to the U.S. Census Bureau, in 1988, the average net worth of a white American family was $43,280. For a black family, it was $4,170, and for Hispanics, $5,520. See Spencer Rich, "Gap Found in Wealth Among Races," *The Washington Post*, January 9, 1991, p. 3.

239 For a black male: The United States leads the world with 426 of every 100,000 American citizens incarcerated. For black men, the number is 3,100 per 100,000. See "U.S. Leads the World in Imprisonment," *The New York Times*, January 7, 1991.

240 9,536 people: This Department of Justice statistic can be found in "Tom Foley, Gun Nut," *The New Republic*, January 28, 1991, p. 7. Were Britain's population similar to that of our own, a U.S.-style murder rate would have resulted in more than 300 times the number it experienced, according to my own imprecise calculations.

240 Given rising costs: The percentage of young Americans able to afford their own homes fell during the Reagan presidency as the "average" first-time buyer earned only 77% of the necessary income to qualify for a mortgage on an "average" starter home. Forty million Americans could not afford to purchase health insurance, and many more were underinsured. The cost of a college education, meanwhile, roughly doubled during the 1980s, reaching a $6,175 mean at public universities and $12,511 at private schools. The (1988) housing and education figures are cited in Alfred J. Malabre, Jr., *Within Our Means* (New York: Random House, 1991), pp. 39 and 47 respectively. The health insurance figure is cited in "The Third Year," *The New York Times*, editorial page, January 31, 1991.

240 "the United States has provided": Leon Wieseltier, "What Went Wrong? An Appraisal of Reagan's Foreign Policy," *The New York Times Magazine*, December 7, 1986, p. 137.

240 "to undermine confidence": Christopher Lasch, "The Costs of our Cold War Victory," *The New York Times*, op-ed page, July 13, 1990.

241 "no money shall be": United States Constitution, Article I, Section 9.

241 "the 1990s will demand": Jessica Tuchman Matthews, "Redefining Security," *Foreign Affairs*, Spring 1989, p. 162. Matthews's article, however, was surrounded by an all too typical *Foreign Affairs* Cold War menu.

242 "whole global warning": "The McLaughlin Group," April 26, 1992.

242 "the litany": Christopher Lehmann-Haupt, "What the U.S. Can Do to Pay for Its Past Mistakes," *The New York Times*, January 28, 1991, p. C24.

243 The Economic Policy Institute: See The Economic Policy Institute, "The State of Working America, 1986," (Washington, DC: EPI, 1986), and Bennett Harrison and Barry Bluestone, *The Great U-Turn* (New York: Basic Books, 1988). See also Eric Alterman, "A Pop(ulist) Quiz," *The New York Times*, op-ed page, July 25, 1990.

244 "the critical weakness": Kevin Phillips, "George Bush and Congress—Brain Dead Politics of 1989," *The Washington Post*, Outlook section, October 1, 1989, p. 1. This article forms the basis of Phillips' introduction to *The Politics of Rich and Poor: Wealth and the American Electorate in the Reagan Aftermath*.

244 "outdated ideologies": Phillips, "George Bush and Congress—Brain Dead Politics of 1989," p. 1.

244 64 percent of Americans: Cited in ibid.

245 "The infant death rate": George F. Will, *Newsweek*, April 9, 1990.

246 "successful schools": George F. Will, January 31, 1991.

246 "It was their emperor": John LeCarré, *The Secret Pilgrim* (New York: Alfred A. Knopf, 1991), p. 321.

12. OPERATION PUNDIT STORM

248 "Nation's Capital": *The Washington Post*, February 18, 1990, p. 1.

248 "refusing to stand up": "The McLaughlin Group," July 28, 1991, and September 13, 1991.

249 Ms. Barr was: "The McLaughlin Group," July 28, 1990.

249 "Thanks Saddam": Ben Wattenberg, August 7, 1990.

249 "In a way": "The Guns of August," *The New Republic*, September 3, 1990, p. 9.

249 "the heavy speculation": R. W. Apple, Jr., quoted in James Bennet, "How They Missed That Story," *The Washington Monthly*, December 1990, p. 16.

249 "Hey, whaddya know": Michael Kinsley, "Kuwaiti Fried," *The New Republic*, October 8, 1990, p. 6.

249 Bush's State Department: See Dean Baquet, "Investigators Say U.S. Shielded Iraqis from Bank Inquiry," *The New York Times*, March 20, 1992, and Anthony Lewis, March 15, 1992.

249 The ruling al-Sabah: See Ernest Hollings, United States Senate, January 12, 1990, and Daniel P. Moynihan's "Letter to New York," May 10, 1991.

250 "Following Bush's conversion": Author's interview with James Fallows.

251–252 "The war between": Quoted in Randall Rothenberg, "The Battle of the Columnists: Telling Leaders How to Think," *The New York Times*, "Week in Review," September 23, 1990.

252 "In order to narrow": Author's interview with Jude Wanniski.

252 "democratism" . . . "idolatry": Patrick J. Buchanan, "America First—and Second, and Third," *The National Interest*, Spring 1990, p. 81.

252 The fervently anti-Soviet: See Zbigniew Brzezinski, "Beyond Chaos, What the West Must Do," *The National Interest*, Spring 1990.

252–253 "Disposable capital is": Edward N. Luttwak, Testimony before the Senate Armed Forces Committee, November 29, 1990. See also Sherle R. Schwenninger and Jerry W. Sanders, "The Democrats and a New Grand Strategy," *World Policy Journal*, Fall 1986.

253 "the unchallenged superpower": See Charles Krauthammer, "The Unipolar Moment," *Foreign Affairs: America and the World*, 1990–91, pp. 23–24. See also "New World Order: What's New? Which World? Whose Orders?" *The Economist*, February 23, 1991, p. 25.

253 "What we find": Daniel Patrick Moynihan, U.S. Senate, January 10, 1991.

253 "it would be crazy": "The McLaughlin Group," July 28, 1990.

253 "We're not going to": "The Capital Gang," August 4, 1990.

253 President Bush told: George Bush quoted in Walker, "Victory and Delusion," *Foreign Policy*, 83, Summer 1991, p. 167, and Thomas Friedman, "Hanging Tough Won't Be the Only Test of Leadership," *The New York Times*, "Week in Review," August 19, 1990, p. 1.

254 "Who will control": Quoted in John B. Judis, "Burden Shirking," *The New Republic*, March 4, 1991, p. 22.

255 TNR editors recommended: "The Guns of August," *The New Republic*, September 3, 1990, p. 10, and "Fighting Dirty," *The New Republic*, September 10 and 17, 1990.

255 "a nightmare not just": Charles Krauthammer, August 17, 1991, and August 3, 1991.

255 "at war with Iraq": A. M. Rosenthal, August 19, August 23, and August 9, 1990.

255 "take Baghdad": Quoted in Otto Friedrich, "The Case Against Going to War," *Time*, September 10, 1990, p. 94.

256 "obviously it is time": Quoted in William Safire, September 3, 1990, and Jeane Kirkpatrick, November 12, 1990.

256 "The United States cannot": Henry Kissinger on "Meet the Press," August 5, 1990, and Henry Kissinger, August 29, 1990.

256 Kissinger's judgment . . .: The material is drawn from "60 Minutes," CBS, March 29, 1992, broadcast. See also Kenneth Timmerman, *The Death Lobby: How the West Armed Iraq* (Boston: Houghton Mifflin, 1991), p. 349.

258 "Bush has been so": Charles Krauthammer, November 25, 1990.

259 "maybe the most important": Richard Cohen, August 23, 1990.

260 If, after more than: See George W. Ball, "The Gulf Crisis," *The New York Review of Books*, December 6, 1990.

261 "dealing with our own": William Safire, November 5, 1990.
261 In any event: See Eric Schmidt, "U.S. Says It Missed 2 A-Plants in Iraq," *The New York Times*, October 10, 1991, p. A7.
261 "There [was] no": Zbigniew Brzezinski, *The New York Times*, September 7, 1991.
262 "almost impossible to": David Broder, November 18, 1990.
262 Richard Cohen . . . : Haynes Johnson, August 10, 1990; Anthony Lewis, January 10, 1991; and Richard Cohen, August 23, 1990.
262 "The conditions that": Charlie Peters, "Stop That Blank Check," *The New York Times*, January 16, 1991.
263 Congress had been: Krauthammer made his comments on "Inside Washington," Barnes and Kondracke on "The McLaughlin Group," November 11, 1990.
263 "almost none": David Broder, December 16, 1990.
263 "right on the fundamental": Leslie H. Gelb, January 2, 1991.
263 "if the alternative": Quoted in Lars-Erik Nelson, March 25, 1991.
263 "Politically," George Bush: The conversations between Bush and Powell were reported in Haynes Johnson, "Book Says Powell Favored Containment," *The Washington Post*, May 2, 1991, p. 1. See also Bob Woodward, *The Commanders* (New York: Simon & Schuster, 1991).
264 Senator Nunn: See Eric Alterman, "Congress' Failure," *Tikkun*, January/February 1991, p. 46, reprinted in James Ridgeway, *The March to War* (New York: Four Walls, Eight Windows, 1991).
264 "this is not": George Mitchell, U.S. Senate, January 10, 1991.
264 "in a manner befitting": David Broder, January 15, 1991.
264 "there have not been": Arlen Specter. U.S. Senate, January 10, 1991.
264-65 "preferred to give": Arlen Specter, U.S. Senate, January 10, 1991.
265 Republican Minority Leader: Cited in James Bennet, "The Senate's Lame Doves," *The Washington Monthly*, March 1991, p. 45.
265 "75 percent or more": John Kerry, U.S. Senate, January 11, 1991.
265 "the most powerful": "Today," NBC, February 26, 1991.
266 Fred Barnes . . . Morton Kondracke: "The McLaughlin Group," March 2, 1991.
266 a "fearsome, transcendent": Rowland Evans and Robert Novak, February 27, 1991.
266 "the most effective": Patrick J. Buchanan, February 28, 1991.
267 *Times* Gulf reporter: Malcolm W. Browne quoted in Timothy M. Phelps, "Many of Gulf Press in Shallow End of Pool," *Newsday*, January 23, 1991, p. 36, and "The Military vs. the Press," *The New York Times Magazine*, March 3, 1991, p. 29.
268 What's more: Dugan made this observation on CBS News on February 13, 1991.
269 A. M. Rosenthal started: See A. M. Rosenthal, January 18, 1991.
269 "technological prowess": George F. Will, January 18, 1991.
269 "a wholly different": Richard Cohen, February 26, 1991.
270 "there's more to": George F. Will on , "This Week with David Brinkley," January 20, 1991.

270 "We need SDI": Fred Barnes on "The McLaughlin Group," January 20, 1991.

270 "When President Bush": Patrick Buchanan, January 23, 1991.

270 "The epic debates": "Bad for Civilians," *The Wall Street Journal*, editorial page, January 21, 1991.

270 the Patriots hit: See Eric Schmitt, "Israel Plays Down Effectiveness of Patriot Missile," *The New York Times*, October 31, 1991, p. A5.

270 "Cold War II": See Charles Krauthammer, February 21, 1991.

270 "reversion to old-style": Rowland Evans and Robert Novak, February 22, 1991.

270 "retain his old pal": A. M. Rosenthal, February 19, 1991.

270 "perfid[ious]": William Safire, February 21, 1991.

270 "rearming Hussein": Morton Kondracke on "The McLaughlin Group," February 23, 1991.

271 "a single pole": Charles Krauthammer, "The Unipolar Moment," *Foreign Affairs: America and the World*, 1990–91, p. 24.

271 "hubris": Patrick Buchanan, February 28, 1991.

271 "to stand up to": See "The Hammer of the Kurds," *The Economist*, April 6, 1991, p. 9.

272 a "large scale": "The Guns of August," *The New Republic*, September 3, 1990, p. 10.

272 price of a barrel: Cited in Walker, "Victory and Delusion," p. 160.

272 In January 1992: See Youssef M. Ibrahim, "Saudis Say They'll Trim Oil Output," *The New York Times*, January 22, 1992, p. D1.

272 Our net indebtedness: See Dennis Healey, "A Bloody Shambles of a War," *The Manchester Guardian Weekly*, March 31, 1991, p. 11.

272 A 1991 Morgan Stanley: See Steven Greenhouse, "World's Finances Facing Strains as Troubled Areas Try to Rebuild," *The New York Times*, March 26, 1991, p. D1.

272 "the United States": James Hoagland, "Bush's America: Welcome to the Post-Gulf World," *The Washington Post*, Outlook section, March 3, 1991, p. 1.

272 "peace and the rule": David Broder, April 10, 1991.

272 CIA Director: Robert Gates quoted in Elaine Sciolino, "Iraq Could Rebuild Weapons Threat Soon, CIA Chief Says," *The New York Times*, January 16, 1992, p. A4.

273 Hussein retained: These are U.S. intelligence estimates as reported by Ann Devroy and Molly Moore, "Winning the War and Struggling with the Peace," *The Washington Post*, April 14, 1991, p. 1.

272 hawkish columnists: See particularly William Safire, January 20, 1992.

273 The Shamir government: See Jackson Diehl, "Israel Boosts Land Seizures," *The Washington Post*, May 14, 1991, p. 1.

273 "the primary gains": Charles Krauthammer, April 19, 1991.

274 By early May: Figures cited in "Kuwait: The War Within," *BusinessWeek*, May 27, 1991, p. 53.

274 According to human rights organizations: See William Branigin and Nora Boustany, "Rights Officials: Kuwaiti Soldiers Commit Abuses," *The Washington Post*, March 16, 1991, p. 1, and Nora Boustany, "Kuwaiti Hospital Said to Cover Up Torture," *The Washington Post*, March 22, 1991.

275 child mortality figures: See Patrick E. Tyler, "Western Health Study in Iraq finds Child Mortality Has Nearly Tripled," *The New York Times*, October 22, 1991, p. A7, and Associated Press, "Iraqi Civilian Deaths in War's Aftermath Estimated at 70,000," *San Francisco Chronicle*, January 9, 1992.

275 "Voice of Free Iraq": See "Operation Desertion," *The Economist*, April 13, 1991, p. 25.

276 The punditocracy did not: See William Safire, April 4, 1991; Haynes Johnson, April 5, 1991; Charles Krauthammer, April 5, 1991; and A. M. Rosenthal, April 5 and April 9, 1991.

276 "enormous disappointment": Charles Krauthammer, April 19, 1991, and May 3, 1991.

277 But the wimp: See, for instance, Fred Barnes, "The Old Bush," *The New Republic*, April 22, 1991, p. 13.

277 "Erstwhile antiwar": Charles Krauthammer, April 19, 1991, and Morton Kondracke, "Kurdled," *The New Republic*, May 13, 1991, p. 10.

277 "The peace": George F. Will, April 4, 1991.

277 "isolationist chickens": Richard Cohen, March 5, 1991.

277 "showed the nation": David Broder, March 6, 1991.

277 "so many elected": "Out of Touch," *The Wall Street Journal*, March 14, 1991, p. A18.

277 "A party that": A. M. Rosenthal, March 15, 1991.

278 his "well conceived": Quoted in David Shribman and James M. Perry, "Conference of Moderate Democrats Finds Party Full of Factions, Undecided on Road Ahead," *The Wall Street Journal*, May 8, 1991, p. A14.

278 "the most influential": Quoted in David Shribman, "Victory in Gulf War Exorcises the Demons of the Vietnam Years," *The Wall Street Journal*, March 1, 1991, p. 1.

278 "nonsense": Charles Krauthammer, March 22, 1991.

278 "the end of the decline": Quoted in Peter Appleborne, "At Home, War Healed Several Wounds," *The New York Times*, March 4, 1991, p. 1.

280 "one of the defining": William J. Bennett, "Rebirth of a Nation," *National Review*, March 18, 1991, p. 41.

280 Britain achieved: See Michael Howard, "Churchill and National Unity," in Michael Howard, ed., *The Lessons of History* (New Haven: Yale University Press, 1991), p. 159.

280 Banks went bust . . . : For the details of these developments, see Andrew Baxter, "U.S. Drops Out of World Machine Tool Top Five," *The Financial Times*, February 12, 1991, p. 4; Louis Uchitelle, "New Jobless Claims at 8-Year High," *The New York Times*, April 5, 1991, p. D1; Suen L. Hwang, "Failures in 90 Jumped 20% Due to Slump," *The Wall Street Journal*, March 13, 1991; "On Recession's Battlefield, The Economy Is Losing Ground," *BusinessWeek*, February 18, 1991, p. 27; John M. Barry, "Recession Deeper in First Quarter," *The Washington Post*, April 28, 1991, p. 1; John Greenwald, "Detroit's Big Three Are Seeing Red," *Time*, May 13, 1991, p. 40, and Reuters, "U.S. Vastly Undercounted Jobless," *San Francisco Chronicle*, March 31, 1992, p. B1.

280 Inside our cities . . . : See Spencer Rich, "Hunger Said to Afflict 1 in 8 American Children," *The Washington Post*, March 27, 1991, p. A4; Robert J. Samuelson, March 14, 1991; Karen Penner, "The Recession Isn't Ready to Pull Out," *BusinessWeek*, March 11, 1991, p. 33; Brooke A. Masters, "Food Program Cuts Thousands in Area," *The Washington Post*, March 12, 1991, p. 1; and Doron P. Levin, "G. M. Picks 12 Plants to Be Shut As It Reports a Record U.S. Loss," *The New York Times*, February 25, 1992, p. 1.

281 The Environmental Protection: See William K. Stevens, "Ozone Loss Over U.S. Is Found to Be Twice as Bad as Predicted," *The New York Times*, April 5, 1991, p. 1.

281 "obsession with": Martin Walker, "Desert Storm over Moscow," *The Washington Post*, Outlook section, February 24, 1991, p. 1.

281 "sob-sisters of journalism": A. M. Rosenthal, February 21, 1991. The column endowed President Bush himself with impressive clairvoyance. On March 6, 1991, the President, speaking before a joint session of Congress, insisted, "We hear so often about our young people in turmoil, how our children fall short, how American products are second class. Well, don't you believe it. The America we saw in Desert Storm was first-class talent."

282 "America's new": Anthony H. Cordesman, "America's New Combat Culture," *The New York Times*, February 28, 1991.

282 "Our best hope": Charles Krauthammer, March 22, 1991.

282 "on the Right": See Bartley, "Is America on the Way Down?" *Commentary*, March 1992, p. 22.

282 Health, employment: See Pfaff, *Barbarian Sentiments: How the American Century Ends*, pp. 24–25.

282 Luttwak bemoaned: See Edward Luttwak, "Is America on the Way Down?" p. 16.

283 "Has it ever": John Lukacs, "Berlin, Future Tense," *Harper's*, March 1991, p. 67.

283 "no-skill, no-money": Edward N. Luttwak, "Bush Has the Momentum, But What About His Mess at Home?" *The Washington Post*, Outlook section, September 9, 1990, p. D1.

283 Grafin Donhoff: Quoted in Francine S. Klefer, "Germany Struggles with Military Role," *The Christian Science Monitor*, March 26, 1991, p. 1.

283 "The great questions": Edward N. Luttwak, Testimony before the Senate Armed Services Committee, November 29, 1990.

284 He continued to mock: See particularly Edward N. Luttwak, "The Shape of Things to Come," *Commentary*, June 1990, p. 25.

284 "Every other nation": Charles Krauthammer, March 22, 1991.

285 "Defense Policy Guidance": See Patrick Tyler, "U.S. Strategy Plan Calls for Insuring No Rivals Develop," *The New York Times*, March 8, 1992, p. 1.

285 "the only effort": See Thomas L. Friedman, "As the World Turns, U.S. Policy Stands Still," *The New York Times*, "Week in Review," March 15, 1992, p. 2.

CONCLUSION

287 "one lonely little": See "Win a Battle, Lose a War," *The Economist*, September 21, 1991, p. 85.

287 "Fuck the Jews": William Safire said he confirmed the substance of the quote, spoken "to two high officials on two different occasions." Safire noted, moreover, that "President Bush and his top staff know he did; it has been agreed that everybody would deny it if it was ever said. But James Baker said it—twice—and meant it." See William Safire, March 19, 1992.

288 "a woolly mammoth": See Charles Krauthammer, March 1, 1992.

288 The tenor of political discussion . . . : Quoted from ABC's "This Week with David Brinkley," December 3, 1991. The "almost criminal" characterization is also Buchanan's.

289 "the taboo against": See Dan Balz and Thomas B. Edsall, "Clinton Charges Administration Arouses 'Overt Antisemitism,' " *The Washington Post*, April 1, 1992, p. 1.

290 "extraordinary burst": Howell Raines, "Battle Report from the Ramparts of the Privacy Zone," *The New York Times*, "Week in Review," February 2, 1992, p. 1.

290 "spinning" the room: Michael Specter, "After Debate, the Masters of 'Spin' Take the Floor," *The New York Times*, February 18, 1992, p. A12.

290 "a deliberate decision": Author's interview with George Stephanopoulos.

291 "below Clinton": See Howard Kurtz, "In Quadrennial Rite, Press Bestows Front Runner Status: It's Clinton," *The Washington Post*, January 12, 1992, p. A6. See also Leslie H. Gelb, December 11, 1991; Rowland Evans and Robert Novak, January 3, 1992; and "The McLaughlin Group," January 5, 1992.

291 "aware of festering": Raines, "Battle Report from the Ramparts of the Privacy Zone," *The New York Times*, "Week in Review," February 2, 1992, p. 1. See also "Sex and the Candidate," *The New Republic*, February 3, 1992, pp. 7–8.

291 Hunt quoted in Ellen Ladowski, "Bill Clinton Is No Victim of the Press," *The New York Times*, op-ed page, March 24, 1992.

291 Rosenthal quoted in Edwin Diamond, "Crash Course," *New York*, February 17, 1992.

291 Blumenthal quoted in Ladowski, "Bill Clinton Is No Victim of the Press."

293 "not a view": "The Clinton Candidacy," *The Washington Post*, editorial page, February 14, 1992.

293 "We've had four": "Nightline," February 25, 1992.

293 "Thank you": Karen De Witt, "A Politician Who Thought He Could," *The New York Times*, February 21, 1992, p. A10.

294 when quizzed: Author's interview with George Stephanopoulos.

294 a "giant bowl": A. M. Rosenthal, April 5, 1992.

294 "a primal scream": Sidney Blumenthal, "The Primal Scream," *The New Republic*, October 2, 1991, p. 22.

294 Next came the hit: Sidney Blumenthal, "The Politics of Self," *The New Republic*, January 20, 1992, pp. 22–27, and Maureen Dowd, "The 1992

Campaign: Democrats; Kerrey Moves to Reinvigorate Campaign," *The New York Times*, January 27, 1992, p. 14.

294 "conspiratorialism": Sidney Blumenthal, "He's a New Age Demagogue," *The New York Times*, op-ed page, April 5, 1992.

294–95 "get-a-diaper crowd": Sidney Blumenthal, "'Losers,'" *The New Republic*, May 4, 1992, p. 16.

295 "unslick . . .": Sidney Blumenthal, "The Survivor," *The New Republic*, April 27, 1992, pp. 18–20. Note: I have changed the tenses of two of these adjectives for grammatical purposes.

296 "tawdry ferocity": Will, *Suddenly: The American Idea at Home and Abroad, 1986–1990*, p. xvi.

297 A decade of public opinion: The figures that follow are taken from the continuous surveys undertaken for the project "Americans Talk Security," published in February 1988. They are cited in Stanley B. Greenberg, "The Struggle for a Democratic Vision," *World Policy Journal*, Summer 1988, pp. 548–54, and in Bruce Russett, *Controlling the Sword: The Democratic Governance of National Security* (Cambridge: Harvard University Press, 1991), p. 168. For a full discussion of this rich body of polling data, see John Martilla, "American Public Opinion: Evolving Dimensions of National Security," in Edward K. Hamilton, ed., *America's Global Interests: A New Agenda* (New York: W. W. Norton, 1989), pp. 261–316.

298 In an extensive: See John E. Reilly, *American Public Opinion and U.S. Foreign Policy* (Chicago: Chicago Council on Foreign Relations, 1991), p. 11.

298 In a November 1990: See ibid., p. 34.

298 "the lead military role": Americans talk security poll cited in Don Oberdorfer, "Strategy for a Solo Superpower," *The Washington Post*, May 19, 1991, p. 1.

300 "crisis of Western Democracy": Lippmann, *Liberty and the News*, p. 5.

300 "what somebody asserts": Ibid., p. 54.

300 "but comes about": Daniel J. Boorstin, *The Image: A Guide to Pseudo-Events in America* (New York: Macmillan, 1961), p. 9.

302 "a pseudo-event": Boorstin, *The Image: A Guide to Pseudo-Events in America*, p. 34.

302 This explains the: See Sut Jhally, Justin Lewis, and Michael Morgan, "The Gulf War: A Study of the Media, Public Opinion and Public Knowledge" (Amherst, MA: The University of Massachusetts, Center for Studies in Communication, 1991). The survey was done between February 2 and 4, 1991.

305 What is defined: See Schudson, *Discovering the News: A Social History of American Newspapers*, pp. 7–9.

305 "the ideology of": See ibid., p. 71.

305 "if objectivity": Quoted in Peter Novick, *That Noble Dream: The "Objectivity Question" and the American Historical Profession* (New York: Cambridge University Press, 1988), p. 416.

305 "Objective journalism": Baker, *The Good Times*, p. 238.

308 The rules of objectivity: Quoted in Novick, *That Noble Dream*, p. 418.

308 "Adolph Ochs' ": Liebling is quoted in James L. Baughman, "The Press and the

Federal Government," presented to the Society for History in the Federal Government session at the Organization of American Historians annual conference, March 23, 1990, Washington, DC.

308 "The purpose of news": See James W. Carey, *Communication as Culture: Essays on Media and Society* (Boston: Unwin Hyman, 1989), p. 79. See also Dewey's review of Walter Lippmann, *Public Opinion*, in *The New Republic*, May 3, 1922, pp. 286–88, and John Dewey, *The Public and Its Problems* (New York: H. Holt and Co., 1927). For an erudite discussion of the Lippmann-Dewey controversy, see also Robert B. Westbrook, *John Dewey and American Democracy* (Ithaca, NY: Cornell University Press, 1991), chapter 9.

309 See Christopher Lasch, "Journalism, Publicity and the Lost Art of Argument," *Gannett Center Journal*, Spring 1990, p. 9. It is historically overgenerous to credit Lippmann's high-minded critiques with changing the course of American journalism when editors had the fantastic moneymaking example of *The New York Times* upon which to concentrate their minds. The dates in Lasch's voting pattern argument are better suited to a *Times*-centric critique as well, to say nothing of the influence on voter rolls of new immigrant, black, and women voters. For a discussion of the larger issue, see Michael E. McGerr, *The Decline of Popular Politics: The American North, 1865–1928* (New York: Oxford University Press, 1986).

INDEX